CONTENTS

Most studies currently published on the career of Elvis Presley tend towards either lightweight fan-worship, or cheap and scurrilous sensationalism. The latter are produced by those who, at the outset, neither like nor understand Elvis Presley, rock 'n' roll, or the origins of both.

What has generally (and conveniently) been ignored is the undeniable fact that Elvis Presley was a significant musician, with a vast output of movies and records, as well as being the most important single pop artist of the 20th century.

After seven years of research and investigation, this is the book that sets the record straight.

Roy Carr and Mick Farren, 1982

Elvis Presley: The Illustrated Record sets out every official Elvis release in chronological order accompanied by composer credits, matrix number, catalogue number, month and year of release, personnel (where known) studio location, precise date of recording and a critical commentary.

After every song title and composer credit is the matrix number—an identification code by which individual tracks are logged in a recording company's tape archive for easy retrieving.

> * 'Heartbreak Hotel' (Axton, Presley, Durden) G2WB 0209
> ** 'I Was The One' (Schroeder, DeMetrius, Blair, Peppers) G2WB 0218
> (US) RCA 47-6420 (45): 20-6420 (78).
> Released: January 1956
>
> Elvis Presley (vcl, gtr), Scotty Moore, Chet Atkins (gtr), Floyd Cramer (pno), Bill Black (bs), D.J. Fontana (dms), Gordon Stocker, Ben & Brock Speer (bv).
> *Recorded: RCA Studios, Nashville, January 10, 1956.
> **January 11, 1956

Abbreviations Of Instruments

acc	accordion
bon	bongoes
bs	bass
bv	backing vocals
clav	clavinet
cong	conga drums
dms	drums
el pno	electric piano
gtr	guitar
har	harmonica
kybs	keyboards
man	mandolin
o	organ
perc	percussion
pno	piano
sax	saxophone
stl gtr	pedal steel guitar
synth	synthesizer
tam	tambourine
tpt	trumpet
ts	tenor sax
tymp	tympani
uke	ukelele
vbs	vibraphone
vcl	vocal

1954-8 THE MEMPHIS FLASH

Nobody, but nobody has to tell the Elvis Presley story one more time. It is the custom-made myth of the second half of the twentieth century. It's a Cinderella story that rapidly turns into something close to a Jacobean saga of the damned prince.

Adolf Hitler, in terms of myth, may have the sombre first half of this century sewn up, but from 1950 onwards it all belongs to Elvis Presley. There have been many other rock 'n' roll stars, but Elvis Presley is already part of history.

The end may have been tragic, but the start was a blinding flash of brilliant hope. A poor white boy, whose idol is Dean Martin, assaults popular music in a way that it has never been assaulted before. He becomes cultural public enemy number one, but also the number one fantasy legend of every high school kid with a dream of rebellion.

In the beginning it was Elvis Presley alone who put the sneer of Marlon Brando and the vulnerability of James Dean, plus the sexual immediacy of his own unique voice, down on a tangible piece of black vinyl that could be bought and taken home.

That was very important. Brando and Dean were fleeting images in a darkened movie house. An Elvis Presley performance was a solid object that could not only be played over and over again, but was also a token of the owner's stake in his or her idol.

When Elvis Aaron Presley was born shortly after noon on January 8, 1935 – his twin brother (Jesse Garon) had been stillborn – it was into a poverty-stricken South that was still struggling to bring itself out of a crippling depression. It was hard times, migration for jobs and all over uncertainty. There was even a spell in jail for Presley's father, Vernon, after a clumsy attempt at cheque forgery. With wicked economic irony, World War II eased the employment situation. The post-war boom brought the first signs of that paper-thin, superficial affluence that is the trademark of the fifties. Cars sprouted fins, household gadgets came on the instalment plan and bulky, first generation televisions flickered out *Dragnet* and *Captain Video* in the corner of the living room.

Elvis Presley was a student of Humes High School in Memphis. By all accounts he was a shy, almost self-effacing kid, except that he did look kind of weird. Long hair by the crewcut standards of the time, a bad case of acne, and cat clothes – the Southern sequel to the zoot suit. Classmates recall that he walked it like a hoodlum but talked it polite and shy. Even then, Elvis Presley was built out of contradictions.

Like every great legend, Presley's has its clearly defined starting point. It was a Saturday afternoon in 1953, Elvis Presley was making a good-for-the-time $42 a week driving a Ford pickup delivery truck for the Crown Electric Company in Memphis. He decided to spend four dollars of his hard-earned salary on a do-it-yourself, one-off disc for his mother, Gladys.

Thus it was that Elvis stopped by the Memphis Recording Service on that historic Saturday in late June, with an acoustic guitar that his mother had given him on his eleventh birthday, paid four dollars to Marion Keisker, who had recently relinquished her role as "Miss Radio Of Memphis" to run the place, and walked into the small recording booth.

He played two songs: The Pied Pipers' million-selling 'My Happiness', and The Inkspots' mawkish, voice-over ballad, 'That's When Your Heartaches Begin', which had been recorded by a country singer, Bob Lamb, some two years earlier. The songs were cut directly onto a ten-inch acetate disc.

That probably would have been the end of Elvis Presley's musical career right there, and today he could well be happy, healthy, and still driving a truck, except for one fact. The Memphis Recording Service was a sideline for Sam C. (Cornelius) Phillips, the owner of Sun Records, a small independent Memphis label that specialized in both R&B and local one-shot hillbilly singles, which he often leased to nationally distributed companies like Chess in Chicago and Modern in Los Angeles.

Marion Keisker doubled as Phillips' assistant at Sun. There was something about the truck-driving teenager's voice – and the boast, "I don't sound like nobody", – that caught her attention, so as well as having the song go directly onto disc, she also recorded the end of 'My Happiness' and the whole of 'That's When Your Heartaches Begin' on a discarded length of recording tape. She also made a note of the singer's address (462 Alabama Street) and phone number (375–630), plus the following comment: "Elvis *Pressley* [sic]. Good ballad singer. Hold."

Seventeen years later Marion Keisker (by then Marion Keisker MacInnes) remembered the incident thus:

"The reason I taped Elvis was this: over and over I remember Sam [Phillips] saying, 'If only I could find a white man who had the Negro feel, I could make a billion dollars.' This is what I heard in Elvis, this . . . what I guess they now call soul, this Negro sound. So I taped it, I wanted Sam to know."

When she played the tape to Sam Phillips the next day, he apparently didn't hear Elvis' soul and basically didn't want to know.

1954

That again might have been the end of it, except that Presley turned up again at Memphis Sound Services situated at 706 Union Avenue, on Friday January 4, 1954 to cut two more songs straight onto disc, 'I'll Never Stand In Your Way' and 'Casual Love Affair'. As before, the operation took less than half-an-hour. This time it isn't clear what the purpose of the disc was supposed to be, another present for mother or whatever.

Also, this time around it was Sam Phillips himself who took the four dollars. Aside from a short conversation during which Phillips suggested the vague possibilities of recording Presley should the right song present itself, it looks as though, once again, he had failed to pick up on the soul in Presley's voice.

A few months later, however, both Presley and Phillips were given a third chance to reach some sort of rapport with each other.

In 1954 a demonstration record was sent in to Sun by Peer Music of a tune called 'Without You'. It had been cut by an unknown singer in Nashville. It has been suggested that the singer was in fact a convict at the Tennessee State Penitentiary who heard about Sun when Phillips visited the Southern slammer to record a group of inmates called The Prisonaires. Although Phillips made quite considerable efforts to trace him, the guy, for all practical purposes, had vanished. According to her account, Marion Keisker jumped in at this point and suggested that Phillips should get hold of Elvis Presley, "the kid with the sideburns."

Presley was summoned by phone, and he hurried around to the Sun studios. Phillips played the demo of 'Without You' to him, Elvis sang it and the result was an unmitigated disaster (Sam Phillips' brother Judd played a tape of this session during a lecture at Memphis State Unviersity on August 16, 1979). Since Presley couldn't seem to handle 'Without You', Sam Phillips suggested he should try a tune called 'Rag Mop'. It was an up-tempo song with exceptionally dumb lyrics that was a hit for The Ames Brothers in 1950 (it also turned up in the late 1970s on *The Muppet Show* sung by a group of mops). Again, Presley didn't seem up to the song.

At this point, instead of giving up, Phillips demanded to know what exactly this 19-year old kid could sing, and if the legend can be believed, Elvis promptly poured out just about every song that the company boss knew. They ranged from R&B through hard-core country to gospel to the inevitable Dean Martin hits. Mr Phillips was impressed.

'Scotty' (Winfield Scott Moore III) Moore (21) and Bill Black (27), then members of a local hillbilly combo called The Starlight Wranglers, were brought in by Phillips to beef up Presley's voice and primitive acoustic guitar strumming with electric guitar and stand-up bass.

They met at Scotty Moore's house one Saturday afternoon in June, which Scotty remembered primarily because of his initial shock when Presley turned up in a jive pink suit and heavily greased hair. (Bill reckoned Presley was a snotty-nosed kid). The threesome fooled around at Moore's for two hours with an assortment of tunes from such diverse sources as Hank Snow ('I Don't Hurt Anymore') Eddy Arnold ('I Really Don't Want to Know') and Billy Eckstine's 'I Apologise' and then arranged a studio audition at Sun for Monday evening. It was Phillips' idea not to drag along the rest of the Wranglers.

Said Phillips to Moore, "We'll just put down a few things and we'll see what it sounds like coming back off the tape recorder."

For the next few weeks Elvis, Scotty and Bill would meet almost every late afternoon or early evening to "develop a style". During this period Elvis also found time to make occasional guest shots with The Starlight Wranglers, but Phillips reckoned the kid didn't sound right with such a large band. They'd patiently routine song after song in the studio – primarily ballads and honky tonk hits – discuss the individual merits of each playback and, come the weekend, present Phillips with acetates of the best takes for his expert opinion.

One evening while they were in the middle of one of these style developing sessions, Phillips called everyone into his office and played them some R&B material which he was considering releasing. He added prophetically between records that one day this kind of music would catch on in a big way.

Elvis then casually remarked that not only did he like this particular kind of music, but he also knew many of the R&B records Sun had previously released, together with the songs of Arthur Crudup, Big Bill Broonzy and Roy Brown. Phillips was impressed. The enthusiasm in

young Elvis' voice made Phillips realize that this liking for R&B was a characteristic of Presley's that had yet to be explored in the studio.

On July 5, 1954 Elvis, Scotty and Bill were back in the studio, but this time with Phillips at the controls. Among the things planned was a country ballad called 'I Love You Because' (the first song they were to get to grips with that evening) plus a new version of the Bill Monroe hit 'Blue Moon of Kentucky'. Also recorded were 'Blue Moon' and the still-unreleased 'Tennessee Saturday Night'.

Fortunately for world history, the epoch-making session was preserved on tape and has been widely bootlegged both in Europe and the USA. At the end of the revolutionary, up-tempo treatment of Bill Monroe's country song, the voice of Sam Phillips can be clearly heard.

"Hell," he yells over the tail-end of Scotty's guitar doodle, "well, that's just fine man . . . well, that's different, that's a pop song now, Little Vi! . . . That's good."

Although the word probably wasn't used for at least another year or more, it was the birth of rockabilly. From some viewpoints, it might even have been the real birth of rock 'n' roll. One thing is for sure: there was electricity in the air and magic all around.

In fact, that first cut of 'Blue Moon Of Kentucky' was never legally released. The version that came out on July 19 on Sun 209 was recorded either later that same night or over the next couple of days once they'd hit their stride on Arthur 'Big Boy' Crudup's 'That's All Right (Mama)'. Whoever decided that the "pop song" had to be done over again made the right decision. If you compare the bootleg with the slightly later official version, it immediately becomes clear that the single version is tougher and far more confident.

On that first take Presley is feeling his way into new and exciting territory, on the second he is sure of a firm beach-head in his new world of rock 'n' roll and he works the music with every ounce of his energy. To this day no artist has ever displayed such consummate style at this juncture in his or her career.

So there we have it, the birth of the legend. How much of it is strictly true remains a matter for conjecture. After a quarter of a century memories fade and the recollections of those involved become merged with oft repeated legend.

It has always been suggested that Elvis Presley had no real motivation to carve himself a career in the music industry. The long interplay between Sam Phillips, Marion Keisker and Elvis Presley is usually presented as a long running miracle, a near divine accident that transformed Presley, almost against his will, into the greatest singing star the world has ever known.

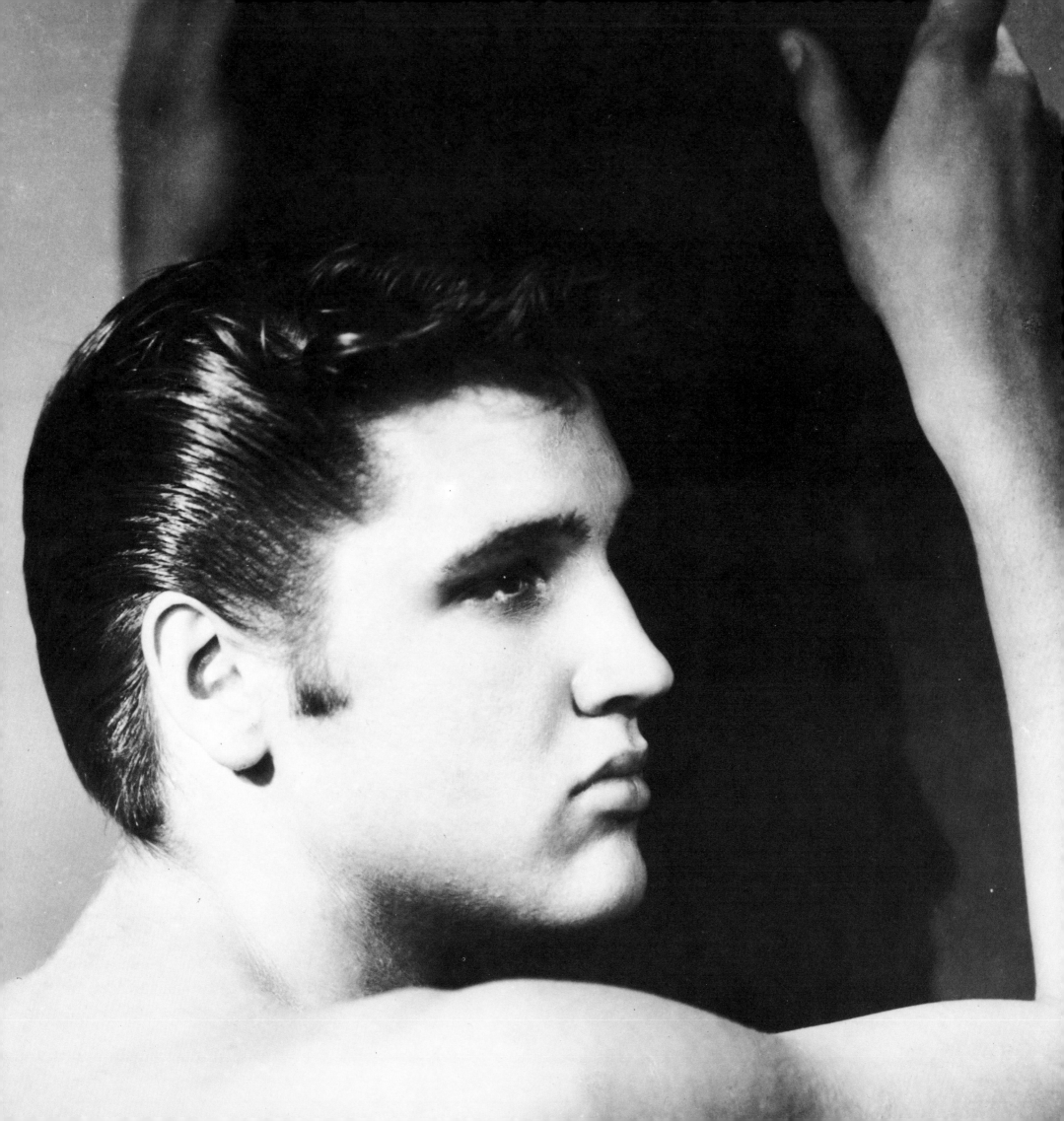

There are, however, a few troublesome little facts that don't quite mesh with the Authorized Version. It could be that far from being the artless, truck-driving Cinderella who had fame thrust upon him, Elvis could have been determinedly hustling himself a singing career well before he happened by Memphis Recording Service.

As early as 1943 he allegedly won first prize for singing 'Old Shep' at the Alabama-Mississippi State Fair. At the age of ten he again entered a talent contest sponsored by a Tupelo radio station, which prompted Vernon and Gladys Presley to gift their only child with a guitar for his eleventh birthday – although he would have preferred a bicycle. Christmas 1952, and Elvis performed 'Cold Cold Icy Fingers' plus an encore of 'Till I Waltz Again With You' during a Humes High benefit variety show.

A former Humes High School friend, the late Johnny Burnette, remembered: "Wherever Elvis went he'd have his guitar slung across his back – never did bother with a case like the rest of us boys. He used to go down to the fire station and sing to the boys there – they were the only ones around Memphis who seemed to have a lot of listening time."

"Every now and then", said Burnette, whose own singing style was redolent of Presley's Sun period (he had also worked locally with both Scotty and Bill), "he'd go into one of the cafes or bars and slouch across a chair. He never sat up straight, he'd just sort of lie there with that mean look on his face. Then some folk would say: 'Let's hear you sing, boy,' and old El would stroll up to the most convenient spot, looking at the ground all the time. Then all of a sudden he'd slide that guitar round to his front and he'd near raise the roof with that real rockin' sound of his."

The first acetate demo was purported to be a birthday gift for his mother (the date of which had long since passed), but what was the intention behind the totally neglected second demo? Also, there's the story told by James Blackwood that Elvis had passed the audition to join The Songfellows – the junior branch of that well-respected Memphis gospel quartet, The Blackwood Brothers. The only reason Presley didn't join The Songfellows is that the singer he was set to replace rescinded his original decision, a move that coincided with Presley being signed by Sun. This again is hardly the behaviour of someone who was totally taken by surprise by his musical ability.

It's a fact that, as early as October 1953, Dewey Phillips introduced a threadbare Elvis on stage at the Eagle Nest club during intermission, as "the poor man's Liberace", and that Elvis crooned a handful of Dean Martin hits, including 'That's Amore'. An uncorroborated rumour also has young Elvis cutting demos with Phineas Newborn at a local radio station.

And then there were his clothes; Lansky Brothers' pink suits and Royal Crown Pomade sideburns were no way the garb of a country boy following in his daddy's humble footsteps. To quote Johnny Burnette once again, "Even in school Elvis used to wear the wildest clothes. He'd always have his shirt collar turned up and wear his hair real long."

Even Elvis' fairly comprehensive knowledge of black R&B, a knowledge that allowed him to slip with consummate ease into the blues shouting style of Arthur 'Big Boy' Crudup, the composer of 'That's All Right (Mama)' and 'My Baby Left Me' (who, incidentally, always claimed that he never got a penny in royalties from the hits Presley had with his songs, only a handout), was hardly conventional. And yet, whenever asked in those early days, Elvis always cited Dean Martin as his biggest idol, with Billy Eckstine running a close second.

It could be that the key to the contradictory enigma that was Elvis Presley from the start right up until his isolated death is a streak of crazed, wildly illogical modesty that continuously surfaced and prevented him from ever revealing anything about himself. At a 1957 press conference he informed the world that Pat Boone was "undoubtedly the finest

voice out now". He even went on to state that Patti Page and Kay Starr were his favourite singers. This, believe it or not, was the man who was outraging the world's oldsters with his wild, onstage, sexual gyrations.

It was this same illogical modesty that caused him to "sir" and "ma'am" everyone to death in public and behave like a scarcely sane despot in private, machine-gunning the barn and running a bulldozer over the summerhouse just because it was there.

After the first release on Sun, a few of the clouds rolled back. Of all periods in Elvis Presley's life, this was the most public. The legend tends to forget that 'Blue Moon Of Kentucky'/'That's All Right (Mama)' wasn't an immediate smash hit. Although, in the end, it notched up more than reasonable regional sales in the South, it wasn't without heavy promotion on the part of both Presley and Phillips.

The first move was to get Presley interviewed on the *Red Hot And Blue* radio show on the local Memphis station WHBQ. The host, Dewey Phillips (no relation to Sam), pointedly asked Presley which high school he attended. When Presley replied "Humes High School", it made it plain to the Southern, still overtly racist, audience that—contrary to first impressions—Elvis was white. This was a very important point in ol' Sam's marketing campaign.

Dewey Phillips also contributed another factor to Elvis Presley's first release. Instead of playing the designated A-side like other Memphis disc jockeys, Phillips, like Sleepy-Eye John over at station WHEM, started spinning 'That's All Right (Mama)'. With advance orders totalling 7000, in a matter of weeks, it was 'That's All Right' that reached the number one slot in the Memphis country chart, where it remained for two weeks.

This, however, was only in Memphis. The word had to be spread and the only way to do it was by a gruelling period of one-night stands at country fairs, National Guard halls, cinemas and high school hops around the South. It was an intense, make-or-break period in the saga of Elvis Presley. Crowded into a beat-up 1954 Chevrolet Bel Air, covering hundreds of miles between dates, eating garbage food and living in cheap motels . . . the pace proved to be crushing.

Although, in that period the public did not associate Elvis with the pills that, in later life, he became so fond of swallowing, there is no doubt that the majority of musicians playing these backroad circuits were depending on amphetamines, benzedrine or caffeine concentrates. It was such a lifestyle that on January 1, 1953 had put the great Hank Williams in an early grave, and the list of Southern artists whose careers were either damaged or terminated by constant use of amphetamines (usually in conjunction with alcohol) runs from Johnny Cash, Carl Perkins, Johnny and Dorsey Burnette, Jerry Lee Lewis, Eddie Cochran and Gene Vincent, right through to Jim Morrison, Janis Joplin, Johnny Winter and The Allman Brothers. If speed didn't get to Elvis Presley, then certainly the strain of the endless one-nighters did. Scotty Moore recounts:

"He [Elvis] had so much energy in those days, we'd have to sit up nights and wear him out so we could go to sleep. There'd be pillow fights, we'd wrestle, anything we could think of. It, like, wore us out.

"Every day, every night was the same. He chewed his fingernails, drummed his hands against his thighs, tapped his feet and every chance he got, he'd start combing his hair."

When this bundle of nerves and energy was pushed out onto a stage, it proved to be the most exciting thing since the Civil War.

Hardly any record remains of these early shows, only a few photographs and the fading memories of people who attended them.

Paul Lichter was at a show at the Overton Park Shell auditorium on August 10, 1954. It

was one of Presley's first major dates, warming up for such conservative country stars as Webb Pierce, Slim Whitman, Minnie Pearl, The Louvin Brothers, Carl Smith and Billy Walker. In his book, *The Boy Who Dared To Rock*, Lichter describes it thus:

"That evening Dewey [Phillips] introduced him to the audience. The curtains parted and, standing on centre stage, Elvis was a sight to behold. He wore a black sport coat trimmed with pink darts and black high rise pants that featured pink pocket flaps and pink lightning bolts lining the outside seam of the leg. He threw one arm above his head and began to move his leg in the now famous corkscrew motion, his smouldering blue eyes peering out at the audience, his thick lips curled into a sexy snarl. He hadn't sung his first note and they were already screaming. Elvis shouted, 'Well-ll-ll', and went right into 'Good Rockin' Tonight'. There was chaos in the audience."

Memphis disc jockey Bob Neal, Elvis's second manager (Scotty had originally held that position for six months), also recalls those early audiences.

"You'd see this frenzied reaction, particularly from the young girls. We hadn't gone out and arranged for anybody to squeal and scream. Not like Frank Sinatra in the forties. These girls screamed spontaneously."

At the Memphis concert Elvis Presley had only been added by Neal as a favour to Sam Phillips, to warm up the crowd for Webb Pierce. In fact, he wasn't even billed. At the earlier matinee performance, it was a different tale. Presley crooned two country standards – 'Old Shep' and 'That's When Your Heartaches Begin' – receiving only polite applause for his efforts. For the second show, Neal instructed Presley to stick to his up-tempo songs and leave the country songs to the real singers. Musicians with that attitude were to pay dearly. When, later that evening, Presley came off that Memphis stage, it was clear to Webb Pierce that there was no point in walking on with the audience close to rioting. By all accounts he walked straight out, pausing only to abuse Presley on the way. Other performers were to suffer similiar experiences. It created a lot of hostility for Presley, but it also ensured that he

was quickly bounced to the top of the bill.

Hostility didn't come only from other performers. Some of the punks in the audience reacted with as much intensity as the girls. It was a kind of negative intensity, though. As Elvis became bigger and bigger throughout the South, so did the number of adolescent rednecks who lay in wait for a chance of punching him out. Their beef was usually concerned with how Presley was getting the local womanhood in an uproar and distracting them from the punks' own small town macho posturing. The fact that Elvis often complemented his wild cat clothes with eye make-up didn't help.

In Lubbock, Texas, one teenage gang even went so far as to fire-bomb Presley's car after a scandal sheet had suggested that he might be sleeping with the police chief's daughter.

Bob Neal frequently found himself involved in these attacks on Elvis.

"It was almost frightening, the reaction that came to Elvis from the teenage boys. So many of them, through some sort of jealousy, would practically hate him. There were occasions in some towns in Texas when he'd have to be sure to have a police guard because somebody'd always try to take a crack at him. Of course, Elvis wasn't afraid of them. He was quite willing to defend himself – and did on occasions."

Afraid or not, the police guard was the start of the impenetrable security that was to cocoon Elvis for the rest of his life.

There were other problems apart from security. By the autumn of 1955 Elvis Presley had five singles out on Sun, and it was becoming clear that Bob Neal, Sam Phillips, Sun Records or even an almost exclusively Southern audience could not fulfill the potential that was Elvis Presley.

On November 22, 1955 the Memphis *Press-Scimitar* ran a story that started: "Elvis Presley, 20, Memphis recording star and entertainer who zoomed into big-time and big money overnight, has been released from his contract with the Sun Record Company of Memphis, and will record exclusively for RCA Victor."

In a deal that involved Neal, Phillips and a new figure that had arrived on Presley's horizon, Colonel Tom Parker, the remaining years still to run on Elvis's contract with Sun, along with all the unreleased recordings, were sold to RCA for the then record sum of $40,000 ($35,000 for Sam Phillips and five grand in back royalties for Elvis). The forty-five-year-old self-styled Colonel also took over Presley's management from Bob Neal.

Tom Parker was a carnival hustler from way back. (He always claimed that he was the son of West Virginia fairground folk. It wasn't until the early 1980s that doubt started to be cast on his origins.) In his chequered career he had cooked up a number of promotions with such unlikely ingredients as ponies, monkeys, dancing chickens and foot-long chili-dogs. His major score prior to Elvis Presley had been in country music. When he signed Elvis, he had already moved Eddy Arnold and Hank Snow into positions of national stardom. Parker had first seen Elvis in Texarkana, Arkansas, and with the instinct of an old carny hand, he went backstage and offered the young singer an informal deal.

Once Presley was safe under his wing, Parker's first move was to put Presley on display at that year's Country And Western Disc Jockeys' Association convention at Nashville's Jackson Hotel. For the first time disc jockeys and promoters from the North were made aware of Elvis Presley. His career had entered a new phase. He was on a set course to become the next golden boy of American entertainment.

Even golden boys, however, need product, and on January 10, 1956 Elvis went into the RCA studios in Nashville and, over the next two days, cut five new tracks. The second song recorded was 'Heartbreak Hotel', written by Tommy Durden and Mae Boren Axton, the mother of Hoyt Axton.

'Heartbreak Hotel', an austere and highly sexual song, was exactly what Presley needed to consolidate the national market that he was now confronting. It was dramatic, strangely spartan and sexually menacing. More than any other record that has gone before (and maybe afterwards) it echoed the strange combination of suppressed violence and self pity that was the hallmark of the James Dean generation. It was the perfect record to launch the international Elvis Presley bandwagon, and teenagers in both the US and Europe climbed on with alacrity. It was a case of instant Presleymania. Britain's *New Musical Express* coined the word in its June 15, 1956 issue.

It was also the only time in Elvis' career that he appeared regularly on television. The

legend has always worked hard on how Ed Sullivan first refused to have Elvis Presley anywhere near his show ("I won't touch Elvis with a long stick"), then relented a month later in an effort to boost his ratings, paid Elvis $50,000 for three appearances on his *Toast Of The Town* CBS-TV programme, and insisted that on the final show (January 6, 1957) Presley should be framed from the waist up because Ed Sullivan only hosted what was, above all, a family show.

The legend doesn't make quite so much of the six appearances on the Dorsey Brothers' shows, and his spots on the Steve Allen and Milton Berle shows. It almost totally neglects to mention the time Elvis appeared live on the Milton Berle programme, with the unlikely combined bill of Esther Williams, Harry James and Buddy Rich. The programme was broadcast live from the flight deck of the aircraft carrier USS *Hancock*. Elvis, unhampered by a studio and censoring camera angles, gave what has to be the wildest and, by television standards, the most alarming display of microphone humping and corkscrewing legs.

Of course, exhibitions like that on the *Milton Berle Show* and his increasingly large public appearances couldn't possibly go unnoticed by the media. Just as 13,000 screaming fans turned out to greet his 1956 arrival in Chicago, the press, the pulpit, radio and television

pundits pulled out every stop to heap abuse on Presley's head. With almost the same alacrity that teenagers turned the Presley image into a battle flag of rebellion, they realized that the singer was a tailor-made target who could be blamed for anything from teenage promiscuity and juvenile delinquency to the decline of western civilization as they knew it.

The *New York Times* demanded a crackdown on riotous rock 'n' roll, describing the music, particularly Elvis Presley's, as "a barrage of primitive jungle beat set to lyrics which few adults would care to hear". The answer, the *Times* piece went on, was to "ban all teenagers from dancing in public" and "enforce a midnight curfew for anyone under 21".

A syndicated magazine article that appeared in both Britain and America in the fall of 1956, by a psychologist, Dr Ben Walstein, attempted to explain why rock 'n' roll was driving western youth bananas! After listening to 'Blue Suede Shoes' with rapt attention, the good doctor opined that "the first impression I get from this has to do with this business of don't step on my blue suede shoes ... don't hurt me ... allow me to have a sense of independence. I think there is also a sexual component in this, in that you might say that the blue suede shoes represent something that has not been tried by the adolescent. There is certainly an anti-formalism in Presley's work, a mood of rebellion."

The magazine *Time*, on the other hand, was surprisingly kind.

"Without preamble, the three piece band cuts loose in the spotlight, the lanky singer flails furious rhythms on his guitar. In a pivoting stance, his hips swing sensuously from side to side and his entire body takes on a frantic quiver, as if he had swallowed a jackhammer."

It took the now-defunct New York *Journal American* to really go for the jugular.

"Elvis Presley wriggled and wriggled with such abdominal gyrations that burlesque bombshell Georgia Southern [a major league stripper of the time] really deserves equal time to reply in gyrating kind. He can't sing a lick, and makes up for vocal shortcomings with the weirdest and most plainly planned suggestive animation short of an aborigine's mating dance."

Even the Russians joined in the mud-slinging with the theory: "Presley is a weapon in the American psychological war . . . To recruit youths with nuclear political views!"

Just so their parents' paranoid fears wouldn't be totally without foundation, the kids went out and obligingly staged a few atrocities of their own. In Jacksonville, Florida, they tore the clothes off Presley's back. In Wichita Falls, Texas, they took his Cadillac apart, and in Fort Worth the local girls carved his name in their flesh with their pen knives. In San José, California, teenagers routed the local police department, injuring eleven cops. There was another riot in sedate Boston at the Massachusetts Institute of Technology, while all over the country a rumour spread that if a girl could actually get to Elvis, he would be more than happy to autograph her breasts, 'Elvis' on the left and 'Presley' on the right. Strangest of all, in Asbury Park, New Jersey (later to be recognized as the home of Bruce Springsteen) twenty-five "vibrating teenagers" were hospitalized after a record hop.

By 1956, Elvis Presley was at his pinnacle. He had revolutionized country music, he had overturned the pop charts, and his live concerts were getting so big that they were fast approaching the point where they would become unmanageable. He had outraged the television audience, he had become the media's favourite whipping boy and was just about the biggest musical phenomenon in the western world. The only world left to conquer was that of Hollywood and motion pictures.

Not that it was that hard a world to conquer. Almost as soon as 'Heartbreak Hotel' was a hit the movie offers had started to flow in Tom Parker's direction. One of the most interesting was a request that Elvis should test for a part in the Joseph Anthony film *The Rainmaker*, where he would star with Burt Lancaster and Katherine Hepburn.

This was interesting. If it had happened, Elvis would have been launched on a movie career as a serious actor with two of the most capable co-stars in the business. Somewhere along the line, though, a decision was made to drop the idea. Instead, 20th Century Fox dusted off a down-at-heel western property called *The Reno Brothers*, added four thinly relevant songs, recruited Richard Egan and Debra Paget as co-stars, re-shot the ending, changed the name to *Love Me Tender* and in the process created something that in later years the world would come to know and worry about: the Elvis Presley vehicle. It was a decision that may have been one of the most disastrous in Presley's whole career.

Two more movies followed, *Loving You* and *Jailhouse Rock*. Both were loose variations on the Presley success story, but the Presley presence and excellent songs made them thoroughly acceptable.

The fourth movie project was a little more ambitious. Adapted from the Harold Robbins novel *A Stone For Danny Fisher*, *King Creole* not only had a good musical score, but also a strong melodramatic plot and experienced performers like Walter Matthau and Carolyn Jones against whom Presley could try his strength.

Unfortunately, while *King Creole* was being made another commitment was fast catching up with Elvis Presley. His military service even had to be deferred for eighty days so that the film could be completed. There was no way, however, that the draft could be avoided forever.

On March 15, 1958 Elvis reported to Fort Chaffee, Arkansas, and was transformed from the Hillbilly Cat into Private US 53310761.

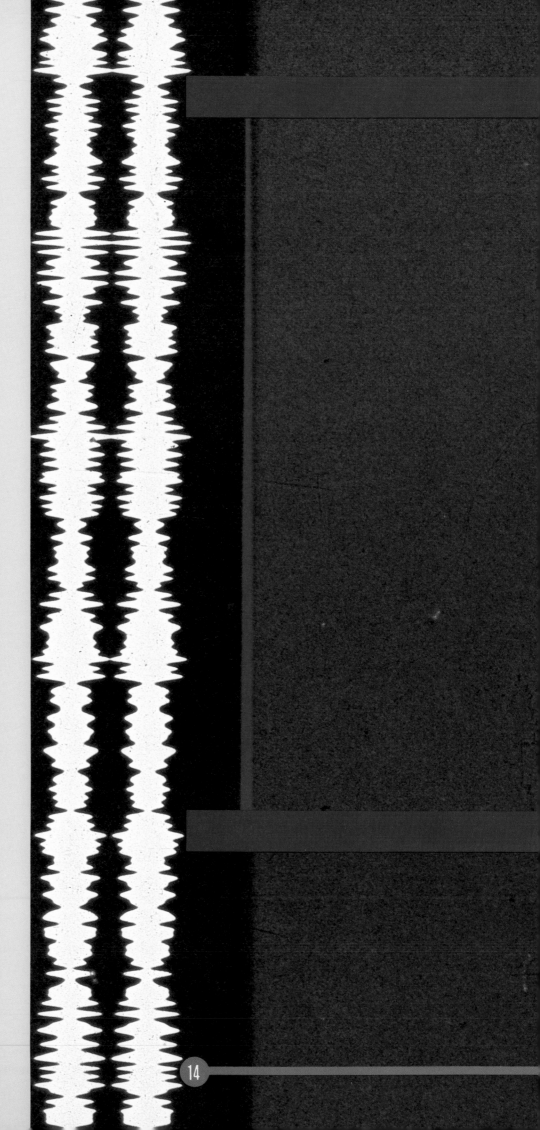

1954

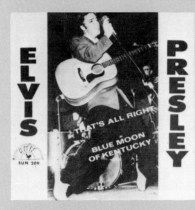

'That's All Right (Mama)' (Crudup) U-128
'Blue Moon Of Kentucky' (Monroe) U-129
(US) Sun 209 (78/45)
Released: July 5, 1954

Elvis Presley (vcl, gtr), Scotty Moore (gtr),
Bill Black (bs)
Recorded: Memphis Recording Service,
Memphis, July 6, 1954

The first song cut at the session which produced the first commercial Elvis Presley single was no revolutionary rocker but a plaintive, somewhat hokey country ballad called 'I Love You Because'. (It never saw the light of day until RCA Victor acquired the entire Presley Sun catalogue later on, but we won't go into that right now.)

What's important is that what was *also* produced on tape during this famous marathon session, while owing its naissance to Southern musical inventiveness in the same way as its hick cousin, contained just that extra degree of creative synthesis which set it immediately, startlingly apart from the rest of the gang.

We're talking about the birth of Rock 'N' Roll.

Sam Phillips didn't know this beforehand, of course. Like other thoughtful musician/producers of his era, he'd been impressed and set to thinking by Bill Haley & the Comets' successful cross-pollination of white country swing and black jump music ('Crazy Man Crazy' and 'Shake, Rattle and Roll'), and it was with a vague idea of following up this promising path that he'd began toying with the idea of persuading the young, directionless Elvis to work out on a couple of Arthur "Big Boy" Crudup numbers.

"Although it seemed incomprehensible to have a white man attempt these songs," Phillips later said, "I just got a notion and called Elvis."

Before springing the Crudup idea, Phillips got on with some gentle breaking-in. First cut, as stated, was 'I Love You Because'. Second was the first of two versions of 'Blue Moon of Kentucky' (subsequently bootlegged, but we won't go into that here, either). Then guitarist Scotty Moore and bassist Bill Black "took five", as was their traditional right about this far into a session.

While they relaxed, Elvis seethed and twitched around the studio in a state of acute hyper-activity. Natural, youthful enthusiasm? Certainly. A metabolism awash with amphetamine? Quite possibly. The "speed" habit had been brought back to the US by ex-combat troops, demobilized after World War II and Korea with a fondness for Government Issue benzedrine and no place particular to go—except back home to whatever small town they had been vacuumed up from. The slender catalogue of virtues possessed by this easily obtainable pick-me-up had long been appreciated by artists, writers and musicians . . . and in addition to all this, Elvis' Mom was being prescribed special diet pills containing this same versatile substance, and her son always seemed to have a pocketful at any given time. Let's just say that those present in the studio drew their own conclusions.

At this instant, as the apocryphal story has it, the racing Elvis suddenly grabbed his ol' guitar and began whacking out a frenetic and frantic version of Crudup's 'That's All Right (Mama)'. Without prompting, Black began slapping out the basic bass notes while Moore applied himself to devising some appropriate licks and flourishes.

According to the story, the dialogue then went like this:

Phillips (in booth): "What the hell's going on?"
Musicians (in studio): "Don't ask us (et cetera)."
Phillips: "Find out real quick and don't lose it. Run through again and I'll put it on tape."
Moore: "Sure, Sam."
Black: "Gotcha."

Elvis: "Yes, sir."
Thus is history made.

Phillips was later to reflect: "We all worked it over and there was a feel at the session—a pleading quality in Elvis' voice—that Crudup's 'That's All Right (Mama)' was just right for him. When we cut, things happened. I said right then, 'That's it.' I knew we had a hit."

Suddenly, the long tedious hours of rehearsal had paid dividends. If 'I Love You Because' and the first slower version of 'Blue Moon of Kentucky' (plus 'Blue Moon', 'Tennessee Saturday Night', 'Satisfied' and 'Harbour Lights', which were also taped during this marathon session) only re-explored old and familiar country music territory, 'That's All Right (Mama)' marked the all-important big breakthrough. It was the blueprint for a unique style which was further to be developed by Elvis, Scotty and Bill over the next four Sun singles before going on to redirect the whole course of popular music.

According to Scotty Moore, the *official* up-tempo version of 'Blue Moon Of Kentucky' materialized in much the same lighthearted manner as 'That's All Right (Mama)'. This time around, it was Bill Black who hit the right groove—doing a falsetto send-up of Bill Monroe which was so infectious that, guitars in hand, Elvis and Scotty immediately picked up the thread and promptly personalized it.

Practically the same tempo as the Crudup song, 'Blue Moon Of Kentucky' displayed even more of the uninhibited vocal mannerisms which, in time, would not only establish the singer as the most instantly recognizable of all recording artists, but serve as a model upon which an entire generation of surrogates would base their own styles.

This hybrid of white country honky tonk and black rhythm 'n' blues would eventually become tagged "rockabilly", but at the moment of inception, Sam Phillips wasn't quite sure what he'd cooked up. Furthermore, he was downright apprehensive about its commerciality.

"We were up a gum stump," said Phillips. "The white disc-jockeys wouldn't touch what they regarded as Negroes' music and the Negro disc-jockeys didn't want anything to do with a record made by a white man. It wasn't western and it wasn't a pop tune . . . there wasn't any ready-made place for it."

So, on Saturday, July 10 Phillips decided to gauge some professional reaction. Armed with acetates of both versions of 'Blue Moon Of Kentucky' and 'That's All Right (Mama)', he strode into Station WHBQ, where good ol' boy Dewey Phillips (no relation) hosted *Red, Hot And Blue*, a regular three-hour Saturday night show devoted exclusively to black music.

"Dewey," said Sam, handing over the acetates, "I've got the best cotton-pickin' record you ever heard."

So scared was Elvis when he discovered Sam Phillips' plan that on the evening in question he took refuge in a local movie house, the Suzore No. 2 Theater—showing, of all things, *High Noon*.

Meanwhile, Dewey Phillips listened intently to the three acetates; nixed the slow version of 'Blue Moon Of Kentucky'; approved the second interpretation of the same tune; but at 9.30 pm decided to air 'That's All Right (Mama)', breaking in over Scotty's guitar solo to inform his listeners that the singer was a local white boy.

Before the record had finished, the radio station's switchboard was jammed with incoming calls, not complaining, but requesting replays and enquiring where they could buy copies.

Dewey then phoned the Presley household and told them to get Elvis over to the Cheska Hotel, where the station was located, pronto. Just before midnight, Elvis found himself seated across the studio microphone from the DJ.

"Sir," confessed the terrified singer, "I don't know nuthin' 'bout being interviewed."

"Just don't say nuthin' dirty," Dewey replied, reassuringly.

Two days later Elvis signed a management contract with Scotty Moore, another with Sam Phillips, and began working out his notice at Crown Electric. By the end of the week, advance orders for 'That's All Right (Mama)' totalled 7000.

'That's All Right (Mama)' backed with 'Blue Moon Of Kentucky' (2nd version) reached the stores on Monday, July 19. To coincide with the release Elvis undertook some local promotion—gigging first at the Eagle Nest Club on Lamar Avenue, with Malcolm

Yelvington's Band, then as the floor show with the band led by Sun Records' engineer Jack Clement. His fee? Ten dollars, each time. (He did better later on.)

Elvis also appeared for a couple of weeks at the Bel Air Club backed by The Starlight Wranglers (which included Scotty and Bill). If audience response during his Bel Air season was minimal, there was plenty of passion brewing backstage. Seems that the remaining Wranglers—Millard Yeow (steel guitar), Tommy Seals (fiddle) and Clyde Rush (guitar)—resented not only Presley's new-found popularity, but also that Scotty and Bill had treacherously participated in the event. They argued that, had it been a proper recording date—like the one the Wranglers had recently done with Doug Poindexter, when they'd cut 'Now She Cares No More For Me' (Sun 202)—then the entire line-up would have been employed. They stubbornly ignored the fact that it had been at Phillips' particular wish that only Scotty and Bill be present at the session.

Anyway, The Starlight Wranglers broke up within a matter of weeks. Scotty and Bill joined Elvis and it was mutually agreed that Elvis would take a 50 per cent share of any monies and that the remainder would be split between the two of them.

On July 28 *Billboard* magazine carried a favourable review of both 'That's All Right (Mama)' and 'Blue Moon Of Kentucky'. It read:

"Presley is a potent new chanter who can sock over a tune for either the country or the R&B markets. On this new disc he comes thru with a solid performance on an R&B-type tune and then on the flip side does another fine job with a country ditty. A strong new talent."

As it transpired, this review more or less coincided with 'Blue Moon Of Kentucky' reaching the coveted No. 1 slot on the Memphis C&W chart and 'That's All Right (Mama)' hitting No. 7.

August 10, 1954 saw Presley steal the thunder from country star Webb Pierce at the aforementioned Overton Park concert, which was quickly followed up by an equally successful guest appearance at the Kennedy Veterans Hospital in Memphis, and a lucrative $65 engagement on September 9, 1954, playing at the grand opening of the Katz Drug Store, in the Airways Shopping Center, from the back of a flatbed truck.

Soon after, Sam Phillips began keeping fairly regular notes of re-orders for Presley's debut single: August 27 (400), October 25 (300). For the year 1955, January 31 (250), April 28 (100), August 22 (100), November 3 (150) and November 25 (700). In total, the original Sun pressing of 'That's All Right (Mama)' sold close to 20,000 copies.

Things were looking up for the 19-year-old ex-trucker.

'Good Rockin' Tonight' (Brown) U-131
(US) Sun 210 (78/45)
'I Don't Care If The Sun Don't Shine'
(David) U-130
Released: September 1954

Elvis Presley (vcl, gtr), Scotty Moore (gtr),
Bill Black (bs)
Recorded: Memphis Recording Service,
Memphis, September 9, 1954

GOOD ROCKIN' TONIGHT
I DON'T CARE IF THE SUN DON'T SHINE

The one professional bad habit that Elvis never broke throughout his entire career was that of constantly finding himself emotionally unprepared for studio work.

At the beginning of September 1954, when Sam Phillips arranged for Elvis to cut a follow-up to 'That's All Right (Mama)', he first had to persuade his protégé that a mere "covering" of the latest juke-box favourites wasn't the best way to further a career.

Despite the localized success of Presley's first single, Phillips was aware of mounting reluctance—on the part of many radio station programmers—to play racially integrated material. Nevertheless, Phillips chose to adhere to his proven policy of coupling an R&B standard with a souped-up country song. And, after some deliberation over material,

'Good Rockin' Tonight'—one of the songs instrumental in Elvis' Overton Park triumph—was selected as the A-side, and 'I Don't Care If The Sun Don't Shine' as the flip. A third track, 'Just Because', was also cut, but remained in the can until the RCA takeover, whilst another Bill Monroe song 'Uncle Pen' was taped, which still remains unheard.

'Good Rockin' Tonight', written and first made famous in 1948 (by New Orleans R&B shouter Roy Brown), is perhaps best remembered as an integral part of the repertoire of that master of the *double-entendre*, Wynonie Harris.

Elvis' version makes no bones about what is implied. As country music commentator Nick Tosches observed, Elvis' treatment of 'Good Rockin' Tonight' was not merely a party song, but an invitation to a holocaust. It is a statement of intent, revealing the kind of self-assured confidence that comes with the first flush of public acceptance.

Elvis Presley, The Hillbilly Cat, and the Blue Moon Boys, as they were soon to be billed, display the kind of arrogant recklessness that hitherto had only been heard on the most risqué black R&B records. Though still something of a novice, Elvis seemed aware of what aroused the primitive instincts in the girls in his audience and, in collusion with Scotty and Bill, was intent on transferring this sensuality onto wax.

If Elvis sings as though his entire nervous system is centralized two feet nine inches above ground level, Bill slaps bass with a vengeance, and Scotty cuts up just as rough. Indeed, the aggression with which these three played later caused people to assume that at least five musicians were involved.

For the flip, 'I Don't Care If The Sun Don't Shine', they again return to country terrain. And, as the three false-starts that emerged on the infamous Dutch bootleg corroborate, the performers stay just the right side of a tongue-in-cheek put-on.

However, it wasn't all plain sailing.

To coincide with this release Phillips arranged for Elvis to appear on the nation's foremost country music show, the *Grand Ol' Opry*, beamed by station WSM out of Nashville.

On September 25, 1954, Elvis was introduced to the discerning Opry audience by Hank Snow, and belted out both sides of his first Sun single. The audience all but sat on their hands. Afterwards, the Opry's top talent scout/MC Jim Denny suggested to Elvis that he should seriously consider returning to his previous occupation as a truck driver.

The young singer was almost destroyed. Not only did he sob all the way back to Memphis, but was so distraught that he left behind—in a gas station—a case containing his brand new cat clothes. (Much later, Jim Denny had the audacity to tell Elvis to his face that he knew all along that the singer possessed star quality.) Elvis made his second and final Opry appearance on October 22, 1954. The audience reaction was no better.

Prior to the release of 'Good Rockin' Tonight', and on Slim Whitman's personal recommendation, Elvis had made the first of what was to prove to be a long string of highly successful appearances on Station KWKH's *Louisiana Hayride*, in Shreveport.

For his Hayride debut he sang 'That's All Right (Mama)' plus a song he'd recorded at the same session, the Rodgers & Hart ballad, 'Blue Moon'.

An instant hit, Elvis, Scotty and Bill were promptly booked for a return engagement, and then contracted on a regular basis—$18 a show for Elvis, and $12 each for Scotty and Bill. On October 16, the first appearance under the terms of this new agreement, Elvis performed five numbers: 'I Forgot To Remember To Forget' (which was to become the flip of his fifth and final Sun single), 'Blue Moon Of Kentucky', 'I Love You Because', 'Just Because' and 'Uncle Pen'.

Before long not only was Elvis guaranteed more money and his act extended to 20 minutes, but he was being invited to sing the commercial for a brand of southern-made doughnuts.

Indeed, the sound of Elvis singing:

You can get 'em pipin' hot, after four pm
You can get 'em pipin' hot, after four pm
You can get 'em pipin' hot,
Southern-made doughnuts hit the spot,
You can get 'em pipin' hot at four pm

became almost as familiar, locally, as the hook-line of his latest single.

1955

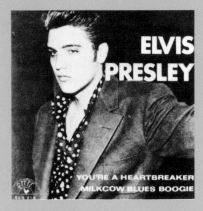

'Milkcow Blues Boogie' (Arnold) U-140
'You're A Heartbreaker' (Sallee) U-141
(US) Sun 215 (78/45)
Released: January 1955

Elvis Presley (vcl, gtr), Scotty Moore (gtr),
Bill Black (bs)
Recorded: Memphis Recording Service,
Memphis, December 18, 1954

Necessity, it has been said, makes strange bedfellows. By the time Elvis Presley's third Sun single ('Milkcow Blues Boogie') was released, guitarist Scotty Moore had willingly relinquished his legal duties as band manager to Bob Neal. A top-rated disc jockey at Station WMPS, Neal had a lucrative sideline regularly promoting schoolhouse hops within a 200-mile radius of Memphis. Though Elvis realized that for a mutually agreed commission of 15 per cent off the top plus expenses, Bob Neal was in a privileged position to guarantee the act regular employment, that privilege didn't extend to Neal being able to spin his *client's* records on WMPS. It wasn't a matter of conflicting interests, just that the station's reactionary boss objected quite vehemently to what he considered to be Presley's bastardization of country music. Moreover, it is said that secretly Elvis disliked Neal for not attempting to use his position to pressurize his stiff-necked boss to rescind his ban. Nevertheless, Elvis had to admit that not only were bookings much better since Neal took charge, but so was the money.

Elvis may still have only been a local celebrity, but there's reason to believe that he was infinitely happier than when the isolation of full-blown success eventually claimed him. At this early juncture, for Elvis, Scotty and Bill, the zenith of their career was not when Elvis burst into tears the first time he was handed a factory-fresh copy of his first single and saw his name on the label, but the night they first earned $300 between them. On the way back home from the gig, which had been held in a high school gym, they stopped off and changed their total take into one-dollar bills. Just before reaching the outskirts of Memphis, Elvis suddenly instructed a friend who was driving to pull off the highway and stop the engine. As Elvis piled out of the car dragging Scotty and Bill along with him, he shouted to the driver to switch the headlights on full. Then, amidst noisy youthful jubilation, all three knelt in the blinding glare and examined their fistfuls of dollars. As they rolled around, slapping one another on the back and laughing fit to cry, they agreed they'd never seen so much money in their entire lives. And, what's more, it was all *theirs*. Ironically, it was at this point that Scotty and Bill came very close to dumping their vocalist.

Sam Philips always maintains that from the outset of his relationship with Elvis, Scotty Moore was of great importance in enabling the young greenhorn to perfect his unique style.

"The reason," says Sam Phillips, "I put Elvis with Scotty in the very first place was because you could suggest an idea to Scotty and he'd give his all to accomplish what you had in mind. He was a fine man. Scotty never tried to be a leader as such, but he was extremely adaptable and that's the kind of guitarist that Elvis needed.

"Playing around with Elvis during those early auditions before we cut and released 'That's All Right (Mama)' I realized that Elvis ran the whole gamut.. he loved blues, he loved gospel and country and also some pop. Now, even though Scotty idolized guitarist Chet Atkins, he wasn't in the least bit reticent about trying to broaden his own style. He realized that if he was going to work successfully with Elvis, he couldn't stay with just the one basic style and he didn't. They developed together. I told him that any musician who plays with a singer must get to know the feel of how that singer will interpret particular songs, so that their accompaniment never gets in the way. I taught them how to feel at ease with themselves in a studio situation." Not being as conversant as Phillips in such subtle matters, Bob Neal thought otherwise. For having managed to get Elvis' twelve-month residency on

the *Louisiana Hayride* extended to eighteen months, Neal persuaded Elvis to seriously review the 25 per cent-each deal he had with Scotty and Bill.

Even though the money was coming in, Neal, having discussed the situation with Presley's parents, insisted that Scotty and Bill should take a cut in salary. After much hassling, it's rumoured that Scotty and Bill changed their minds about quitting and agreed to a guaranteed weekly wage: $200 a week on the road, $100 a week when they weren't working, which was now very seldom. Various fringe benefits, like a record royalty of one-fourth of one per cent a piece, were discussed, but such small talk never amounted to a binding agreement.

That wasn't the only problem to beset the young and inexperienced singer. A paternity suit was slapped on the young stud by a Mississippi belle, but was promptly dismissed, while his ever-watchful mother dissuaded him from marrying Dixie Locke, his Humes High sweetheart.

On a professional level, in an effort to refine the quality of Presley's extremely raw and natural style, Sam Phillips would often try out different recording techniques, even though he seldom used more than one microphone per instrument. "I made it my business to study the dynamic characteristics of every particular microphone I used – how and where it had to be positioned and at what angle. Though, by today's standards, we were working with limited resources and equipment, I knew how to mike up each instrument correctly.

"When it came to Elvis' tenor voice I became aware that it had a certain cancellation characteristic about it – he had power, but at the same time a very soft feel to it, and I had to record him so as it wouldn't get too mixed up with the instrumental overtones.

"I didn't depend on echo too much, even though I had my own special little slapback. I was trying to get the feel in the studio that Elvis, Scotty and Bill got onstage and then try to capture it faithfully on tape.

"If ever I saw any of the three getting a little bit uptight and trying to perform in a manner that didn't have that natural feel to it, I'd stop them. I believed in stylism and the economic use of it. If one note will suffice, don't slip in four or five and try and over-compensate because you were trying to cover up for something else that didn't quite happen.

"I wanted to retain the natural quality in their music because for me, there's nothing more pure than what a person instinctively feels."

As such, it was often left up to the musicians themselves to supply the appropriate natural dynamics. When it came to an instrumental break, Scotty Moore would either turn around and adjust the volume control on his amplifier or, if time didn't allow, just pick at the guitar strings harder than before.

"As far as Elvis was concerned, on something like 'I Don't Care If The Sun Don't Shine, he'd quit playing rhythm, turn his guitar over and commence beating out the tempo on the back. Bill Black would just follow what Scotty was doing and would just slap away at his bass a bit harder than before."

It could be that money was still in short supply so soon after Christmas, but whatever the reason, 'Milkcow Blues Boogie' bombed. It failed to secure a much-needed mention in *Billboard*'s weekly reviews section and eventually sold considerably less than either of Elvis' previous two Sun releases.

Originally written and recorded 20 years earlier by Kokomo Arnold, 'Milkcow Blues Boogie' had, over the years, been subsequently re-recorded by innumerable blues and country stars. Prefaced with a well-rehearsed 'spontaneous' slow, bluesy eight bar intro, the mood of this version of 'Milkcow Blues Boogie' is abruptly shattered when Elvis stops and instructs Scotty and Bill, "Hold it, fellas! That don't *move* me. Let's get real, real gone for a change!" Whammo! The tempo immediately switches to a breakneck gallop. The first real example of Presley's *real goneness*, he only interrupts his wild hiccuping and howling to yell encouragements to Scotty Moore, who furiously picks away at his guitar in manic Merle Travis fashion. Not to be left out, Bill Black applies brute force to the strings of his bass.

At the time it must have sounded every bit like an apocalyptic fanfare! As before, the flip, 'You're A Heartbreaker', didn't break with tradition, in that it was a country muse. But, instead of having been *borrowed* from someone else's repertoire, it had been written by Jack Sallee especially for Presley.

It was now February, and one of the very first things Bob Neal did, in his new managerial role, was to get the trio booked onto a show in Carlsbad, New Mexico. During the same month Elvis also recorded 'Baby, Let's Play House' and 'Mystery Train'. Furthermore, on March 5, 1955 (the same month as the movie *Blackboard Jungle* was released) Elvis Presley was featured on that segment of the *Louisiana Hayride* that was televised.

By now, Elvis, Scotty and Bill had struck up a bond with the *Hayride's* house drummer, 'Don' D.J. (Dominic Joseph) Fontana. He'd already helped them out whenever the trio played the Shreveport area, as he was only too pleased (prior commitments allowing) to supply an added back-beat. At first, it took Fontana some time to re-adjust his style to Presley's *real-gone* rockin'. But come mid-summer, Fontana had become a full-time member of the Presley entourage and was driving his fellow-musicians to new peaks of devilry.

Unbeknown to Bob Neal, a certain Colonel Tom Parker, then the manager of both Eddy Arnold and Hank Snow, had begun to take more than a passing interest in the one they called The Hillbilly Cat. As it transpired, it was Oscar 'The Baron' Davis who had initially brought the singer's exploits to the attention of the Colonel. Davis was the Colonel's dapper advance promotions man and, on a business trip to Memphis, he stumbled across Bob Neal while recording radio promo spots at Station WMPS for a forthcoming Eddy Arnold Show. After Neal had played Davis all three of Presley's records, he invited Davis out to the local Memphis Airport Inn, where Elvis was appearing. There, Davis witnessed Elvis whipping up a capacity all-female audience into a sexual frenzy. He was impressed. Davis asked to meet Elvis. But Neal informed his guest that as Elvis' records were banned on WMPS, the singer was liable to throw a moody. Nevertheless, Davis got to meet Elvis and, when Neal wasn't around, arranged a further meeting the following Sunday before the Eddy Arnold concert.

It seemed as though Davis was interested in making some kind of side-deal with Elvis, but when the time came for his appointment, the Colonel insisted on tagging along to the coffee shop where they were due to meet. It was there that Elvis and the Colonel met for the very first time.

The Colonel's first words were, "Well, the guy will get nowhere on Sun Records!" At that time it appears that the Colonel wasn't very interested in getting professionally involved with another singer. But, being a shrewd operator, he kept tabs to see if Elvis looked like being more than just a local flash-in-the-pan who gave the girls the hots.

Once Elvis achieved the eighth position on *Billboard's* "most promising" new country artist category of its annual poll and professional reports started to filter through that The Hillbilly Cat was knockin' 'em dead in the aisles wherever he appeared, the Colonel began to give Bob Neal the benefit of his expert advice and, whenever possible, work. In retrospect, it can be seen that the Colonel was protecting his future investment, but the time wasn't yet right for him to make his move.

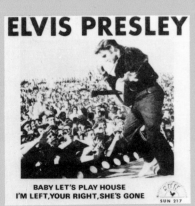

ELVIS PRESLEY

BABY LET'S PLAY HOUSE
I'M LEFT, YOUR RIGHT, SHE'S GONE

SUN 217

** **'Baby, Let's Play House'** (Gunter) U-143 (US) Sun 217 (78/45)
* **'I'm Left, You're Right, She's Gone'** (Kesler, Taylor) U-142
Released: April 1955

Elvis Presley (vcl, gtr), Scotty Moore (gtr), Bill Black (bs)
**Recorded: Memphis Recording Service, Memphis, February 5, 1955
Elvis Presley (vcl, gtr), Scotty Moore (gtr), Bill Black (bs), Johnny Bonnero (dms)
*Recorded: Memphis Recording Service, Memphis, December 18, 1954

By now, the artful Colonel Tom Parker had all but made up his mind that once Bob Neal's contract with Elvis expired (November 1955), he'd personally take over management. The fact that Arnold Shaw—general professional manager of Edward B. Marks Music Corp. and

one of the most influential music industry moguls of the period—approved what he heard the instant the Colonel had played him Presley's records was all the reassurance the Colonel required. The Colonel's intuition to smell out a dollar hadn't malfunctioned, it had just got keener.

This snake-hipped Memphis greaseball who slapped on as much eye make-up as a B-girl, wore the kind of flashy threads that would have gotten other white kids his age arrested on any number of morals charges, and who could grind his nether regions with more natural vigour than the strippers at Minsky's, possessed whatever it was that caused cash register repair men to work overtime.

However, the Colonel still wanted to test-run Elvis Presley in fast professional company, so he promptly booked him as a support on a ten day trek of the Southwest headlined by the ubiquitous Hank Snow and featuring Jimmie Rodgers, Mother Maybelle, The Duke of Paducah and The Carter Sisters. The Colonel reckoned wisely that if Elvis Presley was the raw material from which box office stars were moulded, such exposure would help speed up the process. If he wasn't, then he'd find out real quick before committing himself further For whatever reasons (possibly a piece of any future action), a lot of people suddenly became very interested in expediting Elvis' elevation from the corn-belt circuit into the major league.

If Elvis could cause the kind of female ruckus he did locally, then there was every reason to believe he could repeat the procedure nationally. Arnold Shaw was one of the first people with any muscle to start the momentum, discussing Presley's potential with a leading disc jockey, Bill Randle.

Responsible for discovering and renaming The Crew Cuts (whose cover version of The Chords' 'Sh-Boom' was a national hit), and persuading Coral Records to sign Johnny Burnette, Randle had built up a large listening audience in both Cleveland (WERF) and New York (CBS). Perhaps, being extremely cautious of his own reputation as a star-maker, Randle decided to first try and break Presley's records in Cleveland, rather than risk a (possible) negative reaction in New York, where his show was monitored by the music industry.

Another celebrity DJ who also worked extensively around Cleveland was Tommy Edwards. Every Saturday night, Edwards presented a Country Music Jamboree at The Circle Theater. On Randle's recommendation Edwards booked Presley.

Talk about perfect timing! Presley's visit to Cleveland coincided with that of a Universal Pictures film crew. Intrigued by the burgeoning rock 'n' roll phenomenon and how it was transforming the nation's clean-cut youth into a pack of wild savages, Universal decided to shoot a documentary featuring some of those acts responsible for instigating such disturbances!

Bill Randle had been hired as musical adviser, and part of his job was to book and compere two shows that Universal would film at the St Michael's Hall and Cleveland's Brooklyn High School. The shows were headlined by Bill Haley & the Comets, the inoffensive The Four Lads, and Pat Boone, and there was also Elvis Presley.

Having filmed the afternoon rehearsals, the crew then shot extensive footage of the shows, during which Elvis, realising the importance of the situation, annihilated the crowd with 'Blue Moon Of Kentucky', 'I Forgot To Remember To Forget', 'That's All Right (Mama)' and 'Good Rockin' Tonight'.

Though he was by no means as famous as the other three featured artists, once they'd seen the rushes it was evident to the movie's producers that not only had Elvis stolen the show, but his presence illuminated the screen. Universal, in its wisdom, therefore decided to edit the appropriate footage so that Elvis Presley would emerge as the true hero of the hour. As fate decreed, before this exploitation quickie (tentatively entitled *The Pied Piper of Cleveland* or *A Day In The Life of A Famous Disc Jockey*) was completed for national distribution, the Colonel had taken command of Elvis' business affairs, signed him to RCA and, quite probably at the Colonel's instigation, this movie was never screened commercially.

Soon after the Cleveland episode, Bob Neal flew Elvis to New York City to audition for the highly popular *Arthur Godfrey Talent Show*. It was a case of the old, familiar 'don't-call-us-we'll-call-you' routine. Arthur Godfrey never rang.

1955

Nevertheless, the trip gave Elvis an opportunity to check out both The Big Apple and Bo Diddley, who was appearing uptown in Harlem at the Apollo Theater. Having been invited backstage, Elvis watched the show from the wings and then retired to Bo's dressing room for an impromptu jam. It has been suggested that following that eventful evening Presley promptly incorporated a number of the extrovert R&B star's crowd-pleasing antics into his own high voltage stage routine. To this day Bo Diddley doesn't deny such well-founded theories. The mongrelization of black and white popular music wasn't, at this period, anything particularly new. It had been in a metamorphic state since the first slave ships unloaded their human African cargo in the New World. However, the way in which Elvis Presley unknowingly galvanized both popular music cultures most definitely was innovative.

Elvis taped, 'Baby, Let's Play House' during the very same February session that was also responsible for his fifth, and last, Sun record, 'Mystery Train'.

The former, though credited to Excello recording artist Arthur Gunter, was, in truth, an adaptation of Eddy Arnold's 1951 release for RCA, 'I Want To Play House With You'. Similarly, 'Mystery Train' was also a hybrid. Junior Parker and Sam Phillips may have put their own names to it, but the original source of this song has been traced right back to the '30s, to The Carter Family's 'Worried Man Blues'.

Since he first commenced recording commercially for Sun, the impetuous Elvis had strewn a plethora of half-realized vocal characteristics over a number of recordings. 'Baby, Let's Play House' was the first occasion when he reassembled all those components into one irrepressible torrent of inspired bedlam with which to assault the senses. For Elvis Presley, recording sessions were no longer trial-by-ordeal affairs.

Almost everything recorded with a back-beat, from Jackie Brenston's 'Rocket 88' (incidentally, produced by Sam Phillips in March 1951 and leased to Chess) right through to Elvis' own 'That's All Right (Mama)' has been nailed-to-the-wall as being the *first* rock 'n' roll record; that debate is a matter of personal opinion. The importance of 'Baby, Let's Play House' is that it stands undisputed as the embodiment of the genre. This is where Elvis, Scotty, Bill and rock 'n' roll won their wings. In just 2.13 minutes Elvis rampages through an entire catalogue of every familiar mannerism he'd pioneered: from the delirious over-exaggeration of both vocal and rhythmic nuances and the stuttered '*bub-bub-bub-bub, baby, baby, baby*' mumblings right on through to the sheer cocksure, good-humoured arrogance with which he gleefully celebrates such hedonism. Elvis might well enjoy much bigger selling singles over the next couple of years, but they never quite matched 'Baby, Let's Play House' in terms of the mettlesome adrenalin rush.

All this was achieved without the use of drums. This prompted purists to argue that with the subsequent move to RCA and the addition of drummer D.J. Fontana, Elvis Presley lost, forever, the basic elements that made him the greatest of all popular music's natural talents.

Elvis' enthusiasm on this session was contagious, inspiring the two musicians who flanked him to more than match the magic of the moment. Guitarist Scotty Moore, like Elvis, had now defined his characteristic role in rock music. For those who followed, there were only two choices: you played either like Chuck Berry or Scotty Moore. Few could ever play quite as deftly as either.

Bill Black was a revelation in himself. No longer content to just whack the bass in time to the rhythm, he had developed, with the aid of Phillips, a full-bodied percussive approach. When Bill Black hit his stride, it was difficult to tell whether or not drums were present in the studio. Such confusion led many promoters to assume that Elvis used at least four or five musicians, when, in fact, he had only Scotty and Bill (and much later D.J. Fontana) in tow. Contrary to legend, D.J. Fontana *never* played on any of the three Presley Sun tracks that featured drums.

"That was Johnny Bonnero," revealed Sam Phillips, speaking of the Dean Beard Band's drummer, "and I only used him when I was experimenting with a rim-shot snare drum sound. It was never my intention to use a drummer with Elvis – I was much more interested in what could be achieved with Bill Black's slap bass." The highly distinctive rhythm sound derived from carefully miking-up the instrument to pick up the sonorous rattle of the thick gut strings bouncing off the ebony finger board when Black slapped them with the heel of his palm instead of employing the more orthodox manner of plucking them with the first

and second fingers of his right hand.

"I had a certain feel going between Scotty's lead guitar, Bill's slap bass and Elvis' rhythm guitar so that we didn't need the movement of a drum. Though, in the beginning, I didn't know whether other people would accept it or not, I was developing this distinctive rhythm sound that was separate from anything country, separate from anything R&B or pop. I knew I already had it, but I wanted to do it in a most simplistic way.

"I based my approach on the fact that during the Big Band era of Glenn Miller, Count Basie and the Dorsey Brothers, outside of people like Buddy Rich you hardly ever heard the drums. What you heard were riffs based on the rhythm patterns of how the instruments were arranged. That's the feel I was aiming for with just three instruments and Elvis' voice. Sure, it would have been easy to fall into using steel guitars and a fiddle and other things used in country music, but if I'd have used all that stuff on Elvis' records or Johnny Cash's, we'd have just had another country artist!"

The original disc jockey pressings of 'Baby, Let's Play House' that were mailed out differed to the ones that eventually reached the stores a few weeks later. The B-side featured 'My Baby's Gone,' a slower, haunting blues version of the more familiar flip.

Sam Phillips needed two strong sides on every Presley single, so that if one song didn't conform with a radio station's programming policy, the other side most definitely did. 'My Baby's Gone' didn't spark any reaction and was replaced with 'I'm Left, You're Right, She's Gone'. Incidentally, the discarded 'My Baby's Gone' is to be found on the Dutch Bopcat bootleg.

Having passed the litmus test on his first road tour with Hank Snow, on May 1, 1955 Elvis again packed his cat clothes, hot-footed it down to New Orleans to join Hank Snow and, up until the 20th, when they closed in Chattanooga, was featured along with Slim Whitman, Faron Young, Jimmie Rodgers, The Carter Sisters, The Wilburn Brothers, The Davis Sisters, Martha Carson, Mother Maybelle and Onie Wheeler.

Immediately afterwards, Elvis teamed up again with Hank Snow, and and by mid-June was travelling through Texas with Ferlin Huskey, Marty Robbins, Sonny James, The Maddox Brothers, Rose and Retta, The Belew Twins and The Texas Stompers.

On some occasions his fellow artists requested that, though he was billed as supporting artist, Elvis closed the show. Once Elvis had stirred up audiences into restless mobs, it was impossible, as Ferlin Huskey discovered, for other acts to get any reaction other than apathy and, on occasion, threats of violence.

By the first week in July, the exposure Elvis had received on such one-nighters had pushed 'Baby, Let's Play House' to No.10 on *Billboard's* country music chart and motivated the young singer to begin investing in what would become his insatiable taste for flashy cars – in particular, all pink and two-tone pink and black Cadillacs.

If he was about to "arrive", then Elvis was determined to do so in his own inimitable style.

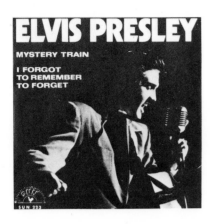

* **'Mystery Train'** (Parker, Phillips) U-156
** **'I Forgot To Remember To Forget'**
(Kesler, Feathers) U-157
(US) Sun 233 (78/45)
Released: August 1955

Elvis Presley (vcl, gtr), Scotty Moore (gtr),
Bill Black (bs)
*Recorded: Memphis Recording Service,
Memphis, February 5, 1955
Elvis Presley (vcl, gtr), Scotty Moore (gtr),
Bill Black (bs), Johnny Bonnero (dms)
**Recorded: Memphis Recording Service,
Memphis, July 11, 1955

Elvis' choice of Little Junior Parker's 'Mystery Train', wasn't so much of a run-of-the-mill cover as a pagan invocation. Set against a clipped, forbidding cloven-hoof gallop, Elvis abandons his more familiar lascivious swashbuckling stance to conjure up the kind of demonic supernatural blues power that years earlier gave rise to the fearsome legend that Mississippi Delta blues singer Robert Johnson sold his soul to the Devil in exchange for his unique ungodlike talent.

Regrettably, the voodoo intensity generated in this performance was a facet of his talent that Elvis would seldom exploit so vividly in later years.

Though there was still 12 months or more to run on Elvis' Sun contract, Arnold Shaw's unbridled enthusiasm had mobilised almost every major New York-based record label to try and set up a parley with Presley concerning his future. Erroneously assuming that apart from managing Elvis, Bob Neal also had a financial stake in Sun, all overtures were made direct to his office. In turn, Neal promptly passed all such communiqués over to Phillips for consideration.

Amongst the first to make a serious offer were Mercury Records' Dee Kilpatrick, who put in a respectable bid of $10,000, and Mitch Miller (of *Singalong With Mitch* fame), who said Columbia would raise that figure to $15,000. When Miller heard the word that Phillips had something more like $20,000 in mind, he rebuffed, "Forget it. No artist is worth that kind of money!" and dropped out of the auction.

In these days of multi-million dollar talent investments, $20,000 may sound like petty cash, but in the mid-'50s, such an advance for the exclusive services of a comparatively unknown singing hilljack, with only a local following, was a small fortune. Nevertheless, Atlantic Records' Ahmet Ertegun was the next person to enter the running. So keen was Ertegun to sign Presley that he not only raised the price to $25,000 – all the ready cash he had – but also offered to throw in his desk! Both this and subsequent deals were rejected by the Machiavellian Colonel Parker, who one observer tagged: "one sharp medicine man."

Acting at the behest of Vernon and Gladys Presley in negotiating a favourable deal for their legally under-age off-spring, the Colonel insisted $45,000 was a much more realistic price. Anything less than that, he intimated (while playing one label off against another), wasn't worth discussing.

'Mystery Train' was released in August 1955, and one can pinpoint the actual circumstances that contributed to Elvis Presley being considered a gilt-edge security – the abrupt termination of the career of someone just four years his senior.

At precisely 5.45 pm on Friday, September 30, 1955 – just four days before the opening of *Rebel Without A Cause* – movie actor James Dean was killed when his silver Spyder Porsche was involved in an accident at the intersection of Routes 466 and 41 in Cholame, on the road to Salinas.

This was the period when America had recently discovered an alien race in its midst – the teenager. And, more than anyone else, James Dean personified the stereotype of this *mixed-up* breed which was seen as an even bigger threat to The American Way than the Reds. A nation's youth mourned the tragic passing of The First American Teenager with such moribund mass-hysteria that it even rivalled the scenes of public mortification that had accompanied Rudolph Valentino's death in August 1926. Once a certain level of sanity

had again been established, the frantic search for Dean's logical successor ensued. Elvis Presley may not have possessed the same sensitive classic features as Dean, but he exuded a rare animal magnetism, and a brooding sensuality even more potent than Dean's pained aura of misunderstood and vaguely androgynous adolescence. Furthermore, Elvis could hold a tune!

'Mystery Train' entered *Billboard*'s country chart (where it remained for 34 weeks) on Saturday, October 8, the very same day as James Dean was laid to rest in his hometown of Fairmount, Indiana. By now, Elvis was starting to attract a certain amount of national notoriety and media attention, and the nicknames of *The Hillbilly Cat*, *The King Of Western Bop*, *Mama Presley's Son*, *The Memphis Flash* and *The Bopping Hillbilly* were automatically made redundant when, somewhat drolly, Humphrey Bogart re-christened him, *Elvis The Pretzel*.

It was obvious to everyone, especially Bob Neal and Sam Phillips, that Elvis Presley now required the machinery of a much larger organisation behind him, if he was to ever realize his true value. Therefore, with the power-of-attorney vested in him by the Presleys, the Colonel set off for New York City, checked into the Hotel Warwick and drew up his final battle plan.

With Hank Snow and Eddy Arnold both signed to RCA, the Colonel set his sights on placing Presley with that company. It has been said that RCA weren't particularly interested to begin with. This isn't quite correct. RCA executive vice-president Larry Kanaga, the company's executive trouble-shooter Frank Folsom, and most notably, the label's A & R chief Steve Sholes had their ear to the ground.

Sholes anticipated the rock 'n' roll explosion that would soon rock the nation, and notified Kanaga that RCA must get involved as early and as quickly as possible. He named Elvis Presley as being the most obvious artist to sign. Apparently, Folsom had a "fund" for such emergencies, and both Kanaga and Folsom gave Sholes the go-ahead.

During this period, the Colonel befriended German-born music publishers Jean and Julian Aberbach. Amongst the Aberbach Brothers' lucrative holdings was Hill & Range, a publishing company specialising in country music. Eventually, a three-way pact was established between the foxy Colonel, Steve Sholes and the Aberbachs, and a verbally agreed transfer fee of $35,000 (plus a $5,000 bonus for Elvis) was negotiated. In actual fact, the five grand bonus was really a back-royalty settlement. The money was split accordingly: RCA put up $25,000 plus the five big bills for Elvis, the Aberbachs chipped in with the remaining $10,000. For this, RCA would acquire all five previously released Sun singles, an unspecified number of unreleased recordings, and exclusive rights to everything Elvis would record over the next three years. However, before inking any formal agreement, the Colonel wanted to wait until the expiration of Bob Neal's contract with Elvis.

By now, 'Mystery Train,' 'Baby, Let's Play House' and 'I Forgot To Remember To Forget' were all well placed on the charts, affording Elvis sufficient box office appeal to headline his own two week road show, accompanied by Wanda Jackson, Johnny Cash, Floyd Cramer, Jean Shepard, Bobby Lord and Jimmy Newman. And just to make certain RCA didn't get cold feet and back out of their (still secret) agreement, the Colonel took Elvis to Nashville at the beginning of November and placed him on display at the Country & Western Disc Jockey Association's annual convention. Not only did Elvis pick up an award as the No.1. *Most Promising New Star*, but ironically, being unaware of their company's pending deal, two smitten RCA talent scouts offered right there and then to buy Elvis' Sun contract on the basis of, "we haven't seen anything so weird in a long time!"

With Elvis poised on the threshold of more than just regional success, the question of why Sam Phillips agreed to put Elvis' contract up for grabs has often been argued. In terms of practicality, with only 12 months still to run, Phillips would have been ill-advised not to have accepted RCA's benevolent offer.

"I had to either sell it, or give up everything else I was doing and just go with Elvis," confessed Phillips.

Marion Keisker is on record as stating that her boss found himself in a Catch 22 situation, in that he desperately needed to raise considerable capital to expand Sun quickly, if he were to give Presley (and any future signings) the same degree of promotion as a major label – or else be content to forever remain a back-water operation.

1955

"It was a moment of decision," Keisker remembers. "Sam decided, and I think wisely, that he could use the money. He could make other stars just as he made Elvis. And, it wasn't six weeks later that Sun came out with Carl Perkins' 'Blue Suede Shoes'."

When, after Elvis moved to RCA, Phillips was asked why he sold Elvis' contract, he may have just been putting everyone on when he replied that he really didn't expect Presley's popularity to last, but perhaps at the time of the big pay-out he seriously contemplated such a possibility.

It has been suggested that one of the reasons why the Colonel schlepped Elvis away from Sun with such haste, was because he detected fierce competition from such new Phillips' protegés as Carl Perkins, Jerry Lee Lewis, Johnny Cash and Charlie Rich, plus the likes of such Memphis wildcats as Johnny Burnette's Rock 'N' Roll Trio, who in 1952 had been responsible for coining the term Rockabilly.

Therefore, if the Colonel didn't get Elvis fixed-up immediately with a major label before the end of the year—and achieve it with maximum publicity—then interest could easily wane and another label could accidentally discover some other barbaric cracker-barrel cowboy just as marketable as Elvis. Therefore, there could be a great deal of truth in the rumour that, for his second RCA record date (and first TV appearance), Elvis was instructed to cover 'Blue Suede Shoes', not simply because it was an ace rockin' tear-up, but to draw media attention away from the undeniable fact that Sam Phillips had just succeeded in scoring a massive Top 5 national hit with Carl Perkins—something he hadn't achieved with Elvis!

In fact, when Perkins released his original version of 'Blue Suede Shoes,' RCA thought they had purchased the wrong artist. Steve Sholes went so far as to ring Phillips, who assured him RCA had bought the right artist! Anyway, on November 20, 1955, Bob Neal's contract with Elvis expired. The Colonel promptly took command and, on November 22, Elvis Presley was *officially* signed to RCA.

At the same time, the Aberbachs pacted a separate deal with Sun Records' music publishing subsidiary Hi-Lo, acquiring the rights to 'Mystery Train,' 'I'm Left, You're Right, She's Gone' and 'You're A Heartbreaker.' Next, the brothers launched Elvis Presley Music, Inc., to publish any future songs Elvis would wax. Once that was settled, Hill & Range began planning a song folio of *Elvis Presley's Jukebox Favourites* which was to include the trio of tunes purchased from Hi-Lo together with, 'Blue Guitar,' 'Always Late (With Your Kisses),' 'Tennessee Saturday Night,' 'Gone, Gone, Gone,' 'Give Me More, More, More (Of Your Kisses),' 'Oakie Boogie' and 'That's The Stuff (You Gotta Watch).'

Meanwhile, there were mutterings coming from Steve Sholes' office that RCA were about to release an album made up almost entirely from the unreleased titles they'd bought from Sun. Amongst the songs shortlisted for inclusion were, 'Just Because,' 'Blue Moon,' 'Tryin' To Get To You,' 'I Love You Because,' 'I'll Never Let You Go,' 'Uncle Pen,' 'Oakie Boogie,' 'Tomorrow Night' and 'Tennessee Saturday Night.' However, there were certain doubts about the overall quality of the album, and so the project was scrapped. Except for the last four titles, the remaining tracks resurfaced a few months later on *Elvis Presley* (LPM-1254).

All of this intense activity has led to wild speculation that aside from the aforementioned unavailable songs, for over a quarter of a century, RCA has been sitting on a treasury of unreleased Sun tapes with titles like: 'Night Train To Memphis,' 'Tennessee Partner,' 'Rock Around The Clock,' 'Sway,' 'Down The Line,' 'Ooby Dooby,' 'Juanita,' 'Tweedlee Dee,' 'Fools Hall Of Fame,' 'Flip, Flop And Fly,' 'Rockin' Little Sally,' 'Cryin' Heart Blues,' 'Cold, Cold Icy Fingers,' 'Cool Disposition' and 'Rock Me Mama.'

Sam Phillips is adamant that he never taped most of the titles alleged to be Sun masters (though a session sheet for December 8, 1954, confirms that 'Uncle Pen' was taped at the same session which produced 'Tomorrow Night').

"We never recorded excessively," says Phillips, "simply because Elvis and I worked on things very diligently. Never recorded for quantity . . . never recorded for recordings' sake . . . just tried to get into the things we did properly."

It's Phillips' belief that many of the titles claimed to have been recorded in his studio were of songs Elvis either featured on stage or on many of his *Louisiana Hayride* broadcasts.

Just prior to the release of 'Mystery Train,' a Niagara Falls radio station claimed that Elvis Presley's newly-recorded rendition of Bill Monroe's 'Uncle Pen' was amongst their most requested discs. The flip was the soon-to-become-familiar, 'I Forgot To Remember To Forget.'

Precisely how this record station acquired such a record has never been satisfactorily explained. Sam Phillips denies that it was an advance demo sent out by Sun to test a specific market. The most obvious explanation is that it was either a studio acetate that had somehow gone astray(!) or, more likely, a bootleg. Even this early in Elvis' career, his most ardent admirers were taping his frequent *Louisiana Hayride* broadcasts and privately pressing up commercially unreleased songs in extremely small quantities. Bootleg singles of 'Uncle Pen' backed with 'Gone, Gone, Gone' circulated around Memphis, as did the coupling of 'Tennessee Saturday Night' with 'Night Train To Memphis'.

As soon as 'Mystery Train' was released, the unofficial 'Uncle Pen' disappeared for a dozen years until a news item appeared in the June 23, 1967 edition of *New Musical Express* that claimed that the British-based Pyramid label were about to release Elvis' waxing of 'Uncle Pen' backed by a medley of Presley's Greatest Hits, 'Tribute To The King,' performed by the Anthony Hedley Orchestra. The record never reached the stores. Pyramid issued a statement insisting that the master had been "irreparably damaged." A likely tale!

Furthermore, Phillips refutes suggestions that at the time of the RCA take-over he was preparing an album tentatively entitled, *Rockin' With Elvis.*

"I didn't feel Elvis needed the exposure on so many songs. As things were, it was difficult for us to do the things that we did and have them sounding as natural as they should be. To take an 'amateur' and say, 'Man, we gotta have an album'—Elvis just wasn't ready. And to expose somebody, with inferior material and inferior interpretations, would distinctively hurt him later on when he was more established. There was a quality in the music that I wanted to retain, because there's nothing more pure than what a person instinctively feels. Therefore, I was even careful about the number of singles I released on him, let alone start thinking about albums—which at that time weren't a big thing. I was careful never to over-expose any of my artists. I wanted the distributors and the people who bought Elvis' records to really want them, to believe in what we were trying to achieve with each one. That's why I never followed hot on the heels of every release—just wanted them to have a fair chance, and leave it up to the public to decide."

For many fans, following the release of 'Mystery Train', this is where the real story ends.

THE SUN RECORDS SESSIONS

		Released
July 5–7, 1954		
'I Love You Because' (take 1)	(LP) RCA CPL-I-0341	January 1974
'I Love You Because' (takes 2 & 4)	(LP) RCA LPM 1254	March 1956
'I Love You Because' (take 3)	not released	
'That's All Right (Mama)' (2 takes)	(45/78) SUN 209	July 1954
'Blue Moon Of Kentucky' (fast take)	(45/78) SUN 209	July 1954
'Blue Moon Of Kentucky' (slow take)	not released	
'Blue Moon' (2 takes)	(LP) RCA LPM 1254	March 1956
'Tennessee Saturday Night' (2 takes)	not released	
'Satisfied'	not released	
'Harbour Lights' (1 take)	(LP) RCA CPL-I-3082	January 1979
September 9, 1954		
'Good Rockin' Tonight' (2 takes)	(45/78) SUN 210	September 1954
'I Don't Care If The Sun Don't Shine' (3 takes)	(45/78) SUN 210	September 1954
'Uncle Pen(n)' (1 take)	not released	
'Just Because' (2 takes)	(LP) RCA LPM 1254	March 1956
December 8, 1954		
'Oakie Boogie' (1 take)	not released	
'Tomorrow Night' (1 take)	(LP) RCA LPM/LSP-3450	July 1965
December 18, 1954		
'Milkcow Blues Boogie' (1 take)	(45/78) SUN 215	January 1955
'You're A Heartbreaker' (1 take)	(45/78) SUN 215	January 1955
'My Baby's Gone' (1 take)	not released	
'I'm Left, You're Right, She's Gone' (1 take)*	(45/78) SUN 217	April 1955
January 6, 1955		
'I'll Never Let You Go (Little Darlin')'	not released	
'I'll Never Let You Go' (8 takes)	(LP) RCA LPM 1254	March 1956
February 5, 1955		
'Baby, Let's Play House' (3 takes)	(45/78) SUN 217	April 1955
'Mystery Train' (1 take)	(45/78) SUN 233	August 1955
July 11, 1955		
'I Forgot To Remember To Forget' (2 takes)*	(45/78) SUN 233	August 1955
'Tryin' To Get To You' (2 takes)*	(LP) RCA LPM 1254	March 1956

Elvis Presley (vcl, gtr), Scotty Moore (gtr), Bill Black (bs), *Johnny Bonnero (dms)
Recorded: Memphis Recording Service, Memphis, Tennessee

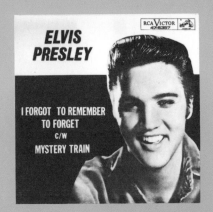

'**Mystery Train**' (Parker, Phillips) F2WB 8001
'**I Forgot To Remember To Forget**'
(Kesler, Feathers) F2WB 8000
(US) RCA 47-6357 (45): 20-6357 (78)
Released: November 1955

'**That's All Right (Mama)**' (Crudup)
F2WB 8040
'**Blue Moon Of Kentucky**' (Monroe)
F2WB 8041
(US) RCA 47-6380 (45): 20-6380 (78)
Released: November 1955

'**I Don't Care If The Sun Don't Shine**'
(David) F2WB 8042
'**Good Rockin' Tonight**' (Brown) F2WB 8043
(US) RCA 47-6381 (45): 20-6381 (78)
Released: November 1955

'**Milkcow Blues Boogie**' (Arnold) F2WB 8044
'**You're A Heartbreaker**' (Sallee)
F2WB 8045
(US) RCA 47-6382 (45): 20-6382 (78)
Released: November 1955

'**Baby Let's Play House**' (Gunter) F2WB 8046
'**I'm Left, You're Right, She's Gone**'
(Kesler, Taylor) F2WB 8047
(US) RCA 47-6383 (45): 20-6383 (78)
Released: November 1955

With Christmas fast approaching and Elvis, potentially the hottest thing on wax, not scheduled to record for his new label until the New Year, RCA decided the time was right to commence recouping their 40,000 bills transfer fee by repressing all five of The Hillbilly Cat's Sun singles.

However, during the remastering, echo was added to certain tracks which hadn't been present in the first instance – a move which, in later years, would greatly annoy the more finicky aesthetes.

Considering Sun still had a selling-off period on excess stock, the sudden appearance of the RCA re-pressings meant that all five Presley singles were simultaneously available on two different labels, and it was those who laid down their 89 cents for the Sun label copies (and looked after them), in preference to the RCA editions, who, much later, would strike the jackpot when these Sun singles became highly-priced collectables. (Sample price: $4000 for all five, mint copies of course.)

Elvis Presley Arrested After Memphis Fist Fight

Rock 'n' Roll Singer Exchanges Blows With Station Attendant Who Told Him to Move

MEMPHIS, Tenn., Oct. 18 (AP) — Teen-age Idol Elvis Presley engaged in a fast fist fight with a service station manager today, leaving the latter with a black eye that "looked like a traveling bag."

Presley, Manager Edd Hopper, 42, and a late comer to the fight, Aubrey Brown, 21, were all charged with assault and battery and disorderly conduct. They made bond of $52 each.

Asst. Police Chief Burns McCarroll said Hopper was trying to open a small pocket-knife at the time officers broke up the fight.

Witnesses said the trouble started when Presley, home from his rock 'n' roll tours, stopped at the station in his sleek, white Continental Mark II automobile and asked Hopper to check the gas tank for leaks.

Asked to Leave

A crowd, drawn by the sideburned singer and the $10,000 car, began to gather. Traffic was blocked. Hopper finally asked Presley to take himself off so the station could get back to normal operation.

A witness, Harvey Huff, told police that Presley, seated in the car signing autographs, agreed to move on but delayed to oblige pressing fans. Huff said Hopper then slapped Presley on the back of the head and said:

"I said, 'Move on.'"

Bob Neal, currently working with Col. Tom Parker on promotion for the Hank Snow show in the South, reports that he has Elvis Presley, Martha Carson, the Carlisles, Ferlin Huskey, J. E. and Maxine Brown and Onie Wheeler set for a week's trek beginning May 29. Neal, who is Presley's personal manager, says the latter has a new release on Sun, "Baby, Let's Play House" b/w "You're Right, I'm Left, She's Gone." Dee-jays may receive a copy by writing him at 160 Union Street, Memphis, Neal says.

Elvis Presley, who bowed into the pro ranks just two months ago, and who since has enjoyed much success with his initial release, "Blue Moon of Kentucky" and "That's All Right," appeared recently on the "Grand Ole Opry" in Nashville on the same segment of the program with Hank Snow, the Davis Sisters and Eddie Hill. Presley, with his guitar and bass-men, Scotty and Bill, made an appearance recently at Texas Bill Strength's nitery in Atlanta, and last Saturday (16) were guests on "Louisiana Hayride" in Shreveport.

HOLLYWOOD, Oct. 20.—"When I stand still I'm dead," said Elvis Presley. He was wearing a black peaked cap—a passerby said, "If you put a red star on it you'd look like a Russian commissar"—and black shirt and suit.

But I can't be sure because his heavy-lidded, half-closed eyes—which I thought were black, though I read later in his studio biography they are blue—were boring deep within me with strange black smudges under them that might have been made up but could have been inherent to his swarthy complexion.

I HAD ASKED HIM, "Why do you think some people object to you?" and that's when he uttered the above-quoted six words that started him off on this interview.

"People," Elvis continued, "say I'm vulgar. They say I use my hips disgustingly. But that's my way of putting over a song. I have to move. When I have a lot of energy, I move more. I lose three or four pounds a performance. I've always done it this way.

ELVIS PRESLEY
Baby Let's Play House 77
SUN 217—A highly distinctive country effort, this is patterned after primitive Southern blues. Great rhythm effects and trick warbling. Should get played. (Excellorec, BMI)
You're Right, She's Gone....71
Presley has the maracas loaded for this unusual, rhythmic country chant. But the content fails to keep pace. (Hi-Lo, BMI)

NBC Rules Out Elvis Presley's 'Offensive Tactics' On TV

New York, June 13. — Elvis Presley can rock 'n' roll to his heart's content and to the whinnies of the teenagers but when he bumps and grinds like a burley queen he'll have to take his shiverin' and shakin' carcass away from NBC-TV.

One of the NBC brass, chagrined at his exhibition of torso tossing on last week's Milton Berle show, today admitted the net received a flood of protests and issued the ultimatum that "we'll have no more of it on our network."

Steve Allen, who has Presley booked on his July 1 network show (replacing Comedy Hour), said today that there has been strong pressure to cancel him out. "If he does appear," said Allen, "he will not be allowed any of his offensive tactics."

CBS had a similar experience two seasons ago with Sheree North, whose wiggles and undulations on a Bing Crosby show brought a wave of censure. The "bump" and "grind" have long been verboten on the networks but on occasion a modified version is sneaked in. It looks like the nets will have to put out a new set of rules to cope with the Presleys and other "nervous" singers who may be coming along.

Jackie Gleason's Stage Show, starring hosts Tommy & Jimmy Dorsey.
'Blue Suede Shoes' and 'Heartbreak Hotel'
Elvis Presley (vcl, gtr), Scotty Moore (gtr), Bill Black (bs), D.J. Fontana (dms), plus The Dorsey Brothers Orchestra
Recorded live: CBS Studios, New York, January 28, 1956

Jackie Gleason's Stage Show, starring hosts Tommy & Jimmy Dorsey.
'Tutti Frutti' and 'I Was The One'
Elvis Presley (vcl, gtr), Scotty Moore (gtr), Bill Black (bs), D.J. Fontana (dms), plus The Dorsey Brothers Orchestra
Recorded live: CBS Studios, New York, February 4, 1956

Jackie Gleason's Stage Show, starring hosts Tommy & Jimmy Dorsey.
'Shake, Rattle And Roll'/'Flip, Flop And Fly' and 'I Got A Woman'
Elvis Presley (vcl, gtr), Scotty Moore (gtr), Bill Black (bs), D.J. Fontana (dms), plus The Dorsey Brothers Orchestra
Recorded live: CBS Studios, New York, February 11, 1956

Jackie Gleason's Stage Show, starring hosts Tommy & Jimmy Dorsey.
'Baby, Let's Play House' and 'Tutti Frutti'
Elvis Presley (vcl, gtr), Scotty Moore (gtr), Bill Black (bs), D.J. Fontana)dms), plus The Dorsey Brothers Orchestra
Recorded live: CBS Studios, New York, February 18, 1956

Jackie Gleason's Stage Show, starring hosts Tommy & Jimmy Dorsey.
'Blue Suede Shoes' and 'Heartbreak Hotel'
Elvis Presley (vcl, gtr), Scotty Moore (gtr), Bill Black (bs), D.J. Fontana (dms), plus The Dorsey Brothers Orchestra
Recorded live: CBS Studios, New York, March 17, 1956

Jackie Gleason's Stage Show, starring hosts Tommy & Jimmy Dorsey.
'Money Honey' and 'Heartbreak Hotel'
Elvis Presley (vcl, gtr), Scotty Moore (gtr), Bill Black (bs), D.J. Fontana (dms), plus The Dorsey Brothers Orchestra
Recorded live: CBS Studios, New York, March 24, 1956
Following the last Tommy & Jimmy Dorsey Show, Elvis was apparently extremely peeved over something, when The Colonel suddenly called "Look what I have for you later". He held out his hand to reveal a bar of chocolate.

Gleason (who observed this bizarre incident), decided to drop his options for six more Elvis guest appearances.

The Milton Berle Show.
'Heartbreak Hotel', 'Money Honey' and 'Blue Suede Shoes'
Elvis Presley (vcl, gtr), Scotty Moore (gtr), Bill Black (bs), D.J. Fontana (dms)
Recorded live: from the flight-deck of the USS Hancock, April 3, 1956

The Milton Berle Show.
'Hound Dog' and 'I Want You, I Need You, I Love You'
Elvis Presley (vcl, gtr), Scotty Moore (gtr), Bill Black (bs), D.J. Fontana (dms), The Jordanaires (bv)
Recorded live: NBC Studios, Hollywood, June 5, 1956

The Steve Allen Show.
'I Want You, I Need You, I Love You' and 'Hound Dog'
Elvis Presley (vcl, gtr), Scotty Moore (gtr), Bill Black (bs), D.J. Fontana (dms), The Jordanaires (bv)
Recorded live: NBC Studios, New York, July 1, 1956

Toast Of The Town, hosted by Ed Sullivan.
'Don't Be Cruel', 'Love Me Tender', Readdy Teddy' and 'Hound Dog'
Elvis Presley (vcl, gtr), Scotty Moore (gtr), Gordon Stoker (pno), Bill Black (bs), D.J. Fontana (dms), The Jordanaires (bv)
Recorded live: CBS Studios, Hollywood, September 9, 1956

Toast Of The Town, hosted by Ed Sullivan.
'Don't Be Cruel', 'Love Me Tender', 'Love Me' and 'Hound Dog'
Elvis Presley (vcl gtr), Scotty Moore (gtr), Bill Black (bs), D.J. Fontana (dms), The Jordanaires (bv)
Recorded live: CBS Studios, New York City, October 28, 1956

Toast Of The Town, hosted by Ed Sullivan.
'Hound Dog', 'Love Me Tender', 'Heartbreak Hotel', 'Don't Be Cruel', 'Too Much', 'When My Blue Moon Turns To Gold Again' and 'Peace In The Valley'
Elvis Presley (vcl, gtr), Scotty Moore (gtr), Bill Black (bs), D.J. Fontana (dms), The Jordanaires (bv)
Recorded live: CBS Studios, New York, January 6, 1957

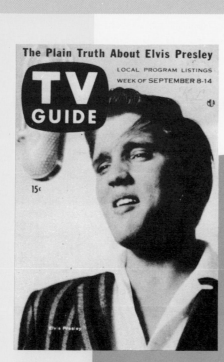

The Plain Truth About Elvis Presley
TV GUIDE
15¢
LOCAL PROGRAM LISTINGS
WEEK OF SEPTEMBER 8-14

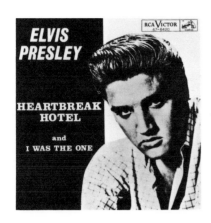

* **'Heartbreak Hotel'** (Axton, Presley, Durden)
G2WB 0209
** **'I Was The One'**
(Schroeder, DeMetrius, Blair, Peppers)
G2WB 0218
(US) RCA 47-6420 (45): 20-6420 (78)
Released: January 1956

Elvis Presley (vcl, gtr), Scotty Moore,
Chet Atkins (gtr), Floyd Cramer (pno),
Bill Black (bs), D.J. Fontana (dms),
Gordon Stoker, Ben & Brock Speer (bv)
*Recorded: RCA Studios, Nashville, January 10,
1956. **January 11, 1956

'ELVIS PRESLEY' (EP)
(US) RCA EPA-747
Released: March 1956

Side 1
*** 'Blue Suede Shoes' (Perkins) G2WB 1230
**** 'Tutti Frutti' (LaBostrie, Penniman, Lubin)
G2WB 1255
Side 2
** 'I Got A Woman' (Charles) G2WB 0208
* 'Just Because' (Shelton, Shelton, Robin)
F2WB 8118

Elvis Presley (vcl, gtr), Scotty Moore (gtr),
Bill Black (bs)
*Recorded: Memphis Recording Service.
July 5–7, 1954
Elvis Presley (vcl, gtr), Scotty Moore,
Chet Atkins (gtr), Floyd Cramer (pno),
Bill Black (bs), D.J. Fontana (dms),
Gordon Stoker, Ben & Brock Speer (bv)
**Recorded: RCA Studios, Nashville, Tennessee.
January 10, 1956.
Elvis Presley (vcl, gtr), Scotty Moore (gtr),
Shorty Long (pno), Bill Black (bs),
D.J. Fontana (dms)
***Recorded: RCA Studios, New York City.
January 30, 1956
****as above. January 31, 1956

Any critical summing up of 'Heartbreak Hotel' has to be just about 100% redundant. If not actually the greatest single recording of all time, it must rank at least in the top five. Lonely Street, the sinister, black-dressed bellhop – and the gloomy hotel itself – all come to surrealistic life, transporting the listener into their sombre world.

It's hard to pin down exactly where the effect came from. Certainly Presley's voice had something to do with it, but although he made hundreds of other records, some awful and some truly great, none of them had quite the same magic as 'Heartbreak Hotel'.

Obviously the song itself was another factor. It was written by Mae Boren Axton (mother of country singer Hoyt Axton) and Jim Durden, who were apparently inspired by a newspaper report of a young man's suicide. He had evidently left a note that included the self-pitying sentence "I walk a lonely street".

On this first session for RCA Records, which also produced 'I Got A Woman', 'Money Honey' and 'I'm Counting On You', the music had a depth and sophistication greatly in advance of the earlier Sun recordings. This was only achieved after the sound engineers had put a call through to Sam Phillips to ask for some technical advice on how to duplicate certain Sun characteristics.

The studio itself was another contributing factor. Housed at 1525 McGovock Street where RCA rented two small rooms from the Methodist Television, Radio and Film Commission – it reverbed with natural acoustics. As a result, the stairwell doubled as RCA's echo chamber. During sessions the Coke machine was apparently placed off-limits, in case the rattle of the dispenser fouled up a crucial take.

This new and innovative echo system was used to great effect and, according to Chet Atkins (at that time running the RCA studios in Nashville), the excitement of the session got to such a peak that Elvis managed to split his newly-acquired pink pants. Not for the first time.

Those first sessions for RCA were a peak for Elvis Presley. He had finally broken out of the southern circuit; he was signed to a major record label for, by the standards of the time, an astronomical sum; and it was clear to anyone with half an ear that he was positively on his way.

For Elvis Presley, the summit of the world must already have been in sight, and the rather sinister magical combination of pain and suppressed violence in 'Heartbreak Hotel' was part of what was going to make sure he got there.

On the reverse side, 'I Was The One' was a near perfect complement. At the same time, it was one of the earliest examples of the throbbing, sobbing drawn-out beat ballad, a form over which Presley always had an undisputed mastery. It also featured vocal echo, very much in the style of the current national heart-throb, pop idol Johnnie Ray, whose career – ironically – was to be eclipsed by the rise of Elvis Presley.

To coincide with this single's release, on January 28 Elvis made the first of six prime-time *live* television appearances on the Tommy & Jimmy Dorsey-hosted *Jackie Gleason's Stage Show*. As a $1250-a-programme guest artist, Elvis opened with Carl Perkins' 'Blue Suede Shoes' and concluded with 'Heartbreak Hotel'. Within a month the latter was on the nation's bestsellers list, where it simultaneously topped both the pop and country music charts before crossing-over into the R&B market where, on April 4, it reached its apogee at No.5.

By March 17, not only had Elvis successfully racked up four more highly-controversial guest shots on the Dorsey Brothers' Show, but between his first and second TV appearances had checked into RCA's New York studio on East 24th Street (January 30–31 & February 3) to record eight more titles – six cover versions and two new songs. With his debut album planned for April and a heavy work-schedule of concert and television appearances ahead, there was some corporate indecision as to what should follow 'Heartbreak Hotel'. Should it be 'Blue Suede Shoes' (which Elvis had already televised on three separate occasions)? Or 'Tutti Frutti' (which he'd also beamed to the nation on February 4 and 18)? The vote was split. Noting that, at $1.29, an EP was only 40 cents dearer than a single – yet offered twice the number of tracks – someone had the inspired notion to launch a two-pronged attack; pairing both 'Blue Suede Shoes' *and* 'Tutti Frutti' on one side of an extended play release and, as a further sales incentive, pressing Presley's version of Ray Charles' 'I Got A Woman' (which he'd premiered on the February 11, Dorsey Brothers' Show), together with an up-tempo unreleased Sun side, 'Just Because', on the flip.

Such a marketing ploy couldn't fail. And it didn't.

Where Carl Perkins' original Sun Records' version of 'Blue Suede Shoes' had been a polite request to tread with caution, Presley's contained a downright threat. Lay off the footwear or else! Simple as that.

A diehard Little Richard fan, Elvis was to cover no less than four of the Georgia Peach's risqué rockers during his first year with RCA. When, in January, Pat Boone (a well-known personal friend of God) attempted publicly to condemn the lasciviousness of 'Tutti Frutti' – by recording a tepid cover – Elvis obligingly illustrated Boone's argument by demonstrating that his own interpretation was just as sexually wanton as the Little Richard original. 'I Got A Woman' was a rabble-rousing stage number which undoubtedly worked better in person than on wax, while the 18-month-old 'Just Because' shot to pieces Sam Phillips' theory that the unreleased tapes he had handed over to RCA were not up to scratch.

This EP cruised confidently into the singles charts and reached a highly-respectable No.24.

N.B. The eight songs Elvis recorded in RCA's New York studio were:

January 30:   'Blue Suede Shoes', 'My Baby Left Me', 'One-Sided Love Affair', 'So Glad You're Mine'.
January 31:   'I'm Gonna Sit Right Down And Cry Over You', 'Tutti Frutti'.
February 3:   'Lawdy, Miss Clawdy', 'Shake Rattle and Roll'.

'ELVIS PRESLEY' (2xEP)
(US) RCA EPB-1254
Released: March 1956

Side I
'Blue Suede Shoes' (Perkins)
*** 'I'm Counting On You' (Robertson) G2WB 0211
Side 2
'I Got A Woman' (Charles)
**** 'One-Sided Love Affair' (Campbell) G2WB 1232
Side 3
'Tutti Frutti' (LaBostrie, Penniman, Lubin)
** 'Tryin' To Get To You' (Singleton, McCoy)
F2WB 8039
Side 4
***** 'I'm Gonna Sit Right Down And Cry (Over You)'
(Thomas, Biggs) G2WB 1254
* 'I'll Never Let You Go' (Wakely) F2WB 8116

Elvis Presley (vcl, gtr), Scotty Moore (gtr),
Bill Black (bs)
*Recorded: Memphis Recording Service.
January 6, 1955.
Elvis Presley (vcl, gtr), Scotty Moore (gtr),
Bill Black (bs), Johnny Bonnero (dms)
**Recorded: Memphis Recording Service.
July 11, 1955.
Elvis Presley (vcl, gtr), Scotty Moore,
Chet Atkins (gtr), Floyd Cramer (pno),
Bill Black (bs), D.J. Fontana (dms),
Gordon Stoker, Ben & Brock Speer (bv)
***Recorded: RCA Studios, Nashville,
Tennessee. January 11, 1956
Elvis Presley (vcl, gtr), Scotty Moore (gtr),
Shorty Long (pno), Bill Black (bs),
D.J. Fontana (dms)
****Recorded: RCA Studios, New York City.
January 30, 1956
*****as above. January 31, 1956

Perhaps because RCA's industrious Special Products department were to put together a whole slew of EPs in October, this rare double-EP is often believed to have been released later in the year. To add to the confusion, there are a number of variations of this specific release in existence, all of which carry the same catalogue number, RCA EPB-1254.

The more common copies have sides 1 and 4 on one record, and sides 2 and 3 on the other. Another variant contains the same songs, but offers a different playing order. Sides 1 and 2 are pressed on one record and sides 3 and 4 on its companion. A third pressing comprised two 45 rpm discs which contain the entire contents of Elvis' debut album (LPM-1254). Though the cover is basically the same as the aforementioned double-EPs, you can recognize this immediately, because strapped across the top is the claim: "The Most Talked About New Personality In The Last Ten Years Of Recorded Music."

Though, as stated, the Special Products compilations weren't made available until October, seeing as the contents were drawn from this cache, perhaps this is an opportune moment to document them.

To capitalize on the Christmas trade and the fact that kids were buying more records than they'd done in years, RCA-Victor introduced their new range of *Elvis Presley Autographed Special* portable Victrolas, which, apart from Elvis' endorsement, were marketed with different packages of Presley's plastic product. The RCA-Victor Automatic Victrola (Model 7EY1) accommodated just 45s and was sold as a job lot. Pay $49.95 instead of $78.29 and you not only received a deluxe boxed set of 15 singles containing (count 'em!) 60 Glenn Miller chestnuts plus carrying cases for both records and record player, but a cute little sales novelty entitled, *Elvis Presley 'Perfect For Parties' Highlight Album. Vol. I* (RCA SPA-7-37). Having purred 'Love Me' Elvis then introduced five other tracks by Tony Cabot & His Orchestra ('Anchors Aweigh'), Tito Puente & His Orchestra ('That's A Puente'), Tony Scott & His Orchestra ('Rock Me But Don't Roll Me'), The Three Suns ('Happy Face Baby') and The Dave Pell Octet ('Prom To Prom'). Should 60 Glenn Miller tracks not be to your liking or should you already own a record player, then 25 cents and a coupon entitled you to a copy of *Perfect For Parties*.

However, the two Victrolas that RCA-Victor were pushing were Models 7EP2 and 7EP45.

The first one was a 4-speed portable that sold for $32.95 and offered as a bonus an Elvis Presley double-EP (RCA SPD-22) which contained the same eight tracks available on EPB-254. The second model was an automatic 45 rpm portable retailing at $44.95 and included an EP triple-pack (RCA SPD-23) which contained:

Side 1: 'Blue Suede Shoes'/'I'm Counting On You'
Side 2: 'I'm Gonna Sit Right Down And Cry Over You'/'I Got A Woman'
Side 3: 'One-Sided Love Affair'/'I'll Never Let You Go'
Side 4: 'Tutti Frutti'/'Tryin' To Get To You'
Side 5: 'I Want You, I Need You, I Love You'/'Don't Be Cruel'
Side 6: 'Hound Dog'/'My Baby Left Me'

ELVIS PRESLEY

RCA VICTOR

A "New Orthophonic" High Fidelity Recording

30

LPM-1254

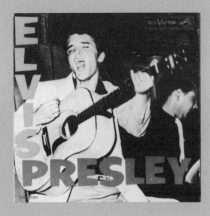

ELVIS PRESLEY (LP)
(US) RCA LPM/LSP 1254
Released: March 1956

Side 1
'Blue Suede Shoes' (Perkins)
'I'm Counting On You' (Robertson)
'I Got A Woman' (Charles)
'One-sided Love Affair' (Campbell)
* 'I Love You Because' (Payne) G2WB 1086
'Just Because' (Shelton, Shelton, Robins)
Side 2
'Tutti Frutti' (LaBostrie, Penniman, Lubin)
'Tryin' To Get To You' (Singleton, McCoy)
'I'm Gonna Sit Right Down and Cry (Over You)'
(Thomas, Biggs)
'I'll Never Let You Go' (Wakely)
* 'Blue Moon' (Rodgers, Hart) F2WB 8117
** 'Money Honey' (Stone) G2WB 0210

Elvis Presley (vcl, gtr), Scotty Moore (gtr),
Bill Black (bs)
*Recorded: Memphis Recording Service.
July 5, 1954.
Elvis Presley (vcl, gtr), Scotty Moore,
Chet Atkins (gtr), Floyd Cramer (pno),
Bill Black (bs), D.J. Fontana (dms),
Gordon Stoker, Ben & Brock Speer (bv)
**Recorded: RCA Studios, Nashville, Tennessee.
January 10, 1956

In less than three chaotic months – during which Elvis had been branded everything from a sex maniac to morally insane, and frequently both – Presleymania had emerged as a full-tilt phenomenon. By comparison, the uncontrollable scenes of mass hysteria, urination, masturbation – and, as former-Presley sidekick-singer P.J. Proby alleges, young girls frantically humping broken-off chair legs – which accompanied Presley's live appearances, made the previous public response yardstick (Frank Sinatra's swooning bobby-soxers) look like a Church picnic.

Following Elvis' sixth and final appearance on the Dorsey Brothers' TV Show (March 24), he was promptly booked for two guest spots (April 3 and June 5) on NBC-TV's *Milton Berle Show* out in Hollywood. Fortunately, the first appearance coincided with Elvis undertaking a Hal Wallis screen-test – a successful audition which resulted in a three-movie deal which guaranteed Elvis with his as-yet-unproven acting talent, $100,000 for his celluloid debut, plus two increments of $50,000 for each subsequent role. When NBC proudly announced that Elvis would appear on the April 3 edition of the *Milton Berle Show* (along with Esther Williams, Arnold Stang and the Harry James Orchestra featuring Buddy Rich), the station was inundated with over 25,000 ticket applications. And when the thoroughly outrageous sight of Elvis doing unspeakable things with both the microphone and the pelvic regions of his supple body while ploughing through 'Heartbreak Hotel', 'Money Honey' and 'Blue Suede Shoes' was transmitted live from the flight deck of the USS *Hancock* aircraft carrier, a viewing audience officially estimated at 40 million (25 per cent of the entire population of the USA) acknowledged Elvis Presley's now undisputed title – The King Of Rock 'N' Roll.

Elvis Presley's first album may have been released with advance orders of 362,000 (automatically making it RCA's biggest-ever LP), but the contents weren't as carefully planned as might have been. However, this doesn't intimate that it wasn't a killer.

All the same, since signing with RCA, Elvis had undertaken only *two* recording sessions: five days that had produced 13 tracks – five of which were *already* in circulation. Here was seed for the future. Of the dozen tracks scheduled for this LP, four were still chart-bound on an EP (EPA-747), while four of the remaining eight had been selected from the Sun booty. That left four titles. 'I'm Counting On You' and 'Money Honey' stemmed from Elvis' first-ever RCA session, and 'One-Sided Love Affair' and 'I'm Gonna Sit Right Down And Cry' came from the January 30–31 date.

Down to basics. The LP was divided seven to five in favour of rockers, with the Sun sides supplying the majority of the ballads.

'I Love You Because', a plaintive country song with minimal accompaniment and allegedly the very first song Elvis cut for Sam Phillips, was a spliced version of takes 2 and 4. The original and unedited rendering (complete with spoken narrative) wasn't released until

January 1976 when it was included on *Elvis – A Legendary Performer Vol. 2* (CPL-I-1349). 'I'll Never Let You Go' is similar in style and treatment to 'I Love You Because', the only deviation being the 16-bar double-tempo pick-up right at the end.

It's been suggested that an unknown bongo player is present on 'Blue Moon'. Quite untrue. Sam Phillips himself has informed one of the authors that it was just Elvis' persistent practice of tapping out the rhythm on the body of his guitar. Elvis' "desecration" of this beloved Rodgers & Hart standard was just the ammunition Presley's critics required. Not only did they consider it an act of *sacrilege* that he attempt to sing a *real* song, but his persisting eerie high-pitched doo-wop wail – it bordered on a ghostly yodel – offended all but The Converted. 'Trying To Get To You' was the only other Sun side (apart from 'Just Because'); it featured an accentuated back-beat (courtesy Johnny Bonnero), which was reminiscent of the now familiar raucous Presley style.

Of the more contemporary RCA material, 'I'm Counting On You' was country-style doo-wop with pounding piano triplets from Floyd Cramer. The piano also dominated the mush-mouthed honky-tonkin' 'One-Sided Love Affair', but this time the boogie beat was supplied by Shorty Long. Set to a spritely four-in-the-bar Bill Black bass beat and some delirious bar-room pianistics, 'I'm Gonna Sit Right Down And Cry Over You' was ideally suited for Presley's body-shakin' St Vitus Bop.

However it was Elvis' serpentine, sexually-overt treatment of Clyde McPhatter & The Drifters' sleazy 'Money Honey' that was both the album's finale and its clincher. Recorded directly after 'Heartbreak Hotel', some of the atmospherics had lingered on, for it evoked the same supernatural sultriness of Elvis' first major hit, defining a style which, on May 4, Gene Vincent & The Blue Caps would copy while recording 'Be-Bop-A-Lula'.

In attempting to maintain interest in the first Presley EP while at the same time going-for-broke behind the album, RCA's Special Products department came up with a practical idea to promote both releases. To focus attention on what RCA reckoned to be the most programmable cuts, three promo-only singles were mailed out. These were:
'Tutti Frutti'/'One-Sided Love Affair' (47-6466) 'I Got A Woman'/'Money Honey' (47/6689) 'Blue Suede Shoes'/'I'm Counting On You' (47-6492).

Then, just when anyone least expected it, Elvis' career took an unforseen set-back, only 20 days after his Milton Berle bonanza. On the strength of his popularity, Elvis was booked for a two week season (at $8500-a-week) to star at the Venus Room in the prestigious Frontier Hotel in Las Vegas.

He opened on April 23, and, by any standards, bombed, being severely mauled by the critics and likened in one review to a "jug of corn liquor at a champagne party."

Furthermore, the management of The Frontier was besieged with complaints from the high-rolling guests, not only about the "sub-standard" live entertainment, but also the disgusting behaviour of those underage fans who either hung around the hotel lobby during the day or gatecrashed the half-empty Venus Room in the evening to scream and weep and generally mess up the place. It was mutually agreed that the entertainer wouldn't play the second week of his engagement, and his contract was torn up.

Thirteen years were to pass before Elvis again set foot on a Las Vegas stage.

1956

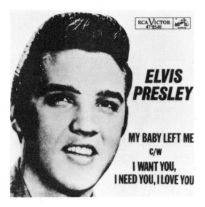

* **'I Want You, I Need You, I Love You'**
(Mysels, Kosloff) G2WB 0271
** **'My Baby Left Me'** (Crudup) G2WB 1231
(US) RCA 47-6540 (45): 20-6540 (78)
Released: May 1956

Elvis Presley (vcl, gtr), Scotty Moore (gtr),
Marvin Hughes (pno), Bill Black (bs),
D.J. Fontana (dms), Gordon Stoker,
Ben & Brock Speer (bv)
*Recorded: RCA Studios, Nashville,
April 11, 1956
Elvis Presley (vcl, gtr), Scotty Moore (gtr),
Shorty Long (pno), Bill Black (bs),
D.J. Fontana (dms)
**Recorded: RCA Studios, New York,
January 30, 1956

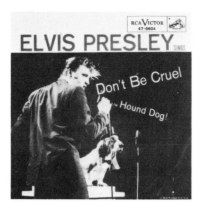

'Hound Dog' (Leiber, Stoller) G2WB 5935
'Don't Be Cruel' (Blackwell, Presley)
G2WB 5936
(US) RCA 47-6604 (45): 20-6604 (78)
Released: July 1956

Elvis Presley (vcl, gtr), Scotty Moore,
Chet Atkins (gtr), Shorty Long (pno),
Bill Black (bs), D.J. Fontana (dms),
The Jordanaires (bv)
Recorded: RCA Studios, New York, July 2, 1956

Elvis Presley's debut album was almost his last. On a flight to Nashville, one of the engines of the twin-engine charter aircraft carrying both Elvis and his musicians cut-out and only an emergency landing on a small deserted airstrip avoided tragedy.

Probably as a result of delayed shock – or something more mundane like touring fatigue – on April 11, as far as we know only one track was completed in the studio; and even then, the eventual master had to be spliced from takes 14 and 17.

'I Want You, I Need You, I Love You' was the precursor of such sultry, heavily-accentuated romancers as 'Playing For Keeps' and, most notably, 'Love Me'.

The flip, 'My Baby Left Me', was a rough-house rendition of yet another Arthur Crudup composition, and a quite uninhibited extension of the original Sun sound which had first brought Elvis to the attention of the public. Recognized as a classic of its kind when first released, it was far too good to be squandered on a B-side. (An alternate take of 'I Want You, I Need You, I Love' was released in January 1976 on *Elvis – A Legendary Performer. Vol.2* (CPL-1349). The reason why this otherwise excellent take was shelved was because of a mistake made when singing the title.

'HEARTBREAK HOTEL' (EP)
(US) RCA EPA-821
Released: May 1956

Side 1
'Heartbreak Hotel' (Axton, Presley, Durden)
'I Was The One' (Schroeder, DeMetrius, Blair, Peppers)
Side 2
'Money Honey' (Stone)
'I Forgot To Remember To Forget' (Kesler, Feathers)

As the unparalleled success of the *Blue Suede Shoes/Tutti Frutti* EP had recently demonstrated, there was a ready-made $1.29 Elvis trade, in this case centred on the hitherto-unexploited 'Money Honey' (a feature of the USS *Hancock* TV special). Nevertheless, to ensure there was no possible sales resistance, 'Heartbreak Hotel' (and its B-side) were added as a bonus while the B-side of 'Mystery Train' ('I Forgot To Remember To Forget') was brought in from the cold to make up a profitable foursome.

In appreciation of the immense power of network television as the most direct means of selling everything Elvis had to offer, the last of his two *Milton Berle Show* appearances (June 5), was effectively deployed (a) to further promote Elvis' current single, 'I Want You, I Need You, I Love You', and (b) to premier a song shortlisted as a possible follow-up, 'Hound Dog'.

A Jerry Leiber and Mike Stoller song (which would later be the subject of complex litigation concerning both ownership and composing credit), 'Hound Dog' had been a huge R&B hit for Willie Mae Thornton on the Peacock label three years earlier.

Elvis may have regularly concluded his riotous stage show with 'Hound Dog', but for some reason was reluctant to record it for a single. It was only at Steve Sholes' insistence that Elvis finally relented. On July 1, the day before Elvis was actually to commit the song to tape, he again plugged 'Hound Dog' on another NBC-TV programme, *The Steve Allen Show*, for which he pocketed $7500.

Following the furore of Elvis' "offensive" antics on the USS *Hancock* and the curtailment of his first disastrous Las Vegas stint, the *Steve Allen Show* was promoted as a tongue-in-cheek ruse, intended to disarm the mounting resentment aimed at Presley. In actual fact, Elvis was in deep trouble.

Having informed the audience that his was a "family show", and the intention wasn't to offend, Steve Allen then announced Elvis, who stepped before the cameras self-consciously decked out in ill-fitting white tie and black tails. However, to belay suspicions that he'd got soft and that this was a total sell-out (which it was), Elvis made it quite clear that he was wearing, what else, blue suede shoes.

To the accompaniment of screams *and* The Jordanaires (thus honouring a promise to retain the singers as a permanent part of his entourage should he Make The Big Time), Elvis opened with 'I Want You, I Need You, I Love You', before ripping into 'Hound Dog'. Nevertheless, the whole charade came dangerously close to backfiring, because many hysterical Elvis fans could see no further than the pathetic sight of their tamed hero dressed up like a clip joint waiter.

Recorded in one day at RCA's New York studio (along with 'Don't Be Cruel' and 'Any Way You Want Me'), 'Hound Dog' may have galvanized Elvis' rock style, but it didn't come easy. The rendering that reached the public may have sounded spontaneous and electrifying, but 31 takes were recorded before a satisfactory one was bagged.

Relentlessly propelled by D.J. Fontana's mule-kick bass drum and regularly strafed with machine-gun snare bursts, the fire of 'Hound Dog' attained even greater intensity when Elvis stepped back from the microphone, The Jordanaires switched from handclapping to sustained chordal harmonies, and guitarist Scotty Moore cut loose over Bill Black's rock-solid pulse beat.

Otis Blackwell's 'Don't Be Cruel' was a truly inspired choice for bedfellow. Depicting Elvis in a salaciously playful mood, it soon became easily as popular as 'Hound Dog'. For if over two million fans promptly went out and bought 'Hound Dog' – and they did – then another two million thought they were buying 'Don't Be Cruel'. The outcome of this resulted in both songs simultaneously holding down both first and second positions on the charts. Combined sales quickly passed five million.

'THE REAL ELVIS' (EP)
(US) RCA EPA-940
Released: September 1956

Side 1
'Don't Be Cruel' (Blackwell, Presley)
'I Want You, I Need You, I Love You'
(Mysels, Kosloff)
Side 2
'Hound Dog' (Leiber, Stoller)
'My Baby Left Me' (Crudup)

For those fans who'd either worn out their copies of Elvis' second and third single, or had them confiscated by their parents, this was a cut-price way of replacing them.

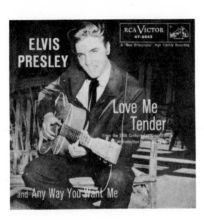

** **'Love Me Tender'** (Presley, Matson)
G2WB 4767
* **'Any Way You Want Me'**
(Schroeder, Owens) G2WB 5937
(US) RCA 47-6643 (45): 20-6643 (78)
Released: September 1956

Elvis Presley (vcl, gtr), accompanied by
The Ken Darby Trio
**Recorded: 20th Century Fox Studios,
Hollywood, August 1956
Elvis Presley (vcl, gtr), Scotty Moore,
Chet Atkins (gtr), Shorty Long (pno),
Bill Black (bs), D.J. Fontana (dms),
The Jordanaires (bv)
*Recorded: RCA Studios, New York,
July 2, 1956

For the first of his three live television appearances on Ed Sullivan's *Talk Of The Town* (September 6, 1956) – he received the then unprecedented inclusive fee of $50,000 – Elvis took the opportunity of introducing the title song from his first-ever movie before a viewing audience of 54 million.

Again, he proved to be a sensation.

Though the record wasn't scheduled for issue for another two months, RCA were forced to bow to public demand in the form of advance orders of 856,237 and rush-release it, even though they argued that in so doing they would immediately kill off still-healthy sales activity for the singer's double-sided smash, 'Hound Dog' and 'Don't Be Cruel'. Of course no such thing happened.

One of the most durable of all early Elvis ballads, both this and 'Any Way You Want Me' – which originated from the 'Hound Dog'/'Don't Be Cruel' record date – revealed a whole new facet of his personality. It was this record alone which was finally responsible for convincing sceptics that Presley could hold a song with the very best of them.

It's interesting to note that the recorded version differs from that in the movie, in that the final verse which he sings over the closing credits,

"If my dreams could all come true/Darling this I know,
Happiness will follow you/Everywhere you go."

is missing.

By this juncture in Elvis Presley's career, there seemed to be almost as many Special Product pressings in circulation as there were commercial releases:

Perfect For Parties Volume 2 (RCA SPA-7-27) includes Elvis' 'I'm Gonna Sit Right Down And Cry Over You'.

(RCA SPD-15) A presentation deluxe boxed set of 10 EPs featuring various artists. Record EP-599-9089 features Elvis Presley – Side 7: 'That's All Right'/'Baby, Let's Play

House', Side 14: 'Mystery Train'/'Milkcow Blues Boogie'.

(RCA SPD-19) A presentation deluxe boxed set of eight records featuring various artists includes 'Heartbreak Hotel'.

(RCA SPD-26) A presentation boxed set of 10 EPs featuring various artists. Elvis is represented by four songs. Side 6: 'Love Me Tender'/'Blue Moon Of Kentucky', Side 15: 'Mystery Train'/'Milkcow Blues Boogie'.

(RCA DJ-7/RCA 47-6643) A radio promo EP. Side 1: Elvis Presley – 'Love Me Tender'/ 'Any Way You Want Me', Side 2: Jean Chapel – 'Welcome To The Club'/'I Won't Be Rockin' Tonight'.

(Motion Picture Service 1206) *Good Rockin' Tonight* EP. Side 1: 'Good Rockin' Tonight'/ 'I Don't Care If The Sun Don't Shine', Side 2: 'Blue Moon Of Kentucky'/'Shake, Rattle and Roll'.

(March Of Dimes-Galaxy Of Stars) This was a 16-inch transcription disc which contained 'Love Me Tender' plus Elvis Presley's personal campaign message on behalf of the March Of Dimes fund. This record was to be aired once only between January 2 and 21, 1957, after which the station was requested to destroy the record. Unfortunately, far too many radio programmers did just that.

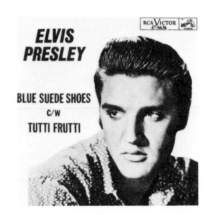

'Blue Suede Shoes' (Perkins)
'Tutti Frutti' (LaBostrie, Penniman, Lubin)
(US) RCA 47-6636 (45): 20-6636 (78)
Released: September 1956

'I Got A Woman' (Charles)
'I'm Counting On You' (Robertson)
(US) RCA 47-6637 (45): 20-6637 (78)
Released: September 1956

'I'll Never Let You Go' (Wakely)
'I'm Gonna Sit Right Down And Cry (Over You)' (Thomas, Biggs)
(US) RCA 47-6638 (45): 20-6638 (78)
Released: September 1956

'Tryin' To Get To You' (Singleton, McCoy)
'I Love You Because' (Payne)
(US) RCA 47-6639 (45): 20-6639 (78)
Released: September 1956

'Blue Moon' (Rodgers, Hart)
'Just Because' (Shelton, Shelton, Robin)
(US) RCA 47-6640 (45): 20-6640 (78)
Released: September 1956

'Money Honey' (Stone)
'One-Sided Love Affair' (Campbell)
(US) RCA 47-6641 (45): 20-6641 (78)
Released: September 1956

'Lawdy, Miss Clawdy' (Price) G2WB 1293
'Shake, Rattle And Roll' (Calhoun)
G2WB 1294
(US) RCA 47-6642 (45): 20-6642 (78)
Released: September 1956

Elvis Presley (vcl, gtr), Scotty Moore (gtr),
Shorty Long (pno), Bill Black (bs),
D.J. Fontana (dms)
Recorded: RCA Studios, New York,
February 3, 1956

There's absolutely no escaping the fact that the continuity of Presley's almost weekly appearances on prime-time TV was not only a crucial element in his mercurial elevation from cracker-barrel curiosity to the most powerful media star of the era, but an important factor in the network ratings war. Not only was Elvis commanding the highest fees ever paid to an entertainer for small screen appearances, but in concert his price was guaranteed at $25,000, a figure which topped the previous all-time high of $10,000 (against 60 per cent of the take) paid to the "comedy" team of Dean Martin and Jerry Lewis.

Presley's ability to match that of the President when it came to securing massive viewing audiences was clearly manifested when *TV Guide Magazine* gave its public approval, not

1956

only by carrying a front-cover interview with the singer, but also in collaborating with RCA to press-up a limited edition of 500 open-ended interview singles (RCA SP-8705). These were mailed out (accompanied by a two-page sheet containing the questions to Presley's pre-recorded replies,) to selected major radio stations with instructions that this promotional device was only to be broadcast between September 6 and 14, after which it was to be returned to RCA.

The demand for Presley product by now far exceeded supply. It was at this juncture – just eight months since the release of 'Heartbreak Hotel' – that his phenomenal popularity was put to the first really acid test.

If – as Colonel Tom Parker argued – the public demanded product, then product they would have. In an unprecedented move, the entire contents of Elvis' chart-topping debut album was simultaneously redistributed on six singles. If that wasn't enough to cause a stampede, a brand new single which coupled Presley's highly-personalized treatments of Joe Turner's 'Shake, Rattle And Roll' (which he'd featured on the February 11 edition of the Dorsey Brothers Show) together with Lloyd Price's 'Lawdy, Miss Clawdy', was also shipped.

While the sceptics in the industry argued that such a move was sheer lunacy, that it would spell commercial suicide for The Man Who Would Be King, it quickly became very apparent that the Colonel's theory was correct: there was no foreseeable saturation level for anything with Presley's voice or image pressed on it.

This was corroborated by the fact that while Presley was completing work on both his debut movie (*Love Me Tender*) and a brand new album, *all* seven singles quickly sold well in excess of 100,000 copies each. The final total amounted to over one million.

From this one remarkable instance, everyone connected with Presley's career realized the commercial desirability of selling the same thing twice – even three times – over.

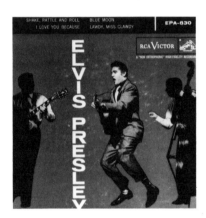

'ELVIS PRESLEY' (EP)
(US) RCA EPA-830
Released: September 1956

Side 1
'Shake, Rattle And Roll' (Calhoun)
'I Love You Because' (Payne)
Side 2
'Blue Moon' (Rodgers, Hart)
'Lawdy, Miss Clawdy' (Price)

'Shake, Rattle And Roll' and 'Lawdy, Miss Clawdy' may well have been the all-new follow-up to the fantastically successful pairing of 'Hound Dog' and 'Don't Be Cruel', but nonetheless it failed to generate any noticeable reaction.

The blame for this shouldn't be attributed to the single being sub-standard – quite the reverse – but to other circumstances. Firstly, this EP was released simultaneously with the six singles drawn from Elvis' debut album. Secondly, Elvis only ever featured 'Shake, Rattle and Roll' on television once. Repackaged within a month of its original release, it did much better second time around thanks to the inclusion of the decidedly melancholic 'Blue Moon'.

'ELVIS' (LP)
(US) RCA LPM-1382
Released: October 1956

Side 1
**** 'Rip It Up' (Blackwell, Marascalco) G2WB 4932
  ** 'Love Me' (Leiber, Stoller) G2WB 4921
 *** 'When My Blue Moon Turns To Gold'
     (Walker, Sullivan) G2WB 4925
 *** 'Long Tall Sally' (Johnson) G2WB 4926
**** 'First In Line' (Schroeder, Weisman) G2WB 4931
 *** 'Paralyzed' (Blackwell) G2WB 4922
     Side 2
   * 'So Glad You're Mine' (Crudup) G2WB 1233
 *** 'Old Shep' (Foley) G2WB 4927
**** 'Ready Teddy' (Blackwell, Marascalco)
     G2WB 4930
**** 'Anyplace Is Paradise' (Thomas) G2WB 4929
  ** 'How's The World Treating You'
     (Atkins, Boudleaux, Bryant) G2WB 4924
  ** 'How Do You Think I Feel' (Pierce) G2WB 4923

Elvis Presley (vcl, gtr), Scotty Moore (gtr),
Shorty Long (pno), Bill Black (bs),
D.J. Fontana (dms) The Jordanaires (bv)
*Recorded: RCA Studios, New York,
January 30, 1956
Elvis Presley (vcl, gtr), Scotty Moore (gtr),
Dudley Brooks (pno), Bill Black (bs),
D.J. Fontana (dms), The Jordanaires (bv)
**Recorded: Radio Recorders, Hollywood,
September 1, 1956. ***September 2, 1956.
****September 3, 1956

Elvis' first album proper – no more falling back on the dependable (now depleted) stock of Sun tapes to make up the quota. With the exception of the eight month old 'So Glad You're Mine', all the tracks on this, Elvis' second album for RCA, originate from a highly productive three day session held in Radio Recorders' Studio B, immediately after he completed filming *Love Me Tender*, and less than a week away from making the first of three Ed Sullivan TV appearances. If that in itself wasn't sufficient to satisfy RCA's accounts department, Elvis also found time to stockpile both sides of his next single, 'Playing For Keeps' and 'Too Much'. Contrary to Sam Phillips' warning, that if Elvis was to consider a long-term recording career, he'd need to suppress his fondness for singing other artists' songs, Elvis seemed to be doing just fine the way things were. For, apart from serving notice on Arthur Crudup's 'So Glad You're Mine', and Red Foley's nauseatingly sentimental 'Old Shep', Elvis and company also turned in no less than three rowdy covers of recent Little Richard hits – 'Rip It Up', 'Long Tall Sally' and 'Ready Teddy'.

In comparison with today's sophisticated recording procedures, Elvis' sessions were just one step up from glorified demo dates. But it was this casual spontaneity and 'hit but seldom miss' approach to the job at hand that was responsible for producing records of unequalled excellence. This is roughly how an Elvis Presley record date operated: song publishers Jean and Julian Aberbach, or Freddie Beinstock (Hill & Range's professional manager and unofficial A&R man), would arrive at the studio (at approximately the same time as the MacDonalds and Cokes), armed with a stack of demo discs. They'd be played for Elvis' consideration, during which time Elvis would commit-to-memory the lyrics, melody and chord changes of those songs that appealed. Once all the songs had been selected and re-spun, Elvis and his musicians would commence recording – making anything up to a couple of dozen takes of each title, before choosing the best.

At this stage in his career, seldom did Elvis deviate from the publishers' demos, which in many instances had been custom-designed by Elvis soundalikes, right down to his highly-stylized vocal mannerisms. The reason why Elvis recorded so many takes of a song wasn't due to any personal musical shortcomings. In his effort to achieve the desired effect, Elvis invariably got so carried away that he'd give a full-scale stage performance right there on the studio floor, to the point where his gyrations took him right off mike and technically ruined an otherwise splendid take. He also had the tendency to send himself up something wicked, causing his musicians to break down mid-number in fits of uncontrollable laughter.

Though at these early sessions Steve Sholes or Chet Atkins are often credited as the producers, they were basically minders. It was Elvis himself who called the shots, whilst they just kept an expert eye on the mechanical details. The only officially available album to accurately capture the pure adrenalin rush that detonated Presleymania (all Elvis' live TV appearances have been widely bootlegged), it vividly depicts the 21-year-old Elvis, not only caught up in his own self-perpetuated momentum, but thoroughly relishing the seemingly unreal experience.

No longer did the sly ol' Colonel have to pay impressionable young girls a few dollars to feign hysteria in Elvis' presence and rip the expensive designer cat-clothes from off the back of his precious meal ticket or, as was common practice, shove their eager little hands down the front of Elvis' pants and grab hold of anything that moved! The problem that now presented itself was how best to protect Elvis from serious physical harm every time he appeared in public, and also keep him out of the clutches of the packs of worldly women who pursued him for all manner of unmentionable reasons.

Whilst reminiscing, Elvis later told a confidante: "Girls would just lose all sense of cool. They were wild . . . take their clothes off and everything. I'll never forget one show where this lady was down front really freakin' out. She jumped up on stage and knocked me on my back. She was bigger than me, wore this full skirt and was sittin' astraddle me. I couldn't get up and she was really goin' wild. Eventually, Scotty and D.J. got her off me and threw her back off stage. When I rolled over to get up, I couldn't because the front of my pants were all wet. She'd peed all over me . . . drowned me. I couldn't go on with the show 'cause I was too embarrassed to face the crowd!"

But while female audiences treated Elvis' appearances as an excuse for unchaste behaviour, according to Elvis, the Colonel did everything in his power to keep his boy in a state that approximated *divine innocence*! This was achieved by keeping Elvis locked up in his hotel and dressing rooms, right up until showtime, before the jittery star was let loose. "People don't realise," said Elvis, "that it was a lot of hard work, tears and sleepness nights. I was always very nervous, hyper-type . . . always had trouble sleeping . . . calming down. There were many times when we'd drive 200 miles to the next city, set up, do the show, pack up and drive another 200 miles to do the next show. I'd often be far too pent-up to sleep. I was an only child—a very protected and spoiled only child. I wasn't used to all this excitement. And, though I was constantly excited, I never had a woman. Had Dixie (Locke) back home, but Colonel Parker wouldn't let me have a steady girlfriend. Didn't want me gettin' married. I wasn't permitted to have girls with me. None. Never had and I needed it . . . it would have helped . . . done me a lotta good!" With no other natural outlet for this apparent excess of youthful energy, Elvis channelled all his juices and frustrations into what he was now being paid a King's ransom for doing. Despite one or two technical misgivings, everything that Elvis was capable of doing—better than any other performer working in rock 'n' roll—is encapsulated on this album.

By now, RCA had given up its attempts to reproduce an acceptable facsimile of Sam Phillips' Sun Sound. Indeed, the engineers who worked on some of the earliest Nashville sessions confided in Phillips that they had encountered insurmountable difficulties in trying to faithfully duplicate his technical expertise. Therefore, on such rockers as 'Paralyzed', 'How Do You Think I Feel', and the trio of Little Richard covers, the guys at Radio Recorders opted for a much more brash, drum-powered production than either the Nashville or New York sessions, by placing even greater emphasis on the separation of piano, guitar, bass and drums. In the transition, Sun's more intimate guitar-dominated textures, and the familiar percussive clatter of Bill Black's bass, were sacrificed, and replaced by, in the case of the bass, the more traditional resonance of the instrument, whilst D.J. Fontana's drums were miked-up to produce full impact. Once the mix was fixed, it was only the mood of a particular song that dictated any slight deviation from the formula. 'So Glad You're Mine' may give the impression of having been recorded in a sleazy strip joint, but for a sensuous ballad like 'Love Me,' the instrumentation is pushed back in the mix in order to bring the vocals of both Elvis and The Jordanaires to the fore. On 'First In Line,' 'Anyplace Is Paradise' and 'How's The World Treating You' the only addition is a spacious bathroom echo that envelops everything.

Contrary to speculation, whilst establishing himself as the King Of The Rock 'N' Roll Jungle, Elvis hadn't forsaken his country music origins. On this album, he played piano on 'Old Shep,' gave an impassioned rendition of 'How's The World Treating You', and evoked vivid memories of the country stance of his Sun Records output.

Not only has this LP the distinction of entering the charts at No.1. but it also produced a million-plus selling EP (*Elvis Vol.I*), with three out of the four tracks achieving chart positions: 'Love Me' (6), 'When My Blue Moon Turns To Gold Again' (27) and 'Paralyzed' (56).

By now, Elvis Presley may have become the most publicity-saturated rock and roll performer of the time, but he was by no means the only one—young and ambitious hip-shakin' hilljacks were virtually falling out of the trees by the thousand.

When, by 1957, it became impractical for Elvis to tour (movies were now very high on his list of priorities), a piano pounder called Jerry Lee Lewis—always a much more violently committed performer than Elvis—began scoring just as many hard rockin' hits over at Sun, with such hoary humdingers as 'Whole Lotta Shakin' Goin' On,' 'Great Balls Of Fire' and 'Breathless'. Songs of brutally overt sexuality that left nothing to the imagination. Lewis, who to this day is convinced he's doomed to an eternity of hell and damnation because of his *unchristian* decision to rock 'n' roll, performed as though he was possessed by all manner of devils. Whereas Elvis always played his part very much tongue-in-cheek, Lewis played flat out, never once drawing the line. Dousing the piano in lighter fuel and then igniting it as an encore was a not uncommon occurrence.

It has been argued, that when Elvis was drafted, had it not been for the career-shattering scandal which, in May '58, surrounded Jerry Lee Lewis' marriage (his third) to his 13-year-old cousin Myra, then Lewis may have become a much more serious threat to the exiled King's popularity than ever Ricky Nelson was.

N.B. In Britain, early copies of the album *Rock 'N' Roll. No.2.* (HMV-1105) contained the very much sought after alternate version of 'Old Shep.'

'ANY WAY YOU WANT ME' (EP)
(US) RCA EPA-965
Released: October 1956

Side 1
'Any Way You Want Me' (Schroeder, Owens)
'I'm Left, You're Right, She's Gone'
(Kesler, Taylor)
Side 2
'I Don't Care If The Sun Don't Shine' (David)
'Mystery Train' (Parker, Phillips)

As the B-side of 'Love Me Tender', the equally romantic 'Any Way You Want Me' may have made No.27 on the national sales barometer, but such was the concentrated attention given to the A-side that all thought of the flip repeating the unprecedented two million plus sales of 'Don't Be Cruel' quickly diminished. Therefore, this EP was intended to give 'Any Way You Want Me' a life of its own. It may have been given star billing over three Sun sides, but it was 'I Don't Care If The Sun Don't Shine' that was chiefly responsible for this record charting.

1956

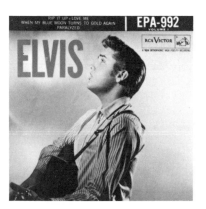

'ELVIS VOLUME I' (EP)
(US) RCA EPA-992
Released: October 1956

Side 1
'Rip It Up' (Blackwell, Marascalco)
'Love Me' (Leiber, Stoller)
Side 2
'When My Blue Moon Turns To Gold'
(Walker, Sullivan)
'Paralyzed' (Blackwell)

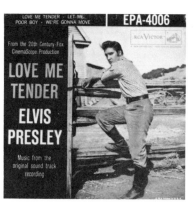

'LOVE ME TENDER' (EP)
(US) RCA EPA-4006
Released: November 1956

Side 1
'Love Me Tender' (Presley, Matson) G2WB 4767
'Let Me' (Presley, Matson) G2WB 7225
Side 2
'Poor Boy' (Presley, Matson) G2WB 7223
'We're Gonna Move' (Presley, Matson)
G2WB 7260

Elvis Presley (vcl, gtr), accompanied by
The Ken Darby Trio
Recorded: 20th Century Fox Studios,
Hollywood, August 1956

Such was the hysteria that now surrounded Elvis Presley that nobody was quite sure which way the market would jump next. For instance, it suddenly became quite evident that in 'Love Me' (originally cut by black duo Willie & Ruth) Elvis had yet another, if unexpected, runaway hit on his hands – though in its original manifestation as an album track, it had not been selected for the attention of RCA's hyper-active Special Products boffins. Dilemma City. Due to public demand following a preview of the September 9 *Ed Sullivan Show*, 'Love Me Tender' (the title song of Elvis' first movie) was now being rush-released ahead of schedule. It was argued that if 'Love Me' were to be issued concurrently, the similarities of style and title might well cause consumer confusion. But the growing demand for this specific title couldn't be ignored. So when on Elvis' second *Ed Sullivan Show* appearance (October 28), he performed 'Love Me' immediately after singing 'Love Me Tender', RCA gave in.

Seeing as plans to re-sell the *Elvis* album as three EPs were already well in the pipeline, 'Love Me' was given priority on the first instalment.

Despite EPs being titled like albums, fans invariably named the first track to indicate the record they wanted. So, in order to minimize any possible confusion between (a) the 'Love Me Tender' single, (b) the EP containing 'Love Me' *and* (c) the upcoming 'Love Me Tender' soundtrack EP, 'Rip It Up' was chosen as the first track with 'Love Me' programmed to follow.

It's been argued that had the batting order been reversed, 'Love Me' would have not only topped the charts (instead of peaking at No.6) but would have sold even more than the million copies for which it was awarded a gold disc.

Thematically, 'Love Me' followed the same pattern as 'Any Way You Want Me'. In the tear-filled eyes of his permanently distraught female admirers Elvis may have seemed out of reach to all except an endless stream of big-breasted starlets and strippers (and the ubiquitous Natalie Wood). Yet despite the implied narcissism of his image and the self-obsessiveness of this song, 'Love Me' somehow took on the form of a most intimate one-to-one *billet-doux*.

On stage, Elvis prefaced this song by first raising his arms above his head and twisting a leg before frantically slapping his crutch and dropping to his knees – an action which on numerous occasions caused so much mayhem in the audience that his performance was brought to an abrupt end. On disc it was different; here was Elvis Presley actually begging for attention instead of the other way around.

Hal Wallis may have guaranteed The Hillbilly Cat a cool 100,000 bills for his screen debut, but initially *Love Me Tender* wasn't envisaged as a musical vehicle. Any music, if incorporated, was intended to be purely incidental. Nevertheless, between the April screen-test and going into production on August 22, not only had the property been changed, from *The Rainmaker* (starring Burt Lancaster) to *Love Me Tender*, but Elvis had been given four songs to sing.

The change of policy wasn't purely coincidental. Elvis signed a $50,000 pact with Ed Sullivan – who a few months earlier, remember, had insisted "I won't touch Elvis with a long stick" – to help stimulate the sagging ratings of his *Toast Of The Town* programme. Hollywood's newest hearthrob was now in a position to give *Love me Tender* the kind of peak time publicity that no studio budget could ever stretch to.

Though on the *Love Me Tender* record label, Elvis shares the songwriting credits for all four songs with Vera Matson, not only did he not co-write these songs, neither did Vera! It was Vera Matson's husband, Ken Darby – the movie's musical director – who was solely responsible for the soundtrack score. The reason for such contortions was strictly a question of finance – specifically, the practice of the publishing arm of the Elvis Empire receiving total or shared publishing royalties in return for Elvis agreeing to record *any* song (check out Elvis' co-author credits on 'Hearbreak Hotel' and 'Don't Be Cruel').

If a mutually satisfying agreement had been reached over the songs Elvis should feature in *Love Me Tender*, the problem of precisely who should play them now had still to be resolved. When the time came for Elvis to record the soundtrack, Ken Darby refused to employ Scotty, Bill and D.J. in any capacity. Darby argued that they were neither capable nor sufficiently experienced to be entrusted with the task of doing justice to his score. Instead, it just so happened that Ken Darby's own Trio was eventually given the task of supplying backtrack. They – and Darby – also got their names splashed about.

Musically, aside from the plaintive title song (based on the traditional air, 'Aura Lee'), the remainder of Darby's score was typical Tinsel Town pseudo-hoedown frivolity.

Love Me Tender/
20th Century Fox

Cast

Vance	Richard Egan
Cathy	Debra Paget
Clint	Elvis Presley
Siringo	Robert Middleton
Brett Reno	William Campbell
Mike Gavin	Neville Brand
The Mother	Mildred Dunnock
Major Kincaid	Bruce Bennett
Ray Reno	James Drury
Ed Galt	Russ Conway
Kelso	Ken Clark
Davis	Barry Coe

Produced by David Weisbart
Directed by Robert D. Webb
Running Time: 89 minutes
Released: November 16, 1956

Love Me Tender was produced by David Weisbart, who had also been responsible in the same capacity for the late James Dean's Rebel Without A Cause. Like so many other young Americans, Elvis was obsessed with the whole James Dean mystique which had, in less than a year since his fatal auto-smash, run almost parallel to his own career in terms of mass hysteria, blind allegiance and commercial exploitation.

Weisbart wasn't Elvis' only link with those who'd known and worked with the late actor. Not only was Elvis dating Dean's Rebel co-star, Natalie Wood, but was also hanging out with Dean's former room-mate, actor Nick Adams (who had enthusiastically bestowed upon himself both the mantle of James Dean and his Rebel red bomber jacket). Incidentally, Adams failed an audition as a Reno Brother because he was considered too young.

From these three people Elvis attempted to extract every possible reminiscence, no matter how trivial, of the late teen idol.

Though Elvis' romance with Natalie Wood eventually cooled, he maintained a long and close relationship with Nick Adams. After both Elvis and Nick died (the latter in 1968 from an OD of paraldehyde and tranquilizers), the inevitable dirt-diggers alleged that this relationship had, like the one Adams shared with Dean, a bisexual basis. It's further alleged that the number of handsome male "cousins" that used to hang out on the periphery of the Presley movie-lots weren't blood relatives but there at Adams' invitation should they be needed for discussions of an exotic nature.

Such subjects are better left to the imagination of scurrilous biographers.

Elvis had ulterior motives for working extremely hard on the set of Love Me Tender. David Weisbart had let it be known that he was contemplating filming The James Dean Story. It also seemed that George W. George and Robert Altman had precisely the same idea. While the latter had chosen Robert Conrad as the possible star, Weisbart had yet to announce who'd play Dean. Above anything, Elvis wanted to be considered for the role. Indeed, it was whispered that Elvis was willing to finance the project whatever the cost.

Weisbart never made his movie, The James Dean Story eventually being made by George and Altman as a rostrum camera documentary, which was withdrawn from circulation soon after release.

N.B. The demand from movie house managers for Love Me Tender was so great that 20th Century Fox distributed an unprecedented 550 prints—almost double that of any other first-run movie. The critics may have crucified Love Me Tender, but before most of the reviews appeared the movie had recouped its one million dollar production cost and was showing a handsome profit.

Love Me Tender

There's little point in pretending that the motion picture career of Elvis Presley was a runaway success. Possibly the kindest thing that anyone can say about it was that it was patchy. The really inferior films didn't, however, start to hit the cinemas until the early sixties. In the fifties the four films that Presley made prior to his induction into the Army, although possibly not great cinema, were certainly a great deal better than the average, cranked out, catchpenny efforts that were released around the same time to cash in on the brand new rock craze.

Originally, Elvis' first break in Hollywood was planned as a supporting role in the Katherine Hepburn, Burt Lancaster picture, The Rainmaker. It's all too possible that if this scheme had come to fruition Presley's career might have gone in a totally different direction, following more closely that of, say, Frank Sinatra, who managed to combine being a singing star and a serious actor.

Certainly, if the flashes he exhibited in some of his films are anything to judge by, Presley had enough talent to make himself a far greater reputation as an actor than he did. Perhaps if he had started his Hollywood career alongside Hepburn and Lancaster, he might have gained greater insight and respect for the craft.

Sadly, this wasn't to be. Somewhere along the line it was decided, almost certainly by Colonel Tom Parker, that Elvis the Singer was too big to make his movie debut in a supporting role. Instead, he should be given a starring vehicle of his own.

20th Century Fox took a not overly impressive Western property titled The Reno Brothers, changed its name to Love Me Tender, (though it was still advertised by its original

Signing film contract with Hal Wallis.

title in some countries) installed David Weisbart as producer and Richard Egan and Debra Paget as co-stars, and the first Elvis Presley movie project was under way.

The plot was unnecessarily complicated. The Reno brothers of the original title are part of a band of Confederate marauders who, in the closing days of the Civil War, are so out of touch with their headquarters that they are not even aware the war is over when they rob a Union train and make off with the Federal payroll.

One Reno brother, Clint (Elvis Presley), was too young to go off to war and stayed home to mind the farm. Hearing mistakenly that the oldest brother, Vance, has been killed in action, Clint marries Vance's fiancée (Debra Paget).

When Vance and the other brothers return to the farm, instant and seemingly unresolvable confusion breaks out, not only over the unfortunate emotional triangle but also over the ultimate fate of the stolen payroll.

Before the final confrontation in which Clint is killed, Elvis also gets the chance to perform four songs. It takes a great stretch of imagination to fit rockabilly tunes into a Western movie, and, indeed it was only accomplished with some sacrifice of plausibility.

From the start to the tearjerk finale—where Egan and Paget walk away from Clint's grave, while a huge ghostly Elvis is superimposed behind them—Love Me Tender is far from being one of the world's greatest movies. It was, however, a good deal better than the kind of vehicles like High School Confidential and Hot Rod Gang that other contemporary stars like Jerry Lee Lewis and Gene Vincent found themselves saddled with.

1956

'ELVIS VOLUME 2' (EP)
(US) RCA EPA-993
Released: December 1956

Side 1
'So Glad You're Mine' (Crudup)
'Old Shep' (Foley)
Side 2
'Ready Teddy' (Blackwell, Marascalco)
'Anypláce Is Paradise' (Thomas)

What with all the commotion of the last 12 months, the idea of a Christmas record had yet to manifest its tinseled head in the Presley scheme of things. However, as the season of good will and reckless spending approached, it was agreed that, as dog was man's best friend, 'Old Shep' – a corny ol' heart-tugging weepie about a faithful-to-the-end mutt – was the *one* Presley record kids could play around the house without parental objections.

Seeing as RCA's Special Products agents had serviced radio stations with truncated single-sided 'Old Shep' promos (CR-15), there was a distinct possibility that parents looking for a cheap stocking-filler would shell out just two bucks and be thankful to receive change.

They did. It reached No. 47.

P4147-11

ELVIS PRESLEY

eclipsed when the second tune came out just under three months later.

It did, however, make No.2 in the charts, and was the first major single hit since 'Hound Dog', breaking the run of non-charting releases (mainly old Sun material and album cuts) that flooded the market in late 1956.

The B-side was a ballad taken from the second album.

At this time, a radio station promo-only DJ-56 (RCA 47-6800) was circulated featuring two of RCA's most popular recording stars.

Side 1. Elvis Presley: 'Too Much'/'Playing For Keeps'
Side 2. Dinah Shore: 'Chantez, Chantez'/'Honky Tonk Heart'

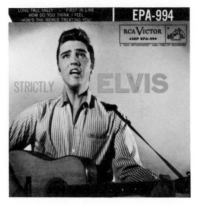

'STRICTLY ELVIS' (EP)
(US) RCA EPA-994
Released: January 1957

Side 1
'Long Tall Sally' (Johnson)
'First In Line' (Schroeder, Weisman)
Side 2
'How Do You Think I Feel' (Pierce)
'How's The World Treating You'
(Atkins, Boudleaux, Bryant)

This release was an opportunity for the owners of *Elvis Volumes 1 and 2* to obtain the last four remaining *Elvis* LP cuts in mini form. If, like the aforementioned EPs, Elvis had chosen to plug one of the titles on TV, then *Strictly Elvis* might have repeated the success of its predecessors.

* **'All Shook Up'** (Blackwell, Presley)
H2WB 0256
** **'That's When Your Heartaches Begin'**
(Fisher, Hill, Raskin) H2WB 0260
(US) RCA 47-6870 (45): 20-6870 (78)
Released: March 1957

Elvis Presley (vcl, gtr), Scotty Moore (gtr),
Dudley Brooks (pno), Bill Black (bs),
D.J. Fontana (dms), The Jordanaires (bv)
*Recorded: Radio Recorders, Hollywood,
January 12, 1957. **January 13, 1957

'Too Much' (Rosenburg, Weisman)
G2WB 4928
'Playing For Keeps' (Kesler) G2WB 4920
(US) RCA 47-6800 (45): 20-6800 (78)
Released: January 1957

Elvis Presley (vcl, gtr), Scotty Moore (gtr),
Bill Black (bs), D.J. Fontana (dms),
The Jordanaires (bv)
Recorded: Radio Recorders, Hollywood,
September 1, 1956

Recorded at the same Hollywood sessions which produced Elvis' second album, 'Too Much' was a more-than creditable solid rocker to start the New Year. The combination of Elvis' vocal and The Jordanaires' backing voices was much the same balance as on 'Don't Be Cruel' and it's very hard to fault the song on any technical level. In actual fact he sang 'Too Much' after 'Don't Be Cruel' on his last-ever *Ed Sullivan Show* (January 6). But since a similar sound and arrangement was used on 'All Shook Up' to far greater effect, 'Too Much' was

'All Shook Up' is still one of those great songs that will be associated with Elvis Presley for as long as he is remembered. Cut at Radio Recorders in Hollywood on January 12 and 13, 1957, the session was part gospel, part rock 'n' roll. Some of the tracks were held for the *Loving You* album. Others found a place on the *Peace in the Valley* EP, while 'All Shook Up', along with the weepie, voice-over B-side, 'That's When Your Heartaches Begin', was picked out for single release.

This was a shrewd, if uninspired move. 'All Shook Up' was Elvis' biggest chart hit, staying in the US No.1 spot for eight weeks straight.

The song also clearly marked Presley's final departure from the sparse, rockabilly sound of the three-piece band, and his adoption of fuller, classic rock 'n' roll arrangements that, from then to his induction into the Army, leaned heavily on the vocal backing of The Jordanaires.

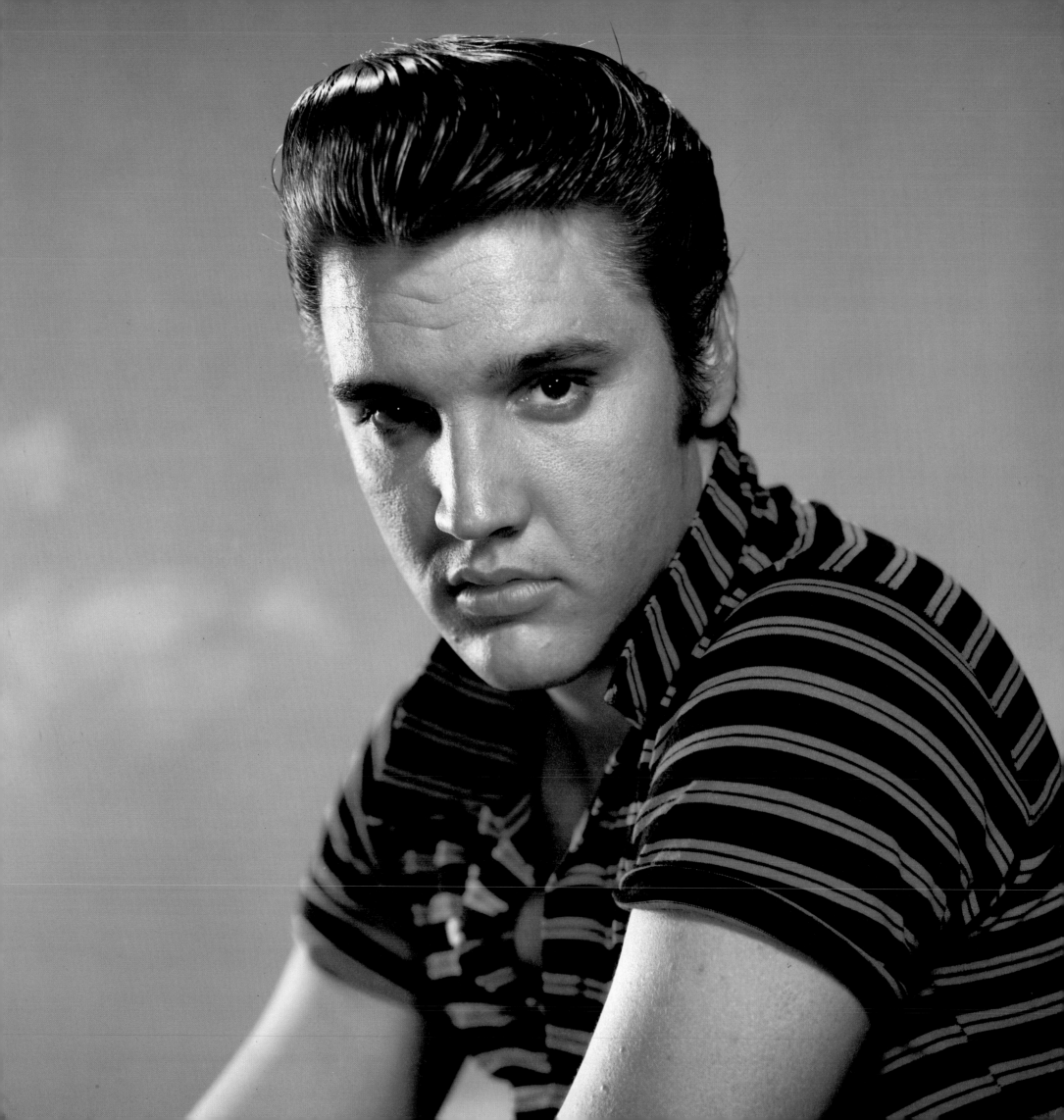

1957

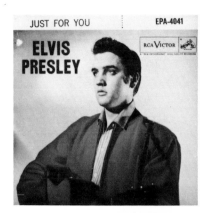

'JUST FOR YOU' (EP)
(US) RCA EPA-4041
Released: April 1957

Side 1
** 'I Need You So' (Hunter) H2WB 0417
* 'Have I Told You Lately That I Love You?'
(Weisman) H2WB 0284
Side 2
* 'Blueberry Hill' (Lewis, Stock, Rose) H2WB 0283
* 'Is It So Strange' (Young) H2WB 0285

Elvis Presley (vcl, gtr), Scotty Moore (gtr),
Dudley Brooks (pno), Bill Black (bs),
D.J. Fontana (dms), The Jordanaires (bv)
*Recorded: Radio Recorders, Hollywood,
January 19, 1957. **February 23, 1957

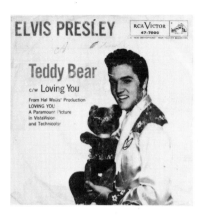

* **'(Let Me Be Your) Teddy Bear'**
(Mann, Lowe) H2WB 2193
** **'Loving You'** (Leiber, Stoller) H2WB 0418
(US) 47-7000 (45): 20-7000 (78)
Released: June 1957

Elvis Presley (vcl, gtr), Scotty Moore (gtr),
Dudley Brooks (pno), Bill Black (bs),
D.J. Fontana (dms), The Jordanaires (bv)
*Recorded: Paramount Studios, Hollywood,
February-March, 1957
**Recorded: Radio Recorders, Hollywood,
February 24, 1957

All through his career Elvis had a habit of indulging in massive bouts of recording at often breakneck speed and then leaving it either to RCA or the Colonel to sort out when and in what form the material would be released.

As with most of the songs recorded during the Hollywood sessions in the spring of 1957, the packaging was carried out in a fairly intelligent manner. This EP represents the country quota of the songs that were put on tape in early 1957.

A sneak preview of the tunes from the movie *Loving You*, at this time poised for release. Apparently the thinking behind the selection was centred on Elvis' widely publicized collection of toy stuffed bears. It was probably the most pop-angled song in the whole movie. The B-side was the slow, drawn-out title ballad that, with the full deep register and hiccup treatment, was a natural sequel to 'Love Me Tender'. The single went to No.1.

Special *Your Dealer Preview* copies of this single were circulated among retailers in limited quantities with a different catalogue number (RCA SDS-57-24).

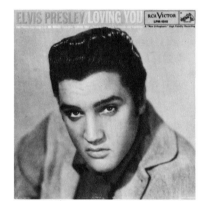

'LOVING YOU' (LP)
(US) RCA LPM-1515
Released: July 1957

Side 1
** 'Mean Woman Blues' (DeMetrius) H2WB 0257
**** '(Let Me Be Your) Teddy Bear' (Mann, Lowe)
H2WB 2193
*** 'Loving You' (Leiber, Stoller) H2WB 0418
* 'Got A Lot O' Livin' To Do'
(Schroeder, Weisman) H2WB 0255
'Lonesome Cowboy' (Tepper, Bennett)
H2WB 2194
**** 'Hot Dog' (Leiber, Stoller) H2WB 2196
**** 'Party' (Robinson) H2WB 2195

Side 2
'Blueberry Hill' (Lewis, Stock, Rose)
*** 'True Love' (Porter) H2WB 0416
*** 'Don't Leave Me Now' (Schroeder, Weisman)
H2WB 0414
'Have I Told You Lately That I Love You?'
(Weisman)
'I Need You So' (Young)

Elvis Presley (vcl, gtr), Scotty Moore (gtr),
Dudley Brooks (pno), Bill Black (bs),
D.J. Fontana (dms), The Jordanaires (bv)
*Recorded: Radio Recorders, Hollywood,
January 12, 1957. **January 13, 1957.
***February 2, 1957. ****February and March
1957

'PEACE IN THE VALLEY' (EP)
(US) RCA EPA-4054
Released: April 1957

Side 1
** '(There'll Be) Peace In The Valley (For Me)'
(Dorsey) H2WB 0258
*** 'It Is No Secret' (Hamblen) H2WB 0282
Side 2
* 'I Believe' (Drake, Graham, Shirl, Stillman)
H2WB 0253
** 'Take My Hand Precious Lord' (Dorsey)
H2WB 0261

Elvis Presley (vcl, gtr), Scotty Moore (gtr),
Dudley Brooks (pno), Bill Black (bs),
D.J. Fontana (dms), The Jordanaires (bv)
*Recorded: Radio Recorders, Hollywood,
January 12, 1957. **January 13, 1957.
***January 19, 1957

Another package from the early 1957 sessions, this time the gospel material. From his childhood Sundays at the First Assembly of God Church, Elvis had acquired a definite taste for "sacred" music. The presentation was tastefully handled, right up to the point of getting Elvis to wear a collar and tie for the cover picture. Sales were sufficiently good (No. 39 in the US charts) for RCA to encourage Elvis to make further excursions into the gospel field.

Without doubt, *Loving You* contained the best collection of rock 'n' roll songs of any movie that Presley ever made. From the pens of writers like Jerry Leiber and Mike Stoller, Doc Pomus and Mort Shuman came tunes like 'Mean Woman Blues', 'Got A Lot O' Livin' To Do' and 'Party'. It was some of the toughest rock 'n' roll material that Elvis ever got to handle. The quality of the music was further enhanced by the fact that, in the context of the film, the majority of the songs was presented in live-on-stage settings, minus any clutter of go-go girls, spurious dance routines or barnyard animals (in later years, the hallmark of the musical performances in the routine Presley film). In *Loving You*, he was given good material and then left alone to sell the songs as best he might.

In addition to the hard rock tunes, the soundtrack album also includes the statutory slow title track and a high drama, hillbilly epic, 'Lonesome Cowboy'. In the US the album was padded out with four country-flavoured songs, 'Don't Leave Me Now', (due to surface

later in the same year in the movie *Jailhouse Rock*), (three from the *Just For You* EP) 'Blueberry Hill', 'Have I Told You Lately That I Love You?' and 'I Need You So'. The US album was a full 12-inch disc; in other territories, however, the package was cut down to a 10-inch record, and the only filler was the somewhat substandard 'True Love', a song that first saw the light of day as a nautical duet between Bing Crosby and Grace Kelly in the film musical *High Society*.

N.B. One of the most illuminating of all Elvis bootlegs is a superbly packaged LP comprised almost entirely of Elvis working on slow, fast and jazzy versions of this movie's title track. The listener is afforded a unique fly-on-the-wall insight of Elvis and his musicians developing a song in the studio until they've finally set the familiar recorded treatment.

Today, Elvis' legacy would be better served if RCA authorized LPs of this nature, rather than re-packaging the same easily-available hits.

Loving You/Paramount

Cast
Deke Rivers......................Elvis Presley
Glenda.........................Lizabeth Scott
Tex Warner..............Wendell Corey
Susan Jessup.................Dolores Hart
Carl.............................James Gleason
Tallman.........................Ralph Dumke
Skeeter................................Paul Smith
Wayne...........................Ken Becker
Daisy.................................Jana Lund

Produced by Hal B. Wallis
Directed by Hal Kanter
Running Time: 101 minutes
Released: July 9, 1957

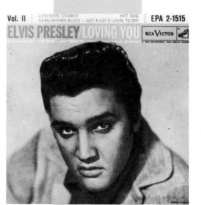

In many ways *Loving You* is one of the most interesting of all the Elvis Presley films. Basically, it is a sanitized version of Presley's own rise to fame on the backroads rockabilly circuit.

A young man with the unlikely name of Deke Rivers is spotted by a down-at-heel country swing band leader (Wendell Corey) and his ex-wife manager (Lizabeth Scott). Rivers joins the band, but is kept as a fake "local talent" who is encouraged to jump up from the audience at the small town fairs and political rallies that the band has sunk to playing.

The impact that the kid has on the young people in the audience leads Scott and Corey to realize that they may be on to a good thing. Alternately exploiting and promoting him, they ride Deke Rivers' talent all the way back to the big city theatres.

Somewhat dazed by sudden success and the resulting fan hysteria, Rivers has difficulty dealing with the girls who thrust themselves at him, the young hoodlums who want to beat him up and the dubious business deals that his new managers involve him in.

There is also an emotional tangle in which Rivers is torn between his lady manager – the older, more experienced, manipulative woman – and the counterpoint ingenue (Dolores Hart).

The whole situation is finally, if less than realistically, resolved on a network TV show that pompously seeks to discover if rock 'n' roll is a force for good or evil.

On the surface *Loving You* seems to be little more than an old-fashioned showbiz romantic drama, updated for the first rock generation. Fortunately, neither the plot nor the acting is the most important thing about this film. What matters about *Loving You* is that it provides the world with something that approaches a visual record of Presley's early stage performances.

Only fleeting and badly-shot clips exist of the young Presley's explosive live performances as a legacy of that era. In *Loving You* these performances, although possibly a little watered down, are consciously recreated for the cinema audience. Certainly you do get enough of the wildly swinging hips and corkscrewing leg (but not crutch slap) to realize what exactly it was that drove the girls crazy back in those early days.

Loving You is also the only colour movie that Presley made before he was drafted.

N.B. In the final concert sequence, Elvis' mother can clearly be seen as a member of the audience. Following her death, Elvis refused to watch the movie ever again.

'LOVING YOU. VOLUME I' (EP)
(US) RCA EPA-1-1515
Released: August 1957

Side 1
'Loving You' (Leiber, Stoller)
'Party' (Robinson)
Side 2
'(Let Me Be Your) Teddy Bear' (Mann, Lowe)
'True Love' (Porter)

'LOVING YOU. VOLUME 2' (EP)
(US) RCA EPA-2-1515
Released: August 1957

Side 1
'Lonesome Cowboy' (Tepper, Bennett)
'Hot Dog' (Leiber, Stoller)
Side 2
'Mean Woman Blues' (De Metrius)
'Got A Lot O' Livin' To Do'
(Schroeder, Weisman)

Although, the market-cautious British settled for an eight-song 10-inch LP (RCA RC-24001) to present the entire *Loving You* soundtrack, in the US it was fleshed out into a costlier 12-incher by the addition of aforementioned non-movie titles. In future "bonus songs" – as such a padding procedure was termed – would become a common if sometimes irritating occurrence. Whether this brace of EPs was another method of extracting additional cash from Elvis fans on a tight budget, or a means of pandering to soundtrack buffs, is open to speculation. Whatever, this was the only means of obtaining the entire *Loving You* score sans frills.

August 1957
Elvis Presley selects his gold lame suit (and matching gold Cadillac convertible) for a four-day North-West Pacific Coast mini-tour. Opening in Spokane, Seattle (30), he plays Vancouver, B.C. (31), and Seattle, Washington (Sept 1). The following day, his show in Portland Oregon is stopped after 15-minutes because of hysterical fans. On this tour (which grossed $147,000), Elvis' repertoire comprised: 'Tutti Frutti', 'Don't Be Cruel', 'I Got A Woman', 'Heartbreak Hotel', Tryin' To Get To You', 'Old Shep', 'Blue Suede Shoes', 'I'm Counting On You', 'Blueberry Hill', '(Let Me Be Your) Teddy Bear', 'Loving You', 'I Love You Because', 'Rip It Up', 'When My Blue Moon Turns To Gold Again', 'I Was The One', 'So Glad You're Mine', 'Love Me' and 'Hound Dog'.

Jailhouse Rock

To some extent *Jailhouse Rock* was another version of Presley's own rise to fame. Although the Presley character, Vince Everett, was far more hard-bitten, violent and cynical than the bemused and naive Deke Rivers in *Loving You*, the resemblance is still there.

Jailed for manslaughter, Vince is taken under the wing of a long term con (Mickey Shaughnessy) and finds himself involved in a prison TV show where he performs a song with Shaughnessy's inmate country band. He also finds himself involved in a prison riot, which results in a brutal flogging.

This notwithstanding, Shaughnessy encourages Vince to take up a musical career once he gets out of the slammer. They decide to become partners on the outside and accordingly sign a fifty-fifty contract.

Vince is the first of the pair to hit the bricks, and, struggling on his own to get ahead in the music business, is abused by drunken hecklers and ripped off by a dishonest record label. On the plus side, he is also befriended by Peggy (Judy Tyler), a record industry promoperson who works with him on his career.

Together they form a small independent record label, a single disc jockey gives them a break and Vince finds that he's taken his first step on the fairytale road to teen idoldom.

Teen idoldom, however, doesn't do too much to improve Vince's personality. He throws his money around, surrounds himself with fast blondes and a tight coterie of

professional hangers-on (sound familiar?); he also dumps all over the loyal and loving Peggy.

Eventually Shaughnessy gets out of jail, and confronts Vince with their jailhouse contract. Vince charmlessly tells him that it's worthless, and instead, offers him the job of flunkey. Shaughnessy quickly graduates to being Vince's less-than-wanted conscience. They fight over Vince's treatment of Peggy and after a blow to the throat, Vince undergoes an emergency operation.

The big ending comes when Vince has to find out whether or not he can still sing. Of course he can, and not only that, he also realizes that Peggy is the one that he's needed all along. The credits are free to roll.

Elvis himself is on record as commenting that, "We had more excitement making this film than I could have believed possible". By the standards of a Presley movie it definitely stands out for its tight scripting, balance between action, humour and music, and supporting cast. The tough, moody, resentful Presley comes across better on the screen than the amiable cretin that he was to play so many times in years to come.

Even the music was robust and energetic rock 'n' roll. Although the songs were presented rather more stagily than in *Loving You*, Presley was still wild and energetic, and, if anything, more confident and assured in the musical numbers than he had been in the previous film.

N.B. The 'Jailhouse Rock' sequence was a rare occasion when Elvis was given a free hand to choreograph the action.

1957

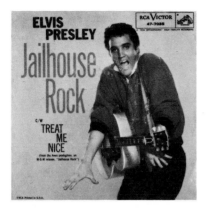

* **'Jailhouse Rock'** (Leiber, Stoller) H2WB 6779
** **'Treat Me Nice'** (Leiber, Stoller) H2PB 5523
(US) 47-7035 (45): 20-7035 (78)
Released: September 1957

Elvis Presley (vcl, gtr), Scotty Moore (gtr),
Dudley Brooks (pno), Bill Black (bs),
D.J. Fontana (dms), The Jordanaires (bv)
*Recorded: MGM Sound Studio, Culver City,
Los Angeles, May 2, 1957
Elvis Presley (vcl, gtr), Scotty Moore (gtr),
Dudley Brooks (pno), Mike Stoller (*pno),
Bill Black (bs), D.J. Fontana (dms),
The Jordanaires (bv)
**Recorded: Radio Recorders, Hollywood,
September 5, 1957

outing as a single, 'Don't Leave Me Now' had been on the *Loving You* album in the US and on an EP in most other areas (although this is an entirely different version). That just left three new cuts for Presley's by then massive international public.

'Young And Beautiful' was the slow, romantic ballad that by now seemed a mandatory ingredient of every Presley picture. 'I Want To Be Free' was something else again. Relying on sonorous, pounding triplets, it was almost a throwback to the clean, uncluttered Sun sound that, after Presley's switch to RCA, seemed to have been lost in a welter of echo and Jordanaires' wop-shoo-wah harmonies.

The standout cut – with the exception of the title song – had to be 'Baby I Don't Care', a rocker in the great classic tradition. Over the years, this has become one of the great standards of rock 'n' roll. And despite all other attempts, the Presley treatment of it has yet to be equalled.

N.B. In 1982, RCA's British wing re-issued this EP with the addition of 'Treat Me Nice'.

The movie *Jailhouse Rock* followed hot on the heels of *Loving You*, and, following the normal practice of the times, the first solid hint of its existence came in the form of a preview single.

There would come a time when an Elvis Presley movie title song would elicit nothing more than resigned groans from everyone but (including?) the hardest of hardcore fans. At the time of *Jailhouse Rock*, though, this was part of a distant and unsuspected future. The song 'Jailhouse Rock' was an all-time Elvis Presley rock 'n' roll classic. At maximum stretch, Elvis' voice turned what, in anyone else's hands, would have been a fairly average R&B tune into one of the most impressive, raucous singles in rock history.

In the original movie soundtrack, the song was saddled with an overblown brass and choral back-up (like most of the screen songs that differed from recorded versions, it has been widely bootlegged). The RCA single was, however, stripped down to the bone, and all Presley had to contend with was a streamlined backing track featuring – guess who? – Scotty Moore, Bill Black, D.J. Fontana, Dudley Brooks and The Jordanaires.

The B-side, 'Treat Me Nice', was a rolling, arrogant rocker with Stoller's piano well to the fore. It was a classic of the fifties' I-want-to-get-laid genre, and the lyrics, with lines like "scratch my back and run your pretty fingers through my hair" scandalized those moralists who were already trying hard to prove that Elvis was a corrupting influence on Western youth in general, and US youth in particular.

Special *Your Dealer Preview* copies of this single were circulated amongst retailers in limited quantities with a different catalogue number (RCA SDS-57-39). 'Jailhouse Rock' was also featured on another RCA Special Products' 'various artists' EP (RCA SPA-7-61).

'JAILHOUSE ROCK' (EP)
(US) RCA EPA-4114
Released: November 1957

Side 1
'Jailhouse Rock' (Leiber, Stoller) H2WB 6779
*'Young And Beautiful' (Silver, Schroeder)
H2WB 6777
Side 2
'I Want To Be Free' (Leiber, Stoller) H2WB 6781
*'Don't Leave Me Now' (Schroeder, Weisman)
H2WB 6783
'Baby, I Don't Care' (Leiber, Stoller) H2WB 6782

Elvis Presley (vcl, gtr), Scotty Moore (gtr),
Dudley Brooks (pno), Mike Stoller (pno),
Bill Black (bs), D.J. Fontana (dms),
The Jordanaires (bv)
Recorded: MGM Sound Studios, Culver City,
California, May 2, 1957

Jailhouse Rock/
20th Century Fox

Cast
Vince Everett..................Elvis Presley
Peggy Van Alden................Judy Tyler
Hunk Houghton......................................
..........................Mickey Shaughnessy
Sherry Wilson..........Jennifer Holden
Eddy Talbot.....................Dean Jones
Laury Jackson............ Anne Neyland
Warden........................Hugh Sanders

Produced by Pandro S. Berman
Directed by Richard Thorpe
Running Time: 96 minutes
Released: October 21, 1957

Although *Jailhouse Rock* was – without question – one of Elvis' finest films, it was undeniably light on songs. In the context of the film, however, this was quite acceptable, and the balance of plot and music was maintained quite carefully.

In recording terms, though, the film was not exactly jam-packed with new material. What there was proved to be little short of magnificent. 'Jailhouse Rock' had already had an

'ELVIS' CHRISTMAS ALBUM'
(US) RCA LOC-1035
Released: November 1957

Side 1
*** 'Santa Claus Is Back In Town' (Leiber, Stoller)
H2PB 5532
** 'White Christmas' (Berlin) H2PB 5526
** 'Here Comes Santa Claus'
(Autry, Haldeman, Melka) H2PB 5527
*** 'I'll Be Home For Christmas' (Kent, Gannon, Ram)
H2PB 5533
* 'Blue Christmas' (Hayes, Johnson) H2PB 5525
*** 'Santa, Bring My Baby Back (To Me)'
(Schroeder, DeMetrius) H2PB 5531
Side 2
*** 'O Little Town Of Bethlehem' (Redner, Brooks)
H2PB 5530
** 'Silent Night' (Mohr, Gruber) H2PB 5528
**** '(There'll Be) Peace In The Valley (For Me)'
(Dorsey) H2WB 0258
**** 'I Believe' (Drake, Graham, Shirl, Stillman)
H2WB 0253
**** 'Take My Hand Precious Lord' (Dorsey)
H2WB 0261
**** 'It's No Secret' (Hamblen) H2WB 0282

Elvis Presley (vcl, gtr), Scotty Moore (gtr),
Dudley Brooks (pno), Bill Black (bs),
D.J. Fontana (dms), The Jordanaires,
Millie Kirkham (bv)
*Recorded: Radio Recorders, Hollywood.
September 5, 1957. **September 6, 1957.
***September 7, 1957. ****Previously released
on 'Peace In The Valley' (EPA-4054)

In the fifties, nobody could accuse the men behind Elvis Presley of being reluctant to jump on to any available marketing bandwagon. At a time when Tom Parker was still personally hawking souvenirs at Presley concerts, Christmas – more importantly, the Christmas spending orgy – was something that simply couldn't be passed up.

The success of the *Peace in the Valley* EP had demonstrated that the public was quite willing to accept Elvis singing gospel songs. So if gospel could work, then why not . . . er . . . Christmas carols?

In fact, the Christmas album was simply a straightforward collection of carols and Yuletide standards. There was 'Silent Night', 'O Little Town Of Bethlehem', 'White Christmas', 'Here Comes Santa Claus', 'I'll be Home For Christmas', and even four cuts from *Peace in the Valley* were dragged around for a second time to pad out the album to a full dozen tracks.

Any innovation in the set was confined to rock 'n' roll Christmas songs, virtually the first of their kind. But the country-flavoured 'Blue Christmas' – on which Presley comes uncomfortably close to yodelling – was fairly predictable. Nashville had, after all, been turning out similar festive fodder for years. 'Santa Bring My Baby Back' is somewhat less predictable. A bouncy if lightweight rocker, it pranced along in a similar rhythmic vein to 'Don't Be Cruel', but revealed nothing to the fans that they hadn't seen before.

For the rock enthusiasts, however, the real surprise of the whole Christmas album was the cut 'Santa Claus Is Back In Town', a Leiber and Stoller collaboration. It was a cut without tinsel or sleighbells. Santa arrived in a big black Cadillac, and Elvis turned in just about the most down-and-dirty blues that he would commit to vinyl until he cut Lowell Fulson's 'Reconsider Baby' after he returned from the army in 1960.

Ever since it was first released, the Christmas album has been one of Presley's perennial sellers, and each holiday season it still faithfully shows up in the stores.

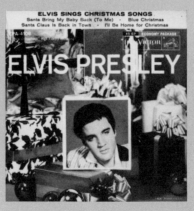

'ELVIS SINGS CHRISTMAS SONGS' (EP)
(US) RCA EPA-4108
Released: December 1957

Side 1
'Santa, Bring My Baby Back (To Me)'
(Schroeder, De Metrius)
'Blue Christmas' (Hayes, Johnson)
Side 2
'Santa Claus Is Back In Town' (Leiber, Stoller)
'I'll Be Home For Christmas' (Kent, Gannon, Ram)

For the secularists who demanded change out of two bucks, RCA astutely packaged together four of the more contemporary cuts from Elvis' first (and most successful) dabble in seasonal schlock. To promote both this EP and the album from which it had been culled, RCA's Special Products department serviced radio stations with promo-only singles of 'Blue Christmas' (RCA 0808).

1958-60 ROCK'N'ROLL

ROOKIE

1958

The drafting into the United States Army of Elvis Presley was a massive public relations project for everyone involved, not least the United States Army. The normal practice, particularly during World War II, when Uncle Sam had come a-knocking on the doors of show business personalities, was either to exempt them on medical grounds (as had happened in the case of "lucky" Frank Sinatra) or to place them in some special category unit where (like unlucky Glenn Miller) their talents could be made use of by the military.

At first it seemed as though Elvis would follow one of these routes. An Army spokesman in Memphis asked what would be the fate of the famous Presley haircut, announced that Presley would, in all probability, be assigned as an entertainer to Army Special Services and that his hair was therefore likely to remain unmolested. This immediately triggered off a storm of protest. A Republican Senator, Clifford Case, angrily demanded to know why Presley should be given preferential treatment. And so on.

The problem fell into the lap of one Brigadier General J.E. Bastion Jr. who, in late 1957, gave out the final word on the Army's attitude towards its controversial recruit. Presley would receive no special treatment, and if Elvis Presley passed all the induction tests, he would receive his basic training at Fort Chaffee, Arkansas, in company with draftees inducted at the same time.

Furthermore, the hair would go.

Elvis himself concurred humbly with their plans. From the set of *Jailhouse Rock*, he told reporters, "I'm not worried about my hair or sideburns or what the army is going to do with me. Everybody who goes into the service gets their hair cut. I expect it, and I wouldn't have it any other way. I'm just a normal healthy guy like all the rest. Only thing is, I got a little break outta life.

"Whatever the army people want me to do is fine. I don't expect any special privileges or favors. Those people in the service are fair. They demand discipline and respect, and that's what I'll give them.

"Maybe the army will put me in a motor pool. I used to be a truck driver, you know. One thing's sure, I don't really believe they're going to try to make life any harder for me than anybody else. They don't run that kind of outfit."

If, however, either Elvis or the military believed that that was the end of the matter, they were sadly mistaken. Despite all protests to the contrary, there was no way that Elvis Presley could be treated like any other private soldier. The process of transforming The Hillbilly Cat into Private US 53310761 was turned into a circus complete with hysterical fans, equally hysterical media, crowds of onlookers and Colonel Tom Parker with his eye open to every angle. The circus reached its peak during the first few days at Fort Chaffee when photographers were allowed a final rampage. Private Benny St Clair, an inductee from Texarkana, Arkansas, was seated next to Elvis during lunch. When photographers did everything but come to blows for pictures of the new Presley, he turned to Elvis in amazement.

"Is it always like this?"

"Yep."

"Doesn't it bother you?"

This time Elvis shook his head.

"Nope. I figure I better start worrying when they don't bother me any more."

Elvis may not have been worrying, but plenty of people were. Most vocal in their anguish were, of course, the fans.

"You didn't draft Beethoven!" was the scream of one midnight caller who had decided that Milton Bowers, the chairman of Local Board 86, (the Board that had both drafted and deferred Elvis in the same week) was to blame.

This was only one of a few hundred cranks who felt compelled to either write or call Bowers. One young woman even went so far as to threaten to come down to Memphis and personally murder the entire board if Elvis was drafted. Bowers passed the letter on to the police.

Not only the fans were worried. Tom Parker and RCA Records were seriously concerned that a two year disappearance might kill off Elvis altogether and there'd be no more golden eggs from their boy goose. Strategies were plotted, rumours circulated and a massive re-issue operation organized.

The IRS couldn't have been all that happy either. In the act of turning Elvis from a $105,000-a-week rock 'n' roll star into a $83.20 GI the US Government lost approximately half a million dollars in taxes.

Then, abruptly, the insanity stopped. The reporters and photographers were barred from the Army posts and, just like the army said in the first place, Elvis was a private in basic training. It seemed that, when the chips were down, the army could beat out the media any time.

In fact, the Presley life in the army was far from the normal, no frills, no favours routine that had been so widely touted. Invoking an army regulation which specified that if a soldier has dependants living nearby he was entitled to live off camp, Elvis was to return each evening to the full spectrum of rock star comforts. All he had to do was move his father, Vernon Presley, to a convenient point near the base, claim Pa as a dependant and that was it. This gave Elvis the ability to enjoy the prolonged company of, among others, starlet Anita Wood, a boon not granted to many servicemen.

While in the US the Presley off-camp residence only amounted to a three bedroomed mobile home. In Germany, however, it was the full star treatment of a luxury apartment, a chauffeur-driven black Mercedes to drive Private Presley to and from the camp, and a seemingly limitless supply of the cream of fraüleins.

Thus, while the world was being fed a perfect patriotic picture of Elvis the model dogface, mucking in with the rest of the guys, the truth had a far more schizophrenic flavour. From nine to five Elvis performed the usual military duties – in his case, acting as driver for his company sergeant. By night, though, it was the life of a rock 'n' roll idol, albeit somewhat low-profile and without interruptions for live shows and recording dates.

Another plus was the slightly less than conventional relationship with Priscilla Beaulieu, the then fourteen-year-old daughter of a US Air Force major. It certainly wasn't every GI who got to hang around with an officer's underage daughter.

In many ways these double standards – a public image of shining his army boots and keeping out of barrack room crap games so as not to set a bad example to his fans, and a private life of starlets, strippers, private afterhours nightclub parties, a rumoured undercover Christmas vacation in London and even a projected trip to Paris to date Brigitte Bardot (Bardot declined) – began to set a pattern for the secretive, reclusive life that was to become so much a part of the Presley image in later years. (In 1978, a book of candid photographs by Rudolf Paulini appeared, showing Presley posing with models, B girls and strippers in a Munich fleshpot.)

There was one other problem created by the determined efforts to present Elvis as the model soldier. The almost total embargo on recording sessions meant that by the end of 1959, there was precious little material with which to feed the hungry public. There was a considerable slump in record sales. Suddenly, as Elvis prepared to return to civilian life, it became clear that an awful lot hinged on what Elvis did immediately he got out of the service.

The only blight on this period, which had otherwise proved to be an overwhelming public relations exercise for both Presley and the US Army, was the untimely death of Elvis' mother Gladys on August 14, 1958. Bereavement would appear to have been a traumatic experience. Certainly, his attachment to his mother was legendary; her death must have had a very far-reaching and lasting effect.

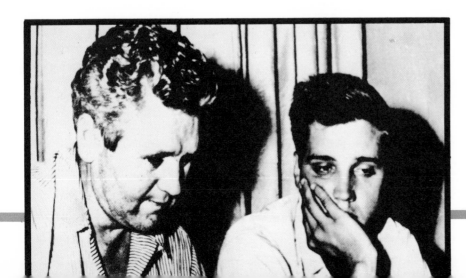

1958

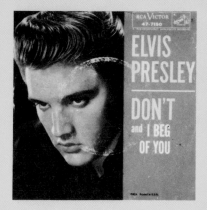

** **'Don't'** (Leiber, Stoller) H2PB 5529
* **'I Beg Of You'** (McCoy, Owens) H2WB 0259
(US) 47-7150 (45): 20-7150 (78)
Released: January 1958

Elvis Presley (vcl, gtr), Scotty Moore (gtr),
Dudley Brooks (pno), Bill Black (bs),
D.J. Fontana (dms), Millie Kirkham,
The Jordanaires (bv)
*Recorded: Radio Recorders, Hollywood,
February 23, 1957. **September 6, 1957

For the first time since 'Love Me Tender', an Elvis Presley single came out with a ballad on the A-side. This might have seemed a strange move at a time when Presleymania and rock 'n' roll mass hysteria were just about at their peak.

'Don't', however, wasn't any ordinary single. It was a heavy, ponderous song that built from a deceptively leaden beginning to a simmering frenzy of repressed passion. Maybe its success was due in part to Elvis' first showing of his sub-operatic, Mario Lanza voice that would later be given full rein on songs like 'It's Now Or Never' and 'Surrender'.

Much more likely, though, was that, on a subliminal level, 'Don't', either deliberately or accidentally, exactly caught the stop-go, don't-touch-me-there rhythm of back seat sex that was so familiar to a great many fifties teens.

It was ironic that the heavily sexual 'Don't' was recorded at the same September, 1957 sessions that produced the carols and religious songs for the Christmas album.

Those who were still hungry for an up-tempo cut could be more than satisfied with 'I Beg Of You', a robust rocker that was recorded at the same time as 'All Shook Up', shelved, and then dusted off as the first B-side of 1958.

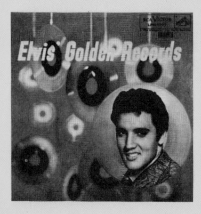

'ELVIS' GOLDEN RECORDS VOLUME I'
(LP)
(US) RCA LPM-1707
Released: March 1958

Side 1
'Hound Dog' (Leiber, Stoller)
'Loving You' (Leiber, Stoller)
'All Shook Up' (Presley, Blackwell)
'Heartbreak Hotel' (Axton, Durden, Presley)
'Jailhouse Rock' (Leiber, Stoller)
'Love Me' (Leiber, Stoller)
'Too Much' (Rosenberg, Weisman)
Side 2
'Don't Be Cruel' (Blackwell)
'That's When Your Heartaches Begin'
(Fisher, Hill)
'(Let Me Be Your) Teddy Bear' (Mann, Love)
'Love Me Tender' (Presley, Matson)
'Treat Me Nice' (Leiber, Stoller)
'Anyway You Want Me' (Schroeder, Owens)
'I Want You, I Need You, I Love You'
(Mysels, Kosloff)

First of the line of hit collections and one that accurately documents the first two years of Presleyitis. It crashed *Billboard's* albums chart at No.3 and remained in the listings for 50 straight weeks.

'Wear My Ring Around Your Neck'
(Carroll, Moody) J2WB 0181
'Don'cha Think It's Time' (Otis, Dixon)
J2WB 0179
(US) RCA 47-7240 (45): 20-7240 (78)
Released: April 1958

Elvis Presley (vcl, gtr), Scotty Moore,
Tiny Trimbrell (gtr), Dudley Brooks (pno),
Bill Black (bs), D.J. Fontana (dms),
The Jordanaires (bv)
Recorded: Radio Recorders, Hollywood,
February 1, 1958

This rock 'n' roll plea to go steady wasn't exactly the greatest Presley single, but it was a fairly creditable rocker. Unfortunately, it only made No.3 in the US charts, the first single that hadn't hit the No.1 slot for over a year.

'Hard Headed Woman' (DeMetrius)
J2PB 3603
'Don't Ask Me Why' (Wise, Weisman)
J2PB 3610
(US) 47-7280 (45): 20-7280 (78)
Released: June 1958

Elvis Presley (vcl, gtr), Scotty Moore (gtr),
Bill Black(bs), D.J. Fontana (dms),
The Jordanaires (bv),
Paramount Studio Orchestra
Recorded: Radio Recorders, Hollywood,
January 1958

This first preview single from the *King Creole* movie soundtrack suffered from the same problems as most of the songs from the film. The amalgam of rock 'n' roll and Dixieland jazz which had been cooked up to give the movie a supposedly authentic New Orleans flavour simply didn't work.

On the screen, the impact of the film was largely sufficient to overcome the shortcomings of the music, but on record it was all too apparent that something didn't quite fit.

King Creole

In his fourth film, *King Creole*, Elvis was finally given a property on which to cut his musical and acting teeth. Sure, it was still the story of the mixed fortunes of a young singer, but at least it wasn't simply a rise-to-fame story. Also, Elvis was blessed by a supporting cast that included such veterans as Walter Matthau, Carolyn Jones and Dean Jagger.

Presley has always cited this movie as his favourite out of all that he made. Indeed, it does show Elvis moving towards serious acting. Unfortunately, like so many other promising directions, it was one that was abandoned after his emergence from the Army.

In the original Harold Robbins novel, the Elvis Presley character, Danny Fisher, was a struggling boxer. When producer Hal Wallis secured Presley to take the starring role in the film for Paramount Pictures, it was deemed the boxer should be transformed into a singer. After all, this was 1958, when people still cared what an Elvis Presley film came out like, not 1962, when he was casually shoehorned into the less than appropriate *Kid Galahad* boxing role.

Another change in *King Creole* is that the young singer, Danny Fisher, is not strictly trying

Recording for *King Creole*.

to make it as a rock 'n' roll star. In fact, his prime motivation is to make it through high school. With an unemployed father, Fisher's only way to accomplish this is to work as a bus boy in a shabby night club.

This work environment puts him in contact with a broad cross-section of the New Orleans low life. One of these is Ronnie (Carolyn Jones), a hooker with a (proverbial) heart of gold whom Danny Fisher protects from a bunch of early morning drunks. When Ronnie drives him to school, insults from schoolyard punks involve Danny in a fight and that results in his losing his chance to graduate.

For Danny Fisher, however, life holds no dull moments. Later the same night he is attacked by a teenage gang, led by Shark (Vic Morrow). He acquits himself so well in the ensuing rumble that the gang does a complete turn-around and invites him along on a shoplifting expedition the next day. Danny's slightly implausible role in the operation is to sing and play his guitar while the rest of the gang plunders the counters of a department store.

It's at this point that the device of switching the central, Danny Fisher character from a boxer to a singer starts to put a rather serious crimp in the plot.

In between bouts of being a reluctant, trainee juvenile delinquent, falling deeper into the sinister clutches of local mafia chieftain Maxie Fields (Walter Matthau), conducting a torrid affair with Ronnie, and a much more innocent one with the ingenue Nellie (Dolores Hart in her second Presley film), he also manages to embark on a career as a singer.

At a club called the King Creole, Danny turns out to be an instant success and starts packing in capacity crowds. Maxie Fields, who owns a rival nightspot, the Blue Shade, doesn't like this one little bit. He tries to win Fisher away from the King Creole by devious means, and the plot thickens to the point of being almost impenetrable.

Danny is blackmailed into taking part in a robbery, the victim of which, unknown to him, is his own father. With Pop badly hurt, Danny has no option but to accept Maxie Fields' offer to pay the hospital bills. Danny is now totally in hock to Fields. For a while he goes along with the situation, but when Fields tells Fisher Senior that his own son was one of the attackers, Danny freaks out and beats up the gangster.

Fields turns the heavies loose on Danny, and he holes up with Ronnie in a remote bayou cabin. Finally, the hoodlums catch up with him and Ronnie is shot dead. Fortunately, Maxie Fields is also killed, and Danny is able to return to the King Creole where he is reconciled with both his father and the ever loyal Nellie.

Confusing? Maybe, but *King Creole* is a masterpiece of dramatic structure compared with some of the later movies.

One of the least appealing facets of *King Creole* is the music. Although Elvis himself is in fine form, his wilder stage routines are toned down quite considerably, and many of the arrangements are a forced and scarcely workable fusion of rockabilly and Dixieland.

Despite the raucously blaring jazz band horns, some songs, particularly 'Trouble' and 'New Orleans', manage to cut through the cacophony.

This, once again, seems to be an example of Hollywood high-handedness. If anybody had bothered to ask any of the musicians involved in the making of the film, they would have discovered that a young singer in New Orleans in 1958 would have been more likely to be singing against a booting back-up band akin to Fats Domino, Little Richard or Professor Longhair than the bastardized Dixieland rock 'n' roll that seems to have been specifically invented to give the film ersatz local colour.

All this notwithstanding, *King Creole* was still the last great Presley film until the Las Vegas and live tour movies of the 1970s.

1958

King Creole/Paramount

Cast
Danny Fisher .... Elvis Presley
Ronnie .... Carolyn Jones
Nellie .... Dolores Hart
Mr. Fisher .... Dean Jagger
"Forty" Nina ..... Liliane Montevecchi
Maxie Fields .... Walter Matthau
Mimi .... Jan Shepard
Charlie LeGrand .... Paul Stewart
Shark .... Vic Morrow

Produced by Hal B. Wallis
Directed by Michael Curtiz
Running time: 115 minutes
Released: June 4, 1958

'KING CREOLE' (LP)
(US) RCA LPM-1884
Released: August 1958

Side 1
'King Creole' (Leiber, Stoller) J2PB 3612
'As Long As I Have You' (Wise, Weisman)
J2PB 3611
'Hard Headed Woman' (DeMetrius) J2PB 3603
'Trouble' (Leiber, Stoller) J2PB 3604
'Dixieland Rock' (Schroeder, Frank) J2PB 3608
Side 2
'Don't Ask Me Why' (Wise, Weisman) J2PB 3610
'Lover Doll' (Wayne) J2PB 3609 new matrix
number J2WB 3262
'Crawfish' (Wise, Weisman) J2PB 3607
'Young Dreams' (Kalmanoff) J2PB 3613
'Steadfast, Loyal And True' (Leiber, Stoller)
J2PB 4228; new matrix number J2WB 3261
'New Orleans' (Tepper, Bennett) J2PB 3605

Elvis Presley (vcl, gtr), Scotty Moore (gtr),
Bill Black (bs), D.J. Fontana (dms),
The Jordanaires, Kitty White (bv),
Paramount Studio Orchestra
Recorded: Radio Recorders, Hollywood,
January 1958

immediately reversed his original decision.

Actually, before being transformed into an all-action musical, the original screen treatment of *A Stone For Danny Fisher* was going to be James Dean's next vehicle after *Somebody Up There Likes Me*. With regard to the latter, Dean's death resulted in the role of real-life prize-fighter Rocky Graziano being given to a likeable young actor named Paul Newman, who also picked up another movie part scheduled for Dean, *The Left-Handed Gun*.

N.B. The take of 'Lover Doll' is different to that on the *King Creole* soundtrack album.

The hybrid of pseudo-Dixieland and rock 'n' roll made this a peculiarly mixed album. On the plus side there were tracks like the magnificent 'Trouble', 'Crawfish' and 'New Orleans'.

Without the raucous traditional jazz horns, 'Hard Headed Woman' and 'Dixieland Rock' might have had a chance at being average Presley rockers, but as they came out on the album, they had a forced, unreal air to them that was a lot less than acceptable.

'As Long As I Have You' and 'Don't Ask Me Why' were the standard, and infinitely forgettable, slow ballads that seemed obligatory for any Elvis film. 'Lover Doll' and 'Young Dreams' were a pair of lightweight rock tunes in the style of 'Teddy Bear', and hardly amounted to much more than musical candy floss.

Then, of course, there was 'Steadfast, Loyal and True', the school song of the (fictional) Royal High School. It may have been mildly amusing in the context of the movie plot, but it hardly needed to be put on record except as a filler.

It was pretty much of a shame that one of Presley's better dramatic movies should have been saddled with music that was, with few exceptions, substandard.

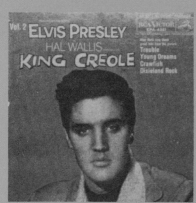

'KING CREOLE VOLUME 1' (EP)
(US) RCA EPA-4319
Released: October 1958

Side 1
'King Creole' (Leiber, Stoller)
'New Orleans' (Tepper, Bennett)
Side 2
'As Long As I Have You' (Wise, Weisman)
'Lover Doll' (Wayne)

'KING CREOLE' VOLUME 2' (EP)
(US) RCA EPA-4321
Released: October 1958

Side 1
'Trouble' (Leiber, Stoller)
'Young Dreams' (Kalmanoff)
Side 2
'Crawfish' (Wise, Weisman)
'Dixieland Rock' (Schroeder, Frank)

The second and last occasion when an Elvis Presley soundtrack would be broken down into Economical Packs.

As a matter of interest, Michael Curtiz – best known for being the director of *Casablanca* – initially refused to direct Elvis in *King Creole*. The Hungarian-born moviemaker's reason was that he was only accustomed to working with actors who, Curtiz insisted, possessed more "dignity" than this rather flashy singer. However, after he had met and been completely charmed by the ever-so-respectful star of the production, Curtiz

1958

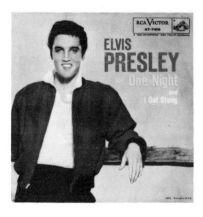

** **'One Night'** (Bartholomew, King) H2WB 0415
* **'I Got Stung'** (Schroeder, Hill) J2WB 3257
(US) 47-7410 (45): 20-7410 (78)
Released: October 1958

Elvis Presley (vcl, gtr), Scotty Moore (gtr),
Dudley Brooks (pno), Bill Black (bs),
D.J. Fontana (dms), The Jordanaires (bv)

Elvis Presley (vcl, gtr), Hank Garland,
Chet Atkins (gtr), Floyd Cramer (pno),
Bob Moore (bs), D. J. Fontana (dms),
Murrey "Buddy" Harman (bon),
The Jordanaires (bv)
Recorded: RCA Studios, Nashville, June 10, 1958

After the disappointment of the *King Creole* music, 'One Night' came like a shot in the arm. Elvis' reworking of Smiley Lewis' notorious loud R&B hit had to be, even with the lyrics considerably toned down, his most awesomely down and dirty single. Pumping twelve-string guitar and, yes, pounding piano provided exactly the right backing, against which Elvis wrung the last ounce of sexuality from his tonsils.

'I Got Stung' was also a treat, being one of the most frantic rockers since the great days of 'Hound Dog' and 'All Shook Up'.

'ELVIS' CHRISTMAS ALBUM' (LP)
(US) RCA LPM-1951
Released: November 1958

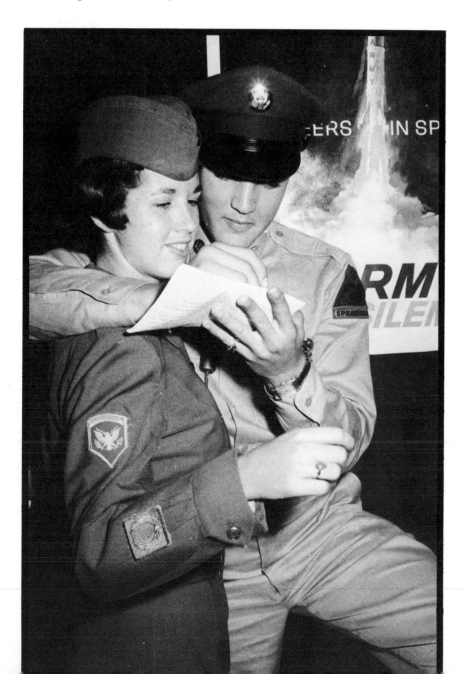

Could be that RCA were in the midst of an economy drive, or maybe they were just being realistic by taking into account that as this very album had topped the bestsellers the previous year, it was safe to assume that every self-respecting Elvis fan already owned a copy. Second time around, the corporate decision dictated that the original deluxe ten page book gatefold be abandoned in favour of a single sleeve with four colour shots of Private Presley on the back just to remind the folks back home that Uncle Sam's favourite son was off in a distant land still defending the cause of truth and justice and the American way.

Despite the new cover and catalogue number, the contents were precisely the same as that found on RCA LOC-1035. This, it seemed, was RCA's logical interpretation of the American way.

'CHRISTMAS WITH ELVIS' (EP)
(US) EPA-4340
Released: December 1958

Side 1
'White Christmas' (Berlin)
'Here Comes Santa Claus'
(Autry, Haldeman, Melka)
Side 2
'O Little Town Of Bethlehem' (Redner, Brooks)
'Silent Night' (Mohr, Gruber)

This, plus two previous EPs – *Peace In The Valley* and *Elvis Sings Christmas Songs* – added up to the entire contents of *Elvis' Christmas Album*.

'FOR LP FANS ONLY' (LP)
(US) RCA LPM-1990 (LSP-1990)
Released: February 1959

Side 1
'That's All Right (Mama)' (Crudup)
'Lawdy, Miss Clawdy' (Price)
'Mystery Train' (Parker, Phillips)
'Playing For Keeps' (Kesler)
'Poor Boy' (Presley, Matson)
Side 2
'My Baby Left Me' (Crudup)
'I Was The One'
(Schroeder, DeMetrius, Blair, Peppers)
'Shake, Rattle & Roll' (Calhoun)
'I'm Left, You're Right, She's Gone'
(Kesler, Taylor)
'You're A Heartbreaker' (Sallee)

The logic behind this, the first of three re-issue compilations, was to gather together ten assorted tracks that hitherto hadn't been recycled on albums. Considering that, for songs like 'Shake, Rattle And Roll', 'Mystery Train' and 'My Baby Left Me', this was third time around, the album did remarkably well in making No. 23 on the nation's bestsellers list.

'ELVIS SAILS' (EP)
(US) RCA EPA-4325
Released: March 1959

Side 1
Press Interview with Elvis Presley
Side 2
Elvis Presley's Newsreel Interview; Pat Hernon Interviews Elvis

This piece of product was strictly for the devoted fan. No music, just Elvis in three separate interviews as, fully installed in the US Army, Elvis leaves the US for his stretch in Germany as a defender of the free world.

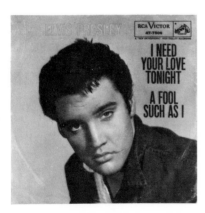

'A Fool Such As I' (Trader) J2WB 3256
'I Need Your Love Tonight'
(Wayne, Reichner) J2WB 3253
(US) RCA 47-7506
Released: March 1959

Elvis Presley (vcl, gtr), Hank Garland,
Chet Atkins (gtr), Floyd Cramer (pno),
Bob Moore (bs), D.J. Fontana (dms),
Murrey "Buddy" Harman (bon),
The Jordanaires (bv)
*Recorded: RCA Studios, Nashville,
June 11, 1958

Once Elvis had made the switch from public idol to private soldier, the problem that faced both Colonel Parker and RCA Records was how to keep the pot boiling—and the excitement up—for two long, long years.

It had already been made abundantly clear that no official deals were going to be made

over Elvis' stretch in the service. As far as was humanly possible, he would serve out his time just like any other young man who'd had his life interrupted by the draft. Neither Elvis nor his management wanted him to drop into some tailor-made, Glenn Miller Special Service entertainer role (there was absolutely no way that the Colonel was going to give it away for free!). This was all very laudable, but it did make it doubly difficult to maintain Presley's pre-eminent position in the changeable world of rock 'n' roll.

The tightrope that had to be walked was, on the one hand, to keep enough product in the stores so the fans wouldn't forget about Elvis, and, on the other, to keep those same fans sufficiently hungry for new product so Elvis' eventual re-emergence would be looked forward to as a major event.

The first area was adequately covered, at least to Colonel Parker's satisfaction, by scheduling a series of second-time-around compilations, which, while not actually giving the fans any new material, at least re-packaged most of what had gone before in a way that maintained some sort of continuity of releases. The second phase of the campaign was a little more difficult. Obviously, if the myth of Elvis being just an "ordinary" soldier was to be maintained, then he couldn't simply duck into a convenient studio each time new product was needed and still retain any level of soldier-boy credibility.

Somewhere along the line a compromise was reached, as compromises usually are, and on June 10 and 11, 1958, on a weekend pass, Elvis was rushed into the RCA Nashville Studios where he cut an amazing five sides of the highest quality, even without his regular band (which had split up when he'd been drafted). The first of these cuts to see the light of day as an A-side was the country standard 'A Fool Such As I', and of all Presley's ventures into straight C&W, it is probably one of the most successful. The interplay between Elvis' lead vocal and The Jordanaires' back-up singing is about as close to perfection as it is possible to get. They manage to maintain an ideal balance between light, wistful sentimentality and the more familiar Presley dramatics.

The B-side, far from being some tack-on afterthought, could easily have been a single in its own right. 'I Need Your Love Tonight' was a direct, straight to the point, full stretch rock 'n' roll tune that could have been interchanged with the next A-side, 'Big Hunk O' Love'.

Certainly, if he could produce singles of that quality while on furlough from the army, there was absolutely no chance that the US Army would turn Elvis Presley into the forgotten man of rock 'n' roll.

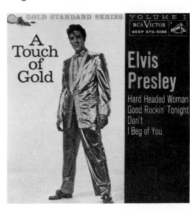

'A TOUCH OF GOLD. VOLUME I' (EP)
(US) RCA EPA-5088
Released: April 1959

Side 1
'Hard Headed Woman' (DeMetrius)
'Good Rocking Tonight' (Brown)
Side 2
'Don't' (Leiber, Stoller)
'I Beg Of You' (McCoy, Owens)

In keeping with the true spirit of American enterprise, the attitude behind this, the first in a trilogy of re-issue EPs, semed to be: why be content with selling something once, when it could be sold at least three times over? Sadly, we've said this before: we'll be saying it again.

For starters, there's Elvis' first 45 of 1958 ('Don't' and 'I Beg Of You') which commenced the re-issue route with this release before being recycled just eight months later on the *50,000,000 Elvis Fans Can't Be Wrong* LP.

As 'Hard Headed Woman' had initially been released as a single to preview the *King Creole* soundtrack, it escaped shortlisting when eight of the 11 movie songs were subsequently redistributed on a brace of EPs.

Surprisingly enough, though 'Good Rockin' Tonight' had been around for well over three years, this was the first time it was reserviced. However, in September it would be re-employed yet again to open the second side of *A Date With Elvis*.

Apparently there was a ready-made market for the *Touch Of Gold* series, because two more EPs were quickly prepared.

* **'A Big Hunk O' Love'** (Schroeder, Wyche) J2WB 3254
** **'My Wish Came True'** (Hunter) H2PB 5524
(US) RCA 47-7600
Released: June 1959
Elvis Presley (vcl, gtr), Hank Garland,
Chet Atkins (gtr), Floyd Cramer (pno),
Bob Moore (bs), D.J. Fontana (dms),
Murrey "Buddy" Harman (bon),
The Jordanaires (bv)
**Recorded: RCA Studios, Nashville, June 10, 1958
Elvis Presley (vcl, gtr), Scotty Moore (gtr),
Dudley Brooks (pno), Bill Black (bs),
D.J. Fontana (dms), Millie Kirkham,
The Jordanaires (bv)
*Recorded: Radio Recorders, Hollywood, September 6, 1957

Rumour went round the world of Elvis Presley fans that these two cuts were the last of the Presley material in the can until the man came out of the army. In fact, this whisper, which seems to have had its start somewhere in the Tom Parker organization, was simply untrue. At that time – June, 1958 – RCA still held at least six unissued tracks. (One of them, 'Ain't That Loving You Baby', would not be released until 1964.)

'A Big Hunk O' Love', although a fairly powerful rocker, was far from being one of Presley's greatest efforts. There was a certain raucous grossness about the song that smacked of formula rather than inspiration.

The B-side, 'My Wish Came True', was also far from being one of Presley's greatest ballads, even after three attempts at cutting it. Unfortunately, this was the Presley single that was going to have to keep the customers satisfied for the next ten months, as RCA would not put out any more new material until 'Stuck On You' in April 1960.

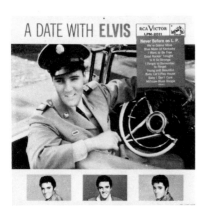

'A DATE WITH ELVIS' (LP)
(US) RCA LPM-2011
Released: September 1959

Side 1
'Blue Moon Of Kentucky' (Monroe)
'Young And Beautiful' (Silver, Schroeder)
'Baby, I Don't Care' (Leiber, Stoller)
'Milkcow Blues Boogie' (Arnold)
'Baby, Let's Play House' (Gunter)
Side 2
'Good Rockin' Tonight' (Brown)
'Is It So Strange' (Young)
'We're Gonna Move' (Presley, Matson)
'I Want To Be Free' (Leiber, Stoller)
'I Forget To Remember To Forget' (Kesler, Feathers)

This could be retitled: *Son Of For LP Fans Only*, because once again it gathered together (only) ten already issued tracks. True, they hadn't previously been available in *album* form. As to their origins: there were five Sun sides, three *Jailhouse Rock* titles, plus one apiece from the *Love Me Tender* and *Just For You* EPs.

However this album's main point of sale was the lavish gatefold sleeve profusely illustrated with pix of Private Presley, a "personal" telegram to the (loyal) fans he'd left behind and a calendar on the back to enable the purchaser to tick off the days until The King's triumphant return from Over The Water.

Clearly, movie mogul Harold Mirisch was greatly impressed with the way Presley's popularity was being kept alive, for he tried to persuade the singer to head the all-star cast for the screen adaptation of *West Side Story*. The idea was to cast Presley, Paul Anka, Fabian, Frankie Avalon and Bobby Darin as the two opposing gangs, the Jets and Sharks.

Elvis said he'd only consider it if Natalie Wood got the female lead. She did, but Presley still passed.

'A TOUCH OF GOLD. VOLUME 2' (EP)
(US) RCA-EPA-5101
Released: October 1959

Side 1
'Wear My Ring Around Your Neck' (Carroll, Moody)
'Treat Me Nice' (Leiber, Stoller)
Side 2
'One Night' (Bartholomew, King)
'That's All Right (Mama)' (Crudup)

Four familiar single sides, two of which – 'Treat Me Nice' and 'That's All Right (Mama)' – had already seen active service on two recent albums (*Elvis' Golden Records* and *For LP Fans Only*, respectively).

Unbeknown to purchasers, both 'Wear My Ring Around Your Neck' and 'One Night' had, at the time of this release, already been scheduled for the upcoming *50,000,000 Elvis Fans Can't Be Wrong* collection. And still nobody complained of being shortchanged!

'50,000,000 ELVIS FANS CAN'T BE WRONG' (LP)
(US) RCA LPM-2075
Released: December 1959

Side 1
'I Need Your Love Tonight' (Wayne, Reichner)
'Don't' (Leiber, Stoller)
'Wear My Ring Around Your Neck' (Carroll, Moody)
'My Wish Came True' (Hunter)
'I Got Stung' (Schroeder, Hill)
Side 2
'One Night' (Bartholomew, King)
'A Big Hunk O' Love' (Schroeder, Wyche)
'I Beg Of You' (McCoy, Owens)
'A Fool Such As I' (Trader)
'Doncha Think It's Time' (Otis, Dixon)

Elvis' second and last Christmas in exile and, as before, RCA didn't possess any new material with which to ensnare the seasonal dollar. Instead they chose (successfully) to promote a statistic: that Elvis had sold fifty million records since joining the label three years earlier.

In terms of re-issues, this album had some semblance of form and continuity in that it gathered together all the A and B sides from Elvis' last five hit singles. If the sight of the King resplendent in his gold lamé suit on the sleeve grabbed them at the browser bins, RCA were determined to focus radio attention on this package by narrowing programmers choice down to just two cuts. Accordingly, 'Wear My Ring Around Your Neck' and 'Don't' were picture-sleeved as a radio promo-only single (RCA SP-45-76). On January 23, 1958, Elvis worked on both 'My Wish Came True' (J2WB 0178) and 'Doncha' Think It's Time' (J2WB 0179). Being dis-satisfied with the results, he again re-recorded them on February 1, along with 'Your Cheatin' Heart' and 'Wear My Ring Around Your Neck'. It's believed that this first version of 'Doncha' Think It's Time' is the one that appeared on this album, as it's different to the single release. (In 1979 both the title and cover concept were accurately spoofed for an Elvis Costello bootleg double album.)

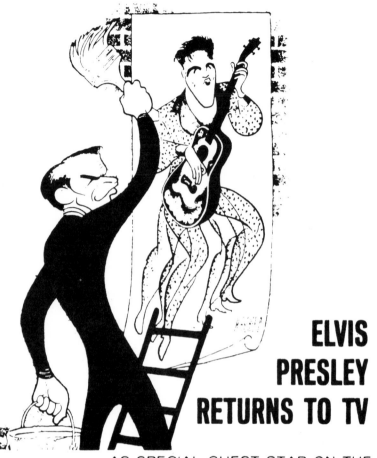

The Frank Sinatra – Timex Show/
Welcome Home Elvis (ABC)
'Fame And Fortune', 'Stuck On You' and a duet
of 'Witchcraft' (Presley) and 'Love Me Tender'
(Sinatra)

Elvis Presley (vcl), Scotty Moore (gtr),
Floyd Cramer (pno), Bob Moore (bs),
D.J. Fontana, Murrey "Buddy" Harman (dms),
The Jordanaires (bv), plus
The Nelson Riddle Orchestra
Recorded: The Fontainebleau Hotel,
Miami Beach, March 26, 1960
Transmitted: May 12, 1960

1960-8 HOLLYWOOD HOSTAGE

1960

For Elvis Presley, getting out of the army was as much of a circus as going in. When the plane bringing in "the most publicized soldier since General MacArthur" reached Fort Dix, New Jersey, the eastern seaboard was in the grip of a raging blizzard. Nevertheless, TV crews, newsmen, photographers, 2000 fans and Nancy Sinatra turned out to greet it. Seemed like business as usual; but, in fact, Elvis was returning to a very different world.

It was no longer 1958, but March 1960. Most of the wild men of rock 'n' roll had been edged out of the picture. Buddy Holly, The Big Bopper, Ritchie Valens and Eddie Cochran were dead. Chuck Berry was in jail. Little Richard had taken up religion. Jerry Lee Lewis had just about managed to scandalize himself clear off the major concert circuits. Gene Vincent had fled to Europe. Even DJ Alan Freed, always the mass media champion of rock, had been run off the air by the payola scandals.

On the radio just about all you could hear was a new form of soft-centred pop music. Its perpetrators were a sorry bunch: Bobby Vee, Connie Francis, Fabian, Frankie Avalon and Bobby Rydell. It was a period when energy and creativity went out of the window and all the important decisions were made by the record company and radio bosses, not by the musicians or individual disc jockeys.

Although nobody seriously doubted that Elvis still had a position in the world of music, there was quite a lot of speculation as to what that position might be. All the boys who'd refused to give up their leather jackets in the face of Pat Boone's white bucks and college sweater hoped that Elvis would come back to restore the true faith of rock 'n' roll. Sadly, it was not to be. It was quickly revealed that both Elvis and Colonel Tom Parker had decided on a very different course for Elvis' career. From the ABC-TV special *Welcome Home, Elvis*, hosted by Frank Sinatra, onwards, it became clear that the path chosen for Elvis was to be that of the all-round entertainer.

Of course, rock 'n' roll was still going to be part of the package – or so it appeared at first. Unfortunately, with the exception of the magnificent *Elvis is Back* album and two giant, live charity shows in Memphis and Hawaii in early 1961, rock 'n' roll began to take a back seat as Presley was groomed for matinée idolatry.

Initially, though, there was an attempt to turn Elvis into a serious actor with the film *Flaming Star*, in which Elvis landed the fairly meaty part of the half-breed Pacer, torn between warring cowboys and Indians. At one point the part had been offered to Marlon Brando. Brando had declined. The part wasn't that meaty, but for Elvis it could have been a springboard to something better than *Blue Hawaii* or *Kid Galahad*.

However, the attempt was, at least in Colonel Tom's balance-sheet eyes, less than an outstanding success. Elvis gave a creditable performance but, for some reason, the crowds didn't flock into the movie houses the way they had done for *GI Blues*. Even then there was one more attempt to promote Elvis the thespian. *Wild In The Country* turned out to be simply an inferior picture, an implausible, watered-down *Peyton Place* with rural country-boy substituted for small-town New England girl. Elvis as a singing Allison Mackenzie didn't draw the public either, so the Colonel's decree went forth: no more serious films for Elvis. Light romantic comedies with lots of songs and lots of girls were what brought in the bucks, so light romantic comedies with lots of songs and lots of girls it was going to be. Elvis was to remain shackled to that formula for close to a decade – a decade during which the King of Rock 'N' Roll, to all outward appearances, handed in his self-respect and allowed himself to be led by the nose through a series of cinema atrocities. The standard Elvis movie was brightly coloured, loaded with big-breasted, go-going women and infinitely forgettable songs. Even Elvis developed an intense loathing for them, and he attempted to race through them with the minimum effort, and in the minimum time. Between 1962 and 1968 Elvis averaged three films a year. Each one was completed in under three weeks. The customers kept coming, and no one in the Presley camp saw any reason to change their policy. Red West, Elvis' bodyguard and stand-in, tells how his attitude towards the films deteriorated.

"At first it was something new to him. After a while it got to be the same, a pick-up from the last movie. It really got so he didn't like doing them. At first he liked making movies, but when it didn't get any better and the songs were all the same, it kinda got bogged down. Actually, some of the films he couldn't wait to get through. Most of 'em. He liked *Wild In The Country*. He liked *Flaming Star* and he liked *King Creole* and I can't think of too many more that he enjoyed doing."

Later, in his book *Elvis – What Happened*, Red West painted a far bleaker picture of Elvis the movie star. According to West, Presley moved through the seemingly endless series of films almost like a pill-popping zombie, literally speeding through each sequence, disgusted with what he had to do and anxious to be away from the set as quickly as possible.

Lance LeGault, a Louisiana singer who was a double for Presley and choreographed some of his song routines through the sixties, points out how the Presley talent was being criminally wasted.

"We shot *Kissin' Cousins* in seventeen days, and I think that film was the turning point as far as shooting was concerned. Up until that time certain standards had been maintained, but it seems to me that from *Kissin' Cousins* on, we were always on short schedule. Once they realized that they could take this guy and do a film that quickly, we were on quick pictures.

"The first time I noticed it for real was in *Roustabout*. Elvis rode a Honda in it. Which is pretty silly, when you think about it, because Elvis rode Harleys. Always rode a big Harley. Yet in this film they put him on a 350 Honda. And this is a guy who's playing the part of a drifter whose only mode of transportation is his bike. This is a guy who supposedly goes across country on a machine that's about right for the driveway, a 350 Honda.

"It's just a little simple example. They never used Elvis to his full capacity in these films . . . in these songs that were given to him to do . . . never, never used the guy. I always had the feeling: okay, here's a schedule and because it's Elvis we're gonna make so much money with the film regardless of whether he rides a Honda or he rides a Harley-Davidson, whether he sings a groovy tune like 'Don't Be Cruel' or 'All Shook Up', as opposed to any piece of crap you want to name that he sang in the film. I kept seeing incident after incident after incident of taking somebody and treating him like it's good enough because it's Elvis and it's in *colour*. And so we're going to make two and a half times the negative cost plus another two and a half times . . . you see?"

Gerald Drayson Adams, who had the dubious honour of writing both *Kissin' Cousins* and *Harum Scarum*, also underlines the almost obsessive quality of cheapness that surrounded the production of an Elvis Presley movie.

"There were never any story conferences. They consisted of money – the first act, second act, third act, money. They were all conducted by Colonel Parker."

In 1963 Elvis himself seemed quite happy to go along with the Colonel's master plan.

"I've had intellectuals tell me that I've got to progress as an actor, explore new horizons, take on new challenges, all that routine. I'd like to progress, but I'm smart enough to know that you can't bite off more than you can chew in this racket. You can't go beyond your limitations. They want me for an artistic picture, that's fine. Maybe I can pull it off someday, but not now. I've done eleven pictures and they've all made money. A certain type of audience likes me. I entertain them with what I'm doing. I'd be a fool to tamper with that kind of success."

There were other things that would tamper with that success. Out in the real world, beyond the closed movie sets, the walls of Graceland and the bought-and-paid-for camaraderie of the Memphis Mafia, it was the 1960s and the times they were a' changing.

This meant problems for Elvis. The US Army was quite probably his last contact with the real world until the seventies. He moved in a totally private world. His working life was a careless amble from one mediocre movie to the next. The formula never changed and new ideas were never introduced.

His private life was equally isolationist. He moved in a continuous circle from Memphis to Hollywood to Palm Springs. It was a life of parties, pills, sex, eating and horseplay with his good ol' buddies who took their salaries and did what was expected of them. If Elvis took it into his head to blow away the TV set with a six-shooter, they'd just laugh it up and bring in a new set. If he decided to purchase a totally redundant ranch so he could go horse-riding, they'd tell him that it was a swell idea and let him go ahead whatever the consequences.

In the Memphis Mafia, Elvis had himself the perfect pampering service. It was a set-up more suited to a spoiled brat than a grown man.

All through the sixties, Elvis was cocooned in a tight coterie of small-minded men, tenaciously clinging to their jobs. It was of paramount importance to everyone in the Presley camp that Elvis should never be allowed to take a good look at the real world, or to get a perspective on his own life and work. If he did that, he might just come to realize their true worth and dump them, replacing the yes-men and hangers-on with people who had some real ability.

Instead, he carried on regardless, doing things the way he had always done them. While President John F. Kennedy was moving Federal troops into Birmingham, Alabama to quell violent civil rights demonstrations, Elvis was making *Viva Las Vegas*. When, later the same

year, Kennedy was assassinated, Elvis was putting the finishing touches to *Kissin' Cousins*. As the Beatles drew a record crowd to Shea Stadium, and the Watts area of Los Angeles was being put to the torch by angry blacks, Elvis was cutting the soundtrack to *Frankie And Johnny*. The Summer of Love saw him working on *Clambake, Speedway* and *Stay Away Joe*. It was at exactly the same time that the Beatles were making 'Sergeant Pepper', and Bob Dylan was recovering from a motorcycle accident, and a British judge was trying to jail Mick Jagger and Keith Richard of the Rolling Stones on drug charges.

It had only taken Elvis seven short years since he came out of the army to turn into what seemed a total anachronism. If Elvis had ever even heard Bob Dylan, the Beatles or the Rolling Stones, no sign of it ever showed in his work. The man who, in the fifties, had done so much to make the first cracks that were eventually to widen into the generation gap seemed totally unaware that large sections of western youth, both black and white, were not only in open revolt against authority, but were also using rock 'n' roll as a symbolic battleflag. He just went on making the films and playing with the Memphis Mafia as though nothing was happening.

Although it didn't show in his music, not even Elvis Presley could remain in absolute isolation. In August 1965 he even played host to the Beatles in his Bel-Air home. The Beatles were on tour and Elvis was doing nothing much of anything.

John Lennon recalled "We spent about four hours talking, listening to records and jamming. During the jam session Elvis played piano and drums. We ate a lot, shot some pool and had a ball. The whole time we were jamming he had the tape machine running."

There was also a personal tragedy. In 1966 Bill Black, who had played bass with Elvis on and off since the earliest days, died of a brain tumour at the age of thirty-nine.

But the major upheaval in the Presley lifestyle throughout the 1960s had to be his marriage.

In 1966 Priscilla Beaulieu, the child sweetheart of his army days in Germany, finally graduated from Immaculate Conception High School in Memphis. As well as dating her steadily through the sixties, Elvis had also, at some point, taken control of her education. It almost seemed as though, from the start, Priscilla had somehow been groomed for the role of Mrs Presley. By all accounts the relationship was a stormy one. There were frequent rows, and a particular bone of contention was the procession of groupies, starlets and nubile whoevers that streamed constantly through Elvis' life and Elvis' bed. At regular intervals Priscilla would flounce back to her parents at Travis Air Force Base near San Francisco.

It would seem that true love does, on occasions, conquer all; on May 1, 1967 Elvis Presley, debatably the world's most eligible bachelor, was married at the Aladdin Hotel, Las Vegas. In February of the following year his daughter Lisa Marie was born at the Baptist Memorial Hospital in Memphis. The wheel had turned full circle. Elvis Presley, The Hillbilly Cat, the one-time corrupter of youth, was a pillar of the entertainment industry establishment.

Pillar maybe, but a pillar with support problems of its own. The formula films and the rotten records were finally starting to take their toll. The box office receipts were dwindling and even hard-core fans were starting to drift away.

Tom Parker hadn't minded too much when the more discerning rock 'n' rollers had abandoned Elvis, despairing of his ever making a quality record again. So they were off after the Jaggers, Lennons, Dylans and Hendrixes? Who needed them? The idea was to clean up Elvis' image, anyway. Elvis could well do without the kind of bums who smoked LSD and burned draft cards. Even then, the one time Presley attempted to do a more than adequate job on a Bob Dylan song ('Tomorrow Is A Long Time'), it was relegated by the powers that were to the position of filler on the *Spinout* soundtrack album.

It wasn't only the hippies who had deserted Elvis, however. More seriously, it was also the broad mass of the record-buying public. Elvis didn't make the No. 1 slot on the US singles or albums charts once between spring of 1962 and the winter of 1969.

Still, the Colonel didn't seem to be particularly bothered. He frequently asserted his belief that there were "a quarter of a million dyed-in-the-wool Elvis Presley fans who'd see every picture three times". If they didn't care that the movies were trash, why should anybody else bother?

Unfortunately, the gospel according to Parker was starting to break down. Even the dyed-in-the-wool couldn't take the later pictures once, let alone three times. They'd been burned too often.

The first signs of breakdown came with *Kissin' Cousins*. Lance LeGault had noticed, from one side of the camera. The director, Gene Nelson, had also noticed it. When he suggested to Parker that maybe the script was "a bad choice", the Colonel had wanted to include a talking camel. That was his best offer.

The distributors were also noticing that the formula Elvis Presley movie was losing its grip. In a number of areas *Kissin' Cousins* was double-billed with *Ghidram The Three-Headed Monster*, a Japanese creature-feature from the same studio that produced *Godzilla*. In fact, Elvis and Godzilla were getting to have a little too much in common. Both worked to cheap formulas, both found themselves sinking into the second-feature bracket, and both were dinosaurs looking for a home. Elvis fortunately didn't show any inclination to eat Tokyo.

By 1967/68 the rot had taken over almost completely. Elvis wasn't even going out double-billed. His movies were being run strictly as second features; not only second features, but second features at the drive-in. *The Trouble With Girls* had reached such an all time low that it wasn't even shown in most of the major American cities. One move that was made to stop the rot was the film *Charro*. For the first time since *Wild In The Country* the formula had been junked. *Charro* was a Western without a song in sight. Elvis had a straight dramatic role, and not only that, he appeared in a stained shirt, dirty leather jeans and a four-day growth of stubble, similar to the one that Clint Eastwood sported in the trilogy of "Dollars" movies.

Unfortunately, *Charro* was still a turkey. Not even James Dean, brought back from the dead to play the lead, could have saved that picture. It was a cheap Hollywood copy of the kind of Italian spaghetti Western that had, in the first place, been a cheap copy of a Hollywood Western, cross-pollinated by Japanese samurai flicks.

Not even Elvis could fight against those odds. In Britain, the distributors turned down *Charro* without even looking at it. Elvis Presley films had such a bad reputation that it wasn't even worth lacing them into the projector.

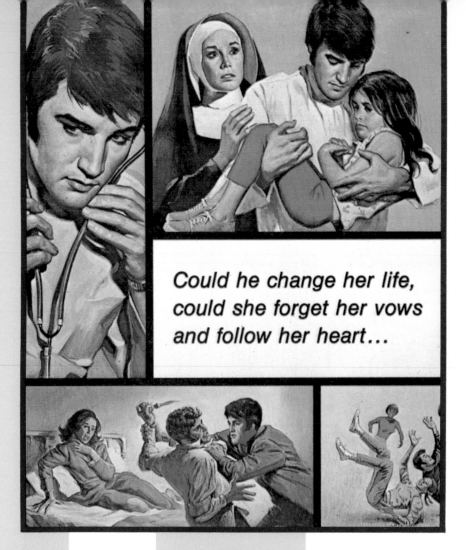

Could he change her life, could she forget her vows and follow her heart...

Change Of Habit was another attempt to upgrade the Presley cinema product. Although Elvis as a ghetto doctor was less than plausible, it did have a better script plus the added attraction of the toothsome Mary Tyler Moore, then riding high in the TV ratings on the strength of the *Dick Van Dyke Show*. She played a nun.

Not even a scene where Mary is raped (or nearly raped) by teenage Puerto Rican hoodlums could bring back the crowds. Elvis had reached the pits. The world could write him off as a first, fine, careless rapture that went downhill forever after.

Or could it?

In January 1968 Colonel Parker announced that NBC-TV, with sponsorship from the Singer Sewing Machine Company, would finance and produce a one-hour Elvis Presley Special to go out on the air the following Christmas.

The Colonel's idea was that the show would be simply another rip-off, just like the movies had become. Elvis would walk on, introduce himself, sing twenty-four Christmas songs, wish everyone a Merry Christmas and split.

Fortunately for everyone involved, particularly the viewing public and Elvis Presley, there was someone on the show who was prepared to fight with the Colonel.

Steve Binder had been appointed by the network as producer and director of the Presley Special. Far from being prepared to go along with Parker's concept, Binder had very positive ideas of his own.

"I felt very, very strongly that the television Special was Elvis' moment of truth. If he did another MGM movie on the Special, he would wipe out his career and he would be known only as that phenomenon who came along in the Fifties, shook his hips and had a great manager. On the reverse side, if he could do a special and prove that he was still number one, he could have a whole rejuvenation thing going.

"If we could create an atmosphere of making Elvis feel he was part of the Special, that he was creating the Special himself, the same way he was originally involved in producing his own records in the old days, before the movies, then we would have a great special. People would really see Elvis Presley, not what the Colonel wanted them to see.

"I, in no way, wanted to do a Christmas show full of Christmas songs. I wanted to leave that to the Andy Williamses and Perry Comos. The one thing I knew that I wanted was that

Elvis should say something; let the world in on that great secret, find out what kind of man he really was."

Binder's strong resolve was not so easy to maintain. The major problem was the constant interference by Parker, who seemed determined to block all originality and innovation. NBC even appointed a special executive producer, Bob Finkel, whose sole task was to keep the Colonel happy, and, where possible, diverted.

The situation was also not helped by Elvis' own seeming inability to stand up to the Colonel. An example of this came when Parker demanded that the show should end with Elvis singing 'Silent Night'. Unknown to Parker, Elvis and Binder had already agreed the finale should be the new composition 'If I Can Dream'. In the middle of a prolonged bout of angry blustering, Parker suddenly pointed to Elvis and declared that 'Silent Night' would have to be kept in the show because Elvis wanted it that way. Binder recalls, "Elvis was just sitting there with his head hanging down. The Colonel said, 'Isn't that right, Elvis?' Elvis just nodded, and when the Colonel left, he looked up and said, 'That's all right, we'll take it out.'"

Despite all the pitfalls, Binder did manage to get the finished show looking very much the way he had first conceived it. A scene where Elvis, symbolizing the young man trying to make his way in the world, lands up in a brothel was cut out, but apart from that, Binder just about did it his way.

As everyone is now aware, Binder was absolutely right. He did manage to present a new Elvis to the world, or, at least, an Elvis who hadn't been seen for nearly ten years. The power, charisma and magnetism that had been missing from Elvis' work for so long was back with a vengeance. It was as though Presley had found something in himself that he'd been out of touch with for most of the sixties.

The response after the show was aired, on December 3, 1968, was phenomenal. NBC wiped out the other networks in terms of ratings, and all doubts that Elvis could still do it were completely swept aside.

In his book *Mystery Train*, rock critic Greil Marcus remembers, "The finest music of his life. If there was ever music that bleeds, this was it. Nothing came easy that night and he gave everything he had – more than anyone knew was there."

that Elvis was taking now his military service was over. This was the first Elvis single released in stereo.

'ELVIS IS BACK' (LP)
(US) RCA LSP/LPM-2231
Released: April 1960

Side 1
* 'Make Me Know It' (Blackwell) L2WB 0081
*** 'Fever' (Davenport, Cooley) L2WB 0098
**** 'The Girl Of My Best Friend' (Ross, Bobrick) L2WB 0101
**** 'I Will Be Home Again' (Benjamin, Leveen, Singer) L2WB 0108
**** 'Dirty, Dirty Feeling' (Leiber, Stoller) L2WB 0102
**** 'The Thrill Of Your Love' (Kesler) L2WB 0103
Side 2
* 'Soldier Boy' (Jones, Williams Jr) L2WB 0082
**** 'Such A Night' (Chase) L2WB 0105
** 'It Feels So Right' (Wise, Weisman) L2WB 0086
**** 'The Girl Next Door Went A'Walking' (Rice, Wayne) L2WB 0107
*** 'Like A Baby' (Stone) L2WB 0099
**** 'Reconsider Baby' (Fulson) L2WB 0109

Elvis Presley (vcl, gtr), Scotty Moore (gtr), Hank Garland (gtr & bs – March sessions only), Floyd Cramer (pno), Bob Moore (bs), D.J. Fontana, Murrey "Buddy" Harman (dms), Homer "Boots" Randolph (ts – April sessions only), The Jordanaires (bv)
*Recorded: RCA Studios, Nashville, March 20, 1960. **March 21, 1960.
***April 3, 1960. ****April 4, 1960

'A TOUCH OF GOLD. VOLUME 3' (EP)
(US) RCA EPA-5141
Released: February 1960

Side 1
'Too Much' (Rosenburg, Weisman)
'All Shook Up' (Presley, Blackwell)
Side 2
'Don't Ask Me Why' (Wise, Weisman)
'Blue Moon Of Kentucky' (Monroe)

Any trepidation that Elvis' hard core rock 'n' roll fans may have had after the release of 'Stuck On You' was totally allayed when *Elvis Is Back* reached the shops. It was nothing less than a masterpiece. Recorded partly at the Nashville sessions that produced 'Stuck On You' and 'Fame and Fortune', the album was a virtual *tour de force* of just about every vocal style that Presley could bend his voice to. There were ballads, blues, up-tempo rockers and even near gospel style tunes like 'The Thrill Of Your Love'.

Picking an outstanding track has to be a matter of pure taste. The production was so full and crisp, and each cut was treated with such care and attention, that it becomes almost impossible to make a value judgement between, say, the rather sweaty exhilaration of the way Presley treats the controversial Johnny Ray hit 'Such A Night', the no-holds-barred rocker 'Dirty, Dirty Feeling' and the measured, atmospheric sexuality of Peggy Lee's celebrated, bass and drums only, treatment of 'Fever'.

On one level, though, the Lowell Fulsom blues 'Reconsider Baby' does merit particular note, if only in so far as it proves beyond any shadow of doubt that Presley was one of the greatest white blues singers of all time. In a relaxed, low register he demands that the woman who has walked out on him take the time to reconsider. Two-thirds of the way through the song he gives way to tenor man 'Boots' Randolph, whose solo not only perfectly complements Presley's voice, but is also one of his finest on record.

With Elvis due for imminent demobilization from Uncle Sam's service, this was the last opportunity for RCA to plunder the back-catalogue.

Actually, they hadn't done too badly. In just 12 months the company had shoved out no less than three sharply sleeved albums and the same number of EPs of old gold.

This was to be the last of such releases for quite some time.

'Stuck On You' (Schroeder, McFarland) L2WB 0083
'Fame And Fortune' (Wise, Weisman) L2WB 0084
(US) RCA 47-7740/stereo 61-7740
Released: March 1960

Elvis Presley (vcl, gtr), Scotty Moore (gtr), Floyd Cramer (pno), Bob Moore, Hank Garland (bs), D.J. Fontana, Murrey "Buddy" Harman (dms), The Jordanaires (bv)
Recorded: RCA Studios, Nashville, March 21, 1960

Nobody quite knew what Elvis would do when he came out of the army in 1960. There was speculation that military service might have changed, or even tamed him. Certainly both RCA and Tom Parker's first consideration was to feed something to the product-hungry fans. 'Stuck On You' was rushed into the shops within two days of the song being recorded.

It might have been better had everyone concerned remembered the homily "more haste, less speed". Although the A-side was a relatively tough rocker, it was noticeably inferior to the great pre-army hits, and despite selling more than a million copies before it was even released, it left many fans feeling disappointed and concerned about the direction

The insistent twelve-string guitar that carries the rhythm through the entire song even predates the way the Rolling Stones used the same effect on songs like 'Good Times, Bad Times' some five years later.

Blues, though, isn't the only measure of Presley's creativity on this album. The mid-tempo, soft-rock ballad 'Girl Of My Best Friend' showed the way to a lot of similar, but infinitely inferior material that had been released by people like Bobby Rydell and Bobby Vee while Presley had been overseas in Germany.

Boots Randolph also featured strongly on the cut 'Like A Baby'. This was another example of Presley turning a song that in anyone else's hands would have been little more than a slightly ridiculous, over-dramatic beat ballad into a memorable event.

The only weak track on the album has to be 'Soldier Boy', and even that is an understandable lapse. A slow crooning country weepie that could almost be a leftover from Nashville's World War II output, it is custom-built for the swooners in the vast Presley audience. Although Elvis is more than capable of handling the song, it doesn't measure up to the rest of the material, particularly when contrasted with 'Fever' or the slowly rolling 'I Will Be Home Again'.

Despite this single lapse, *Elvis Is Back* has to be a milestone in Elvis Presley's career. Sadly it also proved to be something of an epitaph – his last quality album for nearly ten years, until the NBC TV special in 1968.

All through that bleak period, *Elvis Is Back* provided a point of reference that proved that Presley was not only a pop idol but also an outstanding musician.

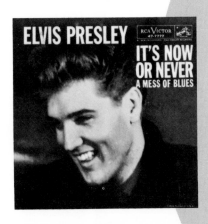

** **'It's Now Or Never'** (Schroeder, Gold)
L2WB 0100
* **'A Mess Of Blues'** (Pomus, Shuman)
L2WB 0085
(US) RCA 47-7777
Released: July 1960

Elvis Presley (vcl, gtr), Scotty Moore (gtr),
Hank Garland (gtr), Floyd Cramer (pno),
Bob Moore (bs), D.J. Fontana,
Murrey "Buddy" Harman (dms),
Homer "Boots" Randolph (ts),
The Jordanaires (bv)
**Recorded: RCA Studios, Nashville,
April 3, 1960
Elvis Presley (vcl, gtr), Scotty Moore (gtr),
Floyd Cramer (pno), Bob Moore,
Hank Garland (bs), D.J. Fontana,
Murrey "Buddy" Harman (dms),
The Jordanaires (bv)
*Recorded: RCA Studios, Nashville,
April 3, 1960

Even before he went into the army, Elvis had shown the occasional, alarming tendency to lapse into what can only be described as an operatic bellow. On songs like 'Don't' he did manage to keep it in check, only pulling out the stops for a few bars and then dropping back into his more familiar, bent-note beat ballad style. When the two techniques were coupled together they brought a measure of contrast and dynamic, but on 'It's Now Or Never' the dynamic depends on Elvis starting out loud and winding up sounding as though an alligator had him by the foot.

Maybe it was an exercise in pure ego, or maybe Elvis was just exploring the full Mario Lanza route – whatever, an anglicized version of 'O Sole Mio' was hardly what was expected from the man who could belt out 'One Night'. It proved to be a harbinger of worse to come.

The B-side, got back to familiar and much more acceptable rock territory. Although not one of Presley's greatest rockers, it was a creditable, medium tempo performance with most of the familiar Elvis mannerisms.

Sincerely
Elvis Presley

AN ORIGINAL SOUNDTRACK RECORDING

HAL WALLIS PRESENTS

ELVIS
in
G.I. BLUES

AN ORIGINAL SOUNDTRACK RECORDING

LPM-2256

RCA VICTOR
A "New Orthophonic" High Fidelity Recording

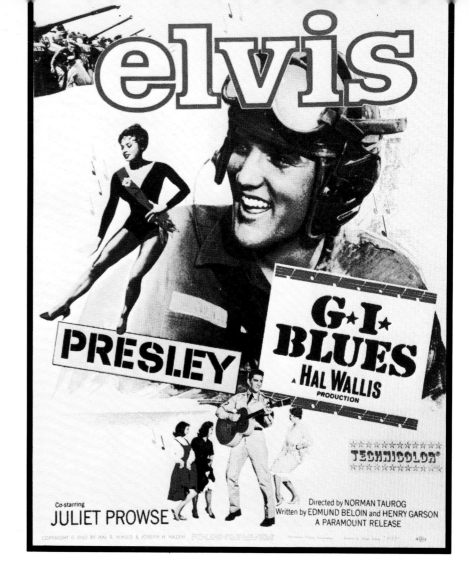

'GI BLUES' (LP)
(US) RCA LSP/LPM-2256
Released: October 1960

Side 1
** 'Tonight Is So Right For Love' (Wayne, Silver)
12PB 3678
** 'What's She Really Like' (Wayne, Silver)
12PB 3679
*** 'Frankfurt Special' (Wayne, Edwards) 12PB 3680
** 'Wooden Heart'
(Wise, Weisman, Twomey, Kaempfert)
12PB 3681
* 'GI Blues' (Tepper, Bennett) 12PB 3682
Side 2
*** 'Pocketful Of Rainbows' (Wise, Weisman)
12PB 3683
*** 'Shoppin' Around' (Tepper, Bennett, Schroeder)
12PB 3684
*** 'Big Boots' (Wayne, Edwards) 12PB 3685
* 'Didja' Ever' (Wayne, Edwards) 12PB 3686
** 'Blue Suede Shoes' (Perkins) 12PB 3687
** 'Doin' The Best I Can' (Pomus, Shuman)
12PB 3688

Elvis Presley (vcl, gtr), Scotty Moore,
Tiny Timbrell, Neil Mathews (gtr),
Dudley Brooks (pno), Ray Siegel (bs),
D.J. Fontana, Frank Bode (dms),
Jimmie Haskell (acc), Hoyt Hawkins (tam),
The Jordanaires (bv)
*Recorded: RCA Studios, Hollywood,
April 27, 1960. **April 28, 1960
Elvis Presley (vcl, gtr), same personnel as above,
except Bernie Mattinson replaces
Frank Bode (dms)
***Recorded: Radio Recorders, Hollywood,
May 6, 1960

GI Blues was the very first of the predictable Elvis movies. He had just come out of the army, hadn't he? He'd served in Germany and probably chased girls, hadn't he? So why not make a movie about a bunch of girl-chasing GIs stationed in Germany with Elvis Presley in the leading role, hah? It's one of the purest examples of the kind of 'creative' thinking that was to direct Elvis' career for the next nine years.

The *GI Blues* soundtrack LP was interesting in so far as it was the first Presley album without a single full-bodied new rock 'n' roll song anywhere on it. A couple of tracks, 'Shopping' Around' and the title song, plus maybe 'Frankfurt Special', came close, but even they leaned closer to show tunes. There was a brief snatch of a poor arrangement of 'Blue Suede Shoes', and that's about as far as it went. More typical of the mood of the film are 'Tonight Is So Right For Love' – almost a rerun of 'Such A Night' on the *Elvis Is Back* album but without its power – and 'Didja Ever', which might suit something like *South Pacific* better than a rock 'n' roll movie.

But then again, this wasn't a rock 'n' roll movie, but a light-weight musical comedy with a fairly traditional soldiers-and-girls plot. Tracks like 'Big Boots', 'Pocketful Of Rainbows' and 'Wooden Heart' made that perfectly clear.

GI Blues/Paramount

Cast
Tulsa McLean .... Elvis Presley
Rick .... James Douglas
Cooky .... Robert Ivers
Lili .... Juliet Prowse
Tina .... Leticia Roman
Marla .... Sigrid Maier
Sgt. McGraw................. Arch Johnson

Produced by Hal B. Wallis
Directed by Norman Taurog
Running Time: 104 minutes
Released: October 20, 1960

'Are You Lonesome Tonight'
(Turk, Handman) 12WB0106
'I Gotta Know' (Evans, Williams) 12WB0104
(US) RCA 47-7810/stereo 61-7810
Released: November 1960

Elvis Presley (vcl, gtr), Scotty Moore,
Hank Garland (gtr), Floyd Cramer (pno),
Bob Moore (bs), D.J. Fontana,
Murrey "Buddy" Harman (dms),
Homer "Boots" Randolph (ts),
The Jordanaires (bv)
Recorded: RCA Studios, Nashville, April 4, 1960

'Are You Lonesome Tonight', cut at the same session that gave the world the bulk of the *Elvis Is Back* material, seems to have been an aberration of that period. It must be Presley's most saccharine weepie since 'That's When Your Heartaches Begin'. It seems scarcely credible that the man who delivers the hackneyed extended monologue which makes up the bulk of the song is the same man who cut 'Reconsider Baby'.

1960 seems to have been a pivotal year for Elvis Presley. He appeared to have come out of the army determined to try a variety of musical directions. It was a period when he managed to produce some of his best work – *and* some that was positively substandard. He'd tried fake opera, featherweight musical comedy, some creditable rock 'n' roll, and equally creditable ballads, and even down and dirty blues. What these sessions really do call into question is Elvis' sense of discrimination.

The B-side, 'I Gotta Know', is a pretty standard rocker, albeit somewhat muddied by The Jordanaires' maddening shooby-dooby-doo-wah chorus.

'HIS HAND IN MINE' (LP)
(US) RCA LSP/LPM-2328
Released: December 1960

Side 1
* 'His Hand In Mine' (Lister) 12WB 0374
** 'I'm Gonna Walk Dem Golden Stairs' (Arr/
Adapt: Presley) 12WB 0382
** 'In My Father's House' (Arr/Adapt: Presley)
12WB 0379
* 'Milky White Way' (Arr/Adapt: Presley)
12WB 0373
** 'Know Only Him' (Hamblen) 12WB 0384
* 'I Believe In The Man In The Sky' (Howard)
12WB 0375
Side 2
** 'Joshua Fit the Battle' (Arr/Adapt: Presley)
12WB 0380
* 'Jesus Knows What I Need' (Lister) 12WB 0376
** 'Swing Down Sweet Chariot' (Arr/
Adapt: Presley) 12WB 0381
* 'Mansion Over The Hilltop' (Stamphill)
12WB 0378
** 'If We Never Meet Again' (Brumley) 12WB 0383
** 'Working On The Building' (Hoyle, Bowles)
12WB 5001

Elvis Presley (vcl, gtr), Scotty Moore (gtr),
Floyd Cramer (pno), Bob Moore (bs),
D.J. Fontana, Murrey "Buddy" Harman (dms),
Homer "Boots" Randolph (ts), The Jordanaires,
Millie Kirkham, Charlie Hodge (bv),
remaining musicians unidentified
*Recorded: RCA Studios, Nashville,
October 30, 1960. **October 31, 1960

Just to add to the confusion, the next offering after 'Are You Lonesome Tonight?' turned out to be a gospel record. Despite attempts to get down to some sacred rocking on cuts like 'I'm Going To Walk Dem Golden Stairs', 'Working On The Building' and 'Joshua Fit The Battle', there was an overall feel of rather well-mannered stiffness about the whole production.

With the release of this album, Elvis may have fulfilled a personal ambition, but instead of recapturing the genuine swing of an old time revival meeting, Presley was as restrained and genteel as the go-to-meeting suit he wore for the cover photograph.

Could this be the very same youngster who just a few short years earlier had been branded The Devil's Advocate?

Flaming Star

Flaming Star was a disaster for Elvis on a whole lot of levels, and virtually none of them was any fault of his. It was the final attempt to let Elvis have a shot at serious acting, and, despite a promising performance from both the star and a solid support of tried and trusted character players, it was, by the Colonel's standards, a financial disaster.

Flaming Star didn't actually lose money; it simply didn't make the kind of profits that the Elvis industry had grown used to. By all accounts, Tom Parker had always insisted that an Elvis film without songs would die the death, and seemed at times to be more interested in seeing himself proved right than working to promote the film's success.

The script, which had previously been offered to Marlon Brando and turned down, wasn't the greatest Western. If Elvis had really wanted to do a great Western he'd have been better advised to have hustled himself a role in *The Magnificent Seven* (a thing the Colonel would never have allowed).

The role of Pacer, the halfbreed son of a rancher (John McIntyre) and his full blooded Kiowa wife (Dolores Del Rio), caught between the Indians and the cowboys, is fraught with just a mite too much shuddering ethnic angst.

Directed by Don Siegal, who was responsible for the original *Invasion Of The Body Snatchers* (and who later pioneered the Clint Eastwood *Dirty Harry* series), the film seemed to be a confused response to the Kennedy era and the contemporary recognition by the media that Race was going to be the major issue of the 60s. Each moral point was delivered on the screen with such directorial fanfares that Siegal might as well have used a flashing neon light.

Nobody exactly expected Elvis to make *High Noon*; but to put him in something so rife with cheap allegory was, to say the least, ill-advised. More action and less morality would have improved the film a hundredfold, particularly as it tended to flag each time Pacer had to cope with his inner torment.

The audiences that came to *Flaming Star* seemed to consist mainly of the curious, who wanted to see how Elvis made out in a dramatic role, and the totally devoted, who were prepared to watch Elvis in absolutely anything.

The surprise was that there really did exist – let's hear it for the Colonel – a large section of Presley fans who wanted nothing more than to see him in the sunshine with songs and girls.

The Colonel seemed almost jubilant; his judgement had, after all, been fully vindicated. The edict went out that from henceforth there would be no more experiments of the *Flaming Star* kind.

From then on, Elvis never deviated from the set formula. It was going to take until the NBC-TV special in 1968 for someone to challenge the Colonel.

Flaming Star/20th Century Fox

Cast
Pacer Burton .... Elvis Presley
Clint Burton .... Steve Forrest
Roslyn Pierce .... Barbara Eden
Neddy Burton .... Dolores Del Rio
Pa Burton .... John McIntyre
Buffalo Horn .... Rudolfo Acosta
Doc Phillips .... Ford Rainey
Dred Phillips .... Karl Swenson
Angus Pierce .... Richard Jaeckel
Dorothy Howard .... Anne Benton
Tom Howard .... L. Q. Jones
Will Howard .... Douglas Dick
Jute .... Tom Reese

Produced by David Weisbart
Directed by Don Siegel
Running Time: 101 minutes
Released: December 20, 1960

1961

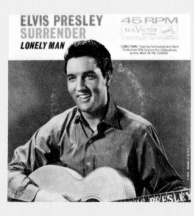

* **'Surrender'** (de Curtis, Pomus, Shuman) 12WB 0377
** **'Lonely Man'** (Benjamin, Marcus) 12PB 5381 (US) RCA 47-7850/stereo 61-7850
Released: February 1961

Elvis Presley (vcl, gtr), Scotty Moore, Hank Garland (gtr), Floyd Cramer (pno), Bob Moore (bs), D.J. Fontana, Murrey "Buddy" Harman (dms), Charlie McCoy (har), Homer "Boots" Randolph (ts), The Jordanaires, Millie Kirkham, Charlie Hodge (bv), remaining musicians unidentified
*Recorded: RCA Studios, Nashville, October 30, 1960
Elvis Presley (vcl, gtr), Scotty Moore (gtr), Floyd Cramer, Dudley Brooks (pno), Bob Moore (bs), D.J. Fontana, Murrey "Buddy" Harman (dms), The Jordanaires (bv), remaining musicians unidentified
**Recorded: 20th Century Fox Studios, Hollywood, November, 1960

It was 1961 and something was slipping. 'Stuck On You' had been a bit of a disappointment, then *Elvis Is Back* had more than made up for it. But now, there was 'Surrender'. It was another exercise in ersatz bel canto. Did Elvis Presley *really* want to become Mario Lanza? The world and its boyfriend wondered when the man intended to put out a hot new rock 'n' roll single. Some even wondered if he ever would again.

Operatic bravado and slow wistful weepies were hardly what one expected from Elvis. Sure, every teenage punk who finds himself on his own at the wrong end of Saturday night could identify with the romantic notion of being a lonely man who wanders all alone, but plenty of discs ran that routine. Roy Orbison had a million of them. Elvis, we remembered, could do better. This was the first of seven compact 33⅓ Elvis singles.

'ELVIS BY REQUEST – FLAMING STAR'
(EP)
(US) RCA LPC-128
Released: April 1961

Side 1
* 'Flaming Star' (Wayne, Edwards) M2PB 1987
* 'Summer Kisses, Winter Tears' (Wise, Weisman, Lloyd) M2PB 1986
Side 2
'Are You Lonesome Tonight' (Tepper, Bennett)
'It's Now Or Never' (Schroeder, Gold)

Elvis Presley (vcl, gtr), Scotty Moore, Tiny Timbrell, Neal Mathews (gtr), Dudley Brooks (pno), Ray Siegel (bs), D.J. Fontana (dms), Jimmie Haskell (acc), The Jordanaires (bv), remaining musicians unidentified
*Recorded: 20th Century Fox Studios, Hollywood, August 12, 1960

The movie *Flaming Star* was yet another crossroads in Elvis' career. The public seemed disinclined to accept Presley in a non-singing, straight-acting, half-decent Western movie; it was a box office flop, and from then on the Colonel made sure that his boy stuck firmly to what had already become the Elvis formula movie.

The film yielded two songs: the title cut, a fairly nondescript Western theme; and a ranch-house hoedown, 'A Cane And A High Starched Collar'. The latter, however, didn't surface until 1976.

Instead, the movie title was coupled with two previous hits, 'Are You Lonesome Tonight' and 'It's Now Or Never' and 'Summer Kisses, Winter Tears', a slow ballad recorded at the same Hollywood sessions.

Another track, 'Britches', was also cut at the same time, but subsequently vanished without trace.

'SOMETHING FOR EVERYBODY' (LP)
(US) RCA LSP/LPM-2370
Released: June 1961

Side 1
** 'There's Always Me' (Robertson) M2WW 0574
** 'Give Me The Right' (Wise, Blagman)
M2WW 0570
** 'It's A Sin' (Rose, Turner) M2WW 0572
*** 'Sentimental Me' (Cassin, Morehead)
M2WW 0576
*** 'Starting Today' (Robertson) M2WW 0575
** 'Gently' (Wizell, Lisbona) M2WW 0568
Side 2
** 'I'm Comin' Home (Rich) M2WW 0567
** 'In Your Arms' (Schroeder, Gold) M2WW 0569
*** 'Put The Blame On Me' (Twomey, Wise,
Blagman) M2WW 0578
*** 'Judy' (Redell) M2WW 0577
** 'I Want You With Me' (Harris) M2WW 0573
* 'I Slipped, I Stumbled, I Fell' (Wise, Weisman)
12PB 5382

Elvis Presley (vcl, gtr), Scotty Moore (gtr),
Floyd Cramer, Dudley Brooks (pno),
Bob Moore (bs), D.J. Fontana,
Murrey 'Buddy' Harman (dms),
The Jordanaires (bv), remaining musicians
unidentified
*Recorded: 20th Century Fox Studios,
Hollywood, October 1960
Elvis Presley (vcl, gtr), Scotty Moore,
Hank Garland (gtr). Floyd Cramer (pno),
Bob Moore (bs), D.J. Fontana,
Murrey 'Buddy' Harman (dms),
Homer 'Boots' Randolph (ts), The Jordanaires,
Millie Kirkham (bv)
**Recorded: RCA Studios, Nashville, March
12,1961, ***March 13, 1961

This undistinguished effort totally lives up to its name. A grab bag of mixed styles, it was obviously aimed to please the widest possible audience, but came closer to pleasing no one. The ballads were weak and the one main rocker, 'I Slipped, I Stumbled, I Fell' was a limp item from the limp movie *Wild In The Country*.

Wild in the Country/
20th Century Fox

Cast
Glenn Tyler .... Elvis Presley
Irene Sperry .... Hope Lange
Noreen .... Tuesday Weld
Betty Lee .... Millie Perkins
Davis............................ Rafer Johnson
Phil Macy........................ John Ireland
Cliff Macy .... Gary Lockwood
Uncle Rolfe.................. William Mims
Dr Underwood ....
.... Raymond Greenleaf
Monica George......................................
.... Christina Crawford
Flossie .... Robin Raymond
Mrs Parsons .... Doreen Lang
Mr Parsons .... Charles Arnt
Sarah .... Ruby Goodwin
Willie Dace...................... Will Corry
Professor Larson.......... Alan Napier
Judge Parker........ Jason Robards, Sr
Bartender .... Harry Carter
Sam Tyler.................. Harry Sherman
Hank Tyler .... Bobby West

Produced by Jerry Wald
Directed by Philip Dunne
Running Time: 114 Minutes
Released: June 15, 1961

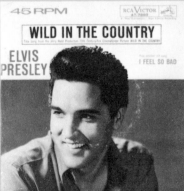

* **'I Feel So Bad'** (Williss) M2WW 0571
** **'Wild In The Country'**
(Peretti, Creatore, Weiss) 12PB 5383
(US) RCA 47-7880
Released: May 1961

Elvis Presley (vcl, gtr), Scotty Moore,
Hank Garland (gtr), Floyd Cramer (pno),
Bob Moore (bs), D.J. Fontana,
Murrey "Buddy" Harman (dms),
Homer "Boots" Randolph (ts), The Jordanaires,
Millie Kirkham (bv)
*Recorded: RCA Studios, Nashville,
March 12, 1961
Elvis Presley (vcl, gtr), Scotty Moore (gtr),
Floyd Cramer, Dudley Brooks (pno),
Bob Moore (bs), D.J. Fontana,
Murrey "Buddy" Harman (dms),
The Jordanaires (bv), remaining musicians
unidentified
**Recorded: 20th Century Fox Studios,
Hollywood, November 1960

After the long lull, Presley finally released another rock 'n' roll single. It wasn't a classic, but at least it had a beat behind the rather relaxed, blues-tinged delivery. The B-side was another movie title, this time from the implausible melodrama *Wild In The Country*.

Blue Hawaii

Blue Hawaii was the Presley film that, once and for all, placed Elvis firmly in the light entertainment, family market. Although in itself a harmless piece of brightly-coloured, candy floss cinema, it set the unbreakable pattern that, in a cheaper, more slapdash form, was to become, for almost ten crucial years, the formula for the Elvis Presley movie and all that this came to stand for.

The story was, to say the least, slight. Chad Gates (Elvis) comes back to Honolulu after his two year stretch in the army, determined not to follow the dictates of his domineering mother (Angela Lansbury). She wants him to settle down into the family pineapple business and marry into the social set. Chad wants to remain faithful to his sweetheart Maile (Joan Blackman), who is definitely unacceptable to Mom, and generally make his own way in the world.

The action is complicated by Chad's taking a job with Maile's tourist agency and having to escort four sexy schoolgirls and their chaperone around the islands' beauty spots. This makes for all kinds of misunderstandings and confusion, particularly when Maile assumes Chad is fooling around with the chaperone (Nancy Walters) and one of the schoolgirls (Jenny Maxwell).

Of course, in the end, all is sorted out. Maile's agency lands a big contract, Chad marries Maile and even Mother is reconciled.

Not that any of this really matters very much. The plot, such as it was, really only provided a loose framework for brightly coloured travelogue shots of the Hawaiian islands, a small army of bikini clad go-go girls, and Elvis' singing and dancing.

No film that has to halt the storyline no less than fourteen times for its star to perform a song can expect to maintain any real sense of continuity. Nothing in the film gave Presley the chance to develop the embryonic dramatic talents that he'd displayed in *King Creole* or even *Jailhouse Rock*; and, saddest of all, with the possible exception of 'Rock-A-Hula Baby', none of the specially written songs in the film could really be described as rock 'n' roll.

Despite all this, though, the public fell, hook, line and sinker, for *Blue Hawaii*'s lightweight appeal. It was a box office smash and the soundtrack album was one of Presley's biggest selling albums, moving some 2½ million copies.

The resulting figures were more than enough to convince the people around Elvis that this was the shape of things to come. If the fans wanted to see Elvis in living colour, against exotic locations and surrounded by pretty, scantily clad girls, then that was exactly what they were going to get.

The success of *Blue Hawaii* and the comparative failure of the non-musical drama *Flaming Star* firmly set Elvis' movie career on the course that would lead directly to atrocities like *Frankie And Johnny*, *Harum Scarum* and *Easy Come, Easy Go*, and the situation where Elvis Presley films were being only reluctantly purchased by drive-in cinemas as second features.

'(Maries's The Name) His latest Flame'
(Pomus, Shuman) M2WW 0860
'Little Sister' (Pomus, Shuman) M2WW 0861
(US) RCA 47-7908
Released: August 1961

Elvis Presley (vcl, gtr), Scotty Moore,
Hank Garland, Neal Mathews (gtr),
Floyd Cramer (pno, o), Gordon Stoker (pno),
Bob Moore (bs), D.J. Fontana,
Murrey "Buddy" Harman (dms),
Homer "Boots" Randolph (ts),
The Jordanaires (bv)
Recorded: RCA Studios, Nashville, June 26, 1961

After the box-office disappointments of *Flaming Star* and *Wild in the Country*, *Blue Hawaii* stuck firmly to the formula of sun, fun, songs and girls and made a mint. On the screen Elvis romped through the surf with a bland grin; all traces of moodiness and rebellion had been purged out of him. The Hillbilly Cat had been fully tamed and sanitized.

The same blandness followed right through to the soundtrack album. The ballads were overbearing and the rock 'n' roll was weak and halfhearted. In the late fifties a cut like 'Rock-a-Hula Baby' would have hardly been acceptable as a B-side. To be the strongest up-tempo track on an entire album was little short of shameful.

On its own *Blue Hawaii* might have been looked at as a harmless Presley excursion into a kind of singing Cary Grant persona. Unfortunately, this was to be the pattern for Presley's deteriorating work over most of the next decade.

About the most significant thing to come out of the whole affair was the song 'Can't Help Falling In Love', an obvious favourite of Presley's, included in his live act when he went back to concert performances in the early seventies.

In total contrast to the *Something for Everybody* LP, 'His Latest Flame' was a minor rock masterpiece. Driven along by a repetitive and insistent guitar figure (á la Bo Diddley), and an energetic piano in the bridge section, the tune pogoed where most of the recent work had plodded.

Even the B-side managed to rock, and even though 'Little Sister' hardly measured up to the standard of 'His Latest Flame', it was a welcome relief from the wilting ballads that occupied the reverse sides of most of Elvis' post-army singles. Compact 33⅓: 37-7908.

In 1979, 'Little Sister' enjoyed a minor renaissance, being covered by Ry Cooder on *Bop Till You Drop*, and Robert Plant (with Rockpile) at the concerts for the people of Kampuchea.

July 26, 1961
During a press interview, Elvis refuses to confirm or deny widespread rumour of a heated quarrel with Frank Sinatra over the affections of actress Juliet Prowse.

Blue Hawaii/Paramount

Cast
Chad Gates .... Elvis Presley
Maile Duval .... Joan Blackman
Abigail Prentace ...... Nancy Walters
Fred Gates .... Roland Winters
Sarah Lee Gates ... Angela Lansbury
Jack Kelman .... John Archer
Mr Chapman .... Howard McNear
Mrs Manaka .... Flora Hayes
Mr Duval .... Gregory Gay
Mr Garvey .... Steve Brodie
Mrs Garvey .... Iris Adrian
Patsy .... Darlene Tomkins
Sandy .... Pamela Alkert
Beverly .... Christian Kay
Ellie .... Jenny Maxwell
Ito O'Hara .... Frank Atienza
Carl .... Lani Kai
Ernie .... Jose De Varga
Wes .... Ralph Hanalie

Produced by Hal B. Wallis
Directed by Norman Taurog
Running Time: 101 minutes
Released: November 14, 1961

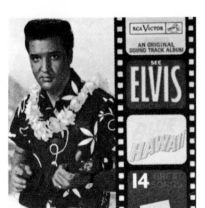

'BLUE HAWAII' (LP)
(US) RCA LSP-LPM-2426
Released: October 1961

Side
** 'Blue Hawaii' (Robin, Rainger) M2PB 2984
** 'Almost Always True' (Wise, Weisman) M2PB 2985
* 'Aloha-Oe' (arr/adapted Presley) M2PB
* 'No More' (Robertson, Blair) M2PB 2987
*** 'Can't Help Falling In Love' (Peretti, Creatore, Wise) M2PBB 2988
*** 'Rock-A-Hula Baby' (Wise, Weisman, Fuller) N2PB 2989
*** 'Moonlight Swim' (Dee, Weisman) M2PB 2990
Side 2
* 'Ku-U-I-Po' (Hawaiian Sweetheart)' (Peretti, Creatore, Weiss) M2PB 2991
* 'Ito Eats' (Tepper, Bennett) M2PB 2992
* 'Slicin' Sand' (Tepper, Bennett) M2PB 2993
* 'Hawaiian Sunset' (Tepper, Bennett) M2PB 2994
*** 'Beach Boy Blues' (Tepper, Bennett) M2PB 2995
** 'Island Of Love' (Tepper, Bennett) M2PB 2996
** 'Hawaiian Wedding Song' (King, Hoffman, Manning) M2PB 2997

Elvis Presley (vcl, gtr), Scotty Moore,
Hank Garland, Tiny Timbrell (gtr),
Floyd Cramer (pno), Dudley Brooks (pno, cel),
Bob Moore (bs), D.J. Fontana, Hal Blaine,
Bernie Mattinson (dms), Bernie Lewis (ps),
Homer "Boots" Randolph (ts),
George Fields (har), Fred Tavares,
Alvino Ray (uke), The Jordanaires, The Surfers,
Dorothy McCarty, Virginia Rees, Louilie-Jean Norman, Jacqueline Allen (bv).
*Recorded: Radio Recorders, Hollywood, March 21, 1961, **March 22, 1961, ***March 23, 1961

'Can't Help Falling In Love'
(Perretti, Creatore, Weiss) M2PB 2988
'Rock-A-Hula-Baby' (Wise, Weisman, Fuller) M2PB 2989
(US) RCA 47-7968
Released: November 1961

Elvis Presley (vcl, gtr), Scotty Moore,
Hank Garland, Tiny Timbrell (gtr),
Floyd Cramer (pno), Dudley Brooks (pno & cel),
Bob Moore (bs), D.J. Fontana, Hal Blaine,
Bernie Mattinson (dms), Bernie Lewis (ps),
Homer "Boots" Randolph (ts),
George Fields (har), Fred Tavares,
Alvino Rey (uke), The Jordanaires,
The Surfers (bv)
Recorded: Radio Recorders, Hollywood, March 23, 1961

This was the required single of the soundtrack of the movie. This A-side, more than any other, became associated with Elvis' public performances (he used it as his grand finale.)

Christmas 1961
The Colonel makes RCA print up one million wallet-size Elvis calendars, distribute them free of charge, and pay Elvis a token royalty on each.

1962

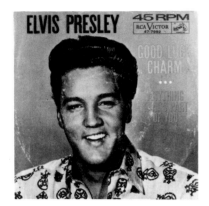

'Good Luck Charm' (Schroeder, Gold)
M2WW 1003
'Anything That's Part Of You' (Robertson)
M2WW 1004
(US) RCA 47-7992
Released: February 1962

Elvis Presley (vcl, gtr), Scotty Moore,
Jerry Kennedy (gtr), Floyd Cramer (pno),
Bob Moore (bs), D.J. Fontana,
Murrey "Buddy" Harman (dms),
Homer "Boots" Randolph (ts & clar),
Gordon Stoker (acc), The Jordanaires, Millie
Kirkham (bv).
Recorded: RCA Studios, Nashville,
October 15, 1961

'POT LUCK' (LP)
(US) RCA LSP/LMP-2523
Released: June 1962

Side 1
** 'Kiss Me Quick' (Pomus, Shuman) M2WW 8854
**** 'Just For Old Time Sake' (Tepper, Bennett)
N2WW 0689
**** 'Gonna Get Back Home Somehow'
(Pomus, Shuman) N2WW 0686
**** '(Such An) Easy Question' (Blackwell, Scott)
N2WW 0687
* 'Steppin' Out Of Line' (Wise, Weisman, Fuller)
M2PB 3038
*** 'I'm Yours' (Robertson, Blair) M2WW 8859
Side 2
**** 'Something Blue' (Evans, Byron) N2WW 0685
***** 'Suspicion' (Pomus, Shuman) N2WW 0694
***** 'I Feel That I've Known You Forever'
(Pomus, Jeffreys) N2WW 0692
**** 'Night Rider' (Pomus, Shuman) N2WW 0690
**** 'Fountain Of Love' (Giant, Lewis) N2WW 0688
** 'That's Someone You Never Forget'
(West, Presley) M2WW 8858

Elvis Presley (vcl, gtr), Scotty Moore,
Hank Garland, Tiny Timbrell (gtr),
Bernie Lewis (ps), Floyd Cramer (pno),
Dudley Brooks (pno, cel), Bob Moore (bs),
D.J. Fontana, Hal Blaine, Bernie Mattinson (dms),
Homer 'Boots' Randolph (ts),
George Fields (har), Alvino Rey,
Fred Tavares (uke), The Jordanaires,
The Surfers (bv)
*Recorded: Radio Recorders, Hollywood,
March 22, 1961
Elvis Presley (vcl, gtr), Scotty Moore,
Hank Garland, Neal Mathews (gtr),
Floyd Cramer (pno, org), Gordon Stoker (pno),
Bob Moore (bs), D.J. Fontana,
Murrey 'Buddy' Harman (dms),
Homer 'Boots' Randolph (claves),
The Jordanaires (bv)
**Recorded: RCA Studios, Nashville,
June 25, 1961. ***June 26, 1961
Elvis Presley (vcl, gtr), Scotty Moore,
Harold Bradley (gtr), Grady Martin (gtr, vibes),
Floyd Cramer (pno), Bob Moore (bs),
D.J. Fontana, Murrey 'Buddy' Harman (dms),
Homer 'Boots' Randolph (ts, vibes),
The Jordanaires, Millie Kirkham (bv)
****Recorded: RCA Studios, Nashville,
March 18, 1962. *****March 19, 1962

1962 was hardly a vintage year, either for Elvis or rock 'n' roll in general. In England there were the first stirrings – on a very word of mouth level – of a group called the Beatles; and a young folk singer who'd given himself the name Bob Dylan was scratching a living in New York's Greenwich Village; but all Elvis seemed to be able to come up with was a rather light-weight rock 'n' roll single coupled with a nostalgic ballad. Artistically, it was hardly an auspicious start to a new year, although the record did get to the No. 1 slot in the charts.

'FOLLOW THAT DREAM' (EP)
(US) RCA EPA-4368
Released: May 1962

Side 1
'Follow That Dream' (Wise, Weisman)
M2WW 0874
'Angel' (Tepper, Bennett) M2WW 0873
Side 2
'What A Wonderful Life' (Wayne, Livingstone)
M2WW 0875
'I'm Not The Marrying Kind' (Davis, Edwards)
M2WW 0876

Elvis Presley (vcl, gtr), Scotty Moore,
Hank Garland, Neal Mathews (gtr),
Floyd Cramer (pno),
Bob Moore (bs), D.J. Fontana,
Murrey "Buddy" Harman (dms), The Jordanaires,
Millie Kirkham (bv)
Recorded: RCA Studios, Nashville, July 5, 1961

A formula Elvis movie that played the conflict between shiftless Florida Poor Folk and corrupt Authority strictly for laughs, *Follow That Dream* only produced a slim EP of songs. These so lacked impact that they were forgotten almost as soon as they had finished playing.

N.B. Throughout his career, Bruce Springsteen has persistently slipped various Presley songs (e.g. 'Heartbreak Hotel' and 'Can't Help Falling In Love') into his concert repertoire. However, in 1981 he surprised audiences with a radically re-worked version of (of all things) 'Follow That Dream'.

March, 1962, saw Elvis back in the RCA studios in Nashville. Two new guitar players, Thomas Grady Martin and Harold Bradley, were brought in to augment Scotty Moore. Apart from this, it was strictly business as usual.

Out of all the cuts on this workmanlike but rather nondescript album, only 'Suspicion' stands out on account of its high sense of drama. The rest are rather dull.

It was starting to look as though Elvis had begun treating his studio obligations as a chore rather than a pleasure. It would be nice to be able to say that Presley was instead diverting his energy into a film career, but the evidence of this was not to be found on the screen.

Follow That Dream/
United Artists

Cast
Toby Kwimper .... Elvis Presley
Pop Kwimper .... Arthur O'Connell
Holly Jones .... Anne Helm
Alicia Claypoole .... Joanna Moore
Carmine .... Jack Kruschen
Nick .... Simon Oakland
Eddy and Teddy Bascomb ....
.... Gavin and Robert Koon
Ariadne .... Pam Ogles

Produced by David Weisbart
Directed by Gordon Douglas
Running Time: 110 minutes
Released: March 29, 1962

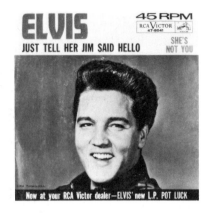

'She's Not You' (Pomus, Shuman, Leiber)
N2WW 0695
'Just Tell Her Jim Said Hello'
(Leiber, Stoller) N2WW 0693
(US) RCA 47-8041
Released: July 1962

Elvis Presley (vcl, gtr), Scotty Moore,
Harold Bradley (gtr), Grady Martin (gtr, vibes),
Floyd Cramer (pno), Bob Moore (bs),
D.J. Fontana, Murrey 'Buddy' Harman (dms),
Homer 'Boots' Randolph (ts, vibes),
The Jordanaires, Millie Kirkham (bv)
Recorded: RCA Studios, Nashville,
March 19, 1962

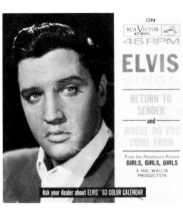

'Return To Sender' (Blackwell, Scott)
N2PB 3279
'Where Do You Come From'
(Batchelor, Roberts) N2PB 3274
(US) RCA 47-8100
Released: October 1962

Elvis Presley (vcl, gtr), Scotty Moore,
Barney Kessel, Tiny Timbrell (gtr),
Dudley Brooks (pno), Ray Siegal (bs),
D.J. Fontana, Hal Blaine, Bernie Mattinson (dms),
Homer "Boots" Randolph (ts, vibes),
The Jordanaires (bv)
Recorded: Radio Recorders, Hollywood,
March 1962

By far the best song to come out of the March '62 sessions (with the possible exception of 'Suspicion') this was the one selected as Elvis' second single for 1962. Unfortunately, all this is not saying very much. Professional but unmemorable.

Finally, in October, Elvis came up with his first really memorable single of 1962. It was recorded in Hollywood in March of the same year, immediately after the completion of the Nashville sessions that had produced 'Pot Luck'.

Part of the same studio stint that laid down the extensive soundtrack for *Girls, Girls, Girls*, 'Return to Sender' was one of those pearls that only turn up once every couple of hundred oysters. With powerful backing from The Jordanaires, it is a classic Presley cut that is still played and remembered long after the rest of the songs from the film are either forgotten or half remembered as fillers for a mediocre sound track.

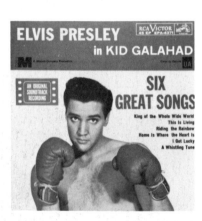

'KID GALAHAD' (EP)
(US) RCA EPA-4371
Released: September 1962

Side 1
'King Of The Whole Wide World'
(Batchelor, Roberts) N2PB 3131
'This Is Living' (Weisman, Wise) N2PB 3132
'Riding The Rainbow' (Weisman, Wise)
N2PB 3133
Side 2
'Home Is Where The Heart Is' (Edwards, David)
N2PB 3134
'I Got Lucky' (Fuller, Weisman, Wise) N2PB 3135
'A Whistling Tune' (Edwards, David) N2PB 3136

Elvis Presley (vcl), Scotty Moore (gtr),
Bob Moore (bs), D.J. Fontana (dms),
The Jordanaires (bv), remaining musicians
unidentified
Recorded: Radio Recorders, Hollywood,
October & November 1961

Here came another movie, in this instance slightly superior to the usual dire formula films — it even had superstar-to-be Charles Bronson in a supporting role. The songs, however, didn't cut it, and the world found itself with a second forgettable movie EP in the same year.

Seeing as no commercial single was scheduled to be lifted from this six song EP, RCA's Special Products team once again attempted to influence radio station programmers by coupling 'King Of The Whole Wide World' and 'Home Is Where The Heart Is' (RCA SP-118) as a promo-only platter.

N.B. *Kid Galahad* was a re-make of a 1937 movie which starred Edward G. Robinson, Humphrey Bogart, Bette Davis and Wayne Morris (in the title role).

Kid Galahad/United Artists

Cast
Walter Gulick.................Elvis Presley
Willey Grogan...................Gig Young
Dolly Fletcher...............Lola Albright
Rose Grogan ....Joan Blackman
Lew Nyack ....Charles Bronson
Lieberman ....Ned Glass
Maynard ....Robert Emhardt
Otto Danzig....................David Lewis
Joie Shakes ....Michael Dante
Zimmerman....................Judson Pratt
Sperling...................George Mitchell
Marvin.........................Richard Devon

Produced by David Weisbart
Directed by Phil Karlson
Running Time: 95 minutes
Released: July 25, 1962

'GIRLS! GIRLS! GIRLS!' (LP)
(US) RCA LSP/LPM-2621
Released: November 1962

Side 1
'Girls! Girls! Girls!' (Leiber, Stoller) N2PB 3272
'I Don't Wanna Be Tied' (Giant, Baum, Kaye)
N2PB 3273
'Where Do You Come From'
(Batchelor, Roberts) N2PB 3274
'I Don't Want To' (Tarre, Spielman) N2PB 3275
* 'We'll Be Together' (O'Curran, Brooks)
N2PB 3276
'A Boy Like Me, A Girl Like You'
(Tepper, Bennett) N2PB 3277
'Earth Boy' (Tepper, Bennett) N2PB 3278
Side 2
'Return To Sender' (Blackwell, Scott) N2PB 3279
'Because Of Love' (Batchelor, Roberts)
N2PB 3280
'Thanks To The Rolling Sea' (Batchelor, Roberts)
N2PB 3281
'Song Of The Shrimps' (Teper, Bennett)
N2PB 3282
'The Walls Have Ears' (Tepper, Bennett)
N2PB 3283
'We're Comin' In Loaded' (Blackwell, Scott)
N2PB 3288

Elvis Presley (vcl, gtr), Scotty Moore,
Barney Kessell, Tiny Timbrell (gtr),
Dudley Brooks (pno), Ray Siegel (bs),
D.J. Fontana, Hal Blaine, Bernie Mattinson (dms),
Homer "Boots" Randolph (ts, vibes),
The Jordanaires (bv).
Recorded: Radio Recorders, Hollywood,
March 1962
*plus Rob Bain, Al Hendricson (gtr),
The Amigos (bv).

If it hadn't been for 'Return to Sender', this whole album could easily and justly have been written off.

The title song, 'Girls! Girls! Girls!', came near to a successful impersonation of a rock 'n' roll track, but even by the greatest stretch of fan worshipping imagination, it was an unworthy effort on the part of a musician who had once released songs like 'All Shook Up' and 'Don't Be Cruel'. Even so, Presley's as yet untarnished popularity could still guarantee an album of such mediocrity a No.3 placing in the nation's best sellers.

Girls! Girls! Girls!/Paramount

Cast
Ross Carpenter .... Elvis Presley
Robin Ganter............. Stella Stevens
Laurel Dodge .... Laurel Goodwin
Wesley Johnson............Jeremy Slate
Chen Yung.............................Guy Lee
Kin Yung........................ Benson Fong
Madame Yung .... Beulah Quo
Sam .... Robert Strauss
Alexander Starvos....... Frank Puglia
Madame Starvos .... Lili Valenty
Leona and Linda Starvos ....
....................Barbara and Betty Beall
Arthur Morgan..............Nestor Paiva
Mrs Morgan.................. Ann McCrea
Mai and Tai Ling.......................................
.... Ginny and Elizabeth Tiu

Produced by Hall Wallis
Associate Producer: Paul Nathan
Directed by Norman Taurog
Running Time: 106 minutes
Released: November 2, 1962

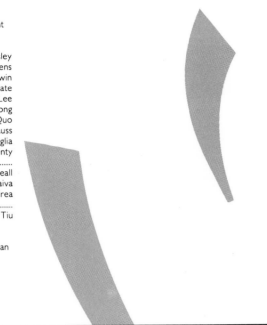

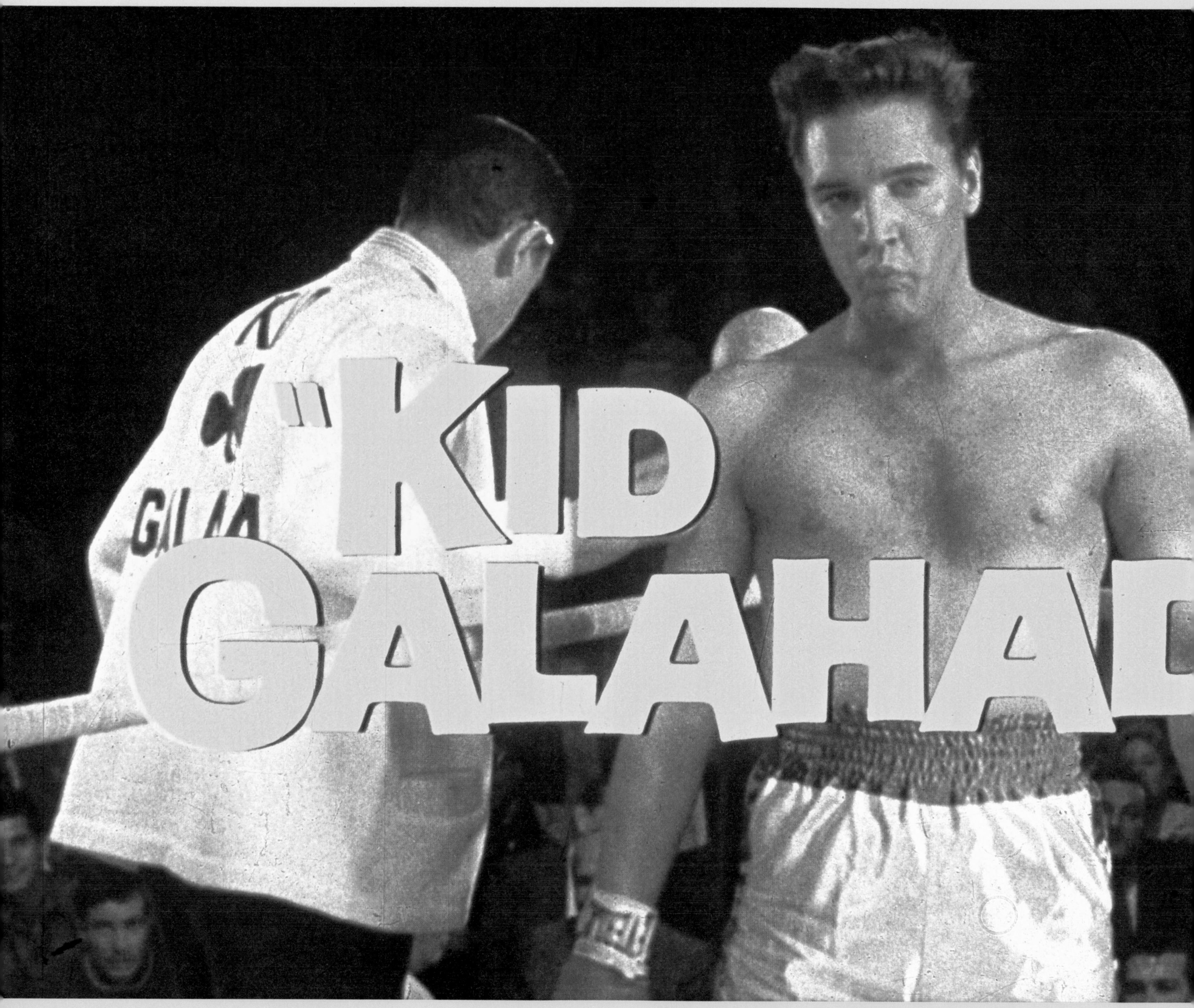
"KID
GALAHA

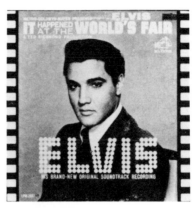

'IT HAPPENED AT THE WORLD'S FAIR'
(LP)
(US) RCA LSP/LPM-2697
Released: April 1963

Side I
'Beyond The Bend' (Weisman, Wise, Fuller)
PPA3 2723
'Relax' (Tepper, Bennett) PPA3 2726
'Take Me To The Fair' (Tepper, Bennett)
PPA3 2718
'They Remind Me Too Much Of You'
(Robertson) PPA3 2725
'One Broken Heart For Sale' (Blackwell, Scott)
PPA3 2724
Side 2
'I'm Falling In Love Tonight' (Robertson)
PPA3 2719
'Cotton Candy Land' (Batchelor, Roberts)
PPA3 2720
'A World Of Our Own' (Giant, Baum, Kaye)
PPA3 2721
'How Would You Like To Be' (Raleigh, Barkan)
PPA3 2722
'Happy Ending' (Weisman, Wayne) PPA3 2717

Elvis Presley (vcl, gtr), Scotty Moore,
Barney Kessel (gtr), Tiny Timbrell (gtr, man),
Dudley Brooks (pno), Ray Siegel (bs),
Ray Siegel (bs), D.J. Fontana, Hal Blaine (dms),
The Jordanaires, The Mello Men (bv), remaining
musicians unidentified
Recorded: MGM Sound Studios, Culver City,
October 1962

This movie soundtrack album—which contained ten less-than-memorable songs—amounted to little more than an out-and-out rip-off. Total running time? Fractionally over twenty tedious minutes.

The lead single, 'One Broken Heart For Sale', ran a mere 1.34 minutes. It was neither the first or last time that Elvis would take the money and run.

It Happened At The World's
Fair/Metro-Goldwyn-Mayer

Cast
Mike Edwards .... Elvis Presley
Diane Warren............... Joan O'Brien
Danny Burke...........Gary Lockwood
Sue-Lin.................................. Vicky Tiu
Vince Bradley ....H. M. Wynant
Miss Steuben...............Edith Atwater
Barney Thatcher ....Guy Raymond
Miss Ettinger............Dorothy Green
Walter Ling.......................... Kam Tong
Dorothy Johnson .... Yvonne Craig

Directed by Norman Taurog
A Ted Richmond Production
Running Time: 105 minutes
Released: April 3, 1963

'One Broken Heart For Sale'
(Blackwell, Scott) PPA3 2724
'They Remind Me Too Much Of You'
(Robertson) PPA3 2725
(US) RCA 47-8134
Released: January 1963

Elvis Presley (vcl, gtr), Scotty Moore,
Barney Kessel, Tiny Timbrell (gtr),
Dudley Brooks (pno), Bob Moore,
Ray Siegel (bs), D.J. Fontana, Hal Blaine (dms),
The Jordanaires, The Mello Men (bv), remaining
musicians unidentified
Recorded: MGM Sound Studios, Culver City,
October 1962

'(You're The) Devil In Disguise'
(Giant, Baum, Kaye) PPA4 0292
'Please Don't Drag That String Around'
(Blackwell, Scott) PPA4 0291
(US) RCA 47-8188
Released: June 1963

Elvis Presley (vcl, gtr), Scotty Moore,
Grady Martin, Jerry Kennedy,
Harold Bradley (gtr), Floyd Cramer (pno),
Bob Moore (bs), D.J. Fontana,
Murrey 'Buddy' Harman (dms),
Homer 'Boots' Randolph (ts, vibes, shakers),
The Jordanaires, Millie Kirkham, Joe Babcock (bv)
Recorded: RCA Studios, Nashville, May 26, 1963

This preview single from Presley's first MGM movie, *It Happened At The World's Fair*, proved very little except that the rocker was by now totally eclipsed by the smiling, would-be all-round entertainer. Even that wouldn't have been too bad, except that the all-round entertainer was being furnished with all-round mediocre songs.

By now, even the public seemed to notice. The single only made No. 2 in the US charts—to date, the lowest-ever position for a new Presley single.

On May 26, 1963, Elvis went into the RCA studios in Nashville with fourteen songs for a full-blown two-day recording session. With the exception of two re-recordings ('Memphis Tennessee' and 'Ask Me', done the following year) and one other track ('It Hurts Me'), this was the last time that Elvis was to attempt anything similar for some time.

Right up until May 25, 1966, Elvis would do nothing except cut soundtracks for movies. With the British Beat invasion poised to launch itself at the US, it was an action that amounted to nothing less than a criminal waste of talent.

One single was selected from these sessions, and that was '(You're The) Devil In Disguise', penned by the ubiquitous trio of Giant, Baum and Kaye. Although not a great Presley rock 'n' roll tune, it was certainly a marked improvement on the material that had been released immediately beforehand.

The original idea had been to follow the single with a studio album but, due mainly to the heavy movie commitments that Presley had taken on (four movies in the next eighteen months), the idea was dumped. The remaining dozen songs were filtered out over the next few years, either as singles or as bonus tracks on the lightweight soundtrack albums.

'(You're The) Devil In Disguise' peaked at No. 3 on the US singles charts – a feat he wasn't to repeat until the release of 'Crying In The Chapel' in 1965.

* **'Bossa Nova Baby'** (Leiber, Stoller) PPA3 4431
** **'Witchcraft'** (Bartholomew, King) PPA4 0295
(US) RCA 47-8243
Released: October 1963

Elvis Presley (vcl, gtr), Scotty Moore, Barney Kessel (gtr), Tiny Timbrell (gtr, mandolin), Dudley Brooks (pno), Ray Siegel (bs), D.J. Fontana, Hal Blaine, Emiel Radocchia (dms), Anthony Terran, Rudolph D. Loera (tpt), The Jordanaires, The Amigos (bv)
*Recorded: Radio Recorders, Hollywood, January 22, 1963
Elvis Presley (vcl, gtr), Scotty Moore, Grady Martin, Jerry Kennedy, Harold Bradley (gtr), Floyd Cramer (pno), Bob Moore (bs), D.J. Fontana, Murrey 'Buddy' Harman (dms), Homer 'Boots' Randolph (ts, vibes, shakers), The Jordanaires, Millie Kirkham, Joe Babcock (bv)
**Recorded: RCA Studios, Nashville, May 26, 1963

Once again, a movie preview single (*Fun In Acapulco* this time). Despite the Leiber and Stoller pedigree, it was another noticeably inferior song. It did, however make No. 8 on the hot hundred.

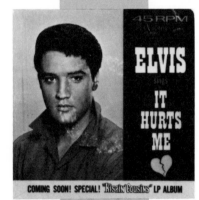

* **'Kissin' Cousins'** (Wise, Starr) RPA3 0219
** **'It Hurts Me'** (Byers) RPA4 1006
(US) RCA 47-8307
Released: October 1963

Elvis Presley (vcl, gtr), Scotty Moore, Harold Bradley, Grady Martin (gtr), Floyd Cramer (pno), Bob Moore (bs), D.J. Fontana, Murrey "Buddy" Harman (dms), Homer "Boots" Randolph (ts), Charlie McCoy (har), The Jordanaires (bv)
*Recorded: RCA Studios, Nashville, October 11, 1963
Elvis Presley (vcl, gtr), Scotty Moore, Harold Bradley, Grady Martin (gtr), Floyd Cramer (pno, org), Bob Moore (bs), D.J. Fontana, Murrey "Buddy" Harman (dms), Homer "Boots" Randolph (ts, vibes), The Jordanaires, Millie Kirkham (bv)
**Recorded: RCA Studios, Nashville, January 12, 1964

This single heralded yet another atrocious movie. The B-side was fairly presentable.

In another galaxy, the Rolling Stones issued 'Not Fade Away'.

N.B. This is another instance (this time in Italy) where both The Jordanaires and parts of the instrumental backing track are missing. The catalogue number is N-1410.

'ELVIS' GOLDEN RECORDS VOLUME 3'
(LP)
(US) RCA LSP/LPM-2765
Released: September 1963

Side 1
'It's Now Or Never' (Di Capua, Schroeder, Gold)
'Stuck On You' (Schroeder, McFarland)
'Fame And Fortune' (Wise, Weisman)
'I Gotta Know' (Evans, Williams)
'Surrender' (De Curtis, Pomus, Schuman)
'I Feel So Bad' (Willis)
Side 2
'Are You Lonesome Tonight?' (Turk, Handman)
'(Marie's The Name) His Latest Flame' (Pomus, Schuman)
'Little Sister' (Pomus, Shuman)
'Good Luck Charm' (Schroeder, Gold)
'Anything That's Part Of You' (Robertson)
'She's Not You' (Pomus, Stoller, Leiber)

The first resmelting of old gold in almost four years. Spanning the period from Presley's army demob ('Stuck On You') right through to the Summer of '62 ('She's Not You'), the package contains eight out of nine consecutive singles plus some flip sides. But precisely why such a massive hit as 'Can't Help Fallin' In Love' was omitted reveals a lack of planning which was to become all too prevalent in the future.

1963

'FUN IN ACAPULCO' (LP)
(US) RCA LSP-2756
Released: November 1963

Side I
** 'Fun In Acapulco' (Weisman, Wayne) PPA3 4423
 * 'Vino, Dinero Y Amor' (Tepper, Bennett)
    PPA3 4424
 * 'Mexico' (Tepper, Bennett) PPA3 4425
** 'El Toro' (Giant, Baum, Kaye) PPA3 4426
 * 'Marguerita' (Robertson) PPA3 4427
 * 'The Bullfighter Was A Lady' (Tepper, Bennett)
    PPA3 4428
** '(There's) No Room To Rhumba In A Sports Car'
    (Wise, Manning) PPA3 4429
Side 2
 * 'I Think I'm Gonna Like It Here'
    (Robertson, Blair) PPA3 4430
 * 'Bossa Nova Baby' (Leiber, Stoller) PPA3 4431
** 'You Can't Say No In Acapulco'
    (Feller, Fuller, Morris) PPA3 4432
** 'Guadalajara' (Guizar) PPA3 4433
*** 'Love Me Tonight' (Robertson) PPA4 0297
**** 'Slowly But Surely' (Wayne, Weisman)
    PPA4 0306

Elvis Presley (vcl, gtr), Scotty Moore,
Barney Kessel (gtr), Tiny Timbrell (gtr, man),
Dudley Brooks (pno), Ray Siegel (bs),
D.J. Fontana, Hal Blaine, Emiel Radocchia (dms),
Anthony Terran, Rudolph D. Lorea (tpt),
The Jordanaires, The Amigos (bv)
*Recorded: Radio Recorders, Hollywood,
January 22, 1963. **January 23, 1963
Elvis Presley (vcl, gtr), Scotty Moore,
Grady Martin, Jerry Kennedy,
Harold Bradley (gtr), Floyd Cramer (pno),
Bob Moore (bs), D.J. Fontana,
Murrey "Buddy" Harman (dms),
Homer "Boots" Randolph (ts, vibes, shakers),
The Jordanaires, Millie Kirkham, Joe Babcock (bv)
***Recorded: RCA Studios, Nashville,
May 26, 1963. ****May 27, 1963

The movie soundtracks were now coming thick and fast and, by the standards of the average Elvis film, this was one of the better examples. At least part of the success of the project was due to its sticking closely to the Mexican theme, rather than trying to shoehorn a bunch of unrelated songs into a minimal plot (the usual scheme of things).

Nevertheless, what is one supposed to make of such instant forgettables as '(There's) No Room To Rhumba In A Sports Car'?

In North America this soundtrack may have only sprouted a solitary single ('Bossa Nova Baby'), but by nature of its overt Mexicali flavour, RCA's Central American *afficionados* chose to re-distribute the entire contents of the soundtrack over a number of singles.

Fun In Acapulco/Paramount

Cast
Mike Windgren .... Elvis Presley
Margarita Dauphine ....
 .... Ursula Andress
Dolores Gomez .... Elsa Cardenas
Maximillian .... Paul Lukas
Raoul Almeido .... Larry Domasin
Moreno .... Alejandro Rey
Jose .... Robert Carricart
Jamie Harkins .... Teri Hope

Produced by Hal B. Wallis
Directed by Richard Thorpe
Running Time: 98 minutes
Released: November 21, 1963

1964

'KISSIN' COUSINS' (LP)
(US) RCA LSP-2894
Released: April 1964

Side 1
** 'Kissin' Cousins (No. 2)' (Giant, Baum, Kaye)
   RAP3 0218
** 'Smokey Mountain Boy' (Rosenblatt, Milrose)
   RPA3 0224
** 'There's Gold In The Mountains'
   (Giant, Baum, Kaye) RPA3 0226
** 'One Boy, Two Little Girls' (Giant, Baum, Kaye)
   RPA3 0223
** 'Catchin' On Fast' (Giant, Baum, Kaye)
   RPA3 0221
** 'Tender Feeling' (Giant, Baum, Kaye) RPA3 0225
Side 2
 * 'Anyone (Could Fall In Love With You)'
   (Benjamin, Marcus, DeJesus) RPA3 0227
** 'Barefoot Ballad' (Fuller, Morris) RPA3 0220
** 'Once Is Enough' (Tepper, Bennett) RPA3 0222
** 'Kissin' Cousins' (Wise, Starr) RPA3 0219
 * 'Echoes Of Love' (Roberts, McMains) PPA4 0290
** '(It's A) Long Lonely Highway' (Pomus, Shuman)
   PPA4 0303

Elvis Presley (vcl, gtr), Scotty Moore,
Grady Martin, Jerry Kennedy, Harold
Bradley (gtr), Floyd Cramer (pno), Bob
Moore (bs), D.J. Fontana,
Murrey "Buddy" Harman (dms),
Homer "Boots" Randolph (ts),
The Jordanaires (bv)
*Recorded: RCA Studios, Nashville,
May 26, 1963. **May 27, 1963
*** October 11, 1963

Prior to the release of both the movie and soundtrack album, the Colonel chose to ignore grassroot grumblings from fans concerning the quality and quantity of Elvis' movie vehicles with a flippant statement about why neither he nor Elvis insisted upon script approval.

"We have approval", chortled the Colonel, "only on money. Anyway, what does Elvis need? A couple of songs, a little story and some nice people to go with him!"

As if to emphasize this precarious stance, the Colonel returned the script of *Kissin' Cousins* unread. Attached to it was a personal memo: "If you want an opinion or evaluation of this script, it will cost you an additional $25,000." It soon became evident that such a short-sighted policy would prove detrimental to Presley's stock as a movie star.

Colonel Parker to Gene Nelson: "We don't know how to make movies. We have you for that. All we want are songs for an album."

Kissin' Cousins/
Metro-Goldwyn-Mayer

Cast
Josh Morgan } .... Elvis Presley
Jodie Tatum }
Pappy Tatum ...... Arthur O'Connell
Ma Tatum .... Glenda Farrell
Capt. Robert Salbo. Jack Alvertson
Selena Tatum.................. Pam Austin
Midge .... Cynthia Pepper
Azalea Tatum............ Yvonne Craig
General Donford... Donald Woods
Sgt. Bailey .... Tommy Farrell
Trudy .... Beverly Powers
Dixie.......................... Hortense Petra
General's Aide............ Robert Stone

Produced by Sam Katzman
Directed by Gene Nelson
Running Time: 96 minutes
Released: March 6, 1964

Where the single led, the movie soundtrack followed. This time it was a Li'l Abner-style hillbilly romp, and with the exception of the ballad, 'It Hurts Me', both movie and music were completely forgettable.

With Elvis playing both an army officer (Josh Morgan) and his hick double (Jodie Tatum) – achieved by the application of a rather tatty blond wig – the main selling point of this quickie was that the fans got two Elvii for the price of one. Quick to chase a fast buck, the Colonel attempted (unsuccessfully) to get Presley's fee doubled for the dual role. The whole exercise might actually have been improved by Tom Parker's talking camel.

 * **'Kiss Me Quick'** (Pomus, Shuman)
   M2WW 0857
** **'Suspicion'** (Pomus, Shuman) N2WW 0694
(US) RCA 47-0639
Released: April 1964

Elvis Presley (vcl, gtr), Scotty Moore,
Hank Garland, Neal Mathews, (gtr),
Floyd Cramer (pno, org), Gordon Stoker (pno),
Bob Moore (bs), D.J. Fontana,
Murrey "Buddy" Harman (dms),
Homer "Boots" Randolph (claves),
The Jordanaires (bv)
*Recorded: RCA Studios, Nashville,
June 25, 1961
Elvis Presley (vcl, gtr), Scotty Moore,
Harold Bradley (gtr), Grady Martin (gtr, vibes),
Floyd Cramer (pno), Bob Moore (bs),
D.J. Fontana, Murrey "Buddy" Harman (dms),
Homer "Boots" Randolph (ts, vibes),
The Jordanaires, Millie Kirkham (v)
**Recorded: RCA Studios, Nashville,
March 19, 1962

For a change, this single didn't emanate from a movie soundtrack. The A-side was, in fact, recorded back in June 1961 – during the same session that produced '(Marie's The Name) His Latest Flame' – and had been lying around the shelf. For some unfathomable reason, it was decided that April 1964 was the right moment for its release.

It only made No. 34 in the US charts; whereas in the perverse ol' UK it was a chart-topper.

The B-side, however, 'Suspicion', showed Presley in fine dramatic form. The fact that a Presley vocal clone (Terry Stafford) later achieved substantial chart success with this same song demonstrates that the wrong side had indeed been selected for promotion.

N.B. On a Spanish EP entitled, *Elvis Presley Canta* (3-20820), one of the stereo channels is missing on both 'Kiss Me Quick' and 'Suspicion' and with it the dulcet tones of Los Jordanaires.

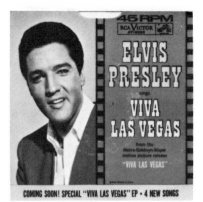

'What'd I Say' (Charles) RPA3 0235
'Viva Las Vegas' (Pomus, Shuman) RPA3 0234
(US) RCA 47-8360
Released: April 1964

Elvis Presley (vcl, gtr), Scotty Moore,
Glen Campbell (gtr), Dudley Brooks (pno),
Bob Moore (bs), D.J. Fontana,
Murrey "Buddy" Harman (dms), The Jordanaires,
The Jubilee Four, The Carole Lombard Quartet
(bv), remaining musicians unidentified
Recorded: MGM Sound Studios, Culver City,
July 7 & 9, 1963

It was ironic that one of the better Elvis formula movies, *Viva Las Vegas* (retitled in Britain *Love In Las Vegas*), should not merit its own soundtrack album, but instead be split into a four-track EP and a single, while the remaining songs were cast to the wind.

'Santa Lucia' was held over for the *Elvis For Everyone* album (August 1965) while 'Yellow Rose Of Texas'/'The Eyes Of Texas', plus two songs dropped from the actual film itself, 'Night Life' and 'Do The Vega', weren't dragged out of cold storage until the *Singer Presents Elvis Singing Flaming Star And Others* collection was sold exclusively through Singer Company shops in November 1968. Meanwhile, the Elvis/Ann-Margret duet 'The Lady Loves Me' plus 'You're The Boss' still languishes in mothballs. It was once again left to enterprising bootleggers to do the job properly, and put together a superbly-packaged, professional quality soundtrack album.

The A-side, the rock 'n' roll classic, 'What'd I Say', unfortunately sounds as though Presley's heart and energy weren't strictly in the project (not at all surprising with Ann-Margret on the set!) and it fails to measure up to the infinitely superior versions by Ray Charles and Jerry Lee Lewis.

The B-side was the title song from the movie and, in that, the fans got exactly what they expected.

N.B. An intriguing little EP entitled *See The USA The Elvis Way* (EPAS-4386) was created in New Zealand, offering the afficionado a true stereo cut of 'Viva Las Vegas' and 'Memphis'. The EP also contained 'New Orleans' and 'Blue Moon Of Kentucky'.

Viva Las Vegas/
Metro-Goldwyn-Mayer

Cast
Lucky Jordan.................. Elvis Presley
Rusty Martin .... Ann-Margret
Count Elmo Mancini ....
.... Cesare Danova
Mr. Martin............ William Demarest
Shorty Farnsworth.......... Nicky Blair

Produced by Jack Cummings and
  George Sidney
Directed by George Sidney
Running Time: 86 minutes
Released: April 20, 1964

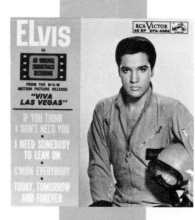

'VIVA LAS VEGAS' (EP)
(US) RCA EPA-4382
Released: July 1964
Side 1
'If You Think I Don't Need You' (West, Cooper)
RPA3 0387
'I Need Somebody To Lean On'
(Pomus, Shuman) RPA3 0386
Side 2
'C'Mon Everybody' (Byers) RPA3 0389
'Today, Tomorrow And Forever'
(Giant, Baum, Kaye) RPA3 0388

Elvis Presley (vcl, gtr), Scotty Moore,
Glen Campbell (gtr), Dudley Brooks (pno),
Bob Moore (bs), D.J. Fontana,
Murrey "Buddy" Harman (dms), The Jordanaires,
The Jubilee Four,
The Carole Lombard Quartet (bv), remaining
musicians unidentified.
Recorded: MGM Sound Studios, Culver City,
July 7 & 9, 1963

Enhanced not only by the dynamic presence of the statuesque Ann-Margret, but also by a slightly better script and songs than many Presley musicals, *Viva Las Vegas* was definitely a cut above the usual Presley cliché-ridden cinema product, and in the opinion of many fans, it remains among the most durable – constantly being re-screened at conventions.

As already pointed out, for some reason RCA didn't bother to put out the fourteen available tracks as a souvenir soundtrack LP. Instead, they cut corners by backing-up the moderately successful 'What'd I Say' single with this EP; and even these four cuts were not exactly the most memorable moments from the film's score. It stiffed at 92.

Perhaps the fact that Elvis – and, more to the point, Ann-Margret – had made no secret about their on-set affair adversely affected sales. Indeed, the lady had gone so far as to inform every gossip columnist within earshot that both Elvis and herself had long passed the "just good friends" stage in their relationship. Hopefully, gushed the star, she would soon be in a position to announce their wedding plans. It was still the era when it was considered unacceptable even to contemplate marrying public property; and the poor sales for this EP may well have been the fans' way of showing displeasure.

Whatever, to the world, their romance abruptly terminated, 'though they still remained on the best of terms right up until his death, with Elvis never forgetting to send her a bouquet of flowers (in the shape of a guitar) whenever she opened in a new show.

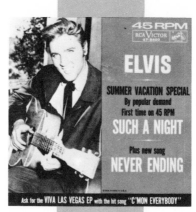

  * **'Such A Night'** (Chase) 12WB 0105
** **'Never Ending'** (Kaye, Springer) PPA4 0293
(US) RCA 47-8400
Released: July 1964

Elvis Presley (vcl, gtr), Scotty Moore,
Hank Garland (gtr), Floyd Cramer (pno),
Bob Moore (bs), D.J. Fontana,
Murrey "Buddy" Harman (dms),
Homer "Boots" Randolph (ts),
The Jordanaires (bv)
*Recorded: RCA Studios, Nashville,
April 4, 1960
Elvis Presley (vcl, gtr), Scotty Moore,
Grady Martin, Jerry Kennedy,
Harold Bradley (gtr), Floyd Cramer (pno),
Bob Moore (bs), D.J. Fontana,
Murrey "Buddy" Harman (dms),
Homer "Boots" Randolph (ts, vibes, shakers),
The Jordanaires, Millie Kirkham, Joe Babcock (bv)
**Recorded: RCA Studios, Nashville,
May 26, 1963

Due to Presley's preoccupation with recording virtually nothing but soundtracks, RCA were forced to re-release yet another back-catalogue track. This time they plundered the *Elvis Is Back* album, coupling it with one of the shelved cuts from the May '63 studio sessions. 'Such A Night', complete with false starts, later reappeared, in January 1976, on *Elvis – A Legendary Performer. Volume 2* (RCA CLP-1-1349).

1964

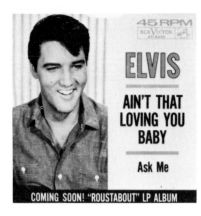

* **'Ain't That Loving' You Baby'**
(Otis, Hunter) J2WB 3255
** **'Ask Me'** (Modugno, Giant, Baum, Kaye)
RPA4 1005
(US) RCA 47-8440
Released: September 1964

Elvis Presley (vcl, gtr), Hank Garland,
Chet Atkins (gtr), Floyd Cramer (pno),
Bob Moore (bs), D.J. Fontana (dms),
Murrey "Buddy" Harman (bon),
The Jordanaires (bv)
*Recorded: RCA Studios, Nashville,
June 10, 1958
Elvis Presley (vcl, gtr), Scotty Moore,
Harold Bradley, Grady Martin (gtr),
Floyd Cramer (pno, o), Bob Moore (bs),
D.J. Fontana, Murrey "Buddy" Harman (dms),
Homer "Boots" Randolph (ts, vibes),
The Jordanaires, Millie Kirkham (bv)
**Recorded: RCA Studios, Nashville,
January 12, 1964

The May 27, 1963 version of 'Ask Me' was rejected and the song was finally re-recorded in January of the next year with practically the same personnel, only guitarist Jerry Kennedy not making the second date. The B-side rocker dates from the brief June '58 session during a weekend leave from the army which also produced 'I Need Your Love Tonight', 'A Big Hunk O'Love', 'A Fool Such As I' and 'I Got Stung'.

This version of 'Ain't That Loving You Baby' comprises spliced sections from at least two takes.

N.B. Whether by accident or intent, on the single version issued in France (45-567), both The Jordanaires and some of the instrumentation have been deleted, giving extra prominence to both Elvis' vocal and Floyd Cramer's piano.

'ROUSTABOUT' (LP)
(US) RCA LSP-2999
Released: November 1964

Side 1
* 'Roustabout' (Giant, Baum, Kaye) RPA3 5273
'Little Egypt' (Leiber, Stoller) RPA3 5270
'Poison Ivy League' (Giant, Baum, Kaye)
RPA3 5272
'Hard Knocks' (Buyers) RPA3 5267
'It's A Wonderful World' (Tepper, Bennett)
RPA3 5268
'Big Love, Big Heartache'
(Fuller, Morris, Hendrix) RPA3 5265
Side 2
'One Track Heart' (Giant, Baum, Kaye)
RPA3 5271
'It's Carnival Time' (Weisman, Wayne)
RPA3 5269
'Carny Town' (Wise, Starr) RPA3 5266
'There's A Brand New Day On The Horizon'
(Buyers) RPA3 5274
'Wheels On My Heels' (Tepper, Bennett)
RPA3 5275

Elvis Presley (vcl, gtr), Scotty Moore,
Tiny Timbrell, William E. Strange (gtr),
Floyd Cramer, Dudley Brooks (pno), Bob Moore,
Ray Siegel (bs). D.J. Fontana, Hal Blaine,
Murrey "Buddy" Harman, Bernie
Mattinson (dms), Homer "Boots" Randolph (ts),
The Jordanaires, *The Mello Men (bv)
Recorded: Radio Recorders, Hollywood,
February 24–8 & March 2–6, 1964

The movie with the infamous Honda motorcycle also produced an infamous soundtrack. About the only really creditable track was Elvis' version of the Coasters' 'Little Egypt'. Surprisingly, despite the generally low quality – and extremely harsh words of criticism from the press – the album was Presley's first US No. 1 for some time, and has sold consistently over the years. This was to be his last chart-topping album until the release, in 1973, of *Aloha From Hawaii Via Satellite*.

With 'Blue Christmas' released simultaneously to take care of impulse yuletide trade, RCA didn't pull any tracks from this album for a single. Nevertheless, they were astute enough to pair 'Roustabout' and 'One Track Heart' (RCA SP-139) as a radio-only promo single.

Roustabout/Paramount

Cast
Charlie Rogers............Elvis Presley
Maggie Morgan..Barbara Stanwyck
Cathy Lean................Joan Freeman
Joe Lean......................Leif Erickson
Madame Mijanou................................
....Sue Ane Langdon
Harry Carver................Pat Buttram
Marge.............................Joan Staley
Arthur Nielson.............Dabs Greer
Fred...............................Steve Brodie
Sam...................Norman Grabowski
Lou..............................Jack Albertson
Hazel...............................Jane Dulo
Cody Marsh...................Joel Fluellen
Little Egypt...................Wilda Taylor

Produced by Hal B. Wallis
Associate Producer: Paul Nathan
Running Time: 101 minutes
Released: November 12, 1964

* **'Blue Christmas'** (Heyes, Johnson) H2PB 5525
** **'Wooden Heart'**
(Wise, Weisman, Twomey, Kaempfert)
I2PW 3681
(US) RCA 447-0702
Released: November 1964

Elvis Presley (vcl, gtr), Scotty Moore (gtr),
Dudley Brooks (pno), Bill Black (bs),
D.J. Fontana (dms), The Jordanaires,
Millie Kirkham (bv)
*Recorded: Radio Recorders Studio, Hollywood,
September 5, 1957
Elvis Presley (vcl, gtr), Scotty Moore,
Tiny Timbrell, Neal Mathews (gtr),
Dudley Brooks (pno), Ray Siegel (bs),
D.J. Fontana, Frank Bode (dms),
Jimmie Haskell (acc), Hoyt Hawkins (tam),
The Jordanaires (bv)
**Recorded: RCA Studios, Hollywood,
April 28, 1960

As soon as a single had run its natural chart course, it was promptly deleted, invariably to reappear with a new catalogue number as part of RCA's Gold Standard re-issue series. Such was the fate of most Elvis singles. However, from time to time the Gold Standard series offered the A&R department an opportunity to issue certain album tracks in single form for the very first time.

Here is such an instance. A predictable seasonal offering which paired, arguably, the most popular track from *Elvis' Christmas Album* with the cloying 'Wooden Heart', courtesy *GI Blues*.

1965

March 15, 1965
Elvis and The Colonel celebrate their 10th anniversary as a team. To date, they've made 17 movies and sold 100-million records. For their troubles, they are alleged to have made $135-million from the former and $150-million from the latter.

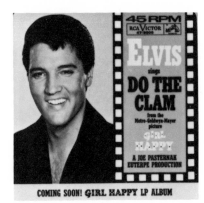

COMING SOON! GIRL HAPPY LP ALBUM

** **'Do The Clam'** (Wayne, Weisman, Fuller) SPA3 2009
* **'You'll Be Gone'** (West, Presley, Hodge) N2WW 0691
(US) RCA 47-8500
Released: March 1965

Elvis Presley (vcl, gtr), Scotty Moore, Tiny Timbrell (gtr), Floyd Cramer, Dudley Brooks (pno), Bob Moore, Ray Siegel (bs), D.J. Fontana, Hal Blaine, Murrey "Buddy" Harman (dms), Homer "Boots" Randolph (ts), The Jordanaires, The Carole Lombard Trio, The Jubilee Four (bv), remaining musicians unidentified
**Recorded: MGM Sound Studios, Culver City, June 5, 1964
Elvis Presley (vcl, gtr), Scotty Moore, Harold Bradley (gtr), Grady Martin (gtr, vibes), Floyd Cramer (pno), Bob Moore (bs), D.J. Fontana, Murrey "Buddy" Harman (dms), Homer "Boots" Randolph (ts), The Jordanaires, Millie Kirkham (bv)
*Recorded: RCA Studios, Nashville, March 18, 1962

1965 promised to be a revolutionary year for rock 'n' roll, with the Beatles, the Rolling Stones and Bob Dylan breaking into previously uncharted territory, while bands like the Who, the Yardbirds and the Byrds were determinedly struggling up the success ladder. Elvis now made his first contribution of the year, and it proved to be anything but innovative.

'Do The Clam' was a linear descendant of all the other dance craze records, 'Dixieland Rock', 'Rock-A-Hula-Baby' and 'Bossa Nova Baby'. Its only distinction in this mixed company was probably that it was the worst. Elvis' contact with reality had come close to zero. Nevertheless, one still encounters many Elvis fans who honestly believe 'Do The Clam' to be one of his finest-ever moments. There's no accounting for taste!

Girl Happy/
Metro-Goldwyn-Mayer

Cast
Rusty Wells....................Elvis Presley
Valerie ....Shelley Fabares
Big Frank...................Harold J. Stone
Andy................................ Gary Crosby
Wilbur..............................Jody Baker
Sunny Daze ....Nita Talbot
Deena ....Mary Ann Mobley
Romano.......................Fabrizio Mioni
Doc............................Jimmy Hawkins
Sgt. Benson.................Jackie Coogan
Brentwood Von Durgenfeld.............
.... Peter Brooks
Mr Penchill.......................John Fiedler
Betsy.................................Chris Noel
Laurie............................ Lyn Edington
Nancy............................Gale Gilmore
Bobbie ....Pamela Curran
Linda.................................Rusty Allen

Produced by Joe Pasternak
Directed by Boris Sagal
Running Time: 96 minutes
Released: January 22, 1965

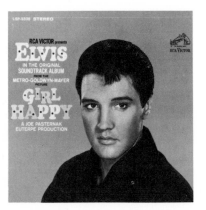

'GIRL HAPPY' (LP)
(US) RCA LSP/LPM-3338
Released: April 1965

Side 1
* 'Girl Happy' (Pomus, Meade) SPA3 2001
** 'Spring Fever' (Giant, Baum, Kaye) SPA3 2002
* 'Fort Lauderdale Chamber Of Commerce' (Tepper, Bennett) SPA3 2003
* 'Startin' Tonight' (Rosenblatt, Millrose) SPA3 2004
* 'Wolf Call' (Giant, Baum, Kaye) SPA3 2005
** 'Do Not Disturb' (Giant, Baum, Kaye) SPA3 2006
Side 2
** 'Cross My Heart And Hope To Die' (Wayne, Weisman) SPA3 2007
** 'The Meanest Girl In Town' (Byers) SPA3 2008
* 'Do The Clam' (Wayne, Weisman, Fuller) SPA3 2009
** 'Puppet On A String' (Tepper, Bennett) SPA3 2010
** 'I've Got To Find My Baby' (Byers) SPA3 2011
*** 'You'll Be Gone' (West, Presley, Hodge) N2WW 0691

Elvis Presley (vcl, gtr), Scotty Moore, Tiny Timbrell (gtr), Floyd Cramer, Dudley Brooks (pno), Bob Moore, Ray Siegel (bs), D.J. Fontana, Hal Blaine, Murrey "Buddy" Harman (dms), Homer "Boots" Randolph (ts), The Jordanaires, The Carole Lombard Trio, The Jubilee Four (bv), remaining musicians unidentified
*Recorded: MGM Sound Studios, Culver City, June 5, 1964. **June 8, 1964
Elvis Presley (vcl, gtr), Scotty Moore, Harold Bradley (gtr), Grady Martin (gtr; vibes), Floyd Cramer (pno), Bob Moore (bs), D.J. Fontana, Murrey "Buddy" Harman (dms), Homer "Boots" Randolph (ts), The Jordanaires, Millie Kirkham (bv)
***Recorded: RCA Studios, Nashville, March 18, 1962

Slap Happy was about the only way that one could describe this stage in Presley's career. The rule seemed to have become: three films a year; no studio records; and if the soundtrack music doesn't fill the quota, the balance can be made up by re-issues.

The films were starting to blur, and neither movies nor music had anything to make them stand out from the rest – unless it was the fact that, for some mysterious reason, the RCA master tape had been speeded up and the Presley voice had accordingly taken on a distinct Mickey Mouse quality.

CRYING IN THE CHAPEL

* **'Crying In The Chapel'** (Glenn) 12WB 0385
** **'I Believe In The Man In The Sky'** (Howard) 12WB 0375
(US) RCA 447-0643
Released: April 1965

Elvis Presley (vcl, gtr), Scotty Moore (gtr), Floyd Cramer (pno), Bob Moore (bs), D.J. Fontana, Murrey "Buddy" Harman (dms), Homer "Boots" Randolph (ts), The Jordanaires, Millie Kirkham, Charlie Hodge (bv), remaining musicians unidentified
*Recorded: RCA Studios, Nashville, October 30, 1960. **October 31, 1960

Hitherto best remembered by rock fans as one of the biggest-ever hits for Sonny Til & The Orioles (Jubilee 5122), the Presley version was an out-take from the 1960 sessions that produced *His Hand In Mine* and gave the singer an unexpected Easter-tide religious hit.

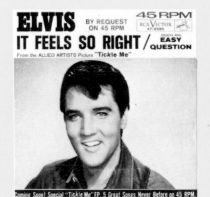

(Such An) Easy Question' (Blackwell, Scott)
N2WW 0687
* **'It Feels So Right'** (Wise, Weisman)
12WB 0086
(US) RCA 47-8585
Released: May 1965

Elvis Presley (vcl, gtr), Scotty Moore,
Harold Bradley (gtr), Grady Martin (gtr, vibes),
Floyd Cramer (pno), Bob Moore (bs),
D.J. Fontana, Murrey "Buddy" Harman (dms),
Homer "Boots" Randolph (ts, vibes),
The Jordanaires, Millie Kirkham (bv)
**Recorded: RCA Studios, Nashville,
March 18, 1962
Elvis Presley (vcl, gtr), Scotty Moore (gtr),
Floyd Cramer (pno), Bob Moore,
Hank Garland (bs), D.J. Fontana,
Murrey "Buddy" Harman (dms),
The Jordanaires (bv)
*Recorded: RCA Studios, Nashville,
March 21, 1960

Tickle Me/Allied Artists

Cast

Lonnie Beale	Elvis Presley
Pam Merritt	Jocelyn Lane
Vera Radford	Julie Adams
Stanley Potter	Jack Mullaney
Estelle Penfield	Merry Anders
Hilda	Connie Gilchrist
Brad Bentley	Edward Faulkner
Deputy Sturdivant	Bill Williams
Henry	Louis Elias
Adolph	John Dennis
Janet	Laurie Burton
Clair Kinnamon	Linda Rogers
Sibyl	Ann Morell
Ronnie	Lilyan Chauvin
Evelyn	Jean Ingram
Mildred	Francine York
Pat	Eve Bruce

Produced by Ben Schwalb
Directed by Norman Taurog
Running Time: 90 minutes
Released: June 15, 1965

A pair of recycled songs from the movie *Tickle Me*, which had originally been available on the *Pot Luck* and *Elvis Is Back* albums respectively.

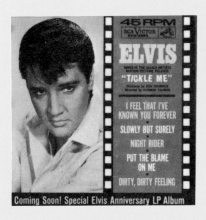

'TICKLE ME' (EP)
(US) RCA EPA-4383
Released: July 1965

Side 1
'I Feel That I've Known You Forever'
(Pomus, Jeffreys)
'Slowly But Surely' (Wayne, Weisman)
Side 2
'Night Rider' (Pomus, Shuman)
'Put The Blame On Me'
(Twomey, Wise, Blagman)
'Dirty, Dirty Feeling' (Leiber, Stoller)

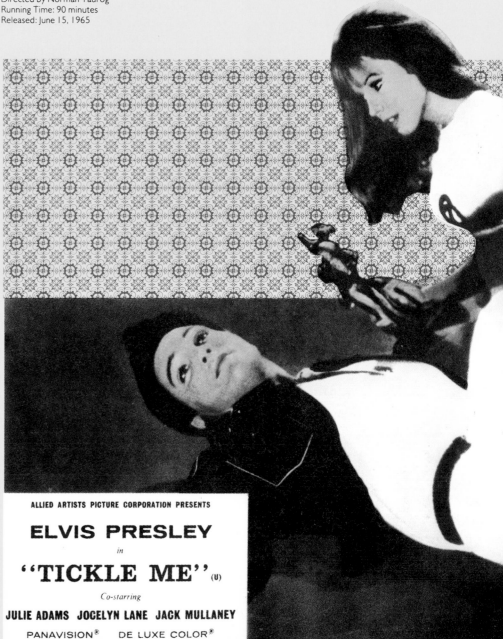

ALLIED ARTISTS PICTURE CORPORATION PRESENTS

ELVIS PRESLEY
in

"TICKLE ME" (U)

Co-starring

JULIE ADAMS JOCELYN LANE JACK MULLANEY

PANAVISION®   DE LUXE COLOR®
RELEASED BY WARNER-PATHE DISTRIBUTORS LTD.

This, his eighteenth movie, was really an all-time something in terms of the Presley quality control unit – an Elvis Presley flick without a single originally commissioned song. (Reportedly, there was neither sufficient time nor budget to accommodate such luxuries.) All nine songs – only a portion of which were released on the Extended Play soundtrack souvenir – were either left over from various studio sessions (from 1960 onwards) or, as already revealed, even recycled from the *Elvis Is Back* album.

The one hopeful sign was that the US fans were starting to wise up. The EP only made a chart showing at No. 70, and within seven weeks had disappeared from the lists.

Abroad, it was a slightly different story. In Britain, the soundtrack was sold as two separate EPs. Volume One (RCA RCX-7173) comprised the same track listing as the US release, while Volume Two (RCA RCX-7174) gathered together the four remaining titles: 'I'm Yours', 'Long Lonely Highway', 'It Feels So Right', and '(Such An) Easy Question'.

Further to confuse the collector, all nine songs were released as a fully fledged soundtrack album in Taiwan (Hai Shan HS-370).

Arguably, the movie's only saving grace was the appearance of British starlet Jocelyn Lane as Presley's girlfriend.

What follows is a list of the original sources from which all these tracks were culled.

'Dirty, Dirty Feeling' and 'It Feels So Right' from *Elvis Is Back*; 'Put The Blame On Me', *Something For Everybody*; 'Night Rider', 'I'm Yours', '(Such An) Easy Question', and 'I Feel That I've Known You Forever' from *Pot Luck*; 'Slowly But Surely', *Fun In Acapulco*; 'Long Lonely Highway', *Kissin' Cousins*.

'ELVIS FOR EVERYONE' (LP)
(US) RCA LSP/LPM 3450
Released: July 1965

Side 1
** 'Your Cheatin' Heart' (Williams) J2WB 0180
*** 'Summer Kisses, Winter Tears
    (Wise, Weisman, Lloyd) M2PB 1986
****** 'Finders Keepers, Losers Weepers' (Jones, Jones)
    PPA4 0296
*** 'In My Way' (Wise, Weisman) I2PB 5384
* 'Tomorrow Night' (Coslow, Grosz) SPA4 2331
***** 'Memphis, Tennessee' (Berry) RPA4 1004
Side 2
**** 'For The Millionth And The Last Time'
    (Tepper, Bennett) M2WW 1002
*** 'Forget Me Never' (Wise, Weisman) I2PB 5385
**** 'Sound Advice' (Giant, Baum, Kaye)
    M2WW 0878
***** 'Santa Lucia' (Trad: arr, Presley) SPAI 6898
**** 'I Met Her Today' (Robertson, Blair)
    M2WW 1005
** 'When It Rains, It Really Pours' (Emerson)
    H2WB 0419

Elvis Presley (vcl, gtr), Scotty Moore (gtr),
Bill Black (bs)
*Recorded: Memphis Recording Service,
Memphis, Tennessee. July 5, 1954
N.B. Under the auspices of producer
Chet Atkins, the original Sun track was
overdubbed at RCA's Studios, Nashville,
Tennessee on March 18, 1965, using the
following musicians: Chet Atkins,
Grady Martin (gtr), Henry Strzelecki (bs),
Murrey "Buddy" Harman (dms),
Charlie McCoy (har) The Anita Kerr Singers (bv)
Elvis Presley (vcl, gtr), Scotty Moore (gtr),
Tiny Timbrell (gtr) (Feb '58 only),
Dudley Brooks (pno), Bill Black (bs),
D.J. Fontana (dms), The Jordanaires (bv)
**Recorded: Radio Recorders, Hollywood,
California.
February 24, 1957 – 'When It Rains, It Really
Pours'
February 1, 1958 – 'Your Cheatin' Heart'
Elvis Presley (vcl, gtr), Scotty Moore (gtr),
Tiny Timbrell & Neal Mathews (gtr) (Aug '60
only), Dudley Brooks (pno), Floyd Cramer (pno)
(Oct '60 only), Ray Siegel (bs) (Aug '60 only),
Bob Moore (bs) (Oct '60 only),
D.J. Fontana (dms), Murrey "Buddy" Harman
(dms) (Oct '60 only), The Jordanaires (bv),
remaining musicians unidentified.
***Recorded: 20th Century Fox Studios,
Hollywood, California.
August 12, 1960 – 'Summer Kisses, Winter Tears'
October 1960 – 'In My Way' and 'Forget Me
Never'
Elvis Presley (vcl, gtr), Scotty Moore (gtr),
Hank Garland & Neal Mathews (gtr) (July '61
only), Jerry Kennedy (gtr) (Oct '61 only),
Floyd Cramer (pno), Bob Moore (bs),
D.J. Fontana, Murrey "Buddy" Harman (dms),
Homer "Boots" Randolph (ts, clar) (Oct '61 only),
Gordon Stoker (acc) (Oct '61 only),
The Jordanaires, Millie Kirkham (bv).
****Recorded: RCA Studios, Nashville,
Tennessee.
July 5, 1961 – 'Sound Advice'
October 15, 1961 – 'For The Millionth And The
Last Time'
October 16, 1961 – 'I Met Her Today'
Elvis Presley (vcl, gtr), Scotty Moore (gtr),
Grady Martin, Harold Bradley (gtr),

Jerry Kennedy (gtr) (May '63 only),
Floyd Cramer (pno, o), Bob Moore (bs),
D.J. Fontana, Murrey "Buddy" Harmen (dms),
Homer "Boots" Randolph (tenor sax, vbs, sha),
The Jordanaires, Millie Kirkam (bv),
Joe Babcock (bv) (May '63 only).
*****Recorded: RCA Studios, Nashville,
Tennessee.
May 26, 1963 – 'Finders keepers, Losers
Weepers'
January 12, 1964 – 'Memphis, Tennessee'
Elvis Presley (vcl, gtr), Scotty Moore,
Glen Campbell (gtr), Dudley Brooks (pno),
Bob Moore (bs), D.J. Fontana,
Murrey "Buddy" Harman (dms), The Jordanaires,
The Jubilee Four,
The Carole Lombard Quartet (bv), remaining
musicians unidentified.
******Recorded: MGM Sound Studios,
Hollywood, California, July 7 & 9, 1963

With Elvis disinclined to record anything but the minimum movie music, RCA was once again forced to scratch through the vaults to keep up the supply of, if not new, at least previously-unheard material.

The title *Elvis For Everyone* covers a general grab-bag of unissued tracks from just about every period since Elvis came out of the army (i.e. 'Sound Advice' was an unreleased song dropped from the soundtrack EP of *Follow That Dream*; similarly, 'In My Way' and 'Forget Me Never' were a brace of *Wild In The Country* left-overs, while 'Santa Lucia' was but one of the five unreleased cuts from the *Viva Las Vegas* soundtrack).

Of the dozen tracks assembled for this album, standouts includes Hank Williams' classic 'Your Cheatin' Heart' and Chuck Berry's much-covered 'Memphis Tennessee', although the latter was marred by poor recording quality.

It's of passing interest to note that on one occasion Elvis not only toyed with the idea of cutting a tribute album to Hank Williams (early in his career, Elvis had been sought to portray the legendary country singer in a Hollywood biopic, but the project was dropped when the Williams estate objected, and George Hamilton was selected for the role), but also a collection of Chuck Berry songs.

However, for Elvis afficionados – and there were a few – this album's main focus of interest was the ballad 'Tomorrow Night', a track excavated and later restored (by Chet Atkins) from among the cache of tapes RCA acquired in November 1955, when they purchased young Presley's entire Sun label output from Sam Phillips.

Recorded on July 5, 1954, 'Tomorrow Night' wasn't originally scheduled for inclusion on *Elvis For Everyone*. Track five, side one was to be 'Tennessee Saturday Night', a Sun side which had been shortlisted for release on two previous occasions (firstly, as an album of Sun tapes to be released while Elvis was in the army, and secondly on *Something For Everybody*), but dropped without explanation. So, on March 18, 1965 Chet Atkins commenced overdubbing and remixing Scotty and Bill's original backing track. For this task, Atkins selected Grady Martin to assist him with the guitar parts, plus Charlie McCoy (harmonica), Henry Strzelecki (bass), Murrey 'Buddy' Harman (drums) and the Anita Kerr Singers. Though the finished result was quite acceptable to most listeners, the purists argued that an overdubbing operation of this nature was tantamount to sacrilege. Whether or not Chet Atkins ever attempted further studio surgery on any other unreleased Sun masters is not known.

Despite being persistently presented with lists of unreleased Sun recordings – in particular 'Tennessee Saturday Night' and 'Uncle Pen' – RCA either officially deny the very existence of such material or, in a less guarded moment, claim that what they *do* possess is unsuitable for commercial purposes.

Those who have had access to such material beg to differ.

Anyway, right up until the inauguration of the *Legendary Performer* series this was to be the last occasion when RCA would delve into the 'non-existent' Sun tapes.

N.B. Not only is 'Summer Kisses, Winter Tears' replaced by 'Wild In The Country' on the British version of this album (RD-7723), but the track features a maracca player not heard on the American version!

'HARUM SCARUM' (LP)
(US) RCA LSP/LPM-3468
Released: October 1965

Side 1
'Harum Holiday' (Andreoli, Poncia) SPA3 6755
'My Desert Serenade' (Gelber) SPA3 6761
'Go East Young Man' (Giant, Baum, Kaye)
SPA3 6751
'Mirage' (Giant, Baum, Kaye) SPA3 6756
'Kismet' (Tepper, Bennett) SPA3 6758
'Shake That Tambourine' (Giant, Baum, Kaye)
SPA3 6752
Side 2
'Hey, Little Girl' (Byers) SPA3 6759
'Golden Coins' (Giant, Baum, Kaye) SPA3 6753
'So Close, Yet So Far' (Byers) SPA3 6754
'Animal Instinct' (Giant, Baum, Kaye) SPA3 6757
'Wisdom Of The Ages' (Giant, Baum, Kaye)
SPA3 6760

Elvis Presley (vcl, gtr), Scotty Moore (gtr),
Floyd Cramer (pno), Bob Moore (bs),
D.J. Fontana, Murrey "Buddy" Harman (dms),
Homer "Boots" Randolph (ts),
The Jordanaires (bv),
remaining musicians unidentified
Recorded: RCA Studios, Nashville,
February 24, 1965

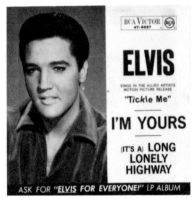

'I'm Yours' (Robertson, Blair)
'Long Lonely Highway' (Pomus, Shuman)
(US) RCA 47-8657
Released: August 1965

The final movie of 1965, and (debatably) the very worst of the Presley output ever to hit the cinema. Since it's hardly possible to say anything good about it, it's probably better to say nothing at all, except that it allegedly took less than two weeks to shoot and that in many countries it was retitled *Harem Holiday*, which did nothing to improve it.

Harum Scarum/
Metro-Goldwyn-Mayer

Cast
Johnny Tyronne............Elvis Presley
Princess Shalimar....................
............................Mary Ann Mobley
Aishah ....Fran Jeffries
Prince Drana...........Michael Ansara
Zacha ....Jay Novello
King Toranshad..............Philip Reed
Sinan...........................Theo Marcuse
Baba.................................Billy Barty
Mohar ....Dirk Harvey
Juina ....Jack Castanzo
Captain Heret............Larry Chance
Leilah.........................Barbara Werle
Emerald.....................Brenda Benet
Sapphire.....................Gail Gilmore
Amethyst......................Wilda Taylor
Sari ....Vicki Malkin

Produced by Sam Katzman
Directed by Gene Nelson
Running Time: 95 Minutes
Released: December 15, 1965

Third time around for both these tracks. Stemming from the very same June '61 sessions that produced 'His Latest Flame', the ballad 'I'm Yours' first appeared on *Pot Luck* before being recycled for the *Tickle Me* soundtrack LP.

'Long Lonely Highway' can be traced right back to *Kissin' Cousins*, before being given a second lease as a *Tickle Me* filler.

For this single, 'I'm Yours' was shortened, the narration (found on *Pot Luck*) having been edited out.

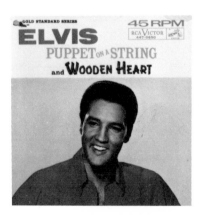

'Puppet On A String' (Tepper, Bennett)
'Wooden Heart'
(Wise, Weisman, Twomey, Kaempfert)
†2PW 3681
Released: October 1965

Yet another re-release. It's interesting to note that the choice of 'Wooden Heart' as a B-side meant that it had actually been re-issued *twice*, in this capacity, inside twelve months.

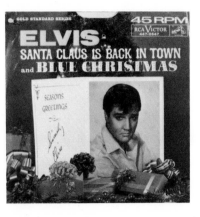

'Blue Christmas' (Heyes, Johnson) H2PB 5525
'Santa Claus Is Back In Town'
(Leiber, Stoller) H2PB 5532
(US) RCA 47-0647
Released: November 1965

Another seasonal re-re-release, with last year's A-side relegated to the flip.

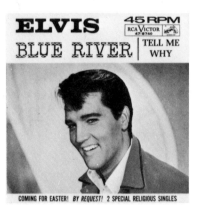

* 'Tell Me Why' (Turner, Titus) H2WB 0254
** 'Blue River' (Evans, Tobias) PPA4 0304
(US) RCA 47-8740
Released: January 1966

Elvis Presley (vcl, gtr), Scotty Moore (gtr),
Dudley Brooks (pno), Bill Black (bs),
D.J. Fontana (dms), The Jordanaires (bv)
*Recorded: Radio Recorders Studios,
Hollywood, January 12, 1957
Elvis Presley (vcl, gtr), Scotty Moore,
Grady Martin, Jerry Kennedy,
Harold Bradley (gtr), Floyd Cramer (pno),
Bob Moore (bs), D.J. Fontana,
Murrey "Buddy" Harman (dms),
Homer "Boots" Randolph (ts, vibes, shakers),
The Jordanaires, Millie Kirkham, Joe Babcock (bv)
**Recorded: RCA Studios, Nashville,
May 27, 1963

RCA went as far back as the January 1957 'All Shook Up' sessions for the A-side of this single and, to everyone's surprise, unearthed a creditable rock performance. Unfortunately, despite coinciding with Christmas, it failed to click with sufficient fans and climbed no higher than No. 33.

Contrary to speculation, the four second longer version of 'Blue River' that appears on a French EP (86508) isn't an alternate take – it's just that a technical malfunction during manufacture slightly slowed down the tape.

'Joshua Fit The Battle' (Trad: arr/
adapted,. Presley)
'Known Only To Him' (Hamblen)
(US) RCA 47-0651
Released: February 1966

'Milky White Way' (Trad: arr/
adapted, Presley)
'Swing Down Sweet Chariot' (Trad: arr/
adapted, Presley)
(US) RCA 47-0652
Released: February 1966

1966 proved to be a low point for Elvis Presley. Not one of his records made it into the US Top 10, and it looked like rock 'n' roll would soon forget him.

The worst thing of all was that neither Colonel Parker nor any of Elvis' advisers seemed to notice what was going on. Releasing one third of the five year old *His Hand In Mine* LP as a pair of gospel singles (that failed to even make the charts) was hardly the way to stop the rot.

'Frankie And Johnny'
(Gottlieb, Karger, Weisman) SPA3 7378
'Please Don't Stop Loving Me' (Byers)
SPA3 7384
(US) RCA 47-8780
Released: March 1966

Elvis Presley (vcl, gtr), Scotty Moore,
Barney Kessel (gtr), Floyd Cramer (pno),
Bob Moore, Ray Siegel (bs), D.J. Fontana,
Hal Blaine (dms), Homer "Boots" Randolph (ts),
The Jordanaires (bv), remaining musicians
unidentified
Recorded: United Artists Studios, Hollywood,
May 13–15, 1965

Once again the single preceded the album of the film, and once again it was inferior, and, unsurprisingly, anachronistic.

'FRANKIE AND JOHNNY' (LP)
(US) RCA LSP/LPM-3553
Released: April 1966

Side 1
'Frankie And Johnny'
(Gottlieb, Karger, Weisman) SPA3 7378
'Come Along' (Hess) SPA3 7374
'Petunia, The Gardener's Daughter'
(Tepper, Bennett) SPA3 7375
'Chesay' (Karger, Weisman, Fuller) SPA3 7376
'What Every Woman Lives For' (Pomus, Shuman)
SPA3 7377
'Look Out Broadway' (Wise, Starr) SPA3 7379
Side 2
'Beginner's Luck' (Tepper, Bennett) SPA3 7380
'Down By The Riverside/
When The Saints Go Marching In'
(Trad: arr Giant, Baum, Kaye) SPA3 7381
'Shout It Out' (Giant, Baum, Kaye) SPA3 7382
'Hard Luck' (Weisman, Wayne) SPA3 7383
'Please Don't Stop Loving Me' (Byers) SPA3 7384
'Everybody Come Aboard' (Giant, Baum, Kaye)
SPA3 7385

Elvis Presley (vcl, gtr), Donna Douglas (vcl),
Scotty Moore, Barney Kessell (gtr),
Floyd Cramer (pno), Bob Moore, Ray Siegel (bs),
D.J. Fontana, Hal Blaine (dms),
Homer "Boots" Randolph (ts),
The Jordanaires (bv). Remaining musicians
unidentified.
Recorded: United Artists Studios, Hollywood,
May 13–15, 1965

The folk tale of Frankie and Johnny, a traditional saga of jealousy, betrayal and murder, was bowdlerized here into a happy-go-lucky musical romp. The songs in the film lapsed to an almost pre-rock vaudeville level that scarcely scratched the surface of Presley's talent.

Frankie and Johnny/
United Artists

Cast
Johnny............................Elvis Presley
Frankie......................Donna Douglas
Nellie Bly..................Nancy Kovack
Mitzi......................Sue Ane Langdon
Braden......................Anthony Eisley
Cully..........................Harry Morgan
Pog............................Audrey Christie
Blackie........................Robert Strauss
Wilbur........................Jerome Cowan
Earl Barton Dancers............................
............Wilda Taylor, Larri Thomas
........Dee Jay Mattis, Judy Chapman

Produced by Edward Small
Directed by Fred de Cordova
Running Time: 87 minutes
Released: July 20, 1966

'PARADISE HAWAIIAN STYLE' (LP)
(US) RCA LSP-3643
Released: June 1966

Side 1
'Paradise, Hawaiian Style' (Giant, Baum, Kaye)
TPA3 3835
'Queenie Wahine's Papaya' (Giant, Baum, Kaye)
TPA3 3834
'Scratch My Back' (Giant, Baum, Kaye)
TPA3 3840
'Drums Of The Islands' (Tepper, Bennett)
TPA3 3837
'Datin' (Wise, Starr) TPA3 3843
Side 2
'A Dog's Life' (Wayne, Weisman) TPA3 3836
'A House Of Sand' (Giant, Baum, Kaye)
TPA3 3843
'Stop Where You Are' (Giant, Baum, Kaye)
TPA3 3841
'This Is My Heaven' (Giant, Baum, Kaye)
TPA3 3838
'Sand Castle' (Goldberg, Hess) TPA3 3839

Elvis Presley (vcl, gtr), Scotty Moore,
Barny Kessel, Charlie McCoy (gtr),
Bernie K. Lewis (ps), Larry Muhoberac (pno),
Ray Siegel, Keith Mitchell (bs), D.J. Fontana,
Hal Blaine, Victor Feldmen (dms),
The Jordanaires, The Mello Men (bv)
Recorded: Radio Recorders, Hollywood,
July 26 & 27, and August 2–4, 1965

Paradise–Hawaiian Style/
Paramount

Cast
Rick Richards.................Elvis Presley
Judy Hudson...............Suzanne Leigh
Danny Kohana..............James Shigeta
Jan Kohana........Donna Butterworth
Lani...............................Marianna Hill
Pau .... Irene Tsu
Lehua...............................Linda Wong
Joanna ....Julie Parrish
Betty Kohana...................Jan Shepard
Donald Belden...........John Doucette
Moki.....................................Philip Ahn
Mr. Cubberson...........Grady Sutton
Andy Lowell....................Don Collier
Mrs. Barrington...........Doris Packer
Mrs. Belden...................Mary Treen
Peggy Holdren...............Gigi Verone

Produced by Hal Wallis
Associate Producer: Paul Nathan
Running Time: 91 minutes
Released: June 8, 1966

* **'Love Letters'** (Young, Heyman) TPA4 0914
** **'Come What May'** (Tableporter) TPA4 0924
(US) RCA 47-8870
Released: June 1966

Elvis Presley (vcl, gtr), Scotty Moore,
Harold Bradley, Chip Young (gtr),
Pete Drake (ps), Floyd Cramer (pno),
David Briggs, Henry Slaughter (o),
Bob Moore (bs), D.J. Fontana,
Murrey "Buddy" Harman (dms),
Charlie McCoy (har, bs), The Jordanaires,
The Imperials, Millie Kirkham (bv)
*Recorded: RCA Studios, Nashville,
May 25, 1966. **May 28, 1966

Paramount Pictures had Elvis back on the beach and (predictably) back among the girls, in an attempt to recreate *Blue Hawaii*, the movie that Colonel Parker seemed to regard as the perfect Elvis money-making epic.

Unfortunately, in terms of film, music and even box office returns, Elvis' second tour of the Islands fell a long way behind the first. Even the soundtrack album had nothing as good as 'Can't Help Falling In Love' or as ludicrous as 'Rock-A-Hula Baby'.

Finally, after three long years, Elvis went back into a recording studio to cut something other than a movie soundtrack. Even before he set foot in the studio, certain improvements had occurred. RCA had radically refitted their Studio B in Nashville, and Felton Jarvis had taken over as Presley's producer.

Although in later years doubts might be cast on the merits of Jarvis' influence, right now the mere presence of new people around him seemed to encourage Elvis to lift his performances.

The first of these sessions ran between May 25 and May 28, 1966. The majority of the seventeen completed masters had a religious theme. One of the few secular tunes was 'Love Letters', and that was selected as the next single.

It was a much better record than many that Presley had put out in the preceding year, but his interpretation (which stuck close to Ketty Lester's original chart-topping arrangement) failed to catch the public's imagination, and only made No. 19 in the charts.

August 9, 1966
A few words from Colonel Tom Parker: "People say Elvis' pictures aren't doing so good these days. I tell you, we've made 22 pictures, 19 have been box office successes, two haven't completed their run yet and the other one hasn't been released. How do you argue with his kind of success? It's like telling Maxwell House to change their coffee formula when the stuff is selling like no tomorrow!"

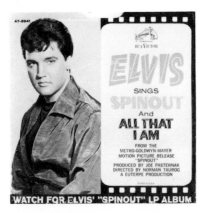

'Spinout' (Wayne, Weisman, Fuller) TPA3 5311
'All That I Am' (Tepper, Bennett) TPA3 5307
(US) RCA 47-8941
Released: October 1966

Elvis Presley (vcl, gtr), Scotty Moore (gtr),
Floyd Cramer (pno), Bob Moore (bs),
D.J. Fontana, Murrey "Buddy" Harman (dms),
The Jordanaires (bv), remaining musicians
unidentified.
Recorded: MGM Sound Studios, Culver City,
February 21, 1966

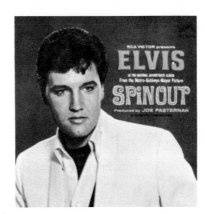

'SPINOUT' (LP)
(US) RCA LPM/LSP 3702
Released: November 1966

Side 1
* 'Stop, Look And Listen' (Byers) (TPA3 5305)
* 'Adam And Eve' (Wise, Starr) (TPA3 5306)
* 'All That I Am' (Tepper, Bennett) (TPA3 5307)
* 'Never Say Yes' (Pomus, Shuman) (TPA3 5308)
* 'Am I Ready' (Tepper, Bennett) (TPA3 5309)
* 'Beach Shack' (Giant, Baum, Kaye) (TPA3 5310)
Side 2
* 'Spinout' (Wayne, Weisman, Fuller) (TPA3 5311)
* 'Smorgasbord' (Tepper, Bennett) (TPA3 5312)
* 'I'll Be Back' (Wayne, Weisman) (TPA3 5313)
** 'Tomorrow Is A Long Time' (Dylan) (TPA4 0913)
** 'Down In The Alley' (Stone & The Clovers)
(TPA4 0912)
*** 'I'll Remember You' (Lee) (TPA4 0983)

Elvis Presley (vcl, gtr), James Burton (gtr),
Floyd Cramer (pno), Bob Moore (bs),
D.J. Fontana, Murrey "Buddy" Harman (dms),
The Jordanaires (bv).
*Recorded: Radio Recorders, Hollywood,
California. February 21, 1966
Elvis Presley (vcl, gtr), Scotty Moore,
Chip Young (gtr), Floyd Cramer,
Henry Slaughter (pno), David Briggs (o),
Bob Moore, Henry Strzelecki (bs),
D.J. Fontana (dms),
Murrey "Buddy" Harman (dms, tymp),
Pete Drake (st gtr), Charlie McCoy (har bs),
Homer "Boots" Randolph, Rufus Long (sax),
Ray Stevens (trmp), The Jordanaires,
The Imperials, Millie Kirkham, June Page,
Dolores Edgin, Sandy Posey (bv).
**Recorded: RCA Studios, Nashville, Tennessee.
May 26, 1966
Elvis Presley (vcl, gtr), Scotty Moore,
Chip Young (gtr), Henry Slaughter (pno),
David Briggs (o), Bob Moore (bs),
D.J. Fontana (dms),
Murrey "Buddy" Harman (dms, tymp),
Pete Drake (st gtr), Rufus Long (sax),
The Jordanaires, The Imperials, Millie Kirkham,
Dolores Edgin, June Page (bv)
***Recorded: RCA Studios, Nashville,
Tennessee. June 10, 1966

This undistinguished title song from an undistinguished movie was released as an undistinguished single and after entering the charts at its highest position, No. 40, took just seven weeks to return whence it came.

Spinout/Metro-Goldwyn-Mayer

Cast
Mike McCoy .... Elvis Presley
Cynthia Foxhugh .... Shelley Fabares
Diane St. Clair .... Diane McBain
Les .... Deborah Walley
Susan .... Dodie Marshall
Curly .... Jack Mullaney
Lt. Tracy Richards .... Will Hutchins
Philip Short .... Warren Berlinger
Larry .... Jimmy Hawkins
Howard Foxhugh .... Carl Betz
Bernard Ranley .... Cecil Kellaway
Violet Ranley .... Una Merkel
Blodgett .... Frederic Warlock
Harry .... Dave Barry

Produced by Joe Pasternak
Directed by Norman Taurog
Running Time: 95 minutes
Released: December 14, 1966

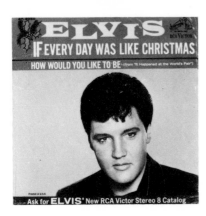

* **'If Every Day Was Like Christmas'** (West)
TPA4 0984
'How Would You Like To Be'
(Raleigh, Baeman)
(US) RCA 47-8950
Released: November 1966

Elvis Presley (vcl, gtr), Scotty Moore,
Chip Young (gtr), Pete Drake (ps),
David Briggs (pno), Henry Slaughter (o),
Bob Moore (bs), D.J. Fontana,
Murrey "Buddy" Harman (dms), Rufus Long (ts),
The Jordanaires, The Imperials, Millie Kirkham,
Dolores Edgin, June Page (bv)
*Recorded: RCA Studios, Nashville,
June 10, 1966

In order to allow ample time for packaging and promotion, it's common practice for artists to record their Christmas offerings in midsummer. And so, to evoke the right seasonal spirit, a Christmas tree (adorned with twinkling fairylights) was erected in the studio for Elvis to croon beneath. It was a wasted effort. This, Elvis' obligatory seasonal single for '66, failed even to nudge the Hot 100. Considering this single had been made for such a specific purpose, it's inexplicable that the flip was culled from the three-year-old soundtrack of *It Happened At The World's Fair*.

This album would have been undistinguished except for one crucial point. Among a selection of predictably *nada* tunes, Elvis presented the world with a totally unheralded and, in fact, almost ignored, cover of a Bob Dylan tune.

'Tomorrow Is A Long Time' was a candidate for Dylan's *Freewheeling Bob Dylan*, but was finally dropped in deference to other songs. Thus Elvis had recorded a Dylan tune which few people had heard before. Cut during that triumphant return to the studio that produced 'Love Letters' and the *How Great Thou Art* album, Elvis turned in an elegant, dignified performance over a tastefully simple modern country backing. It was exactly the kind of record that the people who had thrown up their hands in horror at 'Do The Clam' wanted to hear from Presley.

Amazingly, no one on the Presley management team and nor at RCA saw the potential of the track. Dylan was at his youthful and somewhat crazed peak in 1966. *Blonde On Blonde* had been released, and some of his followers were trying to elect him Messiah of the twentieth century. He had emerged as the biggest solo performer since Presley himself. The news that Elvis Presley was releasing a new Bob Dylan song would certainly have interested many one-time Elvis fans who were now sadly writing him off as a clown or a loser. Without any effort, Presley could have put himself right back into the centre of things. 'Tomorrow Is A Long Time' could have been a turning point. Nobody around him saw it that way, however. The song was buried as a bonus on a mediocre soundtrack album. There would be more bad movies and more bad records before Elvis attempted to pull his act together.

1967

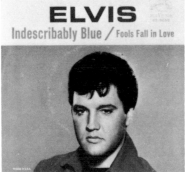

ELVIS
Indescribably Blue / Fools Fall in Love

Coming Soon! Elvis' new Sacred LP Album "How Great Thou Art"

* **'Indescribably Blue'** (Glenn) TPA4 0982
(US) RCA 47-9056
** **'Fools Fall In Love'** (Leiber, Stoller)
TPA4 0925
Released: January 1967

Elvis Presley (vcl, gtr), Scotty Moore,
Chip Young (gtr), Pete Drake (ps),
David Briggs (pno), Henry Slaughter (o),
Bob Moore (bs), D.J. Fontana,
Murrey "Buddy" Harman (dms), Rufus Long (ts),
The Jordanaires, The Imperials, Millie Kirkham,
Dolores Edgin, June Page (bv)
*Recorded: RCA Studios, Nashville,
June 10, 1966
Elvis Presley (vcl, gtr), Scotty Moore,
Chip Young (gtr), Pete Drake (ps), Floyd Cramer,
Henry Slaughter (pno), Bob Moore, Henry
Strzelecki (bs), D.J. Fontana,
Murrey "Buddy" Harman (dms),
Charlie McCoy (bs, har),
Homer "Boots" Randolph, Rufus Long (ts),
Ray Stevens (tpt), The Jordanaires, The Imperials,
Millie Kirkham, Dolores Edgin, Sandy Posey (bv)
**Recorded: RCA Studios, Nashville,
June 28, 1966

Though Elvis had already cut an album's worth of material for the *How Great Thou Art* project in May 1966, a second session had been convened in the June of that year because RCA had argued that, as it had taken 28 months to coax Elvis into recording anything other than soundtracks, the five tracks left over from the May session, in view of future movie commitments (and with the exception of 'Love Letters'), did not leave them a sufficiency of product.

'Indescribably Blue' was one of the three songs produced at this session. Although melodramatic and overworked, at least it gave one the feeling that Elvis was trying again, a quality it shared with the B-side.

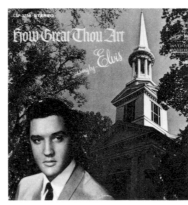

'HOW GREAT THOU ART' (LP)
(US) RCA LSP/LPM-3758
Released: March 1967

Side 1
** 'How Great Thou Art' (Hine) TPA4 0909
**** 'In The Garden' (Miles) TPA4 0918
**** 'Something Bigger Than You And I'
(Lange, Heath, Burke) TPA4 0920
**** 'Farther Along' (Trad: arr Presley) TPA4 0916
*** 'Stand By Me' (Trad: arr Presley) TPA4 0910
**** 'Without Him' (LeFevre) TPA4 0921
Side 2
**** 'So High' (Trad: arr Presley) TPA4 0915
**** 'Where Could I Go But To The Lord' (Coats)
TPA4 0923
**** 'By And By' (Trad: arr Presley) TPA4 0917
***** 'If The Lord Wasn't Walking By My Side'
(Slaughter) TPA4 0922
** 'Run On' (Trad: arr Presley) TPA4 0908
*** 'Where No One Stands Alone' (Lister)
TPA4 0911
* 'Crying In The Chapel' (Glenn) 12WB 0385

Elvis Presley (vcl, gtr), Scotty Moore,
Hank Garland (gtr), Floyd Cramer (pno),
Bob Moore (bs), D.J. Fontana,
Murrey "Buddy" Harman (dms),
Homer "Boots" Randolph (ts), The Jordanaires,
Millie Kirkham, Charlie Hodge (bv),
remaining musicians unidentified
*Recorded: RCA Studios, Nashville,
October 31, 1960
Elvis Presley (vcl, gtr), Scotty Moore,
Chip Young (gtr), Pete Drake (ps), Floyd Cramer,
Henry Slaughter (pno), David Briggs (o),
Bob Moore, Henry Strzelecki (bs),
Charlie McCoy (bs, har), D.J. Fontana,
Murrey 'Buddy' Harman, (dms),
Homer 'Boots' Randolph, Rufus Long (ts),
Ray Stevens (tpt), The Jordanaires, The Imperials,
Millie Kirkham, June Page, Dolores Edgin,
Sandy Poser (bv)
**Recorded: RCA Studios, Nashville,
May 25, 1966. ***May 26, 1966.
****May 27, 1966. *****May 28, 1966

The main result of the May '66 sessions had been the completion of yet another religious album, a much more lively affair than Elvis had produced for several years. Unfortunately, in the year that the Beatles were in the Abbey Road studios recording *Sgt Pepper*, it had to be something of a side-issue. Nevertheless, Elvis was, for once, actively involved on every level in the promotion of this, his first Felton Jarvis-produced project.

To coincide with its release, a very limited edition *Special Palm Sunday Programming* promo-only album (RCA SP-33-461) was pressed, containing selections from *How Great Thou Art* together with a personal message of goodwill from Elvis himself, and half-hour prime time spots were booked on 500 major US radio stations to present it. This entire self-financed project was dedicated by Elvis to the memory of his late mother.

As a further promotional back-up, an airplay special single of 'How Great Thou Art' coupled with 'So High' (RCA SP-162) and sleeved in a black and white reproduction of the album artwork was freely circulated to radio stations.

The operation was to pay dividends. *How Great Thou Art* earned Elvis his only Grammy Award, and went on to sell well in excess of one million albums in the US alone.

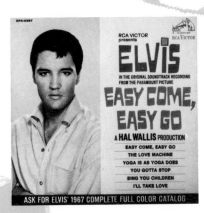

'EASY COME, EASY GO' (EP)
(US) RCA EPA-4387
Released: May 1967

Side 1
'Easy Come, Easy Go' (Weisman, Wayne) UPA3 3805
'The Love Machine' (Nelson, Burch, Taylor) UPA3 3806
'Yoga Is As Yoga Does' (Nelson, Burch) UPA3 3807
Side 2
'You Gotta Stop' (Giant, Baum, Kaye) UPA3 3808
'Sing You Children' (Nelson, Burch) UPA3 3809
'I'll Take Love' (Fuller, Barkan) UPA3 3810

Elvis Presley (vcl, gtr), Scotty Moore, Tiny Timbrell, Charlie McCoy (gtr), Michel Rubini (pno), Bob Moore, Jerry Scheff (bs), D.J. Fontana, Hal Blaine, Murrey "Buddy" Harman, Emil Radocchia (dms), Cal Tjader (vibes, perc), Anthony Terran, William Hood, Mike Henderson, Butch Parker, E. Meredith (horn section), The Jordanaires (bv)
Recorded: Radio Recorders, Hollywood, September 26, 28 & 29, 1966

Right For Love'. The mono pressings (PL-3414) find 'Tonight's All Right For Love' ousted in favour of 'Tonight Is So Right For Love'. The plot does not thicken any further!

Easy Come, Easy Go/
Paramount

Cast
Ted Jackson .... Elvis Presley
Jo Symington .... Dodie Marshall
Dina Bishop .... Pat Priest
Judd Whitman .... Pat Harrington
Gil Carey .... Skip Ward
Schwartz .... Sandy Kenyon
Captain Jack .... Frank McHugh
Cooper .... Ed Griffiths
Ship's Officers ....
.... Reed Morgan, Mickey Elley
Vicki .... Elaine Beckett
Mary .... Shari Nims
Zoltan .... Diki Lawrence
Artist .... Robert Lawrence
Madame Neherina ....
.... Elsa Lanchester

Produced by Hal Wallis
Directed by John Rich
Running Time: 95 minutes
Released: June 14, 1967

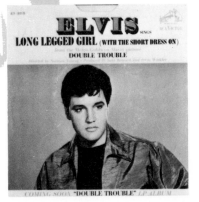

* **'Long Legged Girl (With The Short Dress On)'**
(McFarland, Scott) UPA3 3937
'That's Someone You'll Never Forget'
(West, Presley) M2WW 0858
(US) RCA 47-9115
Released: May 1967

Elvis Presley (vcl, gtr), Scotty Moore, Tiny Timbrell (gtr), Bob Moore (bs), D.J. Fontana, Hal Blaine, Murrey "Buddy" Harman (dms), The Jordanaires (bv)
*Recorded: MGM Sound Studios, Culver City, June 26, 1966

Another movie and another soundtrack EP. They were nothing to shout about. The improvement that had been made in studio production was not matched by the music of the movies. In fact, this EP might even be the worst record Elvis Presley ever made. The vocals were shameful, the sound quality lousy and the arrangements hit or miss. But then, it's alleged that when Elvis entered the Radio Recorders studio to dub the vocal tracks, he turned to one of the engineers and muttered, "What are you supposed to do with shit like this?"

About the only track that might have raised some interest was a version of the Everly Brothers' 'Leave My Woman Alone' (WPA3 1039). This, however, was never released.

N.B. In New Zealand, this soundtrack EP was fleshed out (with the addition of other songs) into a long player. The stereo copies (RPLS-3414) not only offer true stereo *Easy Come, Easy Go* recordings (not available Stateside), but also a true stereo 'Tonight's All

On Thursday, April 27, Elvis all but completed work on the Los Angeles set of *Clambake*.

On Monday, May 1, early in the morning, Colonel Parker and one hundred "close" friends assembled in the private suite of Milton Prell, owner of the Aladdin Hotel, Las Vegas, to witness Nevada Supreme Court Justice David Zenoff marry Elvis Aaron Presley to Priscilla Ann Beaulieu.

Joe Esposito was best man and Michelle Beaulieu, the bride's sister, the maid-of-honour. The ceremony was concluded at 9.41 am.

At 2.50 pm the newly-weds took off for Presley's Palm Springs retreat for a brief honeymoon. On Wednesday, they arrived in Hollywood so that Elvis could complete the final day's shooting on *Clambake*, after which the couple jetted directly back to Memphis (aboard a commercial airline) where, on May 29, a second wedding reception was staged for 125 friends and relatives at Graceland.

In between all this highly-publicized activity, RCA chose to release a trailer for both the soundtrack and movie of *Double Trouble*, in the form of the clichéd rocker, 'Long Legged Girl (With The Short Dress On)' backed with yet another track plundered from *Pot Luck*. It bombed!

Much as the majority of Presley's record-buying fans had chosen to ignore the *Viva Las Vegas* EP when Ann-Margret "leaked" details of her torrid romance with Elvis, they now evinced no interest in his "wedding" single. Perhaps the King had broken a few million hearts by taking himself a Queen. Whatever the reason, 'Long Legged Girl' was one of Presley's poorest sellers to date. It was in and out of the charts in five weeks flat, peaking at No. 63. Not for another 18 months would Elvis reach the US top 20 again.

'DOUBLE TROUBLE' (LP)
(US) RCA LSP/LPM-3787
Released: June 1967

Side 1
* 'Double Trouble' (Pomus, Shuman) UPA3 3934
* 'Baby, If You'll Give Me All Of Your Love' (Byers)
  UPA3 3935
* 'Could I Fall In Love' (Starr) UPA3 3936
* 'Long-Legged Girl' (McFarland, Scott)
  UPA3 3937
* 'City By Night' (Giant, Baum, Kaye) UPA3 3938
* 'Old MacDonald' (Starr) UPA3 3939
  Side 2
* 'I Love Only One Girl' (Tepper, Bennett)
  UPA3 3940
* 'There Is So Much World To See'
  (Tepper, Weisman) UPA3 3941
* 'It Won't Be Long' (Weisman, Wayne)
  UPA3 3942
** 'Never Ending' (Kaye, Springer) PPA4 0293
*** 'Blue River' (Evans, Tobias) SPA4 6768
** 'What Now, What Next, Where To'
  (Robinson, Blair) PPA4 0294

Elvis Presley (vcl, gtr), Scotty Moore,
Chip Young (gtr), Bob Moore (bs), D.J. Fontana,
Murrey "Buddy" Harman (dms),
The Jordanaires (bv),
remaining musicians unidentified
*Recorded: RCA Studios, Nashville,
June 26, 1967
Elvis Presley (vcl, gtr), Scotty Moore, Grady
Martin, Jerry Kennedy, Harold Bradley (gtr),
Floyd Cramer (pno), Bob Moore (bs),
D.J. Fontana, Murrey "Buddy" Harman (dms),
Homer "Boots" Randolph (ts, vibes),
The Jordanaires, Millie Kirkham,
Joe Babcock (bv).
**Recorded: RCA Studios, Nashville,
May 26, 1963. ***May 27, 1963

Double Trouble/
Metro-Goldwyn-Mayer

Cast
Guy Lambert .... Elvis Presley
Jill Conway .... Annette Day
Gerald Waverly.......... John Williams
Claire Dunham....... Yvonne Romain
The Wiere Brothers..... Themselves
Archie Brown............ Chips Rafferty
Arthur Babcock
.... Norman Rossington
Georgie .... Monty Landis
Morley .... Michael Murphy
Inspector DeGrotte...... Leon Askin
Iceman .... John Alderson
Captain Roach.......... Stanley Adams
The G Men .... Themselves

Produced by Judd Bernard and
 Irwin Winkler
Directed by Norman Taurog
Running Time: 90 minutes
Released: May 24, 1967

The *Double Trouble* soundtrack album gave the world tape hiss, the horrific experience of Elvis doing 'Old Macdonald', complete with moos and oinks, and, surprisingly, 'City By Night', a song that was head and shoulders above the average movie tune.

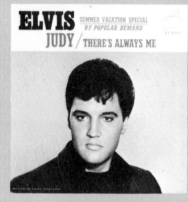

* **'There's Always Me'** (Robertson)
  M2WW 0574
** **'Judy'** (Redell) M2WW 0577
  (US) RCA 47-9287
  Released: August 1967

Elvis Presley (vcl, gtr), Scotty Moore,
Hank Garland (gtr), Floyd Cramer (pno),
Bob Moore (bs), D.J. Fontana,
Murrey "Buddy" Harman (dms),
Homer "Boots" Randolph (ts), The Jordanaires,
Millie Kirkham (bv)
*Recorded: RCA Studios, Nashville,
March 12, 1961. **March 13, 1961

An off-the-shelf single from 1961.

* **'Big Boss Man'** (Smith, Dixon) UPA4 2766
** **'You Don't Know Me'** (Walker, Arnold)
  UPA4 2771
  (US) RCA 47-9341
  Released: September 1967

Elvis Presley (vcl, gtr), Jerry Reed (gtr)
(September 10 only), Scotty Moore,
Harold Bradley, Chip Young (gtr),
Pete Drake (ps), Floyd Cramer (pno),
Bob Moore (bs), D.J. Fontana,
Murrey "Buddy" Harman (dms),
Homer "Boots" Randolph (ts),
Charlie McCoy (har), The Jordanaires,
Millie Kirkham (bv)
*Recorded: RCA Studios, Nashville,
September 10, 1967. **September 11, 1967

At long last Elvis put out a fully fledged rock 'n' roll song. Along with 'Guitar Man', it was included as a makeweight on the *Clambake* soundtrack album but, as singles, both tunes had enough meat to make a lot of people who had virtually written off Presley start taking notice all over again.

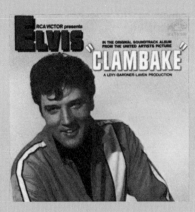

'CLAMBAKE' (LP)
(US) RCA LSP/LPM-3893
Released: November 1967
Side 1
** 'Guitar Man' (Hubbard) (UPA4 2765)
 * 'Clambake' (Weisman, Wayne) (UPA3 8443)
 * 'Who Needs Money?' (Starr) (UPA3 8444)
 * 'A House That Has Everything' (Tepper, Bennett)
   (UPA3 8445)
 * 'Confidence' (Tepper, Bennett) (UPA3 2753)
 * 'Hey, Hey, Hey' (Byers) (UPA3 8446)
Side 2
*** 'You Don't Know Me' (Walker, Arnold)
    (UPA4 2771)
 * 'The Girl I Never Loved' (Starr) (UPA3 8447)
 * 'How Can You Loose What You Never Had'
   (Weisman, Wayne) (UPA3 8448)
** 'Big Boss Man' (Smith, Dixon) (UPA4 2766)
**** 'Singing Tree' (Owens, Solberg) (UPA4 2774)
*** 'Just Call Me Lonesome' (Griffin) (UPA4 2769)
    Elvis Presley (vcl, gtr), Grady Martin,
    Harold Bradley (gtr), Pete Drake (ps),

Murrey "Buddy" Harman (dms), The Jordanaires,
Millie Kirkham, Willie Hutchins, June Page,
Priscilla Hubbard, Dolores Edgin (bv).
*Recorded: RCA Studios, Nashville, Tennessee.
February 21, 1967
Elvis Presley (vcl, gtr), Jerry Reed (ld gtr),
Scotty Moore, Harold Bradley, Chip Young (gtr),
Pete Drake (ps), Floyd Cramer (pno),
Bob Moore (bs), D.J. Fontana,
Murrey "Buddy" Harman (dms),
Homer "Boots" Randolph (ts),
Charlie McCoy (har), The Jordanaires,
Millie Kirkham (bv).
**Recorded: RCA Studios, Nashville, Tennessee.
September 10, 1967
***Same personnel as ** (minus Reed).
September 11, 1967
****Same personnel as ** September 12, 1967

Take away 'Guitar Man' and 'Big Boss Man' and, for your money, you had nothing more than another predictable movie collection. The sound was a little better than average, but the material was still shamefully weak.

Perhaps someone at RCA realized this, because a promotion-only EP (RCA MTR-244) featuring 'Clambake', 'Hey, Hey, Hey', 'You Don't Know Me' and 'A House That Has Everything' was put together and distributed, in limited quantities, around selected American radio stations.

Clambake/United Artists

Cast
Scott Heywood .... Elvis Presley
Dianne Carter .... Shelly Fabares
Tom Wilson .... Will Hutchins
James Jamison III .... Bill Bixby
Sam Burton .... Gary Merrill
Duster Heywood .... James Gregory
Ellie .... Amanda Harley
Sally .... Suzy Kaye
Gloria .... Angelique Pettyjohn

Produced by Levy-Gardner-Leven
  Productions
Directed by Arthur Nadel
Running Time: 99 minutes
Released: December 4, 1967

1968

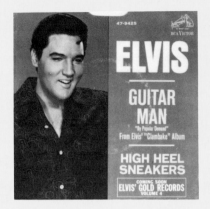

* '**Guitar Man**' (Reed) UPA4 2765
** '**High Heel Sneakers**' (Higgenbottom)
UPA4 2770
(US) RCA 47-9425
Released: January 1968

Elvis Presley (vcl), *Jerry Reed
('Guitar Man' only), Scotty Moore,
Grady Martin (gtr), Pete Drake (ps),
Floyd Cramer (pno), Bob Moore (bs),
D.J. Fontana, Murrey "Buddy" Harman (dms),
Charlie McCoy (har),
Homer "Boots" Randolph (ts), The Jordanaires,
Millie Kirkham (bv)
Recorded: RCA Studios, Nashville,
*September 10. **September 11, 1967

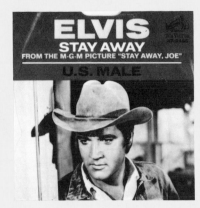

* '**US Male**' (Hubbard) WPA4 1807
** '**Stay Away**' (Tepper, Bennett) WPA1 1002
(US) RCA 47-9465
Released: March 1968

Elvis Presley (vcl), Jerry Reed (ld gtr),
Scotty Moore, Chip Young, Grady Martin (gtr),
Pete Drake (ps), Floyd Cramer (pno),
Bob Moore (bs), D.J. Fontana,
Murrey "Buddy" Harman (dms),
Charlie McCoy (har), The Jordanaires (bv)
*Recorded: RCA Studios, Nashville,
January 17, 1967
Elvis Presley (vcl), Scotty Moore (gtr),
Bob Moore (bs), D.J. Fontana (dms),
The Jordanaires (bv), remaining musicians
unidentified
**Recorded: MGM Studios, Culver City,
October 4, 1967

A significant recording session took place in the RCA Nashville studio in September 1967. After a long time producing nothing except uninspired movie music, Elvis actually returned to the studio to put down some honest-to-God rock 'n' roll. He had attempted the same thing earlier in the same year, but that had been nothing short of disastrous. All that was achieved was a single song, 'Suppose'.

The September attempt proved different. In three days Presley and the band completed ten tracks. Two of these, 'Guitar Man' and Tommy Tucker's 'High Heel Sneakers', were solid rock 'n' roll treatments, and were coupled to give the world one of the best singles that had come from Presley in quite a while.

The slight promise shown by 'Guitar Man' fell flat on its face with the release of 'US Male'. Sure, it was a rock 'n' roll song of sorts, but ponderous and overbearing, with an air of arrogance that left an unpleasant aftertaste. What made it even worse was that the year was 1968. Black ghettos were exploding in flame, the world was still trying to digest the Beatles' *Sgt Pepper* and Nixon was running for President. All Elvis could come up with was this exercise in flabby machismo. How out of touch could a man be?

Whether they were trying to reactivate post-Christmas interest in *Clambake*, or just reinforce Presley's current hard-rockin' image, RCA's Special Products department also pressed up a promo-only EP (RCA MTR-243) which paired both sides of this current single with his last two *Clambake*-derived hits 'Guitar Man' and 'Big Boss Man'.

'**ELVIS' GOLD RECORDS VOLUME 4**' (LP)
(US) RCA LSP/LPM-3921
Released: February 1968

Side 1
'Love Letters' (Young, Hayman)
'Witchcraft' (Bartholomew, King)
'It Hurts Me' (Byers, Daniels)
'What'd I Say' (Charles)
'Please Don't Drag That String Around'
(Blackwell, Scott)
'Indescribably Blue' (Glenn)
Side 2
'(You're The) Devil In Disguise'
(Giant, Baum, Kaye)
'Lonely Man' (Benjamin, Marcus)
'A Mess Of Blues' (Pomus, Shuman)
'Ask Me' (Modugno, Giant, Baum, Kaye)
'Ain't That Loving You Baby' (Otis, Hunter)
'Just Tell Her Jim Said Hello' (Stoller, Leiber)

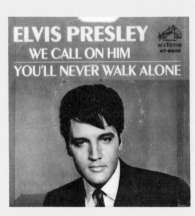

'**You'll Never Walk Alone**'
(Rogers, Hammerstein) UPA4 2773
'**We Call On Him**' (Karger, Weisman, Wayne)
UPA4 2772
(US) RCA 47-9000
Released: April 1968

Elvis Presley (vcl), Scotty Moore,
Grady Martin (gtr), Peter Drake (ps),
Floyd Cramer (pno), Bob Moore (bs),
D.J. Fontana, Murrey "Buddy" Harman (dms),
Charlie McCoy (har),
Homer "Boots" Randolph (ts), The Jordanaires,
Millie Kirkham (bv)
Recorded: RCA Studios, Nashville,
September 11, 1967

On three previous occasions, *Gold Records* compilations had been an obvious method of chronicling Presley's immediate past achievements. However, efforts to produce a fourth such volume presented innumerable problems, due to the fact that a majority of Presley's current releases were drawn from substandard movie soundtracks. This had resulted in a loss of continuity as a hit-maker. Therefore, it came as no big revelation when this album failed to offer the same kind of retrospective as before. The best that could be assembled was seven B-sides (stemming as far back as 1960) as opposed to just five A-sides. Moreover, in attempting to make this a viable release, the entire 1965 output was passed over.

At the same sessions that produced 'Guitar Man' and 'High Heel Sneakers', Elvis also cut a pair of gospel songs. With typical Presley corporate thinking, they were coupled and released as his third single of 1968.

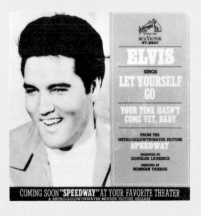

'**Your Time Hasn't Come Yet Baby**'
(Hirschorn, Kasna) WPA1 1023
'**Let Yourself Go**' (Byers) WPA1 1029
(US) RCA 47-9547
Released: May 1968

Elvis Presley (vcl), Scotty Moore (gtr),
Bob Moore (bs), D.J. Fontana (dms),
Floyd Cramer (pno), The Jordanaires (bv),
remaining musicians unidentified.

An eighth-rate single from an eighth-rate movie (*Speedway*).

'SPEEDWAY' (LP)
(US) RCA LSP-3989
Released: June 1968

Side 1
** 'Speedway' (Glazer, Schlaks) WPA1 1026
** 'There Ain't Nothing Like A Song'
(Byers, Johnston) WPA1 1022.
** 'Your Time Hasn't Come Yet Baby'
(Hirschorn, Kasna) WPA1 1023
** 'Who Are You?' (Wayne, Weisman) WPA1 1025
** 'He's Your Uncle, Not Your Dad'
(Wayne, Weisman) WPA1 1030
** 'Let Yourself Go' (Byers) WPA1 1029
Side 2
*** 'Your Groovy Self' (Hazelwood) (WPA1 1038
** 'Five Sleepy Heads' (Tepper, Bennett)
WPA 1024
* 'Western Union' (Tepper, Bennett) PPA4 0305
**** 'Mine' (Tepper, Bennett) UPA4 2767
***** 'Goin' Home' (Byers) WPA1 1001
** 'Suppose' (Dee, Goehring) WPA1 1028

Elvis Presley (vcl, gtr), Scotty Moore,
Grady Martin, Jerry Kennedy,
Harold Bradley (gtr), Floyd Cramer (pno),
Bob Moore (bs), D.J. Fontana,
Murrey "Buddy" Harman (dms),
Homer "Boots" Randolph (ts, vibes),
The Jordanaires, Millie Kirkham, Joe Babcock (bv)
*Recorded: RCA Studios, Nashville,
May 27, 1963
Elvis Presley (vcl, gtr), Scotty Moore (gtr),
Floyd Cramer (pno), Bob Moore (bs),
D.J. Fontana, Murrey "Buddy" Harman (dms),
The Jordanaires (bv), remaining musicians
unidentified.
**Recorded: MGM Studios, Culver City,
June 19, 1967
Nancy Sinatra (vcl), Scotty Moore (gtr),
Floyd Cramer (pno), Bob Moore (bs),
D.J. Fontana, Murrey "Buddy" Harman (dms),
The Jordanaires (bv), remaining musicians
unidentified.
***Recorded: MGM Studios, Culver City,
June 19, 1967 (backing track only)
****Elvis Presley (vcl, gtr), Scotty Moore,
Harold Bradley, Chip Young (gtr),
Pete Drake (ps), Floyd Cramer (pno),
Bob Moore (bs), D.J. Fontana,
Murrey "Buddy" Harman (dms),
Charlie McCoy (har),
Homer "Boots" Randolph (ts), The Jordanaires,
Millie Kirkham (bv)
Elvis Presley (vcl, gtr), Scotty Moore (gtr),
Floyd Cramer (pno), Bob Moore (bs),
D.J. Fontana, Murrey "Buddy" Harman (dms),
The Jordanaires (bv), remaining musicians
unidentified
*****Recorded: MGM Studios, Culver City,
October 4, 1967

The Presley films had sunk to such an all-time low that they began to blur into each other not only in the minds of the public, but also, it would seem, in the minds of those who made them. Elvis always had some mildly jive, romantic job. He always smiled, he usually punched someone and always got the girl (in this case, old flame Nancy Sinatra). He always made a soundtrack album, and always smiled for the cover photograph. This policy generated only enough interest to take the album to No. 72 in the US charts.

Stay Away, Joe/
Metro-Goldwyn-Mayer

Cast
Joe Lightcloud .... Elvis Presley
Charlie Lightcloud ....
.... Burgess Meredith
Glenda Callahan .... Joan Blondell
Annie Lightcloud .... Katy Jurado
Grandpa .... Thomas Gomez
Hy Slager .... Henry Jones
Bronc Hoverty .... L. Q. Jones
Mamie Callahan .... Quentin Dean
Mrs Hawkins .... Anne Seymour
Congressman Morissey ....
.... Douglas Henderson
Lorne Hawkins .... Angus Duncan
Frank Hawk .... Michael Lane
Mary Lightcloud ..... Susan Trustman
Hike Bowers .... Warren Vanders
Bull Shortgun .... Buck Kartalian
Connie Shortgun .... Mourishka
Marlene Standing Rattle ....
.... Caitlin Wyles
Billie-Joe Hump .... Marya Christen
Jackson He-Crow ....
.... Del "Sonny" West
Little Deer .... Jennifer Peak
Deputy Sheriff Matson ....
.... Brett Parker
Orville Witt .... Michael Keller

Produced by Douglas Laurence
Directed by Peter Tewksbury
Running Time: 98 minutes
Released: March 14, 1968

Speedway/
Metro-Goldwyn-Mayer

Cast
Steve Grayson .... Elvis Presley
Susan Jacks .... Nancy Sinatra
Denny Donford .... Bill Bixby
R. W. Hepworth .... Gale Gordon
Abel Esterlake ...... William Schallert
Ellie Esterlake ..... Victoria Meyerink
Paul Dado .... Ross Hagen
Birdie Kebner .... Carl Ballantine
Juan Medala .... Ponice Ponce
The Cook .... Harry Hickox
Billie Jo .... Christopher West
Mary Ann .... Miss Beverly Hills
Ted Simmons .... Harper Carter
Lloyd Meadows .... Bob Harris
Carrie .... Courtney Brown
Billie .... Dana Brown
Annie .... Patti Jean Keith
Mike .... Carl Reindel
Dumb Blonde .... Gari Hardy
Lori .... Charlotte Considine
Race Announcer .... Sandy Reed

Produced by Douglas Laurence
Directed by Norman Taurog
Running Time: 90 minutes
Released: June 13, 1968

1968

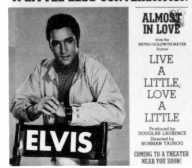

'Almost In Love' (Bonfa, Starr) WPAI 5766
'A Little Less Conversation' (Strange, Davis)
WPAI 5767
(US) RCA 47-9610
Released: September 1968

Elvis Presley (vcl), Scotty Moore (gtr),
Bob Moore (bs), D.J. Fontana (dms),
Floyd Cramer (pno), remaining musicians
unidentified.
Recorded: MGM Sound Studios, Culver City,
March 11, 1968

Another movie single, this time from *Live A Little, Love A Little*. Another flop.

Live A Little, Love A Little/
Metro-Goldwyn-Mayer

Cast
Greg..................................Elvis Presley
Bernice ....Michele Carey
Mike Landsdown............Don Porter
Penlow..............................Rudy Vallee
Harry................................Dick Sargent
Milkman................. Sterling Holloway
Ellen...........................Celeste Yarnall
Delivery Boy...............Eddie Hodges
Robbie's Mother ....Joan Shawlee
Miss Selfridge .... Mary Grover
Receptionist ....Emily Banks
Art Director ....Michael Keller
1st Secretary................ Merri Ashley
2nd Secretary................Phyllis Davis
Perfume Model.........Ursula Menzel

Produced by Douglas Laurence
Directed by Norman Taurog
Running Time: 89 minutes
Released: October 9, 1968

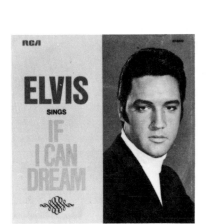

* **'If I Can Dream'** (Brown) WPAI 8029
'Edge Of Reality' (Giant, Baum, Kaye)
WPAI 5769
(US) RCA 47-9670
Released: October 1968

Elvis Presley (vcl), Tommy Tedesco,
Mike Deasy (gtr), Don Randi (kybds),
Larry Knechtal (bs), Hal Blaine (dms),
The Blossoms (bv), The NBC Orchestra:
conductor, W. Earl Brown; musical director,
William Goldenberg
*Recorded: NBC Studios, Burbank,
June 30, 1968

Although nobody knew it at the time, Elvis was poised for the first positive move in almost a decade. 'If I Can Dream' was part of the material recorded for the NBC-TV special. Although it was hardly the finest moment of that finest hour in Elvis' recent career, it did have sufficient impact to make No. 12, which, sad to say, was better than Elvis had done in quite a while. The B-side was, unfortunately, another cut dredged from the soundtrack of *Live A Little, Love A Little*.

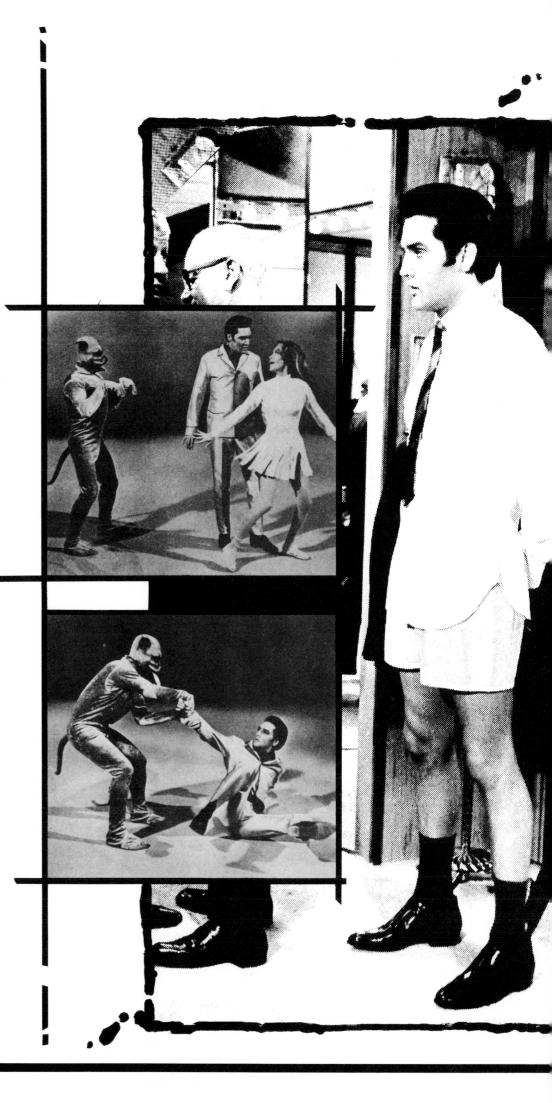

Connor Maas
Rec Soccer
2014

Lommel

'SINGER PRESENTS ELVIS SINGING FLAMING STAR AND OTHERS' (LP)
(US) RCA PRS-279
Released: November 1968

Side 1
* 'Flaming Star' (Wayne, Edwards) M2PB 1987
** 'Wonderful World' (Fletcher, Flatt) WPA1 5768
** 'Night Life' (Giant, Baum, Kaye) WPA1 8023
** 'All I Need Was The Rain' (Weisman, Wayne) WPA1 8026
**** 'Too Much Money Business' (Berry) WPA4 1800
Side 2
** 'Yellow Rose Of Texas/The Eyes Of Texas' (Wise, Starr, Sinclair) WPA1 8024
*** 'She's A Machine' (Byers) WPA1 8027
** 'Do The Vega' (Giant, Baum, Kaye) WPA1 8025
***** 'Tiger Man' (Lewis, Burns) WPA1 8023

Elvis Presley (vcl, gtr), Scotty Moore,
Tiny Timbrell, Neal Mathews (gtr),
Dudley Brooks (pno), Ray Siegel (bs),
D.J. Fontana (dms), Jimmie Haskell (acc),
The Jordanaires (bv), remaining musicians
unidentified
*Recorded: 20th Century Fox Studios,
Hollywood, August 12, 1960.
Elvis Presley (vcl, gtr), Scotty Moore (gtr),
Glen Campbell (gtr – 1963 sessions only),
Dudley Brooks (pno – 1963 only),
Floyd Cramer (pno – 1968 only), Bob Moore (bs),
D.J. Fontana (dms),
Murrey "Buddy" Harman (dms – 1963 & 1967 only), The Jordanaires (bv – 1963 & 1967 only),
The Jubilee Four,
The Carole Lombard Quartet (bv – 1963 only)
**Recorded: MGM Sound Studios, Culver City,
June 7 & 9, 1963. October 4, 1967.
March 11, 1968
Elvis Presley (vcl, gtr), Scotty Moore,
Tiny Timbrell Charlie McCoy (gtr), Michael
Rubini (pno), Bob Moore, Jerry Scheff (bs),
D.J. Fontana, Hal Blaine,
Murrey "Buddy" Harman (dms),
Cal Tjader (vibes, per), Anthony Terran,
William Hood, Mike Henderson, Butch Parker,
E. Meredith (horn section), The Jordanaires (bv)
***Recorded: Radio Recorders, Hollywood,
September 26–29, 1966.
Elvis Presley (vcl, gtr), Scotty Moore,
Chip Young, Jerry Reed (gtr), Pete Drake (ps),
Floyd Cramer (pno), Bob Moore (bs),
D.J. Fontana, Murrey "Buddy" Harman (dms),
Charlie McCoy (har), The Jordanaires (bv)
****Recorded: RCA Studios, Nashville,
January 17, 1968.
Elvis Presley (vcl, gtr), Tom Tedesco,
Mike Deasy (gtr), Don Randi (piano, o),
Larry Knechtal (bs), Hal Blaine (dms), The NBC
Orchestra conducted by W. Earl Brown.
Musical Director: William Goldenberg
*****Recorded: NBC Sound Studios, Burbank,
June 27, 1968

'ELVIS–NBC-TV SPECIAL' (LP)
(US) RCA LPM-4088
Released: December 1968

Side 1
* 'Trouble' (Leiber, Stoller) WPA1 8030
* 'Guitar Man' (Reed) WPA1 8047
** 'Lawdy, Miss Clawdy' (Price) WPA1 8031
** 'Baby What You Want Me To Do' (Reed) WPA1 8032
Dialogue
** 'Heartbreak Hotel' (Axton, Durden, Presley) WPA1 8033
** 'Hound Dog' (Leiber, Stoller) WPA1 8034
** 'All Shook Up' (Blackwell, Presley) WPA1 8035
** 'Can't Help Falling In Love' (Peretti, Creatore, Weiss) WPA1 8036
** 'Jailhouse Rock' (Leiber, Stoller) WPA1 8037
Dialogue
** 'Love Me Tender' (Presley, Matson) WPA1 8038

Side 2
Dialogue
** 'Where Could I Go To But The Lord' (Coats) WPA1 8039
** 'Up Above My Head' (Brown) WPA1 8040
** 'Saved' (Leiber, Stoller) WPA1 8041
Dialogue
** 'Blue Christmas' (Hayes, Johnson) WPA1 8042
Dialogue
** 'One Night' (Bartholomew, King) WPA1 8043
* 'Memories' (Strange, Davis) WPA1 8044
* 'Nothingville' (Strange, Davis) WPA1 8045
Dialogue
* 'Big Boss Man' (Dixon, Smith) WPA1 8046
* 'Guitar Man' (Reed) WPA1 8047
* 'Little Egypt' (Leiber, Stoller) WPA1 8048
** 'Trouble' (Leiber, Stoller) WPA1 8030
* 'Guitar Man' (Reed) WPA1 8047
* 'If I Can Dream' (Brown) WPA1 8029
Elvis Presley (vcl, gtr), Tom Tedesco,
Mike Deasy (gtr), Don Randi (pno, o),
Larry Knechtal (bs), Hal Blaine (dms),
The Blossoms (bv), The NBC Orchestra
conducted by W. Earl Brown, Musical Director:
William Goldenberg
*Recorded: NBC Studios, Burbank,
June 27, 1968
Elvis Presley (vcl, gtr), Scotty Moore,
Charlie Hodge (gtr), D.J. Fontana (dms),
Alan Fortas (tam)
**Recorded: NBC Studios, Burbank
June 28, 1968

Part of the deal negotiated between RCA, NBC, and the sponsors, the Singer company, to present Elvis in his own TV spectacular included Singer getting the rights to release their own Presley album that would be sold exclusively through Singer stores.

The album didn't amount to very much more than a rag-bag of old movie cuts and it didn't augur all that well for the as-yet-unseen TV special. However, the British equivalent (RCA RD-7723) was a better proposition, for it offered both 'Flaming Star' and 'Summer Kisses, Winter Tears' with the entire *Loving You* soundtrack and 'Are You Lonesome Tonight?'

Anyone who harboured any doubts or fears about what exactly Elvis Presley would do with a one hour TV special all to himself had those doubts firmly set to rest during the first few seconds of the show.

There was Elvis, resplendent in black leather, looking every inch the rock 'n' roll star, laying down a dramatic version of 'Trouble', the tune from *King Creole* that had always qualified as one of his meanest rock 'n' roll songs. There wasn't a trace left of the musical comedy clown, the only face of Elvis that the public had been allowed to see for almost a decade.

For the next sixty minutes. Elvis ran through the entire gamut of everything he could do best. He sang hard rock, hip-swivelling in black leather in front of a near-hysterical studio audience. Later in the show, he took the same, theatre-in-the-round stage to sit and jam on old hits like 'Love Me Tender', 'Lawdy Miss Clawdy' and 'One Night' with a relaxed Scotty Moore, Charlie Hodge, D.J. Fontana and Alan Fortas. He even took time to pay a fast verbal tribute to The Beatles and The Byrds, joke about his famous lip, and reminisce about how the vice squad in Florida had threatened to arrest him if he moved anything more than his little finger.

Elvis didn't, however, stick solely to rock 'n' roll. The big mid-show set piece was a romanticized musical biography of the man, complete with big band orchestrations and dance sequences, all built round the song 'Guitar Man'. There was also a gospel interlude, climaxing with a shaking, up-tempo version of 'Saved'.

When re-shown on August 17, 1969, the seasonal 'Blue Christmas' was replaced by

'Tiger Man'. This track can be found on *Elvis Sings Flaming Star* (CAS-2304).

The show ended with what almost amounted to Presley using 'If I Can Dream' as his message to the world, apparently closing the show in this manner directly against the wishes of Colonel Parker. Parker did get his way, though, on the matter of a song routine set against a brothel background. Parker didn't feel that this scene was strictly in keeping with the Presley image, and, despite protests from the show's producer, Steve Binder, who considered the sequence 'one of the best scenes I've ever been responsible for', the whole episode was cut from the show.

Despite these small, unfortunate details, the NBC special was a personal triumph for Elvis Presley. It was like watching a man rediscover his strength, charisma and self-respect. It reminded a world that had been all too near forgetting, just how great Presley could be when he was given the chance. The rock 'n' roll was the wildest he had produced since he'd come out of the army. The gospel music was treated with respect; both it and the ballads were presented without the layers of saccharine that had, all too sadly, become the Presley hallmark over the previous few years.

It was obvious that Elvis had not only reached a turning point in his career, but that he was also actively enjoying being back in front of a live audience. Although Elvis had always been a hard man to predict, it really started to look as though he was ready to return to the real world.

N.B. The theatre-in-the-round sequences were edited from four impromptu mini-gigs held in the studio before an invited audience. Even though extracts have appeared on the *Legendary Performer* compilations, the entire output of those remarkable sessions have surfaced on two bootleg double albums (*The Burbank Sessions*) and offer even further insight into his artistic rebirth.

Soundtrack recording sessions for the NBC-TV Special, *Elvis*.

June 27, 1968

WPAI 8045	'Nothingsville'	LPM-4088
WPKM 8112	'Let Yourself Go'	CPL-1-3082
WPAI 8046	'Big Boss Man'	LPM-4088
WPKM 8113	'It Hurts Me'	CPL-1-3082
WPAI 8047	'Guitar Man'	LPM-4088
WPAI 8048	'Little Egypt'	LPM-4088
WPAI 8030	'Trouble'	LPM-4088
WPAI 8118	'Love Me'	CPL-1-0341
WPAI 8119	'Tryin' To Get To You'	CPL-1-0341
WPAI 8116	'Are You Lonesome Tonight'	CPL-1-0341
WPAI 8117	*'Blue Suede Shoes'	CPL-1-1349
WPAI 8031	*'Lawdy, Miss Clawdy'	LPM-4088
WPAI 8043	*'One Night'	LPM-4088
WPAI 8044	'Memories'	LPM-4088
WPAI 8028	'Tiger Man'	PRS-279
WPAI 8042	*'Blue Christmas'	LPM-4088
WPAI 8032	*'Baby, What You Want Me To Do'	LPM-4088
WPAI 8120	*'Baby, What You Want Me To Do'	CPL-1-1349
KPA5 9564	*Medley: 'Lawdy, Miss Clawdy'/'Baby, What You Want Me To Do'	CPL8-3699(4)

Known unreleased material:

6.00 pm Show
* *'That's All Right (Mama)'
* *'Heartbreak Hotel'
* *'Love Me'
* *'Baby, What You Want Me To Do' (2 takes)
* *'Blue Suede Shoes'
* *'Lawdy, Miss Clawdy'
* *'Are You Lonesome Tonight?'
* *'When My Blue Moon Turns To Gold Again'
* *'Blue Christmas'
* *'Tryin' To Get To You'
* *'One Night'

8.00 pm Show
* *'Heartbreak Hotel'
* *'Baby, What You Want Me To Do' (2 takes)
* *'Blue Moon Of Kentucky'
* *'That's All Right (Mama)'
* *'Are You Lonesome Tonight?'
* *'Blue Suede Shoes'
* *'One Night'
* *'Love Me'
* *'Tryin' To Get To You'
* *'Santa Claus Is Back In Town'
* *'Tiger Man'
* *'When My Blue Moon Turns To Gold Again'

June 28, 1968

WPAI 8039	'Where Could I Go But To The Lord'	LPM-4088
WPAI 8040	'Up Above My Head'	LPM-4088
WPAI 8041	'Saved'	LPM-4088
WPAI 8029	'If I Can Dream'	47-9670

June 29, 1968

WPAI 8033	'Heartbreak Hotel'	LPM-4088
WPAI 8034	'Hound Dog'	LPM-4088
WPAI 8035	'All Shook Up'	LPM-4088
WPAI 8036	'Can't Help Falling In Love'	LPM-4088
WPAI 8037	'Jailhouse Rock'	LPM-4088
WPAI 8038	'Love Me Tender'	LPM-4088
WPAI 8030	'Trouble'	LPM-4088
WPAI 8047	'Guitar Man'	LPM-4088

Known unreleased material:
6.00 pm Show
Medley: 'Heartbreak Hotel'/'One Night'
Medley: 'Heartbreak Hotel'/'Hound Dog'/'All Shook Up'
'Can't Help Falling In Love'
'Jailhouse Rock'
'Don't Be Cruel'
'Blue Suede Shoes'
'Love Me Tender'
'Trouble'
'Baby, What You Want Me To Do'
'If I Can Dream'

8.00 pm Show
Medley: 'Heartbreak Hotel'/'Hound Dog'/'All Shook Up'
'Can't Help Falling In Love'
'Jailhouse Rock'
'Don't Be Cruel'
'Blue Suede Shoes'
'Love Me Tender'
'Trouble'
Medley: 'Trouble'/'Guitar Man'
Medley: 'Trouble'/'Guitar Man'
'If I Can Dream'

Elvis Presley (vcl, gtr), Tom Tedesco, Mike Deasy (gtr), Don Randi (pno, o), Larry Knechtal (bs), Hal Baine (dms), The Blossoms (bv).
The NBC Orchestra conducted by W. Earl Brown.
Musical Direction: William Goldenberg

*Elvis Presley (vcl, gtr), Scotty Moore, Charlie Hodge (gtr), D.J. Fontana (dms), Alan Fortas (tam)

Recorded: NBC Studios, Burbank, California

1969-77 THE RISE & FALL OF THE KING

As the sixties drew to a close, it seemed for the first time in almost a decade that people were prepared to take Elvis Presley seriously. There was absolutely no doubt that the NBC TV Special had convinced the world that Presley was not a spent force and was still a viable entertainer in the world of rock 'n' roll. The obvious next step was for Presley to consolidate his position by returning to the live stage. Many one-time fans waited, if not with bated breath, at least with marked curiosity. All too often Presley, and the organization around him, had failed to take the obvious initiative and for at least five years, his career had drifted, his work becoming a conveyor belt product. Artistically, he had swung closer and closer to the skids. 1969 seemed to present a unique (and possibly last) chance for Elvis Presley to pull out of the downward spin of bad records and even worse movies.

Rumour was rife. There were any number of theories as to why Presley seemed to be entering this new energetic phase in his career. Some people claimed that Elvis was on the verge of dumping Tom Parker and seeking more capable management. Others circulated the story that he had finally become incensed at the success of Tom Jones, a performer whom Presley considered little more than a questionable copy of himself. Many pointed out that Jones was probably the first singer, in terms of style, that Elvis considered a serious rival. There was even talk of Colonel Parker nosing around Jones' management situation. Certainly, on April 6, 1968, Elvis, accompanied by Priscilla, drove to Las Vegas to check out Jones, and it was after this show that Elvis apparently made up his mind to return to the live stage. Directly the decision had been made, the main debate became exactly how he was going to go about it.

The options were varied. 1968 was already witnessing a revival of fifties rock 'n' roll. It was a direct reaction to the forty-minute guitar solos that had become too much the norm of psychedelic experimentation. It wasn't seriously expected that anyone of Presley's stature would hit the boards in the kind of rock 'n' roll package that was currently bringing Bill Haley, Chuck Berry and Bo Diddley back into the public eye, but certainly there couldn't be a better time for Presley to make his move.

Nobody seriously doubted that Elvis could do anything but attract a massive audience. The final year of the sixties was already growing used to huge crowds – Woodstock had become a part of history. Bob Dylan had attracted some 400,000 to an open air festival on England's Isle of Wight and The Rolling Stones had drawn a similar number to a free concert in London's Hyde Park. At the end of the year, a fatal combination of the Stones and the Hell's Angels cast a murderous gloom over another free concert, at the Altamont Raceway, just outside San Francisco.

It might have been possible, at a stretch of the imagination, for Presley to headline open air events in various parts of the world, as Dylan had done at the Isle of Wight. A second alternative could have been for Presley to follow the Shea Stadium, Hollywood Bowl route that The Beatles had taken some four years earlier. As it turned out though, Elvis chose neither of these courses. He and Colonel Parker elected to go straight for middle of the road, heart of tinsel show business. He turned his back on the strictly rock 'n' roll audience and went after Tom Jones, Barbra Streisand, Sammy Davis Jr., Dean Martin, Frank Sinatra and the rest. The venue for Presley's return to his public was the showroom of the International Hotel in Las Vegas.

With 1,519 rooms, the International was the largest hotel in the neon city. It housed the biggest casino in the world, and its 1970 staff payroll was in excess of $23 million. It was an imposing enough setting for the Presley comeback, but like so many other events in Presley's career, it was to set a pattern that would, in the end, prove destructive.

It has never been exactly clear why, when Presley expressed a desire to get out of the dispiriting cycle of movie vehicles because, as he told his first night audience in Vegas, he "got tired of singing to the guys (he) beat up in motion pictures", Tom Parker should steer him straight into the Las Vegas lounges. One possible reason is that the Colonel may have, despite all indications to the contrary, still harboured a basic distrust of the rock 'n' roll world, still considered the music a nine day wonder, even after fifteen years. It had always been Parker's basic intention to turn Presley from a rock 'n' roller into an all round entertainer. Staging the comeback in Las Vegas seemed totally in keeping with this kind of thinking.

Another possible reason for Parker's decision to take Presley to Vegas was that he neither trusted nor had any real contact with people like Bill Graham, Frank Barcelona or Dee Anthony, who were now booking and promoting America's biggest rock shows. The most prosaic explanation, that Parker was lured to Vegas simply because he was a hopelessly compulsive gambler, only became public a number of years after Presley's death, although as early as 1975 there were rumours that Parker was seriously in hock to the Vegas casinos and was having to collateralise a million dollar gambling tab with Elvis' future earnings. Once again we hit one of those desperate ironies that dog the career of Elvis Presley i.e. it would seem that his creative direction took a major (and possibly fatal) turn because his manager couldn't win at blackjack and didn't know enough to stop playing.

For better or for worse, Elvis Presley was booked to play the International Hotel at Las Vegas for a month. On July 26, 1969, just ten days after Neil Armstrong had become the first man to set foot on the moon, Elvis walked out onto a stage in Las Vegas. In his biography, *Elvis*, writer Jerry Hopkins gives an eyewitness account of that first appearance in eight years.

"Elvis sauntered to centre stage, grabbed the microphone from its stand, hit a pose from the fifties – legs braced, knees snapping almost imperceptibly – and before he could begin the show, the audience stopped him cold. Just as he was to begin his first song, he was hit in the face with a roar. He looked. All two thousand people were on their feet, pounding their hands together and whistling, many of them standing on their chairs and screaming."

Before Elvis had even sung a note, his return to the live stage was a triumph.

Behind Presley, sharing his conquest of Las Vegas, was just about the best rock 'n' roll band that money could buy. Leading the back-up musicians was guitarist James Burton, who, to this day, is debatably the world's foremost session picker. Jerry Scheff on bass and Ronnie Tutt on drums were also world class studio musicians, and Larry Muhoberac took care of the keyboard chores (although when Presley returned to the International in January, 1970, he would be replaced by former Cricket Glen D. Hardin).

This nucleus was certainly the best ensemble that Elvis had had in back of him since the golden days of Bill Black, Scotty Moore, D.J. Fontana and Floyd Cramer. In addition to the hard core four there were also John Wilkinson and Charlie Hodge on rhythm guitars. The Jordanaires had been asked to provide the male back-up singing, but had declined due to pressure of Nashville studio commitments. In their place, Elvis had hired the Imperials, the vocal quartet who had worked with him on the *Spinout* and *How Great Thou Art* albums. In addition, Elvis recruited the Sweet Inspirations, a four girl group who had featured on countless Atlantic label soul classics. With fourteen people, in addition to Elvis himself, on the stage, plus the twenty-five piece pit orchestra, the Presley presentation was lavish enough to match the Roman colonnade, the fake Louis XIV decor and plaster cherubs that were the interior design scheme of the International's Showroom.

As the black suited Elvis (the familiar white rhinestoned jump suits were still part of the future) roared through 'Blue Suede Shoes', 'I Got A Woman', 'Jailhouse Rock', 'Don't Be Cruel', 'Heartbreak Hotel' and 'Hound Dog', the capacity crowd knew that they need have no fears as to whether the one-time rock king coud still cut it. He slowed the tempo with 'Love Me Tender', 'Memories', 'I Can't Stop Loving You'. He performed his current hit 'In The Ghetto', previewed a powerful new song, 'Suspicious Minds' and even ventured into the Beatles' songbook with 'Yesterday' and a snatch of 'Hey Jude'. After his initial nervousness, Presley proved that he was fit, well rehearsed and totally on top of the show, and the critics were ecstatic. A headline on *Billboard*'s front page declared, "Elvis Retains Touch in Return to Stage". *Variety* called him a "superstar" and described him as "very much in command of the entire scene". David Dalton, writing in *Rolling Stone*, called Elvis "supernatural, his own resurrection". Suddenly, Elvis Presley was being accorded serious respect and, much more importantly, he was doing something to deserve it. By the end of July he had played to 101,500 paying customers, with scarcely an empty seat through the whole season.

The obvious question was – what was Elvis going to do next? The point had been proved, he had made his comeback and he was right there in the public eye. The problem was that the momentum had to be sustained if the series of International Hotel shows were not to be simply a flash in the pan. Many observers expected that Elvis would follow through with a full scale tour of the USA, if not of the world. The single of 'Suspicious Minds' was a number one hit and had gone gold. The double album, *From Memphis to Vegas/From Vegas to Memphis* had also topped one million sales. The last of the vehicle movies, *Change of Habit* with Mary Tyler Moore, had crawled away to well deserved oblivion, and there were no more contracted. In terms of his career, Elvis was free, loose and riding high. He could do just about anything that he wanted.

It came as something of a surprise when it was announced that there would be no tour in the immediate future and instead, Elvis would return to the International Hotel for the month of January, 1970. It seemed a little soon, and some fans, confronted by the idea of Elvis playing Las Vegas twice in the same six months, wondered if once again, the same sloppy line of least resistance career direction that had embroiled Presley in nearly ten years of bad movies was once again at work. Could it be that Elvis was simply exchanging a well worn Hollywood rut for a new Las Vegas rut?

As 1970 drew closer, these fears appeared to be unfounded. Plans were drawn up for a million dollar-plus close-circuit TV concert to be held at the Las Vegas Convention Centre in August and transmitted by Filmways Concert Associates to 275 cities at $5 a ticket. Elvis would be guaranteed one million bucks. This idea was scrapped because it was decided that there was much more money to be made on the road. Subsequently, 'market tests' were carried out. First, at Houston Astrodome (February 27–March 1st), followed by six September shows (Phoenix, St. Louis, Detroit, Miami, Tampa, Mobile) and a predominantly West Coast trip of eight venues in November.

Although the Astrodome concerts turned out to be little more than freakshows, with atrocious sound and almost unbelievable distances between some sections of the crowd and the performer, Elvis walked away with $1.2 million. At the same time, it was possible to peg seat prices so the cheapest were only a dollar. This was something of a thank-you gesture to the east Texas fans whose loyalty had been so crucial in the early days of 1954–5.

Elvis was clearly back in the live action groove, and working a schedule that would have seemed tough to bands whose members were considerably younger. Through 1970 he played 137 shows. In 1971 he upped the ante and made the year's total 156, while 1972 saw 164 performances, including four triumphant concerts at New York's Madison Square Garden. It seemed as though all America wanted to see Elvis Presley and, in his turn, Elvis was doing his level best to accommodate them.

Beyond America, there was the rest of the world, however. After three years, Europe, Japan and Australia all starting asking, quite rightly, when they were going to see some action. They had, after all, been important markets for Presley ever since the start of his career, but he had never sung a live note in any of these territories, except for some impromptu jamming during his draftee years in Germany.

Obviously something had to be done for these international fans. The solution, formulated in a deal between Parker and NBC, was hardly what the fans expected, though. The devoted millions, spread right across the planet, clearly thought that they were entitled to a full scale, Elvis Presley world tour. Instead, they were given *Aloha From Hawaii*—a live concert, from the Hawaiian International Centre Arena would be beamed across the world via satellite. It had the potential to reach one and a half billion people, more than had watched the first moonwalk. Technology was hardly a substitute for a real live Elvis, but, for the time being, it was the best that the overseas faithful were going to get.

Adding insult to injury, there were a number of countries that declined to subscribe to the NBC space hookup. The most notable to opt out was the United Kingdom. Neither ITA nor BBC, the two British networks, were willing to buy the show and, for years to come, the home of The Beatles and The Rolling Stones had to make do with bootleg video tapes.

Once again, the world had to wait until well after Elvis' death for an explanation as to why Presley never toured anywhere but in the United States and Canada. The major coup of Albert Goldman, the author of the otherwise reprehensible biography *Elvis* (not to be confused with Jerry Hopkin's work of the same title), was in bringing to the attention of the world something that many Presleyphiles had known for years – that Colonel Tom Parker was in fact a Dutch national, an illegal immigrant called Andreas Cornelis Van Kuijk. Parker had always been characteristically cagey about his origins, vaguely claiming that he was the son of "carny folk". If Goldman is correct, the reason that he turned down millions in offers

from all over the world for Elvis to appear in person was simply that Parker could not legally obtain a passport without giving away his secret. (He never once visited Elvis in Germany, but busied himself instead in repackaging back-catalogue.)

Aloha From Hawaii seems, in retrospect, to have been the final peak of Elvis' career. It was a strange and debatable peak unfortunately, that seemed, despite a killer version of 'Blue Suede Shoes' and a reading of 'This Time You Gave Me A Mountain' that didn't leave a dry eye in the house, to have more to do with megalomania than rock 'n' roll.

The Hillbilly Cat had turned into something that might have been dreamt up by Marvel Comics. In his spangled eagle cape and jewelled jumpsuit, the fifties hoodlum had been transformed into something out of science fiction – a superhero, the Handsome Dictator of the Universe. Without question, it was the most colossal one man show ever attempted by an entertainer, and also without question one of the most colossal ego trips in recent history. Sadly, Elvis would do nothing to equal it during the rest of his life.

Despite his continuing successes, even before *Aloha*, a pattern was starting to emerge. Elvis was slipping into a routine that consisted of six months touring and two stints in the Las Vegas Hilton. It hardly boded well, for any time a regular pattern started to show up in the work of Elvis Presley the quality began to suffer. The problem that confronted Elvis Presley throughout his career was that success was never once equated with artistic achievement, but with the acquisition of the biggest bankroll. Whatever spark of inspiration Elvis displayed was quickly damped down by the production line attitude to his work. It was inevitable that Elvis got bored quicker than any other major artist, and that sooner or later the boredom would show. Elvis seemed to run on three year bursts of energy – the three years prior to the army, when he was building his reputation; the first three years of the sixties, when he still seemed interested in what he was doing; and the three years after the NBC Special.

Not only was there concern about his work, but by 1973 other rumours were starting to cloud the previously cleancut Presley image. His wife had left him, and it seemed as though his ego was reeling. If Elvis Presley couldn't find true love, who the hell could?

A significant incident took place during Presley's 1975 stint at the Las Vegas Hilton. The Showroom was, as usual, packed and the show ended, with the usual tumultuous applause. Suddenly, however, the audience was subjected to an abrupt and unexpected change of routine. Instead of sprinting for the dressing room, Elvis remained standing at the microphone. He suddenly announced that he wanted to tell it like it really was, to "set the record straight".

"The other night I had the 'flu real bad. Someone started the report that I was strung out. If I ever find out who started that, I'll knock their goddamn head off. I've never been strung out in my life."

He was like a man with an obsession. It was as though he seriously believed that the world thought of him as a hopeless drug addict. The 2,500 strong crowd watched stunned as Presley ranted on. He had never touched drugs in his life, and had no intention of starting on drugs in the future. Never was there a more perfect case of a man damning himself by protesting too much.

Over the years there had been literally hundreds of rumours about Elvis Presley – it would be unimaginable that it could be any other way. Elvis Presley was the world's greatest rock star. He simply had to be the focal point for speculation, gossip and plain, old fashioned lies, and his bouts of Garbo-like seclusion only served to intensify the talk. At least three times in his career, fictitious stories of his death spread like wild fire. "Elvis is dead" was a recurring theme long before the 1970 lunacy about the death of Paul McCartney.

Ironically, rumours of drug abuse by Presley were comparatively mild. At no point did he flaunt any kind of stoned persona comparable to those of Jimi Hendrix, Jim Morrison or Grace Slick. He was never hauled away on drugs charges like John Lennon, Brian Jones, Keith Richards or Jerry Garcia. Compared to the wild bunch of second generation rock stars, Elvis was a picture of rectitude and conservatism.

Of course, the dopeheads speculated on the kind of drugs Elvis used – the same kind of speculation that attributed an amphetamine habit to John F. Kennedy. Some reasoned that Elvis couldn't have come out of the southern rockabilly circuit without dabbling with the same amphetamines that killed Hank Williams, nearly incapacitated Johnny Cash and

Elvis Presley's Las Vegas/
Lake Tahoe Seasons

July 26–August 28, 1969
The International Hotel, Las Vegas
57 Shows

January 26–February 23, 1970
The International Hotel, Las Vegas
57 Shows

August 10–September 7, 1970
The International Hotel, Las Vegas
58 Shows

January 26–February 23, 1971
The Hilton Hotel, Las Vegas
57 Shows

July 20–August 2, 1971
The Sahara Hotel, Lake Tahoe
28 Shows

August 9–September 6, 1971
The Hilton Hotel, Las Vegas
57 Shows

January 26–February 23, 1972
The Hilton Hotel, Las Vegas
57 Shows

August 4–September 4, 1972
The Hilton Hotel, Las Vegas
63 Shows

January 26–February 23, 1973
The Hilton Hotel, Las Vegas
54 Shows (three cancelled due to illness)

May 5–May 20, 1973
The Sahara Hotel, Lake Tahoe
25 Shows (engagement terminated May 16, due
to illness)

August 6–September 3, 1973
The Hilton Hotel, Las Vegas
59 Shows

January 26–February 9, 1974
The Hilton Hotel, Las Vegas
29 Shows

May 16–May 26, 1974
The Sahara Hotel, Lake Tahoe
22 Shows

August 19–September 2, 1974
The Hilton Hotel, Las Vegas
27 Shows (two cancelled due to illness)

October 10–October 14, 1974
The Sahara Hotel, Lake Tahoe.
8 Shows

March 18–April 1, 1975
The Hilton Hotel, Las Vegas
29 Shows

August 18–August 20, 1975
The Hilton Hotel, Las Vegas
(engagement terminated after 5 shows, due to
illness)

December 2–December 15, 1975
The Hilton Hotel, Las Vegas
17 Shows

helped Jerry Lee Lewis turn himself into an awesome and, at times, demonic legend. Others claimed that they were certain that Elvis was stoned during some of the rehearsal sequences in the movie *Elvis: That's The Way It Is*. Still more pointed out that since, according to all the available information, Elvis didn't drink, he must be into some kind of turn-on—otherwise, what was the point of being the king of rock 'n' roll? Most sensible people dismissed the drug rumours—if they wanted to worry about Elvis Presley at all, they could fret about his broken marriage, the stories of his compulsive eating, his obesity, his deteriorating health, and his wild and bizarre spending sprees that sometimes resulted in total strangers receiving gifts of cars or expensive jewellery.

It was only after Presley's death that the frightening truth about the real extent of his prolonged and massive drug abuse became public knowledge. Sadly for everyone concerned, it was the hippie theorists who were right and the sensible people who were wrong. Not even the hippies, though, had suspected the degree of crazed disregard with which Elvis could swallow almost every variety of pill.

The controversies over Presley's death and drug habits are unlikely to be satisfactorily resolved, if for no other reason than that too many of his fans would prefer their idol laid to rest with an unsullied memory. (Indeed, many still believe the drug stories to be simply a smear campaign.) All reliable information does, however, point to the fact that Presley could (and did) consume drugs in such quantity and variety that he made Keith Richards and Jimi Hendrix look like boy scouts.

Perversely, Presley's drug abuse was strictly confined to prescription stimulants and narcotics. This may have been because he liked to maintain the pretence that he was only taking pills for his health, or could have been a natural precaution against the possibility of arrest (although it would have taken a courageous 'narc' to actually bust Elvis Presley). If exclusively using prescription drugs was an act of caution, once the prescription was handed to the druggist, all caution ceased. Bodyguard Red West recalled in the book "Elvis: What Happened", published before Elvis' death, "He takes pills to go to sleep, he takes pills to get up. He takes pills to go to the john and he takes pills to stop him going to the john. There have been times where he was so hyper on uppers that he had trouble breathing, and on one occasion he thought that he was going to die. His system doesn't work any more like a normal human being's. The pills do all the work for him. He is a walking pharmaceutical shop."

Stories conflict as to when, where and how Elvis' drug habits got their start. Some stories claim that it was as early as his first days of touring with Scotty Moore and Bill Black and hanging out at Sun Records. A less than kind version of these stories was that he would even rip-off his mother's diet pills in order to get sufficiently wired to overcome his chronic shyness and to face an audience.

Red West, on the other hand, denies that Presley took drugs during those early years, and claims that he was "high enough on his natural energy." According to West, Elvis' first dabblings came during his army stint in Germany, when he was given dexedrine by an over-zealous and less than scrupulous sergeant who liked to keep his men snappy and alert during all-night manoeuvres.

Whatever the origins of Presley's drug use, most sources agree that he was pretty much a full blown speed freak, using all kinds of amphetamines and similar uppers during the long haul in the sixties when he turned out one idiot movie after another.

Elvis, however, appeared to thrive on the speed diet. "In the early days the man had a tremendous constitution. He would never stop."—Red West. The main problem seemed to have been to keep him amused. His work demanded so little of his talent that there was a constant need for diversion; a need that almost certainly gave rise to Presley's almost pathalogical promiscuity, the various excesses with guns, cars and other expensive (and sometimes dangerous) toys.

It was only in the seventies, when he had returned to the live stage, that he began switching to tranquillisers and downers and using valium, quaaludes and more powerful pain killers like percodan, demerol and dilaudid (which is normally only prescribed to terminal cancer patients). Obviously much of this downer use was a result of the return to a far more demanding way of life. Touring and playing live shows required more concentration and stamina than the comparatively easy routine of movie work. Elvis

needed to regularly relax, and the downers initially provided a source of instant relaxation. They also, however, brought with them a set of unfortunate and destructive side effects, and much of Presley's mental and physical deterioration in the seventies must have been due to his overkill drug abuse.

Apart from the need to relax there is little doubt that Elvis was well into the recreational side of drug abuse. As early as 1971, Elvis and an unnamed girl fan came close to overdosing after a night of lovemaking and getting high on massive amounts of the cough medicine Hycadan. It is just about possible, in the case of, say, a Jimi Hendrix or a Charlie Parker, if not to condone, at least to ignore an artist's drug habits, so long as his work does not suffer. In the case of Elvis Presley, the drugs appear to have taken over so completely that, toward the end, Presley seemed incapable of doing anything but going through the motions in front of a totally loyal crowd.

The Elvis Presley business operation proved itself far better at cover up than creativity. The world at large heard virtually nothing about Elvis' drug related problems. Even when he was hospitalised on a number of occasions, the fans worried about glaucoma or cancer, obesity and recurrant respiratory complaints. Nobody suspected that Presley had actually OD'ed a number of times, on one occasion only surviving because his father administered artificial respiration.

The disintegration of Elvis Presley clearly starts in earnest after the split with Priscilla in 1972 and the subsequent divorce one year later. No amount of PR work could cover the fact that Presley had suffered a major emotional wound, the only debatable point being whether it was to his heart or to his ego. Aside from his drug taking going into high gear, he also began to show symptoms of full blown megalomania. He became obsessed with uniforms and insignia, even managing to finagle the personal presentation to him of an honorary federal narcotics agent badge by the then President, Richard Nixon.

His behaviour became increasingly erratic and strange. He suffered bouts of irrational, hysterical temper. He went on chronic eating binges, and tried for a while to order a mafia-style hit on Mike Stone, the karate instructor with whom Priscilla had run away. At the same time, he became almost psychotic over the possibility of an attempt on his own life.

When, with Elvis dead, most of his one time entourage had no more reason to keep quiet, the flood gates of rumour were opened wide. At first the problem seemed to be one of chronic boredom. He had once confided to a musician friend that he had no competition left on Earth, there was nothing left to prove. As far as Elvis was concerned, no other performer could challenge him or eclipse his popularity.

Boredom, however, escalated to what can only be described as full scale mental problems. His Dracula-style day (which began at sunset), prompted actress girlfriend Linda Thompson, who lived with him for the majority of the time between his divorce and his death, to comment that "life with Elvis meant living like a bat." He seemed to start seeing himself as some sort of messiah, believing that his shows were not so much entertainment as holy events, during which he could commune with his disciples and they, in turn, could worship him. Religion apparently took hold of him, and he had bouts of reading the Bible to his hangers-on. At extreme moments, he even suffered from delusions that he could heal the sick, and control the weather, by an effort of will.

Even his much vaunted karate seems to have been a myth fostered by the ever present flatterers. Sonny West describes how Elvis turned up at a karate studio—in a heat wave—festooned with jewels and gold, a designer karate suit, a large flashy overcoat and, just to top off the ensemble, an eastern style turban. He was blocked out of his mind and very out of condition. On this and other occasions, the opponents would let him win, and allow him to go on believing that he could whip all comers. In fact, most of the time, the downers made his co-ordination so bad that he was as much a danger to himself as to his sparring partner.

There were even darker rumours—that he would indulge in racist outbursts, and exhibit a level of bigotry that he normally suppressed in public. He was also gun happy, and even in his most relaxed moments (and on stage!) was prone to be armed to the teeth. Gabe Tucker, a Parker employee, and one of the many of Presley's outer circle who rushed into print with a ghosted collection of reminiscences, provides a gauge to the degree of Presley's mania in his book *Up and Down with Elvis.* One morning the Ferrari Elvis owned failed to turn over when he pressed the starter. he walked to the trunk of the car, took out the two pistols he kept there and emptied them into the recalcitrant automobile. Once he was satisfied the car was quite dead, he growled at one of his aids to have it hauled away.

One of his companions sadly asked him, "Why did you do that?"

"I got pressures, man," Elvis mumbled. "I have a demanding family, an expensive life, and I'm lonesome."

The worst occasions of all were when the chemical cocktails in his system would push him well beyond the danger point. He would lose all physical control and fall without warning into deep stupors. He would even lose control of his bowels. Linda Thompson only moved out from Graceland a few months before his death because she could no longer handle his epic drug taking.

"His death could have happened any number of times during the years I spent with him. When a person knocks himself out each night with sleeping pills, he is just as apt to fall asleep face down on the floor as he is to be safely tucked away in bed when the medication hits. For that reason, Elvis required an unfathomable amount of attention. Elvis had a self-destructive vein, and I couldn't watch him self-destruct."

The worst irony of all is, that as far as anyone could tell, the night that Elvis died was only a 'normal" night in the Memphis mansion. Even in a normal night though, Elvis had, according to his step brother Mickey Stanley, been brought sixteen pills, a mixture of valium, quaaludes and barbiturates.

Ironically, there is some reason to suppose that, in the last few months of his life, Elvis may have been making some sort of effort to straighten himself out. Some reports claim that he had attempted a drug rehabilitation course at the Hazleden Foundation, Center City, Minnesota. He had even attempted to enlist the help of Dorsey Burnette (brother of Johnny Burnette), who had given up a life of casual booze, sex and drugs when he had become a born again Christian. Burnette had promised to visit Presley, but by the time he made that visit, Presley was on his way to the morgue. Other stories tell of Presley's intention to make the bi-centennial tour his farewell, and how he was confident that retirement would bring back Priscilla and his daughter. Tragically, if these attempts were made, they all came to nothing.

In the first few hours after Elvis had been discovered dead on the bathroom floor, it would seem that some kind of cover-up had already started. Independent investigators, including Geraldo Rivera of ABC Network News, make the charge that the Presley retainers conspired with Shelby County, Tennessee health officials to conceal the fact that Elvis had OD'ed. Their motive seemed to be that, if the Presley image was tarnished by the scandal of his drug habits, it would not only destroy the legend, but could also hurt Memphis' lucrative Elvis-based tourist trade. Accordingly, County Medical Examiner Jerry Francisco issued the story that Presley had died from a massive heart attack. Dr. Eric Muirhead, Chief of Pathology at the Baptist Memorial Hospital in Memphis, and Dr. Noel Floredo, who attended the autopsy on Presley, both attribute the man's death to "uppers, downers and pain killing drugs ... most probably an interaction of several drugs."

The situation will never be satisfactorily resolved. All notes, reports and photographs of the death scene and the autopsy are missing, and the contents of Presley's stomach had been destroyed without any attempt at analysis. In lieu of hard evidence, the findings by a medical board that George ('Dr. Nick') Nichopolous, the resident doctor at the Presley court, was guilty of grossly overprescribing dangerous drugs to nineteen patients, including Elvis Presley and Jerry Lee Lewis, would indicate that the weight of medical opinion favours the theory that Elvis Presley died of an overdose. Indeed, between January and August 1977, Nichopolous had prescribed some 5,300 pills, mainly amphetamines, quaaludes, tuinol, nembutal, codine, pheno-barbitol and dilaudid to Elvis Presley. In the fall of 1981, Dr. Nick was put on trial in Memphis, but was acquitted when the jury found no evidence of malicious intent.

It is, however, all too easy to make someone like Nichopolous the scapegoat for Presley's death. At worst he can only be regarded as an accomplice or accessory to the rock star's self destruction. Nobody forced Presley to take absurd quantities of drugs. The worst that was done to him was that nobody ever had the courage to point out what he was doing to himself and tell him to stop but, as Graceland's aide David Stanley put it:-

"Nobody ever said no to Elvis Presley."

The morning after his death, the 17th of August, 1977, Elvis Presley lay in state, while 25,000 mourners filed past the solid brass casket. He was dressed in a white suit, light blue shirt and a darker blue tie. The next day, the funeral started at 2 pm. Rex Humbard, the nationally known TV evangelist from Akron, Ohio, conducted the service. It was a private funeral – Jackie Kahane, the comedian who had been compering Presley's shows gave the eulogy, and Kathy Westmoreland, one of his back-up singers, sang two gospel songs. The pallbearers were Charlie Hodge, Joe Esposito, George Klein, Lamar Fike, Felton Jarvis and George Nichopolous.

The death of Elvis Presley produced a multitude of reactions. Obviously there was an enormous amount of genuine pain and grief, but there was also a tinge of craziness and a lot of eyes on a fast buck. One Hollywood cynic exclaimed "great career move" when he heard the news. Of the crowds that gathered on Elvis Presley Boulevard in Memphis in the days that immediately followed August 16th 1977, and the 1½ million who would visit his grave in the first year, by far the greatest percentage had come to pay genuine respect to an idol, a hero, a man who had become so much a part of some lives that he was thought of as a friend. Out on the fringes, however, there were those who had more dubious motives for joining the mourners. At the furthest extreme, there was the crazy who drove his car into part of the crowd outside the gates of Gracelands, killing two fans – Alice Hovatar and Juanita Johnson – and seriously injuring a third, Tammy Baiter. There were also the allegations of a ghoulish plot to kidnap Presley's body and hold it for ransom.

A massive industry in Presley souvenirs and mementos mushroomed, literally overnight. During the days after his death, an estimated 20 million Elvis albums were sold in the USA. World sales increased by something like an amazing 1,000% in the next twelve months (making it the most successful year of Elvis' entire career). In England, where an RCA pressing plant had been marked for closure and the workforce issued with redundancy notices, the demand for Presley records was so heavy that both plant and jobs were reprieved for a number of months.

The media, by and large, treated the death of Elvis Presley with taste and restraint. Typical in response was *The Times* of London, which marked the rock king's passing with a lengthy and dignified obituary. One gross holdout on the generally respectful tone was the *National Enquirer*, which ran a screaming front page complete with what purported to be a picture of Elvis Presley in his coffin, taken with a concealed camera.

True to form, Tom Parker didn't stay in secluded mourning. At the time that Elvis was overdosing on the bathroom floor of Graceland, Parker was in a suite at the Dunfet Sheraton Hotel in Portland, Maine, supervising the advance work on two Presley shows at the Cumberland County Civic Center set for the 17th and 18th of August. According to aides, Parker only muttered "Oh, dear God", and slumped for a few moments when he received the news. That was his only documented display of grief. Within minutes, he was on the phone to Vernon Presley:

"Vernon, I know this is the worst possible time in our lives, and no one will replace Elvis. But you must not fail now, Vernon. There are thousands of unknown people out there who'll move in right now and take advantage of Elvis' life, of his fame. We must protect it not just for ourselves, but for Elvis' child Lisa Marie and for his estate. We must move immediately to make sure that outsiders cannot exploit the name of Elvis Presley. We can mourn, but a prolonged and inactive period of grief over Elvis will prove disastrous for you, for his daughter, for his estate and for his legend. I suggest we move immediately to protect the Elvis image from exploitation by outsiders."

Within a matter of hours, Parker had closed a deal assigning worldwide rights for Elvis Presley merchandising to Factors Incorporated, the international marketing corporation that was, at the time, making a fortune from the Farrah Fawcett Majors poster. This gave Parker the basis for a string of lawsuits that enabled him to corral most of the rights to Presley's image. Possibly Parker's most honest remark was made to Memphis Mafia veteran Lamar Fike shortly after he had heard that Presley was dead:

"Nothing has changed. This won't change anything."

In fact, Tom Parker had been making preparations for Presley's death for some years. Fully aware of Elvis' monstrous drug habit, he did nothing to curb the singer's behaviour. Instead, he organised a financial bale-out that ensured he would suffer no loss if the

THE COLONEL SAYS "HAVE A NICE DAY"

THE COLONEL SAYS "HAVE A NICE DAY"

foreseeable tragedy occurred. As early as 1967, Parker had talked Elvis into giving him an unprecedented 50% of his earnings. In 1973, Parker sold RCA all the rights to the Presley master tapes for $15 million (of which Parker took half.) It was, from his client's point of view, an insane move, that would cost Presley and his heirs a fortune in royalties on his vast and successful catalogue of recordings.

The Colonel made his final move in 1974 when he formed a corporation called Boxcar Enterprises, the sole purpose of which seemed to be to railroad Elvis out of his merchandising royalties. By a baroque division of shares between Parker and a number of his longtime cronies. Elvis was left with a mere 15% of his own earnings in this field.

It's possible that Parker may not get away with his treatment of Elvis Presley. In May of 1980 a 36-year-old Memphis entertainment lawyer, Blancard L. Tual, was appointed by the probate court to represent Lisa Marie's interests, after the executors of Presley's will found it increasingly difficult to deal with the Colonel. An initial investigation not only unearthed Parker's massive commissions, the deal with RCA and the Boxcar Enterprises scam, but also that, on account of his gambling debts, he was selling Presley short in Vegas and had, for years, been grossly inept in even the most simple management tasks. The legal aspects involved – as with the Beatles' Apple empire – will probably not be fully resolved in the foreseeable future.

After the initial shock of Presley's death, many fans were faced with the problem of coping with a world that no longer contained their idol. Some simply refused to believe that Elvis was dead at all. Many clung to the idea put forward by country star Waylon Jennings that the entire death had been faked in order for Presley to retire to a life of quiet anonymity.

Others sought refuge in the occult, and there was such a rash of supposed spirit contacts with Elvis that *Saturday Night Live* ran a sketch in which Lorraine Newman played a TV psychic sob sister with a direct line to Elvis in the netherworld. There were moves to add the image of Elvis Presley to those of the Presidents on Mount Rushmore, and to have his January 8th birthday declared a national holiday in the USA.

There were other, more vengeful fans, who went looking for someone to blame for the seemingly unnecessary death. They're the ones who blamed the women in his life: Priscilla (who had divorced him), Linda Thompson (who had walked out on him just before his death), or Ginger Alden (who had been asleep when Elvis slipped into that final coma). Others looked to Tom Parker, the Memphis Mafia and their grossly insensitive handling of the singer, as the culprits. One group of fans saw George Nichopolous as the arch villain, and one individual even took a shot at the doctor while he was watching a football game in 1979.

In addition to scapegoats, the fans also demanded a continuation of Elvis Presley product. This was not so easy. As a result of Presley's totally lax attitude to recording, there was no wealth of original material in the RCA vaults, as there had been in the case of artists like Buddy Holly or Jimi Hendrix. What was done had to be done with out-takes, re-issues, repackaging jobs and even remixes of the original masters. The bootleggers did their best – to the point that just about every radio or TV show, every interview and every live show was committed to vinyl. Where a set of recordings was blocked by copyright problems (as in the case of the Million Dollar Quartet session, or the Louisiana Hayride tapes) the fans would turn on the pressure until, one way or another, it reached the public.

The music eventually dried up, and the field was left to the phenomena of the Elvis surrogate. In the flesh and in the spangles, there were the Presley imitators. In 1979, it was estimated that some 5,000 individuals were earning a living doing impersonations of Elvis. The movie industry wasn't slow to respond. Kurt Russell in *Elvis* (in the USA a made-for-TV special, in the UK a theatre release) was the first into the market-place. *Elvis* was a carefully planned Hollywood product that reproduced a fair approximation of both the sight and sound of Elvis, but with the exception of a gunned down TV console, it stuck to the most sanitised and orthodox version of the Presley legend.

Following the success of *Elvis* and a follow-up show (that used the same semi-clone docu-drama technique on the early days of the Beatles), the ABC network decided to get into the act. They bought the Ginger Alden version of her affair with Presley and inflicted it on the public as a piece of ludicrous Sunday night soap opera titled *Elvis and the Beauty Queen*. It was mercifully forgotten within seconds of it ending.

The documentary film *This is Elvis* had more of a sense of its own quality. Directors Malcolm Leo and Andrew Solt had the advantage of Tom Parker's co-operation, and were able to use archive film, including clips from *Steve Allen, Ed Sullivan* and the *Dorsey Brothers*. The inclusion of home movies by Joe Esposito with candid and raunchy dialogue attempted to humanise Elvis, but link material (with the now predictable clones in soft focus) brought it in line with general orthodoxy.

It took the medium of print to finally smash the orthodox Presley legend. The rash of quickly produced books that hit the stands immediately after Elvis' death amounted to little more than another form of cheapo souvenir, a variation on the posters, the decals, the junk jewellery, the Elvis radios and bourbon decanters – and the Colonel's most ridiculous project, the line of Elvis Presley wine. Directly the grief and shock had worn off, it seemed that everyone who had so much as brushed past Elvis in an elevator rushed into print with their saccharine memories. These too, though, were little more than souvenirs, mass produced holy relics.

Just prior to Presley's death, the bodyguards – Red West, Sonny West and Dave Hebler (with ghost writer Steve Dunleavy) – had blown the whistle on Presley's drug habits and megalomania. Most of the biographies that followed acknowledged that he had certain problems, but held to the line that Elvis Presley was a wonderful human being. It took four years and New York English professor Albert Goldman to rip down the orthodox legend and attempt an exposé – to the effect that Elvis Presley was a vicious, infantile slob. Unfortunately, much of the value of the allegedly painstaking research that went into his book *Elvis* was negated by gross inaccuracies, and the way that his objectivity was constantly tripped by his own prejudices. Critic Greil Marcus, whose *Mystery Train* contains probably the finest analysis of Presley's creative work, summed up the Goldman book in a *Village Voice* review that was headlined "Lies About Elvis, Lies About Us – The Torrents of Hate that Drive This Book Are Unrelieved":-

"But while Goldman's *Elvis* is not a serious biography, it is a very serious book, if only for what it seeks to accomplish: to exclude Elvis Presley, and the culture of the white working-class South, and the people of that culture, and the culture of rock 'n' roll, and the people of that culture, from any serious consideration of American culture. And the bait is being taken: in the *New York Times* review that will be syndicated all over the United States, Christopher Lehmann-Haupt wrote that after reading Goldman's book 'one feels revolted by American culture for permitting itself to be exemplified by the career of Elvis Presley.' There is no need to feel revolted: American culture has never permitted itself to be exemplified by Elvis Presley, and it never will. But certain Americans (and of course people from all parts of the world) have recognised themselves, and selves they would not have otherwise known, in Elvis Presley."

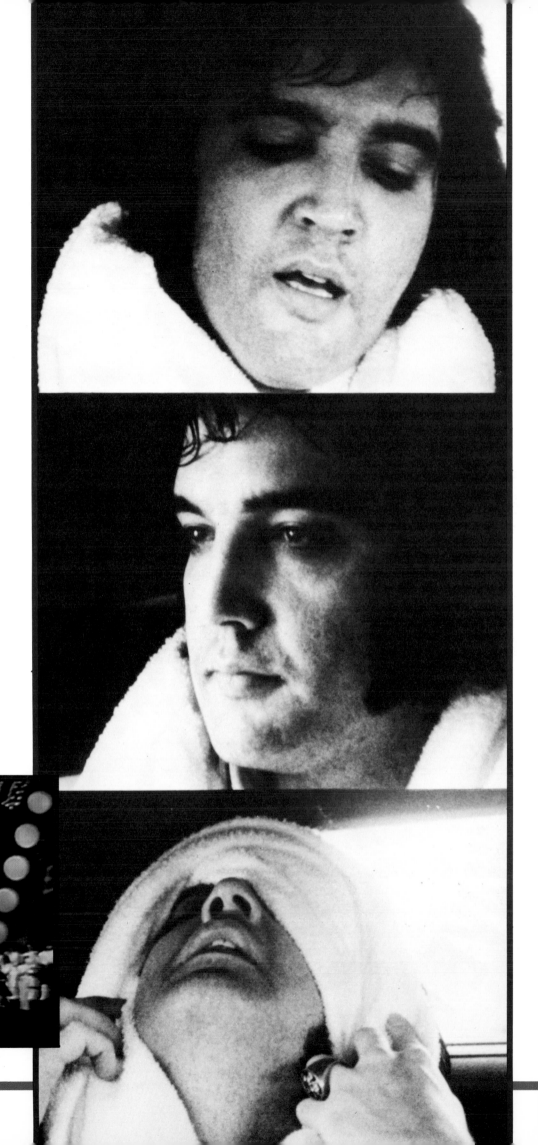

1969

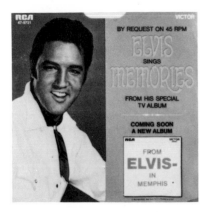

* **'Memories'** (Strange, Davis) WPAI 8044
** **'Charro'** (Strange, Davis) WPAI 8091
(US) RCA 47-9730
Released: March 1969

Elvis Presley (vcl), Scotty Moore, Charlie
Hodges, Tommy Tedesco, Mike Deasy (gtr),
Don Randi (kybds), Larry Knechtal (bs),
D.J. Fontana, Hal Blaine (dms), Alan Fortas (tam),
The NBC Orchestra: Conductor, W. Earl Brown;
Musical Director: William Goldenberg
*Recorded: NBC Studios, Burbank,
June 27, 1968
Elvis Presley (vcl), Scotty Moore (gtr),
The Jordanaires (bv), other musicians and studio
unidentified
**Recorded Hollywood, July 7, 1968

If one takes into account the carnival that accompanied his demobilization from the US Army in March 1960, then the Singer NBC-TV Special amounts to Elvis' second professional comeback in the space of one decade.

This remarkable career-saving TV spectacular had already been successfully previewed with the show's finale, 'If I Can Dream', before the soundtrack album itself was put on sale to coincide with Christmas. Considering the amount of costly preparation that went into both the production and the marketing, the timing of this afterthought was ill-conceived, being a full three months after the event, and five months before its re-screening on August 17, 1969.

That wasn't the only handicap. When taken out of context, 'Memories' was no great shakes as a single. Furthermore, though *Charro* was, by Elvis' shoddy cinematic standards, a better-than-average movie, that particular facet of his declining career had not only become somewhat of a self-derisory embarrassment, but was now greeted with widespread indifference by his fans. And, as such, the title track of *Charro* was only afforded secondary consideration when the A-side was selected for this single. 'Memories' chart run lasted just seven weeks, peaking at No. 37.

Charro/
National General Pictures

Cast
Jesse Wade.................... Elvis Presley
Tracey....................................... Ina Balin
Vince .... Victor French
Sara............................. Barbara Werle.
Billy Roy .... Solomon Sturges
Marcie........................... Lynn Kellogg
Gunner........................... James Sikking
Opie Keetch................. Paul Brinegar
Heff............................... Harry Landers
Lt. Rivera......................... Tony Young
Sheriff Ramsey.......James Almanzar
Mody .... Charles H. Gray
Jerome Selby.................John Pickard
Martin Tilford......... Garry Walberg
Gabe................................ Duane Grey
Lige.............................. Rodd Redwing
Henry Carter ...J. Edward McKinley

Produced and Directed by Charles
  Marquis Warren
Running Time: 98 minutes
Released: September 3, 1969

A different kind of role...

A different kind of man.

Charro

Charro might have been saved if Elvis had taken the whole production to Italy and let Sergio Leone make it for him. It might have been saved if he'd surrounded himself with top Western-movie character actors like Chill Wills, Slim Pickens, Lee Van Cleef, Jack Elam, *et al*.

In fact, if Elvis had simply abandoned *Charro* and done the same as Bob Dylan by getting himself a part in a Sam Peckinpah film (*Pat Garrett & Billy The Kid*), he would have been well ahead on the deal.

Charro was, by anybody's standards, a move of desperation. There was some sense in the idea of getting Elvis, in leather pants and a five-day growth of beard, to do a Clint Eastwood-style bloody spaghetti-Western. It seemed like it could be a lot more fun than the Presley films that had gone immediately before.

Unfortunately writer/producer/director Charles M. Warren didn't seem to know how to make a spaghetti Western. He surrounded Presley with unknowns, particularly mean-looking unknowns. Leone, in his *Dollars* epics, also used unknown support players, but they were always the proud owners of such psychotic faces that the tension was already established before they even opened their mouths.

Nothing so splendidly bizarre happened in *Charro*. Tension was something that simply didn't exist. No one expects a spaghetti Western to have snappy dialogue, and true to type, *Charro* didn't. They are, however, supposed to have long, agonizing build-ups to high-speed and often intricate violence. *Charro* couldn't even manage that. The gun-play was limp to the point of making *The Lone Ranger* seem brutal, melodrama came out tepid, the sets looked cardboard, and the inexplicable plot about a solid gold, Mexican cannon beat anything that came out of Rome for overcomplicated dumbness.

About the only thing that *Charro* had in common with *A Fistful Of Dollars* was the fact of the music being written by Hugo Montenegro.

It was another painful example of how the Elvis Presley Organization seemed able to fumble just about any ball that was thrown at it, and fumble it by being too cheap, so that the finished product was botched and shoddy.

Possibly the greatest tragedy about Elvis Presley was that, far more often than not, he was surrounded by small-minded men who were more concerned with looking after their own penny-ante interests than those of Presley himself.

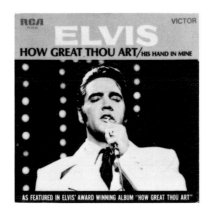

'His Hand In Mine' (Lister) 12WB 0374
'How Great Thou Art' (Hines) TPA4 0909
(US) RCA 74-0130
Released: April 1969

In terms of mass-market consumption, the inherent problem attached to albums aimed specifically for both Christmas *and* Easter holiday sales is that, commercially, they're cold for the remaining eleven months of the year. In a concerted effort to stimulate across-the-counter activity on Presley's religioso back-catalogue, the title tracks of his two "devotional" anthologies were released as a back-to-back appetizer.

* **'In The Ghetto'** (Davis) XPA5 1154
** **'Any Day Now'** (Hilliard, Bacharach)
XPA5 1274
(US) RCA 47-9741
Released: April 1969

Elvis Presley (vcl),
Reggie Young (gtr, electric sitar),
Tommy Cogbill (gtr, bs), John Hughey (ps),
Bobby Wood (pno), Bobby Emmons,
Glen Spreen (o), Mike Leech (bs),
Gene Chrisman (dms), Ed Kollis (har). Over-
dubbed at a later session: Wayne Jackson,
Bob Taylor, Ed Logan (The Memphis Horns),
The Memphis Strings, Sonja Montgomery,
Millie Kirkham, Dolores Edgin, Hursch Wiginton,
Sandy Posey, Mary & Ginger Holladay,
Sandra Robinson, Donna Rhodes, Jeannie Green,
Donna Thatcher, Susan Pilkington (bv)
Recorded: American Studios, Memphis,
*January 21, 1969. **February 21, 1969

In April 1969, when Richard Nixon was just starting to unveil his plans for America, Elvis Presley amazed the world by releasing what almost amounted to a protest song. It was less than a year since the assassination of Robert Kennedy, the murder of Martin Luther King and the riots at the Chicago Democratic Convention. The street radicals who had listened to Presley ten years earlier—and even seen him as some kind of instinctive, gut level revolutionary—had started to assume that Elvis was either ultra conservative, or else totally cut off from the world at large. Now, although 'In The Ghetto' was hardly a searing indictment of capitalist oppression, people started wondering what had happened to Elvis. Could it be that someone had gotten to him?

Sadly, it wasn't so. According to producer Felton Jarvis, the story was a lot more prosaic. The song was presented to Jarvis, Jarvis played the demo tape to Elvis, Elvis took a liking to it and it was included in the marathon recording session that took place between January 13 and 23, when, in the space of ten days, Elvis cut a total of twenty-one songs. Jarvis seems to have masterminded much of what went into the song. At least, that's his story.

"Elvis liked to come in and sing with just the rhythm section. After that he left it to me to put on horns, strings, extra voices, whatever I thought the song needed. Once I'd done this, I'd send the tape round to Elvis for him to listen to and give his approval."

Not that Presley just rubber-stamped the productions that were put out under his name.

"Elvis came into the studio and sang 'In The Ghetto'. He left and we got in these funky girl singers. When Elvis heard the tape, he called me up. Elvis liked to call up at night. He'd call

you at three, four, five in the morning. It never seemed to occur to him that the rest of the world is supposed to be asleep. He just called up when he wanted something.

"Anyway, Elvis called me up and said, 'Felton, those voices are terrible. Take them off, They're really bad.'

"I kept working on the track and as it happened I never quite got around to wiping the girls' voices off the master. Two days later Elvis called back and said, 'Leave 'em on there. The more I listen to 'em the more I like 'em.'

"I guess it was lucky I never wiped off those voices. I guess you could say that Elvis knew what was best for Elvis."

N.B. 'In The Ghetto' was originally sub-titled 'The Vicious Circle', but this was considered a bit too strong for an Elvis single.

'ELVIS SINGS FLAMING STAR' (LP)
(US) RCA Camden CAS-2304
Released: April 1969

Track listing as first released on RCA PRS-279

IN THE GHETTO
Words and Music by SCOTT DAVIS

CARLIN MUSIC CORP. 17 Savile Row London W.1.

3'-

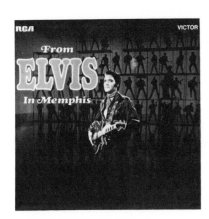

'FROM ELVIS IN MEMPHIS' (LP)
(US) RCA SF-8029
Released: May 1969

Side 1
* 'Wearin' That Loved On Look' (Frazier, Owens) XPA5 1145
** 'Only The Strong Survive' (Gamble, Huff, Butler) XPA5 1272
* 'I'll Hold You In My Arms' (Arnold, Horton, Dilbeck) XPA5 1160
* 'Long Black Limousine' (Stavall, George) XPA5 1142
** 'It Keeps Right On A-Hurtin'' (Tillotson) XPA5 1273
* 'I'm Movin' On' (Snow) XPA5 1147
Side 2
** 'Power Of My Love' (Giant, Baum, Kaye) XPA5 1268
* 'Gentle On My Mind' (Hartford) XPA5 1155
** 'After Loving You' (Miller, Lantz) XPA5 1269
** 'True Love Travels On A Gravel Road' (Owens, Frazier) XPA5 1265
** 'Any Day Now' (Hilliard, Bacharach) XPA5 1274
** 'In The Ghetto' (Davis) XPA5 1154

Elvis Presley (vcl, gtr), Reggie Young (gtr), Tommy Cogbill (gtr, bs), John Hughey (stl gtr), Bobby Wood (pno), Bobby Emmons (o), Ronnie Milsap (pno, vcl, –Jan '69 only), Mike Leech (bs), Gene Chrisman (dms), Ed Kollis (har). Overdubbed at a later session: Millie Kirkham, Sonja Montgomery, Dolores Edgin, Joe Babcock, Sandy Posey, Hursch Wiginton, Mary Holladay, Sandra Robinson, Donna Rhodes, Donna Thatcher, Jeannie Green, Susan Pilkington (bv), The Memphis Horns, The Memphis Strings
Recorded: American Studios, Memphis, Tennessee
*January 1969 sessions.
January 13 – 'Long Black Limousine'
January 14 – 'Wearin' That Loved On Look'
January 15 – 'I'm Movin' On' and 'Gentle On My Mind'
January 21 – 'In The Ghetto'
January 23 – 'I'll Hold You In My Heart'

**February 1969 sessions:
February 17 – 'True Love Travels On A Gravel Road'
February 18 – 'After Loving You' and 'Power Of My Love'
February 20 – 'Only The Strong Survive' and 'It Keeps Right On A-Hurtin''
February 21 – 'Any Day Now'

and (occasionally) Ronnie Milsap were featured on piano. Bobby Emmons played organ, Johnny Hughes the steel guitar, whilst Ed Kollis handled harmonica. It was left to drummer Gene Chrisman to take on the responsibility of expertly holding everything together. *From Elvis In Memphis* is the closest Elvis ever came to recording a full-blown deep soul album, impeccably presenting the artist at the very peak of both physical and artistic maturity.

Thankfully, Elvis was no longer content, at this juncture, to cruise uncommitted through whatever ineffectual conveyor-belt jingles were thrust before him, but was again taking immense pride in a series of performances that echoed the inimitability of his quintessential pre-Army repertoire. His ability to set the appropriate expressive mood, and then meticulously extract every ounce of significance from each lyric had not been so well executed by Elvis since the era of 'Heartbreak Hotel', 'Loving You' and 'I Want To Be Free'. With regard to this recorded dossier, the only other artist ever to cut tracks with such self-assured mastery in the country soul genre was the pre-eminent King Of Rock 'N' Soul, Solomon Burke. Those familiar with Burke's work for Atlantic Records will immediately detect a corollary in the majestic and dramatic interpretive nuances common to both artists: the consummate mercurial switches, from fevered intensity to nonchalant reflectiveness and back again, without any stress. If further confirmation is required, check out both singers' renditions of 'I Really Don't Want To Know' (*Elvis Country*).

To return to *From Elvis In Memphis*, Mr. P. may handle Jerry Butler's prophetic 'Only The Strong Survive', and Chuck Jackson's 'Any Day Now', with as much soulful expertise as the original artists, but it's Elvis' emotive spell-binding readings of the slow blues songs that place him in a class of his very own.

Eddy Arnold's 'I'll Hold You In My Heart' (featuring Elvis on piano), and Joe Henderson's 'After Loving You', are both intoxicating spur-of-the-moment effusions that come within a heated breath of eclipsing even such galvanic classics as 'Don't Leave Me Now', 'One Night', 'Like A Baby' and 'Reconsider Baby' for generating maximum after-hours blues power. It's right here that Elvis pushes himself to the very limits of his talent and takes the kind of risk which, in the hands of lesser artists, would prove embarrassing. From such renditions are reputations fully restored and enriched. Once again, Elvis' evocative, interpretive prowess is rewardingly put to the test on Jody Miller's "Long Black Limousine" – a prophetic Southern rags-to-riches vignette of someone vowing only to return home in a chauffeured long black limo. However, said transportation turns out to be the town hearse!

One cannot write too highly concerning this album – it rates 11 on a scale of 10! Everything about it – right down to the carefully selected NBC-TV Special front cover photograph – displays the kind of sublimity which had been absent for almost a decade. Sadly, never again would Elvis Presley record an album of such overall magnitude.

The closest he would ever come would be *Elvis Country*. Whether or not you're a fully paid-up Elvis fan or just a bystander, discounting for the moment *Greatest Hits* and *Sun Sessions* compilations, *From Elvis In Memphis* ranks alongside of Elvis' first two RCA albums (LPM-1254 and LPM-1382), *Elvis Is Back*, and *Elvis Country* and the soundtracks of both *Loving You* and the *NBC-TV Special* as indispensable acquisitions.

There is a time-honoured theory that at 33, a man is subjected to predestined events which drastically reshape his future. There could well be a modicum of truth in this, because Elvis was exactly 33 years old when he made his triumphant NBC-TV comeback. No doubt, the unqualified success of the special, the fact that the album-of-the-event reached the highest chart position since (ironically enough) the wretched *Harum Scarum* soundtrack, and the fact that plans for his remarkable return to public appearances were in preparation all had a high-motivating effect on Elvis' endeavours.

Save for the still-to-be-screened *Change Of Habit* movie, Elvis had all but disassociated himself from the singin', swingin', synthetic simpleton of the sixties, and was once again endowed with the self-confident skills of a high roller on a winning streak. Still moving in the right direction, Elvis' next major coup was when, one week after his 34th birthday, he chose to cut this – one of his greatest-ever albums – on his home turf. The first occasion since July, 1955, that Elvis had recorded in a Memphis studio.

For this auspicious event, Tommy Cogbill assembled a crack combat unit, comprising some of the South's crackerjack sessioneers. Aside from Cogbill, who doubled on both guitar and bass (check out his nimble-fingered bass breaks on Hank Snow's 'I'm Movin' On'), Reggie Young and Mike Leech also shared guitar and bass parts respectively. Bobby Wood

* **'Clean Up Your Own Back Yard'** (Strange, Davis) XPA1 3976
** **'The Fair Is Moving On'** (Flatt, Fletcher) XPA5 1276
(US) RCA 47-9747
Released: June 1969

Elvis Presley (vcl), Scotty Moore (gtr), Bob Moore (bs), D.J. Fontana (dms), Floyd Cramer (pno), remaining musicians unidentified.
*Recorded: MGM Sound Studios, Culver City, October 15, 1968

Personnel: See 'From Elvis In Memphis' (LP)
**Recorded: American Studios, Memphis, February 21, 1969

Elvis' last-but-one big screen sit-com quickie, *The Trouble With Girls*, gave even less consideration to the soundtrack than to the skimpy story it had to tell. Of the five songs commissioned, only two survived as far as the final print, and only 'Clean Up Your Own Backyard' was chosen to run concurrently with the movie. The remaining survivor ('Almost') was leased out for *Let's Be Friends* (CAS-2408). Over a dozen years later, nothing has officially been seen or heard of the three rejects: 'Swing Down, Sweet Chariot', 'Aura Lee' and 'Sign Of The Zodiac'.

With its cracker-barrel philosophy, 'Clean Up Your Own Backyard' may have been somewhat superior to the sheer rubbish Elvis had crooned in recent movies, but it was still a pale shadow of most of the material this man was now laying down in the studios.

August '69, was a month when rock 'n' roll dominated the media. A large part of America's youth was wallowing in the mud up on Max Yasgur's Woodstock farm, and Elvis Aaron Presley was packing in the remainder, twice nightly, for his first Las Vegas season. Not only that, Elvis was also enjoying his most successful single since he had last topped the US charts, way back in 1962, with 'Good Luck Charm'. Reckoned to be the last title he recorded during his productive 21-song American Studio marathon in January 1969, 'Suspicious Minds' evoked all the old fire.

Career-wise, this release may have coincided with a time when both Elvis' fortunes and his credibility were once more on the upswing, but in several quarters it has been argued that much of this single's success was directly linked to then-persistent press rumours that Elvis' marriage was all over. Not being aware at the time of the full facts of the matter, the

American public appeared to cast a mass sympathy vote in favour of Elvis. Such speculation is difficult to take seriously because, even if such a theory were true, this alone wouldn't account for its rush to the very top of the bestsellers.

The only logical reason is that it was, yep, a great record: performed the way the fans loved to hear their idol, fuelled with a sense of purpose, and matching a magnificent contemporary rock song with an equally magnificent and irresistible interpretation.

For the second half of his career, 'Suspicious Minds' became identified with Elvis' more mature image, as were 'Can't Help Falling In Love' and 'An American Trilogy'. Over the next few years, Elvis was to re-record 'Suspicious Minds' for three in-person albums, while it is estimated that somewhere in the region of two to three dozen alternate in-concert versions are stored in RCA's vaults.

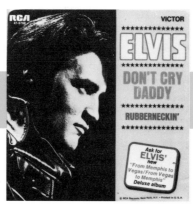

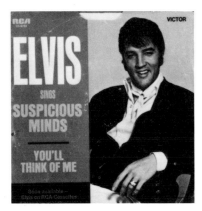

** **'Suspicious Minds'** (James) XPA5 1227
* **'You'll Think Of Me'** (Shuman) XPA5 1146
(US) RCA 47-9764
Released: August 1969

Personnel: 'See 'From Elvis In Memphis' (LP)

Recorded: American Studios, Memphis,
*January 14, 1969. **January 23, 1969

* **'Don't Cry Daddy'** (Scott, Davis) XPA5 1149
** **'Rubberneckin''** (Jones, Warren) XPA5 1156
(US) RCA 47-9768
Released: November 1969

Personnel: See 'From Elvis In Memphis' (LP)

Recorded: American Studios, Memphis,
*January 15, 1969. **January 20, 1969

'Don't Cry Daddy,' together with another Mac Davis composition ('In The Ghetto'), were the first two songs that Elvis personally shortlisted for his magnificent January 1969 American Studio marathon. The reason, Elvis claimed, why he was so attracted to this particular ballad the moment he previewed Davis' demo tape was that it reminded him of his late mother.

Elvis, insisted insiders, never quite recovered from the death of his devoted mother, who died at the age of 46 from her prolonged dependence on a combination of diet pills and alcohol. And it's been suggested, that had she lived a more normal domestic existence, then Elvis may not have so easily fallen victim to such similar excesses. However, that tragedy had yet to be enacted in full.

Such was Elvis' overwhelming vitality and self-confidence when, for the first time since 1955, he chose to record in his hometown of Memphis, that he was able to override the overt sentimentality of 'Don't Cry Daddy' without being encumbered with the effusiveness that, in the latter stages of his recording career, would paint him as a pathetic and directionless figure.

As Elvis embarked upon the "comeback" trail as an in-demand concert artist, it became very apparent that his previous 'career' as a movie star had run its course. Considering that the 'Presley Movie' was no longer a viable proposition, also that Elvis' last three soundtrack albums (*Double Trouble*, *Clambake* and *Speedway*) had peaked at 47, 33 and 82 respectively, here was the second occasion within a year that a movie track had been demoted to the flip side of a single. Of the six songs recorded by Elvis for his appearance opposite Mary Tyler Moore in *Change Of Habit*, only about half survived the final edit. Probably, for that reason, even a soundtrack EP wasn't considered a long-shot bet, so only the boogaloo 'Rubberneckin' was released simultaneously with the movie.

By way of a salvage operation, four of the movie songs ('Let's Forget About The Stars', 'Have A Happy', 'Change Of Habit' and 'Let's Be Friends') were shipped out for the supermarket impulse-purchase trade and shuffled in among the tracks on the Camden compilation *Let's Be Friends* (CAS-2408), while the final song, 'Let Us Pray', found eternal sanctuary on another Camden correlation – the "devotional" *You'll Never Walk Alone* (CAS-2472).

'Don't Cry Daddy' obviously had the desired effect on both the Yuletide heart and wallet. But it wasn't the sight of the toothsome Mary Tyler Moore decked-out in a *haute-couture* nun's habit and carefully applied eyeliner that elevated the record to No. 6 on the bestsellers – the highest point any Presley single would ever achieve (Stateside) from here on in.

'ELVIS – FROM MEMPHIS TO VEGAS/ FROM VEGAS TO MEMPHIS' (LP)
(US) RCA LSP-6020
Released: November 1969

'From Memphis To Vegas'
Side 1
**** 'Blue Suede Shoes' (Perkins) XPA5 2383
* 'Johnny B. Goode' (Berry) XPA5 2314
* 'All Shook Up' (Blackwell, Presley) XPA5 2310
* 'Are You Lonesome Tonight?' (Turk, Handman) XPA5 2316
**** 'Hound Dog' (Leiber, Stoller) XPA5 2384
*** 'I Can't Stop Loving You' (Gibson) XPA5 2320
** 'My Babe' (Dixon) XPA5 2381
Side 2
Medley:
*** 'Mystery Train' (Phillips, Parker)/ 'Tiger Man' (Lewis, Burns) XPA5 2386
* 'Words' (Gibb, Gibb, Gibb) XPA5 2313
*** 'In The Ghetto' (Davis) XPA5 2320
* 'Suspicious Minds' (James) XPA5 2313
** 'Can't Help Falling In Love' (Peretti, Creatore, Weiss) XPA5 2379

Elvis Presley (vcl, gtr), James Burton, John Wilkinson (gtr), Charlie Hodge (gtr, vcl), Larry Muhoberac (pno, o), Jerry Scheff (bs), Ronnie Tutt (dms), The Imperials, The Sweet Inspirations, Millie Kirkham (bv), Bobby Morris & His Orchestra
Recorded: International Hotel, Las Vegas, Nevada.
*August 22, 1969, **August 24, 1969, ***August 25, 1969, ****August 26, 1969

'From Vegas To Memphis'
Side 3
* 'Inherit The Wind' (Rabbitt) XPA5 1151
* 'This Is The Story' (Arnold, Morrow, Martin) XPA5 1143
** 'Stranger In My Own Home Town' (Mayfield) XPA5 1266
* 'A Little Bit Of Green' (Arnold, Morrow, Martin) XPA5 1148
** 'And The Grass Won't Pay No Mind' (Diamond) XPA5 1267
Side 4
** 'Do You Know Who I Am' (Russell) XPA5 1270
* 'From A Jack To A King' (Miller) XPA5 1158
** 'The Fair's Moving On' (Fletcher, Flett) XPA5 1276
* 'You'll Think Of Me' (Shuman) XPA5 1146
* 'Without Love (There Is Nothing)' (Small) XPA5 1159

Elvis Presley (vcl, gtr), Reggie Young (gtr), Tommy Cogbill (gtr, bs), John Hughey (ps), Bobby Wood (pno), Bobby Emmons (o), Ronnie Milsap (pno, vcl, –Jan '69 only), Mike Leech (bs), Gene Chrisman (dms), Ed Kollis (har). Overdubbed at a later session: Millie Kirkham, Sonja Montgomery, Dolores Edgin, Joe Babcock, Sandy Posey, Hursch Wiginton, Mary Holladay, Sandra Robinson, Donna Rhodes, Donna Thatcher, Jeannie Green, Susan Pilkington (bv), The Memphis Horns, The Memphis Strings
Recorded: American Studios, Memphis, Tennessee.
*January 1969 sessions:
January 13 – 'This Is The Story'
January 14 – 'You'll Think Of Me'
January 15 – 'A Little Bit Of Green'
January 16 – 'Inherit The Wind' and 'From A Jack To A King'
January 21 – 'Without Love (There Is Nothing)'
**February 1969 sessions:
February 17 – 'Stranger In My Own Home Town'
February 18 – 'And The Grass Won't Pay No Mind'
February 19 – 'Do You Know Who I Am'
February 21 – 'The Fair's Movin' On'

The Trouble With Girls (And How To Get Into It)/
Metro-Goldwyn-Mayer

Cast
Walter Hale.....................Elvis Presley
Charlene......................Marlyn Mason
Betty.................................Nichole Jaffe
Nita Nix.........................Sheree North
Johnny......................Edward Andrews
Mr Drewcolt...........John Carradine
Caril.................................Anissa Jones
Mr Morality...............Vincent Price
Maude.....................Joyce Van Polten
Willy.................................Pepe Brown
Harrison Wilby.........................
........................Dabney Coleman
Mayor Gilchrist...........Bill Zuckert
Mr Perper.......................Pitt Herbet
Clarence................Anthony Teague
Constable.......................Med Flory

Lige.............................Rodd Redwing
Henry Carter......Edward McKinley

Mamie Callahan........Quentin Dean
Mrs Hawkins.............Anne Seymour
Congressman Morissey.....................

Produced by Lester Welch
Directed by Peter Tewksbury
Running Time: 99 minutes
Released: December 10, 1969

Change of Habit/NBC-Universal

Cast
Dr. John Carpenter......Elvis Presley
Sister Michelle.........................
.........................Mary Tyler Moore
Sister Irene...............Barbara McNair
Sister Barbara..................Jane Elliot
Mother Joseph.............Leorna Dana
Lt. Moretti...................Edward Asner
The Banker...............Robert Emhart
Father Gibbons........Regis Toomey
Rose..........................Doro Merande
Lily..............................Ruth McDevitt
Bishop Finley..........Richard Carlson
Julio Hernandez..............Nefti Millet
Desiree...................Laura Figuerosa
Amanda........................Lorena Rich

Produced by Joe Connelly
Directed by William Graham
Running Time: 93 minutes
Released: January 21, 1970

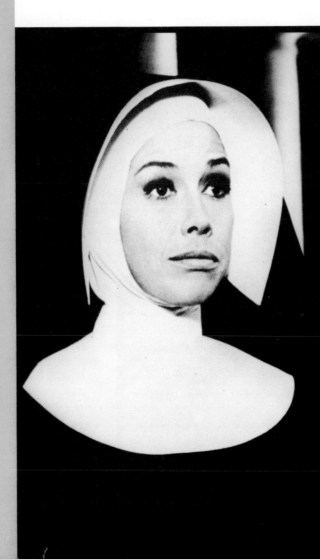

By any reckoning, an awesome enterprise: one in-concert album plus a studio companion. But in the wake of the recent NBC-TV comeback, and the artistically dazzling *From Elvis In Memphis* LP, The King Of Rock 'N' Roll now had to pull out every known stop to match the almost impossible standards he'd publicly set himself earlier in the year. And, for a time, he did so effortlessly. In retrospect, the live *From Memphis To Vegas* segment stands as the prototype for what would quickly seem like an endless succession of repetitive on-stage albums. However, this being the first, overall, it's quite probably the most durable, offering a reflective Golden Oldies look at the roots of Presleymania. It may not ooze the sexual delinquency of either his pre-Army appearances or, for that matter, the rampant chaos of his March 1961, Pearl Harbour appearance, but then, it needs to be remembered that both Elvis and his audience were older and (perhaps!) wiser. On certain evenings, there may still have been sporadic out-breaks of pantie pitching, but this was Las Vegas, so naturally the hysteria was slightly more controlled and up-market. No need here for the National Guard to be called out to restore order as Elvis belts through nine of his certified worldwide hits, two Chess Records' classics – Chuck Berry's 'Johnny B. Goode' and Little Walter's 'My Babe' – plus The Bee Gees' 'Words'.

Elvis may have opened in Las Vegas on July 26, but the recordings that make up the *From Memphis To Vegas* in-concert segment weren't taped until the very last week of his first season. By this time, Elvis had truly hit his stride, and his musicians – without argument, the best backing group ever assembled behind any solo artist – had completed their basic training and were fully broken in as a combat unit.

In former Ricky Nelson guitarist James Burton, Elvis had signed-on (for the duration) a player without peer, whilst Ronnie Tutt could show most drummers the door. With this kind of support, Elvis could – as these tracks reveal – get down to the all-important business at hand. And he did just that.

The studio set, *From Vegas To Memphis*, comprises the second choice of the January–February '69 American Studio sessions which had so far produced *From Elvis In Memphis* and the chart-topping 'Suspicious Minds'.

Though these hitherto unheard cuts veer more towards country, other aspects of Elvis' eclecticism are on display. 'You'll Think Of Me' is a classy mid-tempo Mort Shuman original sung with great sensitivity, 'Without Love (There Is Nothing)' evokes shades of down-home gospelling, and during Ned Miller's 'From A Jack To A King', Elvis exercises some of the vocal gymnastics he'd previously used to startling effect on 'I'll Hold You In My Arms'.

If this album has one unquestionable high-spot, it must surely be the true-grit rendition of Percy Mayfield's 'Stranger In My Own Home Town'. Featuring the electric sitar twang first given chart prominence on Joe South's 'The Games People Play' (courtesy here of Reggie Young), Elvis digs deep into his Southside Chicago blues bag to wail convincingly over the insidious mouth-harp of Ed Kollis. In comparison, the natural essence inherent throughout 'Stranger In My Own Home Town', exposes much of the over-amplified psychedelic blues band posturing of the period for the undignified sham that it was.

To coincide with the drum-beating release of this double set, 50 International Hotel Gift Box Sets – each containing a copy of the double album, the single of 'Kentucky Rain', a 1970 Elvis calendar, an Elvis RCA catalogue, a souvenir photo album, *plus* a specially printed Hotel International Dinner Menu – were presented to those celebrities who'd been personally invited to a special Elvis gala performance.

1970

** **'Kentucky Rain'** (Rabbit, Heard) XPA5 1271
'My Little Friend' (Milete) XPA5 1153
(US) RCA 47-9791
Released: January 1970

Personnel: See 'From Vegas To Memphis'.
Recorded: American Studios, Memphis,
*January 16, 1969. **February 19, 1969

A new decade and a new single – one indicative of the country road Elvis chose to travel for the remainder of his career. That, in itself, would have provided no real cause for dissent, had the overall standard of material, production, and Presley's performances been sustained. But they weren't.

'LET'S BE FRIENDS' (LP)
(US) RCA-Camden CAS-2408
Released: April 1970

Side 1
* 'Stay Away Joe' (Weisman, Wayne) ZPA4 1054
***** 'I'm A Fool' (Kessler) XPA5 1275
****** 'Let's Be Friends' (Arnold, Morrow, March) ZPA4 1057
****** 'Let's Forget About The Stars' (Owens) ZPA4 1055
** 'Mama' (O'Curran, Brooks) WPA1 8122
Side 2

**** 'I'll Be There' (Gabbard, Price) XPA5 1161
*** 'Almost' (Kaye, Weisman) XPA1 3978
****** 'Change Of Habit' (Kaye, Weisman) ZPA4 1058
****** 'Have A Happy' (Weisman, Kaye, Fuller) ZPA 1056

Elvis Presley (vcl, gtr), Scotty Moore (gtr),
Bob Moore (bs), D.J. Fontana,
Murrey "Buddy" Harman (dms)
The Jordanaires (bv), remaining musicians
unidentified
*Recorded: MGM Sound Studios, Hollywood,
California, October 4, 1967
Elvis Presley (vcl, gtr), Scotty Moore,
Tiny Timbrell, Barney Kessel (gtr),
Dudley Brooks (pno), Ray Siegel (bs),
D.J. Fontana, Hal Blaine, Bernie Mattinson (dms),
Homer "Boots" Randolph (ts vib),
The Jordanaires (bv)
**Recorded: Radio Recorders, Hollywood,
California, March 1962
Elvis Presley (vcl, gtr), Scotty Moore (gtr),
Floyd Cramer (pno), Bob Moore (bs),
D.J. Fontana (dms), remaining musicians
unidentified
***Recorded: MGM Sound Studios, Hollywood,
California, October 15, 1968
Elvis Presley (vcl, gtr), Reggie Young (gtr),
Tommy Cogbill (gtr, bs), John Hughey (stl gtr),
Bobby Emmons (o), Bobby Wood (pno),
Mike Leech (bs), Gene Chrisman (dms),
Ed Kollis (har). Overdubbed at a later session:
Millie Kirkham, Sonja Montgomery,
Dolores Edgin, Joe Babcock, Sandy Posey,
Hursch Wiginton, Mary Holladay,
Sandra Robinson, Donna Rhodes, Jeannie Green,
Donna Thatcher, Susan Pilkington (bv),
The Memphis Horns, The Memphis Strings
****Recorded: American Studios, Memphis,
Tennessee, January 23, 1969
*****same personnel and studio as above.
February 21, 1969
Elvis Presley (vcl, gtr), remaining musicians
unidentified
******Recorded: Universal Sound Studios,
Hollywood, California, March 5–6, 1969

This could be viewed as an excuse to wipe the slate clean and dump any remaining debris. Two American Studio escapees ('I'm A Fool' and 'I'll Be There'), plus no less than four of the five songs from *Change Of Habit*, of which this album's title is but one, the other three being, 'Let's Forget About The Stars', 'Have A Happy' and, quite naturally, 'Change Of Habit' itself.

Also present: the theme from *Stay Away Joe* and left-overs from *Girls! Girls! Girls!* ('Mama') and *The Trouble With Girls* ('Almost').

** **'The Wonder Of You'** (Baker, Knight)
ZPA5 1300
* **'Mama Liked The Roses'** (Christopher)
XPA5 1152
(US) RCA 47-9835
Released: May 1970

Elvis Presley (vcl), James Burton,
John Wilkinson, Charlie Hodges (gtr),
Glen D. Hardin (pno), Jerry Scheff (bs),
Bob Lanning (dms),
Bobby Morris & His Orchestra, The Imperials,
The Sweet Inspiration, Millie Kirkham (bv)
*Recorded: The International Hotel, Las Vegas,
February 19, 1970
**Recorded: American Studios, Memphis,
January 16, 1969.
Personnel: See 'From Elvis In Memphis' (LP)

While the rest of the world was at loggerheads over the merits of the Beatles' *Let It Be* album, Elvis again chose to tap the Easter holiday market. Not since 'Crying In The Chapel' (1965), had a seasonal release paid such handsome dividends.

'The Wonder Of You' was a damn-the-torpedoes (full steam ahead) big beat ballad treatment of Ray Peterson's 1959 RCA-Victor hit, and an excerpt from the ready-to-ship *On Stage* album. The schmaltzy flip – a tribute to the memory of his mother, Gladys – possessed all the cloying sentimentality capable of bringing out the maternal instinct in just about every woman who regarded Elvis as the ideal All-American son-substitute.

'ON STAGE – FEBRUARY 1970' (LP)
(US) RCA LSP-4362
Released: June 1970

*** 'See See Rider' (Rainey) ZPA5 1290
**** 'Release Me' (Miller, Stevenson) ZPA 1294
**** 'Sweet Caroline' (Diamond) ZPA5 1293
* 'Runaway' (Crook, Shannon) XPA5 2315
***** 'The Wonder Of You' (Knight) ZPA5 2315
Side 2
**** 'Polk Salad Annie' (White) ZPA 1298
** 'Yesterday' (Lennon, McCartney) XPA5 2318
*** 'Proud Mary' (Fogerty) ZPA 1289
**** 'Walk A Mile In My Shoes' (South) ZPA 1297
*** 'Let It Be Me' (Curtis, Delanoe, Becaud) ZPA 1291

Elvis Presley (vcl, gtr), James Burton,
John Wilkinson (gtr), Charlie Hodge (gtr, vcl),
Larry Muhoberac (pno, o – August '69 recordings only), Glen D. Hardin (pno, – February '70 recordings only), Jerry Scheff (bs),
Ronnie Tutt (dms – August '69 recordings only),
Bob Lanning (dms – February '70 recordings only), The Imperials, The Sweet Inspirations,
Millie Kirkham (bv), Bobby Morris & His Orchestra
Recorded: International Hotel, Las Vegas, Nevada,
*August 22, 1969 **August 25, 1969.
***February 17, 1970 ****February 18, 1970,
*****February 19, 1970

To celebrate his re-enlistment with RCA, Elvis put together what would prove to be his one and only *live* album of all-new material.

They may have been first-runs for Elvis but, without exception, they were all tried and tested tunes. Not a solitary long-shot in sight.

Las Vegas audiences being notoriously conservative, their tastes invariably veer towards a middle-of-the-road repertoire. They only pay out good money to see and hear something they're already familiar with. Offer them anything but that and you'll work to two table napkins and a waiter. So, having edited-out the recorded re-works of his own past glories, Elvis offered a safe-as-milk collection of other artists' Greatest Hits.

Who originally sang what? And when?

1970

'See See Rider', Chuck Willis/1957; 'Release Me', Little Esther Phillips/1962 and Engelbert Humperdinck/1967; 'Sweet Caroline', Neil Diamond/1969; 'Runaway', Del Shannon/1961; 'The Wonder Of You', Ray Peterson/1959; 'Polk Salad Annie', Tony Joe White/1969; 'Yesterday', The Beatles/1965; 'Proud Mary', Creedence Clearwater Revival/1969; 'Walk A Mile In My Shoes', Joe South/1970; 'Let It Be Me', The Everly Brothers/1960.

For the live portion of the *From Memphis To Vegas–From Vegas to Memphis* double album of the previous year, many of the vocal tracks were re-recorded in Nashville. The overall impression gleaned from the extremely casual and good-humoured mood of this new album is that very little, if any, post-op studio surgery has been performed.

Eighty per cent of this LP emanates from the last week of Elvis' second Las Vegas season, while 'Runaway' and 'Yesterday' stem from the last days of his historic first Las Vegas Hilton stint which produced the later release *Elvis In Person At The International Hotel*.

As indicated, this collection of true-to-the-original covers doesn't offer any dramatic surprises, but on the other hand it isn't by any means a let-down.

On Stage 1970 was the right album for the time. In a few short months (on September 10), Elvis was due to embark on his first exploratory coast-to-coast tour (18 concerts in 14 cities), and this album was astutely conceived as a trailer which would attract not only the die-hard fan but, just as important, those potential customers who'd probably never before bought a Presley album. It also acted as a wallet-primer for the hard-sell on Elvis' August release, the four-album *Worldwide 50 Gold Award Hits, Volume 1*.

For those interested in such matters, here is the complete list of the tracks that were mastered from the February 16–19, 1970 Las Vegas sessions:

ZPA5 1286	'All Shook Up'	February 16	unreleased
ZPA5 1287	'In The Ghetto'	February 16	unreleased
ZPA5 1288	'Suspicious Minds'	February 16	unreleased
ZPA5 1289	'Proud Mary'	February 17	LSP-4362
ZPA5 1290	'See See Rider'	February 17	LSP-4362
ZPA5 1291	'Let It Be Me'	February 17	LSP-4362
ZPA5 1292	'Don't Cry Daddy'	February 17	unreleased
ZPA5 1293	'Sweet Caroline'	February 18	LSP-4362
ZPA5 1294	'Release Me'	February 18	LSP-4362
ZPA5 1295	'Kentucky Rain'	February 18	unreleased
ZPA5 1296	'Long Tall Sally'	February 18	unreleased
ZPA5 1297	'Walk A Mile In My Shoes'	February 18	LSP-4362
ZPA5 1298	'Polk Salad Annie'	February 18	LSP-4362
ZPA5 1299	'I Can't Stop Loving You'	February 18	unreleased
ZPA5 1300	'The Wonder Of You'	February 19	LSP-4362 & 47-9835.

* **'I've Lost You'** (Howard, Blaikley) ZPA4 1594
** **'The Next Step Is Love'** (Evans, Parnes)
ZPA4 1619
(US) RCA 47-9873
Released: July 1970

Elvis Presley (vcl, gtr), James Burton, Chip Young (gtr), David Briggs (pno), Norbert Putnam (bs), Jerry Carrigan (dms), Charlie McCoy (har).
Over-dubbed at a later session: The Jordanaires, The Imperials, The Nashville Edition, Millie Kirkham, Jeannie Green, Mary & Ginger Holladay (bv)
*Recorded: RCA Studios, Nashville, June 4, 1970. **June 7, 1970

'WORLDWIDE 50 GOLD AWARDS HITS, VOLUME I' (LP)
(US) RCA LPM-6401
Released: August 1970

Side I
'Heartbreak Hotel' (Axton, Presley, Durden)
'I Was The One'
(Schroeder, DeMetrius, Blair, Peppers)
'I Want You, I Need You, I Love You'
(Mysels, Kosloff)
'Don't Be Cruel' (Blackwell, Presley)
'Hound Dog' (Leiber, Stoller)
'Love Me Tender' (Presley, Matson)
Side 2
'Anyway You Want Me' (Schroeder, Owens)
'Too Much' (Rosenberg, Weinman)
'Playing For Keeps' (Kessler)
'All Shook Up' (Blackwell, Presley)
'That's When Your Heartaches Begin'
(Fisher, Hill, Raskin)
'Loving You' (Leiber, Stoller)
Side 3
'(Let Me Be Your) Teddy Bear' (Mann, Lowe)
'Jailhouse Rock' (Leiber, Stoller)
'Treat Me Nice' (Leiber, Stoller)
'I Beg Of You' (McCoy, Owens)
'Don't' (Leiber, Stoller)
'Wear My Ring Around Your Neck'
(Carroll, Moody)
'Hard Headed Woman' (DeMetrius)
Side 4
'I Got Stung' (Schroeder, Hill)
'(Now And Then There's) A Fool Such As I'
(Trader)
'A Big Hunk O' Love' (Schroeder, Wyche)
'Stuck On You' (Schroeder, Leslie, McFarland)
'A Mess Of Blues' (Pomus, Shuman)
'It's Now Or Never' (Schroeder, Gold, Di Capua)
Side 5
'I Gotta Know' (Evans, Williams)
'Are You Lonesome Tonight?' (Turk, Handman)
'Surrender' (Pomus, Shuman, De Curtis)
'I Feel So Bad' (Willis)
'Little Sister' (Pomus, Schuman)
'Can't Help Falling In Love'
(Peretti, Creatore, Weiss)
Side 6
'Rock-A-Hula Baby' (Wise, Weisman, Fuller)
'Anything That's Part Of You' (Robertson)
'Good Luck Charm' (Schroeder, Gold)
'She's Not You' (Blackwell, Scott)
'Return To Sender' (Blackwell, Scott)
'Where Do You Come From?'
(Batchelor, Roberts)
'One Broken Heart For Sale' (Blackwell, Scott)
Side 7
'(You're The) Devil In Disguise'
(Giant, Baum, Kaye)
'Bossa Nova Baby' (Leiber, Stoller)
'Kissin' Cousins' (Wise, Starr)
'Viva Las Vegas' (Pomus, Shuman)
'Ain't That Loving You Baby' (Otis, Hunter)
'Wooden Heart'
(Wise, Wiseman, Twomey, Kaempfert)
Side 8
'Crying In The Chapel' (Glenn)
'If I Can Dream' (Brown)
'In The Ghetto' (Davis)
'Suspicious Minds' (James)
'Don't Cry Daddy' (Davis)
'Kentucky Rain' (Rabbitt, Heard)
'Excerpts From "Elvis Sails" Interview'

An ambitious and highly successful marketing ploy to sum up the best of Elvis' work (so far) in a single package. Housed in its own cuddly little box, accompanied by a book of, as they used to say, "suitable for framing" photos.

At a time when he should have been exercising cherry-picking discretion over his repertoire, Elvis again squandered his artistry by toying with formularized songs which much lesser talents might well have had second thoughts about recording.

* **'You Don't Have To Say You Love Me'**
(Wickham, Napier-Bell, Donaggio, Pallavicini)
ZPA4 1608
** **'Patch It Up'** (Rabbitt, Bourke) ZPA4 1628
(US) RCA 47-9916
Released: October 1970
*Recorded: RCA Studios, Nashville, June 6, 1970
Personnel: See 'I've Lost You'
**June 8, 1970

The acquisition of previously unrecorded properties of this quality was, even for someone like The King, a constant problem. Be that as it may, the unyielding commitment with which Elvis belted out Dusty Springfield's classic account of the wretchedness of unrequited love, accompanied by Jerry Carrigan's bombastic back-beat and the combined (albeit overdubbed) lung power of The Jordanaires, The Imperials, The Nashville Edition, Millie Kirkham, Jeannie Green and Ginger and Mary Holladay, was the kind of premium performance upon which Presley built up his reputation for the second time in his career.

'Patch It Up' was a stirring soul strut that worked better on stage than on wax. This version is an entirely different take to the one found on *That's The Way It Is*.

'ALMOST IN LOVE' (LP)
(US) RCA-Camden CAS-2440
Released: November 1970

Side 1
'Almost In Love' (Bonfa, Starr)
'Long Legged Girl (With The Short Dress On)'
(McFarland, Scott)
'Edge Of Reality' (Giant, Baum, Kaye)
'My Little Friend' (Milete)
'A Little Less Conversation' (Strange, Davis)
Side 2
'Rubberneckin'' (Jones, Warren)
'Clean Up Your Own Back Yard' (Strange, Davis)
'US Male' (Hubbard)
'Charro' (Strange, Davis)
'Stay Away Joe' (Weisman, Wayne)

This album vividly reveals the kind of haphazard attention that went into programming many Camden compilations. Though the mistake was probably spotted much earlier, it took three years to rectify the fact that 'Stay Away Joe' – the last track on this album – was also the first track on *Let's Be Friends* (CAS-2408). When, in 1973, *Almost In Love* was re-pressed, 'Stay Away Joe' was replaced by 'Stay Away'.

'ELVIS' CHRISTMAS ALBUM' (LP)
(US) RCA-Camden CAL-2428
Released: November 1970

Side 1
'Blue Christmas' (Hayes, Johnson)
'Silent Night' (Mohr, Gruber)
'White Christmas' (Berlin)
'Santa Claus Is Back In Town' (Leiber, Stoller)
'I'll Be Home For Christmas' (Kent, Gannon, Ram)
Side 2
'If Every Day Was Like Christmas' (West)
'Here Comes Santa Claus'
(Autry, Haldeman, Melka)
'O Little Town Of Bethlehem' (Radner, Brooks)
'Santa, Bring My Baby Back (To Me)'
(Schroeder, DeMetrius)
'Mama Liked The Roses' (Christopher)

Though the tracks have been noticeably reshuffled, this is in fact two-thirds of the original November 1957 Christmas Collection (RCA LOC-1035), stripped of the four *Peace In The Valley* EP songs (RCA EPA-4054), and padded out with 'If Every Day Was Like Christmas' (1966) and 'Mama Liked The Roses' (1970).

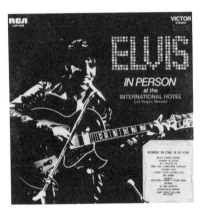

**'ELVIS IN PERSON
AT THE INTERNATIONAL HOTEL,
LAS VEGAS, NEVADA'** (LP)
(US) RCA LSP-4428
Released: November 1970

Side 1
'Blue Suede Shoes' (Perkins)
'Johnny B. Goode' (Berry)
'All Shook Up' (Blackwell, Presley)
'Are You Lonesome Tonight?' (Turk, Handman)
'Hound Dog' (Leiber, Stoller)
'I Can't Stop Loving You' (Gibson)
'My Babe' (Dixon)
Side 2
'Mystery Train' (Phillips, Parker)
'Tiger Man' (Lewis, Burns)
'Words' (Gibb, Gibb, Gibb)
'In The Ghetto' (Davis)
'Suspicious Minds' (James)
'Can't Help Falling In Love'
(Peretti, Creatore, Weiss)

'BACK IN MEMPHIS' (LP)
(US) RCA LSP-4429
Released: November 1970

Side 1
'Inherit The Wind' (Rabbitt)
'This Is The Story' (Arnold, Morrow, Martin)
'Stranger In My Own Home Town' (Mayfield)
'A Little Bit Of Green' (Arnold, Morrow, Martin)
'And The Grass Won't Pay No Mind' (Diamond)
Side 2
'Do You Know Who I Am' (Russell)
'From A Jack To A King' (Miller)
'The Fair's Moving On' (Fletcher, Flett)
'You'll Think Of Me' (Shuman)
'Without Love (There Is Nothing)' (Small)

Now that he had returned to public appearances, Elvis may have been hotter than he'd been in ages, but as 1970 drew to a close and other artists' achievements were assessed, it became quite evident that, recording-wise, aside from five singles, yet another 'live' album (*On Stage*) and the soundtrack for *That's The Way It Is*, Elvis' year had been devoted almost exclusively to a re-issue programme.

By contrast, other 1970 LP releases included: *Let It Be* (The Beatles), *The Man Who Sold The World* (David Bowie), *Willy & The Poor Boys* (Creedence Clearwater Revival), *Deja*

Vu (Crosby, Stills, Nash & Young), *Bitches Brew* (Miles Davis), *Morrison Hotel* (The Doors), *New Morning* (Bob Dylan), *Workingman's Dead* and *American Beauty* (The Grateful Dead), *Volunteers* (Jefferson Airplane), *All Things Must Pass* (George Harrison), *Plastic Ono Band* (John Lennon), *Back in the USA* (MC5), *Moondance* (Van Morrison), *Get Yer Ya-Ya's Out* (The Rolling Stones), *Bridge Over Troubled Water* (Simon & Garfunkel), *Gasoline Alley* (Rod Stewart), *Fun House* (The Stooges), *Live At Leeds* (The Who) and *After The Gold Rush* (Neil Young).

Back in Elvis-land, there had been the trio of budget-price Camden compilations (*Let's Be Friends, Almost In Love* and *Elvis' Christmas Album*), while RCA had offered a boxed four-album refresher course entitled *Worldwide 50 Gold Award Hits Volume I* for those who'd only recently "discovered" Presley.

But that wasn't all. Despite the fact that the latter remained on the nation's bestsellers list for almost six months (reaching as high as No. 12), somebody chose to cleave the double album, *From Memphis To Vegas—From Vegas To Memphis* (RCA LSP-6020) into two separate volumes. It really wasn't worth the effort, for, of the two, only *Back In Memphis* made the charts (just), peaking at No. 183 and then gurgling down the plug and round the u-bend after just three weeks.

* **'I Really Don't Want To Know'**
(Barnes, Robertson) ZPA4 1616
** **'There Goes My Everything'** (Frazier)
ZPA4 1624
(US) RCA 47-9960
Released: December 1970
Personnel as June, 1970, Nashville sessions
*Recorded: RCA Studios, Nashville,
June 7, 1970.
**June 8, 1970

Periodically, Elvis would suddenly delve right back into his past and pull out one of the many songs he used to sing when still at Humes High School in Memphis. In this instance, an Eddy Arnold song later popularized by Tommy Edwards, 'I Really Don't Want To Know'. This was one of the very first things Elvis ever sang when, on a Saturday afternoon in June 1954, he first met up with Scotty Moore and Bill Black, at the former's home, with the purpose of *developing a style of sorts*!

The style having long since been developed and perfected, Elvis is at his balladeering best on this melodramatic country/soul song which acted as a fine precursor for the magnificent *Elvis Country* album.

The flip is slightly more contemporary, being the Dallas Frazier heartbreaker that Engelbert Humperdinck effectively employed in 1967 as the follow-up to his first international hit, 'Please Release Me'.

Both tracks emanate from the Nashville shindig held in June that produced the bulk of three albums – *That's The Way It Is, Elvis Country* and *Love Letters*.

The third prong of the Elvis Presley comeback was *That's The Way It Is*. The first thrust had been the NBC television special, the second, Elvis' decision to return to the live stage, and the third, the movie that showed in graphic detail exactly how he did that.

It was a documentary in the very truest sense of the word. It not only showed the preparation for the show at the Las Vegas International Hilton, but also provided a fairly unusual insight into a man with a unique talent striving to get back to a point where he would be able once again to use that talent.

Although there were large missing chunks, Elvis was filmed clowning at rehearsal rather than rehearsing, and although all the build-up was directed at the Las Vegas show and at least half the live footage was shot at another concert in Phoenix, Arizona, and even though the mechanics of putting Elvis Presley back onto a stage were only examined in the most superficial manner, there was a core of truth that could not be ignored.

Despite being punctuated by rather predictable interviews with gushing fans, and an awful lot of emphasis on proving the greater glory of Elvis Presley, once you got past the promo content of the film, there was an essential fascination in watching Presley, bit by bit, gearing himself up for a show.

The film shot in the hours before the show, when Presley is unable to stop himself compulsively drumming, is almost as electrifying as the concert itself.

In some ways the actual show is something of an anticlimax. There is the obvious temptation to compare Presley in 1970 with Presley in 1958. The emphasis of Presley's movements has switched from his legs to his arms. He has even borrowed a few mannerisms from Tom Jones. Elvis has matured, compromised to a certain extent, but at least has apparently clawed his way out of the morass of bad records, bad films and sagging credibility.

The documentary has its limitations, but on two counts it must be consigned the most successful Presley movie ever made. First, it *is* a film about Elvis Presley – not Elvis-Presley-in-a-film. It shows a side of the man that actually appears to care about what he's doing. The second and most important count is that it documents a crucial time in Presley's life and as a result, provides significant insights for anyone trying to understand the contradictions of his career.

Elvis–"That's the Way It Is"
Metro-Goldwyn-Mayer

Directed by Denis Sanders
Photographed by Lucien Ballard
Running Time: 107 minutes
Released: December 15, 1970

a film about him

'ELVIS–THAT'S THE WAY IT IS' (LP)
(US) RCA LSP-4445
Released: December 1970

Side 1
***** 'I Just Can't Help Believin'' (Mann, Weil) ZPA5 1862
* 'Twenty Days And Twenty Nights' (Weisman, Westlake) ZPA4 1593
** 'How The Web Was Woven' (Westlake, Most) ZPA4 1602
***** 'Patch It Up' (Rabbitt, Bourke) ZPA5 1863
** 'Mary In The Morning' (Cymbol, Lendell) ZPA4 1606
*** 'You Don't Have To Say You Love Me' (Wickham, Napier-Bell, Donaggio, Pallavicini) ZPA4 1608
Side 2
****** 'You've Lost That Lovin' Feelin'' (Mann, Weil) ZPA5 1864
****** 'I've Lost You' (Howard, Blaikley) ZPA5 1865
*** 'Just Pretend' (Flett, Fletcher) ZPA4 1609
** 'Stranger In The Crowd' (Scott) ZPA4 1604
**** 'The Next Step Is Love' (Evans, Parnes) ZPA4 1619
** 'Bridge Over Troubled Water' (Simon) ZPA4 1600

Elvis Presley (vcl, gtr), James Burton, Chip Young (gtr), David Briggs (pno), Norbert Putnam (bs), Jerry Carrigan (dms), Charlie McCoy (harm).
Overdubbed at the later session:
The Jordanaires, The Imperials, The Nashville Edition, Millie Kirkham, Jeannie Green, Mary Holladay, Ginger Holladay (bv)
Recorded: RCA Studios, Nashville, Tennessee.
*June 4, 1970. **June 5, 1970. ***June 6, 1970.
****June 7, 1970
Elvis Presley (vcl, gtr), James Burton, John Wilkinson (gtr), Charlie Hodge (gtr, vcl), Glen D. Hardin (pno), Jerry Scheff (bs), Ronnie Tutt (dms), The Imperials, The Sweet Inspiration, Millie Kirkham (bv), Joe Guercio & His Orchestra.
Recorded: International Hotel, Las Vegas, Nevada. *****August 13, 1970.
******August 14, 1970

For a soundtrack album that's meant to represent a fast-action documentary, this is remarkably pedestrian.

Of the dozen cuts selected from hours of tapes, there's but one song that could be remotely regarded as a rocker ('Patch It Up') while only four tracks were actually recorded before a live audience.

Somewhere in the planning the idea of utilizing the best of the more interesting informal rehearsals was abandoned, and though Elvis' covers of B.J. Thomas' 'I Just Can't Help Believing' and Jackie Lomax's 'How The Web Was Woven' are nothing less than splendid, the overall atmosphere exuded by this album is that of a Vegas-style soporific late show.

It was left to the more enterprising bootleggers to compile the *real* and much more rewarding soundtrack album.

The movie *That's The Way It Is* may have been accepted by both critics and fans alike, but when it came to the *Elvis On Tour* follow-up in 1973, the formula, in the opinion of MGM, had been exhausted. Anyone, they claimed, who wanted to see an Elvis concert could now catch him in the flesh, and therefore an Elvis concert-on-film had limited appeal.

Furthermore, what with all the pre-publicity that surrounded the *Aloha From Hawaii* project, movie house owners were reluctant to book *Elvis On Tour* and, as a result, the movie only received restricted release in off-the-beaten-track areas. Despite having a vested interest in Elvis' career, MGM refused to set aside a promotional budget for a movie which, they argued, would be fortunate to even recoup its original production costs.

As none of the original MGM soundtrack recordings appear on the *That's The Way It Is* album (all the live tracks for this LP being taped by RCA), a list of unreleased MGM material known to exist is hereby supplied as a matter of interest and for reference. One can only assume that MGM must still be in the possession of hours of both film footage and taped recordings.

1970

Studio rehearsals
'Words'
'The Next Step Is Love'
'Polk Salad Annie'
'Cryin' Time'
'That's All Right (Mama)'
'Little Sister'
'What'd I Say'
'Stranger In The Crowd'
'How The Web Was Woven'
'I Just Can't Help Believing'
'You Don't Have To Say You Love Me'

Elvis Presley (vcl, gtr), James Burton, John Wilkinson, Charlie Hodge (gtr),
Glen D. Hardin (pno), Jerry Scheff (bs), Ronnie Tutt (dms).
Recorded: MGM Recording Studios, Culver City, July-August 1970

Concert rehearsals
'Bridge Over Troubled Water'
'You've Lost That Lovin' Feelin''
'Mary In The Morning'
'Polk Salad Annie'

Elvis Presley (vcl, gtr), James Burton, John Wilkinson, Charlie Hodge (gtr),
Glen D. Hardin (pno), Jerry Scheff (bs), Ronnie Tutt (dms). The Imperials,
The Sweet Inspirations, Millie Kirkham (bv), Joe Guercio & His Orchestra
Recorded: International Hotel, Las Vegas, August 1970

Concert performances
'That's All Right (Mama)'
'I've Lost You'
'Patch It Up'
'Love Me Tender'
'You've Lost That Lovin' Feelin''
'Sweet Caroline'
'I Just Can't Help Believing'
'Tiger Man'
'Bridge Over Troubled Water'
'Heartbreak Hotel'
'One Night'
'Blue Suede Shoes'
'All Shook Up'
'Polk Salad Annie'
'Suspicious Minds'
'Can't Help Falling In Love'

Same personnel as concert rehearsals
Recorded: International Hotel, Las Vegas, August 10–16, 1970

Concert performances
ZPA5 1862 'I Just Can't Help Believing'
    August 13 RCA LSP-4445
ZPA5 1863 'Patch It Up'
    August 13 RCA LSP-4445
ZPA5 1864 'You've Lost That Lovin' Feelin''
    August 14 RCA LSP-4445
ZPA5 1865 'I've Lost You'
    August 14 RCA LSP-4445
ZPA5 1866 'Bridge Over Troubled Water'
August 15 unreleased
same personnel as above

Recorded: International Hotel,

Las Vegas August 13–15, 1970

Concert performance
'Mystery Train'/'Tiger Man'

Same personnel as above except
The Hugh Jarrett Singers replace The Imperials
Recorded: Veteran Coliseum, Phoenix,
September 9, 1970

Elvis Presley Concert Appearances:
*Two performances (afternoon & evening)
1969
Las Vegas International (July 26–August 28)

1970
Las Vegas International
(January 26–February 23),
Houston Astrodome (February 27–March 1),
Las Vegas International
(August 10–September 7),

September
Phoenix (9), St. Louis (10), Detroit (11), Miami
(12), Tampa (13*), Mobile (14)

November
Oakland (10), Portland (11), Seattle (12), San
Francisco (13), Los Angeles (14*), San Diego
(15), Oklahoma City (16), Denver (17)

1971
Las Vegas Hilton (January 26–February 23),
Lake Tahoe Sahara (July 20–August 2),
Las Vegas Hilton (August 9–September 6),

November
Minneapolis (5), Cleveland (6*), Louisville (7),
Philadelphia (8), Baltimore (9), Boston (10),
Cincinnati (11), Houston (12), Dallas (13*),
Tuscaloosa (14), Kansas City (15),
Salt Lake City (16)

1972
Las Vegas Hilton (January 26–February 23)

April
Buffalo (5), Detroit (6), Dayton (7), Knoxville
(8*), Hampton Roads (9*), Richmond (10),
Roanoke (11), Indianapolis (13), Charlotte (13),
Greensboro (14), Macon (15*), Jacksonville
(16*), Little Rock (17), San Antonio (18),
Albuquerque (19)

June
New York Madison Square Garden (9, 10*, 11),
Fort Wayne (12), Evansville (13), Milwaukee (14
& 15), Chicago (16* & 17), Fort Worth (18),
Wichita (19), Tulsa (20)

Las Vegas Hilton (August 5–September 4)

November
Lubbock (8), Tucson (9), El Paso (10), Oakland
(11), San Bernardino (12 & 13), Long Beach (14 &
15), Honolulu (17 & 18)

1973
January
HIC Arena, Hawaii–*Aloha From Hawaii Via
Satellite* rehearsal (12) live transmission (14)

Las Vegas Hilton (January 26–February 23, three
shows cancelled due to illness)

April
Phoenix (22), Anaheim (23 & 24), Fresno (25*),
San Diego (26), Portland (27), Spokane (28*),
Seattle (29*), Denver (30)

Lake Tahoe Sahara (May 5–20, season
terminated on the 16th due to illness)

June
Mobile (20), Atlanta (21), Uniondale N.Y. Nassau
Coliseum (22, 23*, 24), Pittsburg (25 & 26),
Cincinnati (27), St. Louis (28), Atlanta (29* & 30*)

July
Nashville (1), Oklahoma City (2)

Las Vegas Hilton (August 6–September 3)

1974
Las Vegas Hilton (January 26–February 9)

March
Tulsa (1 & 2), Houston Astrodome (3*), Monroe
(4), Auburn (5), Montgomery (6), Monroe (7 &
8), Charlotte (9), Roanoke (10), Hampton Roads
(11), Richmond (12), Greensboro (13),
Murfreesboro (14), Knoxville (15*), Memphis
(16* & 17), Richmond (18), Murfreesboro (19),
Memphis (20* & 21)

May
San Bernardino (10), Los Angeles Forum (11*),
Fresno (13)

Lake Tahoe Sahara (May 16–26)

June
Fort Worth (15* & 16*), Baton Rouge (17 & 18),
Amarillo (19), Des Moines (20), Cleveland (21),
Providence (22*), Philadelphia (23*), Niagara
Falls (24), Columbus (25), Louisville (26),
Bloomington (27), Milwaukee (28), Kansas City
(29*), Omaha (30*)

July
Omaha (1), Salt Lake City (2)

Las Vegas Hilton (August 19–September 2, two
shows cancelled due to illness)

September
College Park (27 & 28), Detroit (29), South Bend (30)

October
South Bend (1), St. Paul (2 & 3), Detroit (4),
Indianapolis (5), Dayton (6), Wichita (7), San
Antonio (8), Abilene (9)

Lake Tahoe Sahara (October 10–14)

1975
Las Vegas Hilton (March 18–April 1)

April
Mobile (23), Macon (24), Jacksonville (25),
Tampa (26*), Lakeland (27* & 28),
Murfreesboro (29), Atlanta (30)

May
Atlanta (1 & 2), Monroe (3), Lake Charles (4),
Jackson (5), Murfreesboro (6 & 7),
Huntsville (30 & 31*)

June
Huntsville (1), Mobile (2*), Tuscaloosa (3),
Houston (4 & 5), Dallas (6), Shreveport (7*),
Jackson (8* & 9), Memphis (10)

July
Oklahoma City (8), Terre Haute (9), Cleveland
(10), Charleston (11 & 12*), Niagara Falls (13*),
Springfield (14 & 15), New Haven (16 & 17),
Cleveland (18), Uniondale N.Y. Nassau Coliseum
(19*), Norfolk (20*), Greensboro (21), Asheville
(22, 23, 24)

Las Vegas Hilton (August 18–20, terminated due
to illness)
Las Vegas Hilton (December 2–15)

December
Pontiac (31)

1976
March
Johnson City (17, 18, 19), Charlotte (20),
Cincinnati (21), St. Louis (22)

April
Omaha (22), Denver (23), San Diego (24), Long
Beach (25), Seattle (26), Spokane (27)

May
Bloomington (27), Ames (28), Oklahoma City
(29), Odessa (30), Lubbock (31)

June
Tuscon (1), El Paso (2), Fort Worth (3), Atlanta
(4, 5, 6), Buffalo (25), Providence (26), Largo
(27*), Philadelphia (28), Richmond (29),
Greensboro (30)

July
Baton Rouge (1), Forth Worth (2), Tucson (3),
Tulsa (4), Memphis (5), Louisville (23),
Charleston (24*), Syracuse (25), Rochester (26),
Syracuse (27), Hartford (28), Springfield (29),
New Haven (30)

August
Hampton Roads (1), Charlottesville (2), San
Antonio (27), Houston (28), Mobile (29),
Tuscaloosa (30), Macon (31)

September
Jackson (1), Tampa (2), St. Petersburg (3),
Lakeland (4), Jacksonville (5), Huntsville (6),
Pine Bluff (7 & 8)

October
Chicago (14 & 15), Duluth (16), Minneapolis (17),
Sioux Falls (18), Madison (19), South Bend (20),
Kalamazoo (21), Champaign (22), Cleveland (23),
Evansville (24), Fort Wayne (25), Dayton (26),
Carbondale (27)

November
Reno (24), Eugene (25), Portland (26), Eugene
(27), San Francisco (28 & 29), Anaheim (30)

Las Vegas Hilton (December 2–12)

December
Wichita (27), Dallas (28), Birmingham (29),
Atlanta (30), Pittsburg (31)

1977
February
Miami (12), St. Petersburg (13), West Palm Beach
(14), Orlando (15), Montgomery (16), Augusta
(17), Columbia (18), Johnson City (19), Charlotte
(20)

March
Phoenix (23), Amarillo (24), Norman (25 & 26),
Abilene (27), Austin (28), Alexandria (29 & 30)

April
Greensboro (21), Detroit (22), Toledo (23), Ann
Arbor (24), Saginaw (25), Kalamazoo (26),
Milwaukee (27), Green Bay (28), Duluth (29),
St. Paul (30)

May
Chicago (1 & 2), Saginaw (3), Knoxville (20),
Louisville (21), Largo (22), Providence (23),
Auguste (24), Rochester (25), Binghampton (26 &
27), Philadelphia (28), Baltimore (29), Jacksonville
(30), Baton Rouge (31)

June
Macon (1), Mobile (2), Springfield (17), Kansas
City (18), Omaha (19), Lincoln (20), Rapid City
(21), Sioux Falls (22), Des Moines (23), Madison
(24), Cincinnati (25), Indianapolis (26)

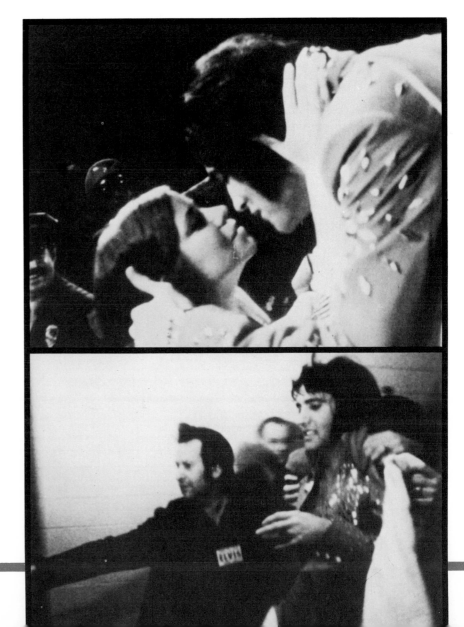

1971

'I'M 10,000 YEARS OLD, ELVIS COUNTRY' (LP)
(US) RCA LSP-4460
Released: January 1971

Side I
***** 'Snowbird' (MacLellan) ZPA4 1797
*** 'Tomorrow Never Comes' (Tubb, Bond) ZPA4 1618
* 'Little Cabin On The Hill' (Monroe, Flatt) ZPA4 1598
***** 'Whole Lotta Shakin' Goin' On' (Williams, David) ZPA4 1799
*** 'Funny How Time Slips Away' (Nelson) ZPA4 1621
*** 'I Really Don't Want To Know' (Barnes, Robertson) ZPA4 1616
Side 2
**** 'There Goes My Everything' (Frazier) ZPA4 1624
** 'It's Your Baby, You Rock It' (Milete, Fowler) ZPA4 1603
* 'The Fool' (Ford, Hazelwood) ZPA4 1597
*** 'Faded Love' (Willis, Willis) ZPA4 1617
*** 'I Washed My Hands In Muddy Water' (Babcock) ZPA4 1622
*** 'Make The World Go Away' (Cochran)

Elvis Presley (vcl, gtr), James Burton, Chip Young (gtr), David Briggs (pno), Norbert Putnam (bs), Jerry Carrigan (dms), Charlie McCoy (har). Overdubbed at a later session: The Jordanaires, The Imperials, The Nashville Edition, Millie Kirkham, Jeannie Green, Mary Holladay, Ginger Holladay (bv)
Recorded: RCA Studios, Nashville, Tennessee, *June 4, 1970. **June 5, 1970. ***June 7, 1970. ****June 8, 1970. *****Elvis Presley (vcl, gtr), Edward Hinton, Chip Young (gtr), David Briggs (pno), Charlie McCoy (o), Norbert Putnam (bs), Jerry Carrigan (dms). Overdubbed at a later session: The Jordanaires, The Imperials, Millie Kirkham, Jeannie Green, Mary Holladay, Ginger Holladay (bv)
*****Recorded: RCA Studios, Nashville, Tennessee, September 22, 1970

For once, the cover – a faded depression-era photograph of the unsmiling, poverty-stricken Presley family – is indicative of the contents.

Elvis Presley's only bona fide concept album, it brilliantly illuminates one specific aspect of his musical heritage. As events demonstrated, it may have been his last truly inspired moment in the studio, but nonetheless, it possesses such rare qualities as to firmly place it amongst his finest canon of recordings.

Apart from *From Elvis In Memphis* (LSP-4155), not since the decade-old *Elvis Is Back* had Presley sounded so totally at ease with himself. And, furthermore, in complete artistic control of the project.

Drawn almost entirely from the June '70 Nashville marathon (34 songs in five days), it was systematic of the modus operandi he'd obsessively pursue right up until his death: stockpiling in excess of a year's worth of releases in practically one breath.

Discounting the two at-home Graceland dates (February and October '76), throughout the seventies, Elvis only ever entered the studio proper on eleven separate occasions*. In fact, discounting the inevitable live albums, he didn't record anything at all during 1974 and 1977.

Elvis' refusal to experiment with more contemporary musical forms was a recurring weakness, but paradoxically, as *Elvis Country* substantiates, it could also bring out his greatest strengths. For whereas many artists become sidetracked by persistent trend-hopping, Elvis never really encountered such dilemmas – simply by refusing to stray too far from base in the first instance. If Elvis exhibited one major deficiency, it was his often infuriating lack of taste in the selection of material. The success or failure of a project had as much to do with this haphazard characteristic as anything else. But, should, as *Elvis Country* vindicates, all the necessary components prove conducive, he'd deliver the goods right bang on the nail. For this unexpected return-to-the-roots odyssey, Elvis assembled his

repertoire from both traditional and contemporary sources: Anne Murray ('Snowbird'), Ernest Tubb ('Tomorrow Never Comes'), Jerry Lee Lewis ('Whole Lotta Shakin' Goin' On'), Jimmy Elledge ('Funny How Time Slips Away'), Bill Monroe ('Little Cabin On The Hill'), Eddy Arnold ('I Really Don't Want To Know'), Timi Yuro ('Make The World Go Away'), Jack Green ('There Goes My Everything'), Sanford Clark ('The Fool'), Bob Wills ('Faded Love'), Stonewall Jackson ('I Washed My Hands In Muddy Water') – and he used the traditional 'I Was Born About Ten Thousand Years Ago' (later released in its entirety on *Elvis Now*) as a kinetic link to fade in and out of every song. One can easily excuse the incongruity of Anne Murray's whimsical 'Snowbird' as the opening cut because the remainder of *Elvis Country* is otherwise filled to overflowing with consistent excellence. Nobly supported by guitarists James Burton and Chip Young, Area Code 615 stalwarts David Briggs and Norbert Putnam on piano and bass respectively, plus Charlie McCoy on harmonica and Jerry Carrigan's strident drumming, Elvis encounters no hardships – slipping effortlessly from the emotionalism of 'Funny How Time Slips Away', 'Make The World Go Away' and the immaculate 'I Really Don't Want To Know', straight into such ebullient rock-outs as 'Whole Lotta Shakin' Goin' On', 'The Fool' and 'I Washed My Hands In Muddy Water'.

Any way one approaches this album, it's clearly evident that Elvis' passion, enthusiasm and dynamism is thoroughly contagious. For example, with Chip Young scratching acoustic rhythm, James Burton picking electric lead and David Briggs bent on demolishing the keyboards, Elvis turns in the *best ever* cover of 'Whole Lotta Shakin' Goin' On'. What results is not a note-for-note facsimile, but a highly-personalized rendition that, in its own way, generates just as much hypertension and sense of purpose as the Lewis original.

In the final analysis, you'll have difficulty locating a better early '70s country rock album.

*1970: June 4–8, RCA Studios, Nashville (34 songs)
September 22, RCA Studios, Nashville (4 songs)
1971: March 15, RCA Studios, Nashville (4 songs)
May 15–21, RCA Studios, Nashville (30 songs)
June 8–9, RCA Studios, Nashville (6 songs plus 2 rejects)
1972: March 27–29, RCA Studios, Hollywood (7 songs plus the unreleased 'For The Good Times' BPA3 1150)
1973: July 21–25, Stax Studios, Memphis (9 songs plus 4 rejects) December 10–16, Stax Studios, Memphis (18 songs)
1975: March 9–12, RCA Studios, Hollywood (10 songs)
1976: February 2–8, Gracelands, Memphis (12 songs)
October 29–31, Gracelands, Memphis (4 songs plus the unreleased 'There's A Fire Down Below' FWA5 1051)

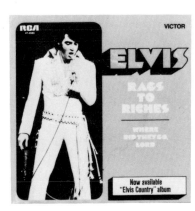

'Rags To Riches' (Adler, Ross) ZPA4 1798
'Where Did They Go Lord' (Frazier, Owens) ZPA4 1800
(US) RCA 47-9980
Released: March 1971

Elvis Presley (vcl,) Edward Hinton (gtr), Chip Young (gtr), David Briggs (pno), Charlie McCoy (o), Norbert Putnam (bs), Jerry Carrigan (dms), The Jordanaires, The Imperials, Millie Kirkham, Jeannie Green, Mary & Ginger Holladay (bv)
Recorded: RCA Studios, Nashville, September 22, 1970

Easter '71 – and Elvis sings an 18-year-old standard which, up until the release of 'I Left My Heart In San Francisco', was instantly recognizable as Tony Bennett's alternative signature tune.

The flip is associated with someone with an even bigger following!

1971

'YOU'LL NEVER WALK ALONE' (LP)
(US) RCA-Camden CALX-2472
Released: March 1971

Side 1
'You'll Never Walk Alone'
(Rogers, Hammerstein)
* 'Who Am I?' (Goodman) XPA5 1278
** 'Let Us Pray' (Wise, Weisman) ZPA4 1957
'(There'll Be) Peace In The Valley (For Me)'
(Foley)
'We Call On Him' (Karger, Weisman, Wayne)
Side 2
'I Believe' (Drake, Graham, Shirl, Stillman)
'It Is No Secret (What God Can Do)' (Hamblen)
'Sing You Children' (Nelson, Burch)
'Take My Hand, Precious Lord' (Dorsey)

Elvis Presley (vcl, gtr), Reggie Young (gtr, sitar),
Tommy Cogbill (gtr, bs), Johnny Hughey (ps),
Bobby Emmons (o), Bobby Wood (pno), Mike
Leech (bs), Gene Chrisman (dms), Ed Kollis (har).
Overdubbed at a later session: Millie Kirkham,
Sonja Montgomery, Dolores Edgin, Joe Babcock,
Hursch Wiginton, Mary Holladay, Sandy Posey,
Sandra Robinson, Donna Rhodes, Jeannie Green,
Donna Thatcher, Susan Pilkington (bv)
*Recorded: American Studios, Memphis,
February 22, 1969
Elvis Presley (vcl, gtr), remaining musicians
unidentified
**Recorded: MCA Studios, Hollywood,
March 6, 1969

Here the main attractions were manifold. The re-availability of all four *Peace In The Valley* EP tracks not seen or heard since *Elvis' Christmas Album*, a couple of rogue soundtrack rejects ('Let Us Pray' from *Change Of Habit* and 'Sing You Children' from *Easy Come, Easy Go*), plus an added bonus of three more unreleased God-rockers, prompted those fans who'd normally cold-shoulder the Camden repertoire to invest.

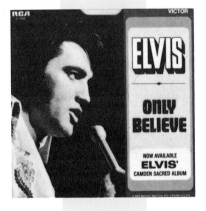

* **'Life'** (Milete) ZPA4 1613
** **'Only Believe'** (Reed, Stephens) ZPA4 1626
(US) RCA 47-9985
Released: May 1971

Personnel as June 1970 Nashville sessions
*Recorded: RCA Studios, Nashville,
June 6, 1970, **June 8, 1970
*June 6, 1970, **June 8, 1970

'Life' was a bizarre, if not totally out-to-lunch, attempt to set Darwinism to music. To Elvis eternal credit, he managed to sing it straight-faced.

The flip, 'Only Believe', was a turgid piece of gimme-dat-ole-time-religion.

⭐ ⭐

'LOVE LETTERS FROM ELVIS' (LP)
(US) RCA LSP-4530
Released: June 1971

Side 1
**** 'Love Letters' (Heyman, Young) ZPA4 1623
**** 'When I'm Over You' (Milete) ZPA4 1615
***** 'If I Were You' (Nelson) ZPA4 1625
** 'Got My Mojo Working' (Foster) ZPA4 1601
*** 'Heart Of Rome' (Stephens, Reed) ZPA4 1614
Side 2
***** 'Only Believe' (Raider) ZPA4 1626
*** 'This Is Our Dance' (Reed, Stephens) ZPA4 1610
* 'Cindy, Cindy' (Kaye, Weisman, Fuller)
ZPA4 1599
** 'I'll Never Know' (Karger, Wayne, Weisman)
ZPA4 1605
*** 'It Ain't No Big Thing (But It's Growing)'
(Merritt, Joy, Hall) ZPA4 1607
*** 'Life' (Milete) ZPA4 1613

Elvis Presley (vcl, gtr), James Burton,
Chip Young (gtr), David Briggs (pno),
Norbert Putnam (bs), Jerry Carrigan (dms),
Charlie McCoy (har). Overdubbed at a later
session: The Jordanaires, The Imperials,
The Nashville Edition, Millie Kirkham,
Jeannie Green, Mary & Ginger Holladay (bv)
*Recorded: RCA Studios, Nashville,
June 4, 1970. **June 5, 1970. ***June 6, 1970.
****June 7, 1970. *****June 8, 1970

Over the years Elvis may have been guilty of quite a number of inexcusable artistic transgressions, but one of the things he'd hitherto avoided was hanging an album's-worth of padding exclusively on a proven hit single.

Nevertheless, by the time whoever it was in charge of such things got around to sifting through the remains of the 34 songs that Elvis had laid down in Nashville between June 4 and 8, 1970, it was quite obvious that practically every meritorious moment had already been distributed on *That's The Way It Is* and, in particular, *Elvis Country*. As Elvis was about to commence his first-ever season at Lake Tahoe's Sahara Hotel (July 20–August 2), before moving back to Las Vegas for a fifth stint (August 9–September 6), the utilization of a re-recording of a still-popular 1966 hit must have seemed the only practical means of charming the would-be customers who, it appeared, revealed an affinity towards the more MOR side of Elvis' repertoire.

It's not that what remained from the Nashville marathon was entirely irredeemable – just that it suffered from the patchiness one would expect of material that had already passed over twice.

Things may not have been planned this way, but the only thing of intrinsic value contained herein is 'Got My Mojo Working' – a pulverizing studio jam of Muddy Waters' veneration of the metaphysical macho-man, which had accidentally been captured on a spool of tape.

'C'MON EVERYBODY' (LP)
(US) RCA-Camden CAL-2518
Released: July 1971

Side 1
'C'mon Everybody' (Byers)
'Angel' (Tepper, Bennett)
'Easy Come, Easy Go' (Weisman, Wise)
'A Whistling Tune' (Edwards, David)
'Follow That Dream' (Wise, Weisman)
Side 2
'King Of The Whole Wide World'
(Batchelor, Roberts)
'I'll Take Love' (Fuller, Barkan)
'Today, Tomorrow And Forever'
(Giant, Baum, Kaye)
'I'm Not The Marrying Kind' (David, Edwards)
'This Is Living' (Weisman, Wise)

These tracks appear to have been selected in much the same manner as many people pick racehorses—with a pin. Three tracks apiece from both *Follow That Dream* and *Kid Galahad*, and two each from *Viva Las Vegas* and *Easy Come, Easy Go*. A much better proposition would have been to lump together the entire contents of the first two soundtracks to replace the deleted EPs.

'ELVIS: THE OTHER SIDES—WORLDWIDE GOLD AWARD HITS, VOLUME 2' (LP)
(US) RCA LPM-6402
Released: August 1971

Side 1
'Puppet On A String' (Tepper, Bennett)
'Witchcraft' (Bartholomew, King)
'Trouble' (Leiber, Stoller)
'Poor Boy' (Presley, Matson)
'I Want To Be Free' (Leiber, Stoller)
'Doncha' Think It's Time' (Otis, Dixon)
'Young Dreams' (Kalmanoff, Schroeder)
Side 2
'The Next Step Is Love' (Evans, Parnes)
'You Don't Have To Say You Love Me'
(Wickham, Napier-Bell, Donaggio, Pallavicini)
'Paralyzed' (Blackwell, Presley)
'My Wish Came True' (Hunter)
'When My Blue Moon Turns To Gold Again'
(Walker, Sullivan)
'Lonesome Cowboy' (Tepper, Bennett)
Side 3
'My Baby Left Me' (Crudup)
'It Hurts Me' (Byers, Daniels)
'I Need Your Love Tonight' (Wayne, Reichner)
'Tell Me Why' (Turner)
'Please Don't Drag That String Around'
(Blackwell, Scott)
'Young And Beautiful' (Silver, Schroeder)
Side 4
'Hot Dog' (Leiber, Stoller)
'New Orleans' (Tepper, Bennett)
'We're Gonna Move' (Presley, Matson)
'Crawfish' (Wise, Weisman)
'King Creole' (Leiber, Stoller)
'I Believe In The Man In The Sky' (Howard)
'Dixieland Rock' (Schroeder, Frank)
Side 5
'The Wonder Of You' (Knight)
'They Remind Me Too Much Of You'
(Robertson)
'Mean Woman Blues' (DeMetrius)
'Lonely Man' (Benjamin, Marcus)
'Any Day Now' (Hilliard, Bacharach)
'Don't Ask Me Why' (Wise, Weisman)
Side 6
'(Marie's The Name) His Latest Flame'
(Pomus, Shuman)
'I Really Don't Want To Know'
(Barnes, Robertson)
'(You're So Square) Baby I Don't Care'
(Leiber, Stoller)
'I've Lost You' (Howard, Blaikley)
'Let Me' (Presley, Matson)
'Love Me' (Leiber, Stoller)
Side 7
'Got A Lot O' Livin' To Do'
(Schroeder, Weisman)
'Fame And Fortune' (Wise, Weisman)
'Rip It Up' (Blackwell, Marascaleo)
'There Goes My Everything' (Frazier)
'Lover Doll' (Wayne, Silver)
'One Night' (Bartholomew, King)
Side 8
'Just Tell Her Jim Said Hello' (Stoller, Leiber)
'Ask Me' (Modugno, Giant, Baum, Kaye)
'Patch It Up' (Rabbitt, Bourke)
'As Long As I Have You' (Wise, Weisman)
'You'll Think Of Me' (Shuman)
'Wild In The Country' (Peretti, Creatore, Weiss)

Although this collection's indispensable Earlier Self (RCA LPM-6401) had made it as high as No. 45 on the bestsellers (quite remarkable considering it was a four-pack), its slovenly-assembled clone lacked the chronological sensibilities of its predecessor; its attempt to

strike the same paydirt fared badly.

As the big money-pulling hits had, for the time being, been exhausted, *The Other Sides* tactic was to disguise the fact that, apart from putting a few hard-to-get items back into circulation the label was really stretching a one-off idea well beyond its limits.

By way of "compensation", the first batch included a remnant of The King's Old Clothes, reverently packaged *à la* Turin Shroud.

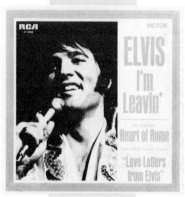

* **'I'm Leavin''** (Jarrett, Charles), APA4 1285
** **'Heart Of Rome'** (Stephens, Blaikley, Howard)
ZPA4 1614
(US) RCA 47-9998
Released: August 1971

Elvis Presley (vcl), James Burton, Chip Young, Charlie Hodges, Joe Esposito (gtr), David Briggs (pno, o) Joe Moscheo (pno), Charlie McCoy (o), Jerry Carrigan, Kenneth Buttrey (dms). Over-dubbed at a later session: The Imperials, Millie Kirkham, Ginger Holladay, Temple Riser, June Page (bv)
*Recorded: RCA Studios, Nashville, May 20, 1971
Personnel as June 1970 Nashville sessions
**Recorded: RCA Studios, Nashville, June 6, 1971

Yet another single that failed to leave any lasting impression.

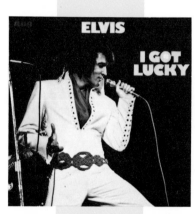

'I GOT LUCKY' (LP)
(US) RCA-Camden CAL-2533
Released: October 1971

Side 1
'I Got Lucky' (Fuller, Weisman, Wise)
'What A Wonderful World'
(Wayne, Livingstone)
'I Need Somebody To Lean On'
(Pomus, Shuman)
'Yoga Is As Yoga Does' (Nelson, Burch)
'Riding The Rainbow' (Weisman, Wise)
Side 2
'Fools Fall In Love' (Leiber, Stoller)
'The Love Machine' (Nelson, Burch, Taylor)
'Home Is Where The Heart Is' (Edwards, David)
'You Gotta Stop' (Giant, Baum, Kaye)
'If You Think I Don't Need You' (West, Cooper)

The companion to *C'Mon Everybody*, in that it supplied the missing pieces to the *Follow That Dream*, *Kid Galahad* and *Viva Las Vegas* puzzles. However, only three of the four remaining *Easy Come, Easy Go* tracks were included, with the non-movie song 'Fools Fall In Love' being substituted for 'Sing, You Children'. The only way to obtain this solitary song was to invest in yet another Camden compilation, *You'll Never Walk Alone*.

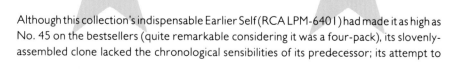

1971

'ELVIS SINGS THE WONDERFUL WORLD OF CHRISTMAS' (LP)
(US) RCA LSP-4579
Released: October 1971

Side 1
* 'O Come, All Ye Faithful' (Trad: arr Presley) APA4 1270
** 'The First Noel' (Trad: arr Presley) APA4 1271
** 'On a Snowy Christmas Night' (Gelber) APA4 1267
** 'Winter Wonderland' (Smith, Bernard) APA4 1268
** 'The Wonderful World Of Christmas' (Tobias, Frisch) APA4 1272
* 'It Won't Seem Like Christmas (Without You)' (Balthrop) APA4 1260
Side 2
** 'I'll Be Home On Christmas Day' (Jarrett) APA4 1266
* 'If I Get Home On Christmas Day' (McCauley) APA4 1261
* 'Holly Leaves And Christmas Trees' (West, Spreen) APA4 1263
* 'Merry, Christmas, Baby' (Baxter, Moore) APA4 1264
* 'Silver Bells' (Evans, Livingston) APA4 1265

Elvis Presley (vcl, gtr), James Burton, Chip Young, Charlie Hodge, Joe Esposito (gtr), David Briggs (pno, o), Joe Moscheo (pno), Charlie McCoy (o), Norbert Putnam (bs), Jerry Carrigan, Kenneth Buttrey (dms).

Personnel as May 1971 Nashville sessions
*Recorded: RCA Studios, Nashville, May 20, 1971.
Personnel as June 1970 Nashville sessions
**Recorded: RCA Studios, Nashville, June 4, 1970

For the second time in his career, Elvis sings the Santa Songbook. Despite the inclusion of a "personal" Christmas card, this collection not only failed to repeat the chart-topping success of the original 1957 *Elvis' Christmas Album*, but failed to chart at all. Seems the Christmas bucks had already been blown on the George Harrison & Friends' *Concert For Bangla Desh* boxed triple.

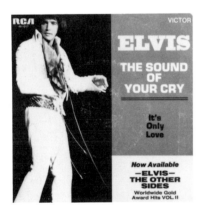

* **'It's Only Love'** (James, Tyrell) APA4 1287
** **'The Sound Of Your Cry'** (Giant, Baum, Kaye) ZPA4 1596
(US) RCA 48-1017
Released: October 1971

The May '71 Nashville sessions
*Recorded: RCA Studios, Nashville, May 20, 9171
The June '70 Nashville sessions
**Recorded: RCA Studios, Nashville, June 4, 1970

With all the promotional emphasis being shoved behind the four-album boxed set *The Other Sides—Worldwide Gold Award Hits Volume 2* (LPM-6402), this unmemorable single came and went so fast that today its very existence is a matter of philosophical debate in various citadels of the intellect.

* **'Merry Christmas Baby'** (Baxter, Moore) APA4 1264
** **'O Come, All Ye Faithful'** (Trad: arranged Presley) APA4 1270
(US) RCA 74-0572
Released: November 1971

Personnel as May 1971 Nashville sessions
*Recorded: RCA Studios, Nashville, May 15, 1971. **May 16, 1971

For the first time since 1966 ('IF Everyday Was Like Christmas'), Elvis chose to schedule a seasonal single. This time around, he placed a two-way bet: rock fans had the choice of the Charles Brown mid-'40s R&B classic 'Merry Christmas Baby' while for the more devout there was the traditional carol 'O Come, All Ye Faithful'.

1972

'ELVIS NOW' (LP)
(US) RCA LSP-4671
Released: January 1972

Side 1
**** 'Help Me Make It Through The Night'
(Kristofferson) APA4 1273
**** 'Miracle Of The Rosary' (Denson) APA4 1259
* 'Hey Jude' (Lennon, McCartney) XPA5 1157
***** 'Put Your Hand In The Hand' (MacLellan)
APA4 1290
**** 'Until It's Time For You To Go' (Saint-Marie)
APA4 1274
Side 2
**** 'We Can Make The Morning' (Ramsey)
APA4 1286
*** 'Early Mornin' Rain' (Lightfoot) APA4 1357
** 'Sylvia' (Stephens, Reed) ZPA4 1627
**** 'Fools Rush In' (Bloom, Mercer) APA4 1276
** 'I Was Born About Ten Thousand Years Ago'
(Presley) ZPA4 1595

Elvis Presley (vcl, gtr) Reggie Young (gtr),
Tommy Cogbill (gtr, bs), John Hughey (ps),
Bobby Wood, Ronnie Milsap (pno),
Bobby Emmons (o), Mike Leech (bs),
Gene Chrisman (dms), Ed Kollis (har).
Overdubbed at a later session:
Sonja Montgomery, Millie Kirkham,
Dolores Edgin, Joe Babcock, Sandy Posey,
Jeannie Green, Hursch Wiginton, Donna Rhodes,
Mary Holladay, Donna Thatcher,
Sandra Robinson, Susan Pilkington (bv),
The Memphis Horns, The Memphis Strings
*Recorded: American Studios, Memphis,
Tennessee. January 22, 1969
Elvis Presley (vcl, gtr), James Burton,
Chip Young (gtr), David Briggs (pno),
Norbert Putnam (bs), Jerry Carrigan (dms),
Charlie McCoy (har). Overdubbed at a later
session: The Jordanaires, The Imperials,
The Nashville Edition, Millie Kirkham,
Jeannie Green, Mary Holladay,
Ginger Holladay (bv)
**Recorded: RCA Studios, Nashville, Tennessee.
June 4, 1970 – 'I Was Born About Ten Thousand
Years Ago'
June 8, 1970 – 'Sylvia'
Elvis Presley (vcl, gtr), James Burton,
Chip Young (gtr), David Briggs (pno),
Norbert Putnam (bs), Jerry Carrigan (dms),
Charlie McCoy (har). Overdubbed at a later
session: The Imperials, The Nashville Edition,
Millie Kirkham, Jeannie Green, Mary Holladay,
Ginger Holladay (bv)
***Recorded: RCA Studios, Nashville,
Tennessee. March 15, 1971
Elvis Presley (vcl, gtr), James Burton, Chip Young,
Charlie Hodge, Joe Esposito (gtr),
David Briggs (pno, o), Joe Moscheo (pno),
Charlie McCoy (o), Norbert Putnam (bs),
Jerry Carrigan, Kenneth Buttrey (dms).
Overdubbed at a later session: The Imperials,
Millie Kirkham, Temple Riser, June Page,
Ginger Holladay (bv)
****Recorded: RCA Studios, Nashville,
Tennessee.
May 15, 1971 – 'Miracle Of The Rosary'
May 16, 1971 – 'Help Me Make It Through The
Night'
May 17, 1971 – 'Until It's Time For You To Go'
May 18, 1971 – 'Fools Rush In'
May 20, 1971 – 'We Can Make The Morning'
Elvis Presley (vcl, gtr), James Burton, Chip Young,
Charlie Hodge, Joe Esposito (gtr).
David Briggs (pno), Charlie McCoy (o),
Norbert Putnam (bs), Jerry Carrigan,
Kenneth Buttrey (dms). Overdubbed at a later
session: The Imperials, Millie Kirkham, June Page,
Sonja Montgomery (bv)
*****Recorded: RCA Studios, Nashville,
Tennessee. June 8,1971

The only half-decent moments on this collection had already been released as an indifferently selling single. That left only 'Fools Rush In' and 'I Was Born About Ten Thousand Years Ago.' The former gives one the impression that, like 'Don't Think Twice, It's Alright', it has resulted out of one of the many May '71 studio jams. It is based fair and square on Ricky Nelson's 1963 hit arrangement, and guitarist James Burton reworked virtually the same set of licks he'd originally picked on the Nelson version.

'I Was Born About Ten Thousand Years Ago' was the unspliced song that had been utilized to great effect as the in-between track on *Elvis Country*.

* **'Until It's Time For You To Go'**
(Sainte-Marie) APA4 1274
** **'We Can Make The Morning'** (Ramsey)
APA4 1286
(US) RCA 74-0619
Released: January 1972

Personnel as May 1971 Nashville sessions
*Recorded: RCA Studios, Nashville,
May 17, 1971. **May 20, 1971

Dissatisfied with his original May 17 recording of this snug Buffy Sainte-Marie love song (plus 'I'll Be Home On Christmas Day' which he'd attempted on May 16), Elvis re-entered RCA's Nashville studio on June 8 to re-cut these two titles along with material for his promised *His Hand In Mine* LP.

For whatever reasons, a second stab proved just as fruitless and so the May 17 tape was cleaned up and put on sale. It only reached No. 40 and, as such, failed to break Elvis' chain of unspectacular singles.

February 23, 1972:
Elvis and Priscilla legally separated

1972

* **'He Touched Me'** (Gaither) APA4 1277
** **'Bosom Of Abraham'**
(Johnson, McFadden, Brooks) APA4 1295
(US) RCA 74-0651
Released: March 1972

Elvis Presley (vcl), James Burton,
Chip Young (gtr), David Briggs (pno),
Norbert Putnam (bs), Jerry Carrigan (dms),
Charlie McCoy (har), The Imperials,
Millie Kirkham, Ginger Holladay,
Temple Riser (bv)
*Recorded: RCA Studios, Nashville,
May 18, 1971
Personnel as June 1971 Nashville sessions
**Recorded: RCA Studios, Nashville,
June 9, 1971

Including the RCA-Camden *You'll Never Walk Alone* compilation, Elvis had now released three "devotional" albums (*His Hand In Mine* and *How Great Thou Art* being the other two) since 1961. While over the years other celebrated rock stars had made much-publicized pacts with almost everyone from cosmic buffoons to Beelzebub, Elvis – true to his First Assembly Of God Church roots – kept faith with the great Jehovah. And seeing as how he was about to reaffirm his belief on record for a fourth time, this single was scheduled as a foretaste of what to expect.

'HE TOUCHED ME' (LP)
(US) RCA LSP-4690
Released: April 1972

Side 1
*** 'He Touched Me' (Gaither) APA4 1277
*** 'I've Got Confidence' (Crouch) APA4 1278
* 'Amazing Grace' (Trad: Newton/arr: Presley)
APA4 1256
**** 'Seeing Is Believing' (West, Spreen) APA4 1280
***** 'He Is My Everything' (Frazier) APA4 1292
***** 'Bosom Of Abraham'
(Johnson, McFadden, Brooks) APA4 1295
Side 2
*** 'An Evening Prayer' (Battersby, Gabriel)
APA4 1279
** 'Lead Me, Guide Me' (Akers) APA4 1275
***** 'There Is No God But God' (Kenny) APA4 1293
**** 'A Thing Called Love' (Hubbard) APA4 1281
***** 'I, John' (Johnson, McFadden, Brooks) APA4 1294
***** 'Reach Out To Jesus' (Carmichael) APA4 1291

Elvis Presley (vcl, gtr), James Burton,
Chip Young (gtr), David Briggs (pno),
Norbert Putnam (bs), Jerry Carrigan (dms),
Charlie McCoy (har).
Overdubbed at a later session: The Imperials,
The Nashville Edition, Millie Kirkham,
Jeannie Green, Mary Holladay,
Ginger Holladay (bv)
Recorded: RCA Studios, Nashville, Tennessee.
*March 15, 1971
Elvis Presley (vcl, gtr), James Burton, Chip Young,
Charlie Hodge, Joe Esposito (gtr),
David Briggs (pno, o), Joe Moscheo (pno),
Charlie McCoy (o), Norbert Putnum (bs),
Jerry Carrigan, Kenneth Buttery (dms).
Overdubbed at a later session:
The Imperials, Temple Riser, June Page,
Millie Kirkham, Ginger Holladay (bv)
Recorded: RCA Studios, Nashville, Tennessee.
**May 17, 1971. ***May 18, 1971.
****May 19, 1971
Elvis Presley (vcl, gtr), James Burton, Chip Young,
Charlie Hodge, Joe Esposito (gtr),
David Briggs (pno), Charlie McCoy (o),
Norbert Putnam (bs), Jerry Carrigan,
Kenneth Buttery (dms).
Overdubbed at a later session: The Imperials,
Millie Kirkham, June Page,
Sonja Montgomery (bv)
Recorded: RCA Studios, Nashville, Tennessee.
*****June 8, 1971. ******June 9, 1971

An exceptionally low chart placing (No. 79) for this all-new full-price album which, as with Elvis' Christmas fare, had milked a once profitable formula to death.

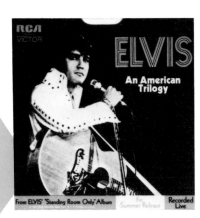

* **'An American Trilogy'** (Trad: arr Newbury)
BPA5 1147
** **'The First Time Ever I Saw Your Face'**
(MacColl) APA4 1255
(US) RCA 74-0672
Released: April 1972

Elvis Presley (vcl, gtr), James Burton,
John Wilkinson (gtr), Charlie Hodge (gtr, bv),
Glen D. Hardin (pno), Jerry Scheff (bs),
Ronnie Tutt (dms), Joe Esposito (perc),
J. D. Sumner & The Stamps, Sweet Inspirations,
Kathy Westmoreland (bv),
Joe Guercio & His Orchestra
*Recorded: Hilton Hotel, Las Vegas,
February 17, 1972
Elvis Presley (vcl, gtr), James Burton,
Chip Young (gtr), David Briggs (pno),
Norbert Putnam (bs), Jerry Carrigan (dms),
Charlie McCoy (har).
Overdubbed at a later session: The Imperials,
The Nashville Edition, Millie Kirkham,
Jennie Green, Mary & Ginger Holladay (bv)
**Recorded: RCA Studios, Nashville,
March 15, 1971

Whenever Elvis used to perform this irredentist musical cavalcade on stage, the effect it had upon certain sections of the audience was quite remarkable. Some people would weep unashamedly – others, their spirits uplifted, would stand to attention as if declaring allegiance to some mythical dynasty.

An amalgam of three traditional songs, it was identical to Mickey Newbury's original 1971 Elektra Records recording. Though Elvis' histrionic treatment was released around Easter – like Christmas, a period when songs containing overt sentimental, religious or nationalistic themes (this possessed all three) have a better-than-average chance of selling – 'An American Trilogy' dumbfounded almost everyone by completely failing to do the expected. There's speculation that the exceptionally lengthy playing time restricted saturation airplay.

'An American Trilogy' was planned as a fail-safe introduction to the scheduled *Standing Room Only* (LSP-4762) – see below – and one of three aces in the pack (the others being 'Burning Love' and 'Separate Ways'). Like *That's The Way It Is*, this album was planned as a half studio/half live soundtrack album to capitalize on the *Elvis On Tour* movie. However, not even Elvis' sensitive B-side interpretation of the Roberta Flack hit 'The First Time Ever I Saw Your Face' could stimulate sales of 'An American Trilogy' beyond No. 66. Confronted with such a commercial disaster, *Standing Room Only* was abandoned and attention promptly diverted to the Madison Square Garden caper.

What follows, by way of a float on your cola, is the original track listing for the unreleased *Standing Room Only* album:-

BPA5 1142 'Never Been To Spain'
February 14, 1972 unreleased
BPA5 1143 'You Gave Me A Mountain'
February 15, 1972 unreleased
BPA5 1144 'A Big Hunk O' Love'
February 15, 1972 unreleased
BPA5 1145 'It's Impossible'
February 16, 1972 APL-1-0283
BPA5 1146 'The Impossible Dream'
February 16, 1972 APL-1-2772
BPA5 1147 'An American Trilogy'
February 17, 1972 74-0672
BPA5 1148 'It's Over'
February 17, 1972 unreleased

BPA3 1149 'Separate Ways'
March 27, 1972 74-0815
BPA3 1150 'For The Good Times'
March 27, 1972 unreleased
BPA3 1151 'Where Do I Go From Here'
March 27, 1972 APL-1-0283
BPA3 1257 'Burning Love'
March 28, 1972 74-0769
BPA3 1258 'Fool'
March 28, 1972 74-0910
BPA3 1259 'Always On My Mind'
March 29, 1972 74-0815
BPA3 1260 'It's A Matter Of Time'
March 29, 1972 74-0769

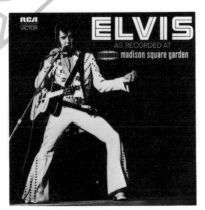

'ELVIS AS RECORDED AT MADISON SQUARE GARDEN' (LP)
(US) RCA LSP-4776
Released: June 1972

Side 1
'Introduction: Also Sprach Zarathustra' (Strauss)
BPA5 6797
'That's All Right (Mama)' (Crudup) BPA5 6774
'Proud Mary' (Fogerty) BPA5 6775
'Never Been To Spain' (Axton) BPA5 6776
'You Don't Have To Say You Love Me'
(Wickham, Napier-Bell, Donaggio, Pallavicini)
BPA5 6777
'You've Lost That Lovin' Feelin'' (Mann, Weil)
BPA5 6778
'Polk Salad Annie' (White) BPA5 6779
'Love Me' (Leiber, Stoller) BPA5 6780
'All Shook Up' (Blackwell, Presley) BPA5 6781
'Heartbreak Hotel' (Axton, Durden, Presley)
BPA5 6782
'Medley: (Let Me Be Your) Teddy Bear'
(Mann, Lowe)/'Don't Be Cruel'
(Blackwell, Presley) BPA5 6783
'Love Me Tender' (Presley, Matson) BPA5 6784
Side 2
'The Impossible Dream' (Leigh, Darion)
BPA5 6785
'Introduction by Elvis' BPA5 6794
'Hound Dog' (Leiber, Stoller) BPA5 6786
'Suspicious Minds' (James) BPA5 6787
'For The Good Times' (Kristofferson) BPA5 6788
'American Trilogy' (Newbury) BPA5 6789
'Funny How Time Slips Away' (Nelson)
BPA5 6790
'I Can't Stop Loving You' (Gibson) BPA5 6791
'Can't Help Falling In Love'
(Peretti, Creatore, Weiss) BPA5 6792

Elvis Presley (vcl, gtr), James Burton,
John Wilkinson (gtr), Charlie Hodge (gtr, vcl),
Glen D. Hardin (pno), Jerry Scheff (bs),
Ronnie Tutt (dms), J.D. Sumner & The Stamps,
The Sweet Inspirations,
Kathy Westmoreland (bv), Joe Guercio & His
Orchestra
Recorded: Madison Square Garden, New York
City, June 10, 1972

Following a fifth Las Vegas season (Jan–Feb), Elvis and his band flew to Buffalo where, on April 5, he kicked off a lengthy coast-to-coast concert tour – a junket which, except for a late summer Vegas residency (Aug–Sept), and a couple of other breaks, would take in thirty cities. Apart from being filmed by MGM for the proposed *Elvis On Tour* movie, this trek's highspot would be Elvis' triumphant return to New York City, where, over the weekend of June 9–11, he would give his first-ever Big Apple concert. Madison Square Garden was selected for this purpose. Over 80,000 tickets were sold in double-quick time for the four shows and a mobile recording unit brought in to capture the hoped-for hysteria.

As a direct result of this top-level decision, the album *Standing Room Only* (LSP-4762) was promptly scrapped to make way. That being the case, it seemed that Elvis was far more interested in being the focal point of what would prove to be the fastest-ever marketing operation in years than in instigating new standards in public performance. The idea behind this project was to record, process, press and ship an album of the Garden gig in less than two weeks. This part of the operation might have been brought in ahead of schedule, but in the rush to get the results of the Saturday night (June 10) concert into the stores, little attention was afforded the back-up matinee tapes, which, aside from including a scorching version of 'Reconsider Baby', revealed (in many instances) performances superior to those released. As to the contents of this album, half of the tracks had previously been available in "live" form on such collections as: *Elvis-NBC-TV* (LPM-4088), *From Memphis To Vegas – From Vegas To Memphis/Elvis In Person At The International Hotel* (LSP-6022), *On Stage* (LSP-4362) and *That's The Way It Is* (LSP-4445), while a "live" recording of 'An American Trilogy' (74-0672) had recently been on the singles chart.

The only tracks hitherto unavailable in any other form were covers of Three Dog Night's

'Never Been To Spain' and Ray Price's 'For The Good Times'. However, such repertoire repetition and the hurried, occasionally sloppy ambience of the proceedings didn't prevent the album from selling a few million worldwide.

For all the brouhaha, this album was regarded by all those actively involved as being nothing more than a production dry-run for an even bigger Presley project, the excruciatingly-titled *Aloha From Hawaii Via Satellite* (VPX-6089).

1972

'ELVIS SINGS HITS FROM HIS MOVIES VOLUME I' (LP)
(US) RCA-Camden CAS-2567
Released: June 1972

Side 1
'Down By The Riverside'/'When The Saints Go Marching In' (Trad: arr Giant, Baum, Kaye)
'They Remind Me Too Much Of You' (Robertson)
'Confidence' (Tepper, Bennett)
'Frankie And Johnny' (Gottlieb, Karger, Weisman)
'Guitar Man' (Reed)
Side 2
'Long Legged Girl (With The Short Dress On)' (MacFarland, Scott)
'You Don't Know Me' (Walker, Arnold)
'How Would You Like To Be' (Raleigh, Barman)
'Big Boss Man' (Smith, Dixon)
'Old MacDonald' (Starr)

Whichever way you approach the problem, it's quite evident that little (if any) artistic discretion was invoked when assembling the Camden budget series. With the exception of a few medium-sized hits and unreleased masters, it would appear that the only qualification a song required for inclusion was that it no longer possessed any further commercial viability to anyone except impulse purchasers.

To state that this album's title is somewhat misleading isn't overstressing the point. Only 'Big Boss Man' and 'Guitar Man' could remotely be termed *bona fide* hits.

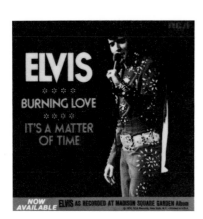

* **'Burning Love'** (Linde) BPA3 1257
** **'It's A Matter Of Time'** (Westlake) BPA3 1260
(US) RCA 74-0769
Released: August 1972

Elvis Presley (vcl), James Burton, John Wilkinson (gtr), Glen D. Hardin (pno), Emory Gordy (bs), Ronnie Tutt (dms), J.D. Sumner & The Stamps (bv)
*Recorded: MGM Recording Studio, Hollywood, March 28, 1972. **March 29, 1972

Contrary to speculation centred around his current inability to pick winners, both 'Burning Love' and the subsequent follow-up, 'Separate Ways' temporarily silenced the cynics by proving that even though they were now few and far between, Elvis still had access to some killer cuts.

A Dennis Linde original (previously waxed by both the composer and Arthur Alexander), 'Burning Love' was a loose-hip swinger, skilfully played and performed with genuine gut passion and peppered by the kind of dynamics by drummer Ronnie Tutt that had become somewhat thin on the ground in Elvis' repertoire. For good measure, Linde overdubbed an extra guitar part in Nashville under Felton Jarvis' supervision.

Justifiably, 'Burning Love' gave Elvis his biggest (and much needed) single smash—it reached No. 2.—since 'Suspicious Minds' topped the charts back in 1969. For some perverse reason, Elvis wasn't particularly enamoured of this gold-plated property. He didn't feel all that comfortable performing it, and took the opportunity to either drop it completely from his stage shows, or just skip through it with the same degree of disinterest with which he handled most of his back-catalogue. It's only other appearance on record is its inclusion on *Aloha From Hawaii*.

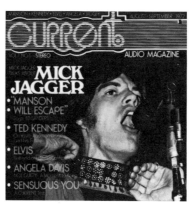

'CURRENT AUDIO MAGAZINE VOLUME I/NUMBER I AUGUST/ SEPTEMBER 1972' (LP)
(US) Buddah CM-VOL-I
Released: September 1972

Side 1
Mick Jagger Speaks About Mick Jagger (interviewer Elliot Mintz)
Manson Will Escape! Says Ed Sanders (interviewer Jamie Friar)
Current Audio Comedy—Robert Klein (interviewer David Goldman)
Teddy Kennedy On Youth, Dope, Abortion And His Future (interviewer Scott Friedman)
Angela Davis Not Guilty! (recorded by Karen McConnell)
The Monty Python Flying Circus
Side 2
Elvis Presley's News Conference (recorded by Hank Neyer)
The Killer Was A Narc (interviewer Larry Bensky)
Bella Abzug Loses (by Jeff Kamen)
Scoop's Column—Audio Mix By Scoop Nisker
Nader Group Hits Vega Despite Recall (by Rich Adams)
Crime Watch: Current Audio's Monthly Crime Column (by Jay Robert Nash and Kevin Mosley)
Sensuous You (by Jaye P. Morgan)

Speaking of totally redundant concepts—and we were—the half-baked idea behind this oddity was to introduce an audio equivalent of *Time* magazine. The trouble was that both radio and television had already got that kind of instant-reporting all sewn up. And, as this "audio magazine" proved, there's nothing less appetizing than yesterday's papers. This was the first and only release in the series.

So rumour has it, apparently Buddah didn't have rights to include the snippets of Elvis' June pre-Madison Square Garden gig press conference, and so the album was promptly withdrawn from circulation.

File under Useless Artifacts (it won't be lonely.)

* **'Separate Ways'** (West, Mainegra) BPA3 1149
** **'Always On My Mind'** (Thompson, James, Christopher) BPA3 1259
(US) RCA 74-0815
Released: November 1972

Elvis Presley (vcl), James Burton, John Wilkinson (gtr), Glen D. Hardin (pno), Emory Gordy (bs), Ronnie Tutt (dms), J.D. Sumner & The Stamps (bv)
*Recorded: MGM Recording Studios, Culver City, March 27, 1972. **March 29, 1972

Priscilla Beaulieu was quite probably the only person ever to stand up to Elvis and refuse to become intimidated and subjugated by his autocratic behaviour.

Priscilla's highly courageous decision—to show her disdain and contempt for Elvis' claustrophobic lifestyle by moving out of his home and into that of karate champion Mike Stone—had a schizophrenic effect on her spouse.

Elvis was regularly stricken with extreme moods of remorse, self-recrimination, fury—and a lust for revenge which, at one point, almost led to Mike Stone's assassination. However, only the first two characteristics were ever paraded in public.

Whether or not Elvis was genuinely heartbroken or just suffering from a deflated ego—having discovered that someone else *could* and *had* replaced him in Priscilla's affections—is debatable. Therefore, all this raises the question as to whether 'Separate Ways'—with its

1973

admission: "Maybe I didn't treat you quite as good as I should have"—is, as most fans interpret it, a bona fide epitaph to one of the Great Love Stories Of The Decade, or a carefully staged public relations exercise to (a) garner maximum sympathy and (b) divert attention from the truth that it was Priscilla that had wanted out and split. .

Whatever the motives, 'Separate Ways' supported by 'Always On My Mind' (an open letter to his young daughter) deals with a delicate subject in a most mature manner without ever becoming emotionally overwrought. A true classic of its kind.

'BURNING LOVE AND HITS FROM HIS MOVIES. VOLUME 2' (LP)
(US) RCA-Camden CAS-2595
Released: November 1972

Side 1
'Burning Love' (Linde)
'Tender Feeling' (Giant, Baum, Kaye)
'Am I Ready' (Tepper, Bennett)
'Tonight Is So Right For Love' (Wayne, Silver)
'Guadalajara' (Guizar)
Side 2
'It's A Matter Of Time' (Westlake)
'No More' (Robertson, Blair)
'Santa Lucia' (Trad: arr Presley)
'We'll Be Together' (O'Curran, Burke)
'I Love Only One Girl' (Tepper, Bennett)

In an effort to perk up the hitherto unspectacular chart success of the Camden re-issue programme, this was the first of two occasions when a recent blockbusting hit would be used as the title track. However, anyone anticipating the same standard to be maintained throughout the rest of the material was in for a big disappointment.

Only in Israel did the *Burning Love* LP appear on the RCA label (CS-2595), as opposed to Camden.

'SEPARATE WAYS' (LP)
(US) RCA-Camden CAS-2611
Released: January 1973

Side 1
'Separate Ways' (West, Mainegra)
'Sentimental Ways' (Cassin, Morehead)
'In My Way' (Wise, Weisman)
'I Met Her Today' (Robertson, Blair)
'What Now, What Next, Where To'
(Robertson, Blair)
Side 2
'Always On My Mind'
(Thompson, James, Christopher)
'I Slipped, I Stumbled, I Fell' (Wise, Weisman)
'Is It So Strange' (Young)
'Forget Me Never' (Wise, Weisman)
'Old Shep' (Foley)

January 8, 1973
Elvis celebrates his 38th birthday by suing Priscilla for divorce.

With 'Burning Love' having greatly contributed to the success of the *Burning Love And Hits From His Movies* Camden compilation (CAS-2595), Elvis' most recent hit single, 'Separate Ways', was employed as this budget album's title and point-of-sales interest. Other than that, it was third time around for 'Is It So Strange' and the dog-eared 'Old Shep'.

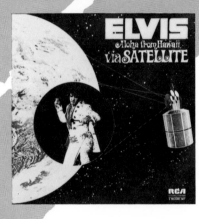

'ALOHA FROM HAWAII VIA SATELLITE' (LP)
(US) RCA VPSX-6089
Released: February 1973

Side 1
'Introduction/Also Sprach Zarathustra' (Strauss)
CPA5 4723
'See See Rider' (Rainey) CPA5 4724
'Burning Love' (Linde) CPA5 4725
'Something' (Harrison) CPA5 4726
'You Gave Me A Mountain' (Robbins)
CPA5 4727
'Steamroller Blues' (Taylor) CPA5 4728
Side 2
'My Way' (Anka, Rivaux, Francois) CPA5 4729
'Love Me' (Leiber, Stoller) CPA5 4730
'Johnny B. Goode' (Berry) CPA5 4731
'It's Over' (Rodgers) CPA5 4732
'Blue Suede Shoes' (Perkins) CPA5 4733
'I'm So Lonesome I Could Cry' (Williams)
CPA5 4734
'I Can't Stop Loving You' (Gibson) CPA5 4735
'Hound Dog' (Leiber Stoller) CPA5 4736
Side 3
'What Now My Love' (Sigman, Becaud, Delanoe)
CPA5 4737
'Fever' (Davenport, Cooley) CPA5 4738
'Welcome To My World' (Winkler, Hathcock)
CPA5 4739
'Suspicious Minds' (James) CPA5 4740
'Introductions By Elvis' CPA5 4741
Side 4
'I'll Remember You' (Lee) CPA5 4742
Medley: 'Long Tall Sally'
(Johnson, Penniman, Blackwell)
'Whole Lotta Shakin' Goin' On' (Williams, David)
CPA5 4743
'American Trilogy' (Newbury) CPA5 4744
'A Big Hunk O'Love' (Schroeder, Wyche)
CPA5 4745
'Can't Help Falling In Love'
(Pretti, Creatore, Weiss) CPA5 4746
'Closing Vamp' CPA5 4747

Elvis Presley (vcl, gtr), James Burton,
John Wilkinson (gtr), Charlie Hodge (gtr, vcl),
Glen D. Hardin (pno), Jerry Scheff (bs),
Ronnie Tutt (dms), J.D. Sumner & The Stamps,
The Sweet Inspirations, Kathy Westmoreland
(bv), Joe Guercio & his Orchestra
Recorded: Honolulu International Centre,
Honolulu, January 14, 1973

1973

This was The Big One. Motivated by the fast-buck success of the recent Madison Square caper, here was the opportunity to transform what had previously been just a grandiose idea into a massive money-spinning reality. Instead of Elvis having to tour the world, the premise of this project was to bring the world (specifically, the affluent Far East) to Elvis.

A television special staged in an exotic location would be transmitted live via telecommunication satellite to participating countries in precisely the same manner as Muhammad Ali's World Heavyweight title fights had made him as big an international Noise in his own right as Presley himself.

The thing Presley had over Ali was that this scheme allowed for a bonus pay-off: within days RCA would follow-through with a live double album of the historic event.

The venue selected was the Honolulu International Centre Arena. A complete dress-rehearsal was staged on January 13, but the actual date of Operation Aloha was the 14th, and the time of transmission, 12.30 am to coincide with Japanese prime-time viewing. For various reasons, presumably financial, only a few European networks screened an edited video the following day. Furthermore, due to programming schedules, it wasn't seen in the United States until April — in many other countries, not until after Presley's death.

Seeing as this was Elvis' second live LP in well under twelve months (his sixth in four years), many fans were becoming openly resentful about the predictable format and the constant duplication of songs. However, on this album, just before singing 'Something', Elvis clearly made a statement of intent, "We're gonna try and do all the songs you wanna hear". Nevertheless, only eight new songs out of the total 23 performed wasn't considered sufficient inducement to make this costly double album a compulsory purchase. What the loyalists didn't appreciate was that this was nothing more than an exercise in market-expansion. Elvis was courting a new and possibly larger audience, and seeking a way of vindicating himself from the stigma of the dreadful movie era. Though (at times), this album exposes the inherent problems of one-off concert recordings, Elvis did prove a point. Not only did the LP go straight to No. 1 on the US charts (selling in excess of two million copies), but the quadrophonic pressing became the first album of its type ever to notch up sales of over one million.

Granted, slightly more thought than usual had gone into the selection of the more familiar material, but the eight new songs didn't offer any revelations. Without exception, they were all second-hand: 'Something' (The Beatles), 'You Gave Me A Mountain' (Marty Robbins and Frankie Laine), 'Steamroller Blues' (James Taylor), 'My Way' (Frank Sinatra), 'It's Over' (Roy Orbison), 'I'm So Lonesome I Could Cry' (Hank Williams), 'What Now My Love' (Gilbert Becaud) and 'Welcome To My World' (Jim Reeves).

Nevertheless, as the mournful 'I'm So Lonesome I Could Cry' rightly affirmed, Elvis Presley still possessed the rare ability to personalize other artists' most familiar work. Indeed, this would have been a much better single choice than James Taylor's effete 'Steamroller Blues'.

The plan for the American TV screening of Aloha From Hawaii was to expand the original live footage into a Chicken-Of-The-Sea Tuna Company-sponsored 90-minute Special. For this purpose, once the live transmission was completed, the auditorium emptied and the orchestra packed off, Elvis — with minimal support from his rhythm section and singers — relaxed and, in a decidedly after-hours mood, recorded five more songs.

Four of them — 'Blue Hawaii', 'Hawaiian Wedding Song', 'KU-U-I-PO' and 'No More' — were sympathetic re-runs from the score of Blue Hawaii. The fifth song was Gordon Lightfoot's reflective 'Early Morning Rain'. In comparison with the Aloha From Hawaii Via Satellite, with the tension of the transmission over, Elvis, despite sounding vaguely tired, offers a much more relaxed approach.

Apart from incorporating all but 'No More' into the American version of the show, the intention was to add these five titles to Elvis (APL-1-0283). However, this idea was scrapped along with the idea of giving them to Camden. All five songs did finally appear on a Camden compilation, albeit Canadian, under the title Mahalo From Elvis (ACL-7064), while 'Blue Hawaii' suddenly popped up on Elvis — A Legendary Performer Volume 2 (CPL-1349).

For the collector, Aloha From Hawaii is a source of plunder. Though the original live transmission on January 14 was a benefit performance for the Kui Lee Cancer Fund, the American screening was "Chicken-Of-The-Sea"-sponsored. Prior to the double album's US release, a small quantity of albums was pressed up for promotional purposes with the "Chicken-Of-The-Sea" company insignia incorporated into the sleeve design and marked "sneak preview". Meanwhile, the nation's jukeboxes were serviced with a six-track EP (RCA 2006) comprising 'My Way', 'What Now My Love', 'I'm So Lonesome I Could Cry', 'Something', 'You Gave Me A Mountain' and 'I Can't Stop Loving You'.

It has never been revealed just how many millions of greenbacks this whole carnival pulled in. Whatever the amount, it wasn't bad going for an evening's work.

'ALMOST IN LOVE' (LP)
(US) RCA-Camden CAS-2440
Released: March 1973

Side 1
'Almost In Love' (Bonfa, Starr)
'Long Legged Girl (With The Short Dress On)' (MacFarland, Scott)
'Edge Of Reality' (Giant, Baum, Kaye)
'My Little Friend' (Milete)
'A Little Less Conversation' (Strange, Davis)
Side 2
'Rubberneckin'' (Jones, Warren)
'Clean Up Your Own Back Yard' (Strange, Davis)
'U.S. Male' (Hubbard)
'Charro' (Strange, Davis)
* 'Stay Away' (Tepper, Bennett) WPA1 1002

Elvis Presley (vcl, gtr), Scotty Moore (gtr),
Bob Moore (bs), D.J. Fontana,
Murrey "Buddy" Harman (dms),
The Jordanaires (bv), remaining musicians
unidentified
*Recorded: MGM Sound Studios, Culver City,
October 4, 1967

See entry for original release (November 1970).

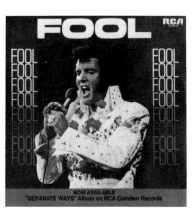

* **'Steamroller Blues'** (Taylor) CPA5 4728
** **'The Fool'** (Sigman, Last) BPA3 1258
(US) RCA 74-0910
Released: March 1973

Elvis Presley (vcl), James Burton, John Wilkinson,
Charlie Hodge (gtr), Glen D. Hardin (pno),
Jerry Scheff (bs), Ronnie Tutt (dms), Joe Guercio
& His Orchestra, The Sweet Inspirations,
J.D. Sumner & The Stamps,
Kathy Westmoreland (bv)
*Recorded: HIC Arena, Honolulu, Hawaii,
January 14, 1973
Elvis Presley (vcl), James Burton,
John Wilkinson (gtr), Glen D. Hardin (pno),
Emory Gordy (bs), Ronnie Tutt (dms),
J.D. Sumner & The Stamps (bv)
**Recorded: MGM Recording Studios, Culver
City, March 28, 1972

For someone who'd once all but been ridden out of town on a rail for daring to unleash unladylike passions in innocent young girls, Elvis' choice of James Taylor's metaphorically clumsy 'Steamroller Blues' was, by his standards of sexuality, quite inexcusable. It was delivered with tongue-in-cheek indifference, and offered titillation that wouldn't have offended even the most prudish of maiden aunts. Possibly, it was this customer-trade that made this single a Top 20 smash and kept it in the charts for three months straight.

Elvis On Tour/
Metro-Goldwyn-Mayer

Produced and Directed by
  Pierre Adidge and Robert Abel
Running time: 93 minutes
Released: June 6, 1973

'ELVIS' (LP)
(US) RCA APL-1-0283
Released: July 1973

Side I
******** 'Fool' (Sigman, Last) BPA3 1258
******* 'Where Do I Go From Here' (Williams)
BPA3 1151
***** 'Love Me, Love The Life I Lead'
(Macauley, Greenaway) APA4 1288
**** 'It's Still Here' (Hunter) APA4 1282
****** 'It's Impossible' (Wayne, Manzanero) BPA5 1145
Side 2
* 'For Lovin' Me' (Lightfoot) APA4 1258
** 'Padre' (Larue, Webster, Romans) APA4 1262
**** 'I'll Take You Home Again, Kathleen'
(Trad: arr Presley) APA4 1283
**** 'I Will Be True' (Hunter) APA4 1284
*** 'Don't Think Twice, It's All Right' (Dylan)
APA4 1269

Elvis Presley (vcl, gtr), James Burton,
Chip Young (gtr), David Briggs (pno),
Norbert Putnam (bs), Jerry Carrigan (dms),
Charlie McCoy (har). Overdubbed at a later
session: The Imperials, The Nashville Edition,
Millie Kirkham, Jeannie Green,
Mary & Ginger Holladay (bv)
*Recorded: RCA Studios, Nashville, Tennessee,
March 15, 1971
Elvis Presley (vcl, gtr), James Burton, Chip Young,
Charlie Hodge, Joe Esposito (gtr),
David Briggs (pno, o), Joe Moscheo (pno),
Charlie McCoy (o), Norbert Putnam (bs),
Jerry Carrigan, Kenneth Buttrey (dms).
Overdubbed at a later session: The Imperials,
Millie Kirkham, Temple Riser, June Page,
Ginger Holladay (bv)
**Recorded: RCA Studios, Nashville, Tennessee,
May 15, 1971. ***May 16, 1971.
****May 19, 1971. *****May 21, 1971.
Elvis Presley (vcl, gtr), James Burton,
John Wilkinson (gtr), Charlie Hodge (gtr, vcl),
Glen D. Hardin (pno), Jerry Scheff (bs),
Ronnie Tutt (dms), Joe Esposito (perc),
J.D. Sumner & The Stamps,
The Sweet Inspirations,
Kathy Westmoreland (bv), Joe Guercio & his
Orchestra
******Recorded: Hilton Hotel, Las Vegas,
Nevada, February 16, 1972
Elvis Presley (vcl, gtr), James Burton,
John Wilkinson (gtr), Glen D. Hardin (pno),
Emory Gordy (bs), Ronnie Tutt (dms),
J.D. Sumner & The Stamps (bv)
*******Recorded: RCA Studios, Hollywood,
California, March 27, 1972.
********March 28, 1972.

all wasting their energies on such rubbish? It might have been a different story if they had. It wasn't until *Our Memories Of Elvis Volume 2* that the almost unedited, full-length (eight-minute) version of 'Don't Think Twice, It's Alright' was officially made available.

This album's only feasible point of entry (the very last track), was manifested more by accident than intent, being a 2.45-minute snippet from a much longer unscheduled impromptu studio jam of Bob Dylan's 'Don't Think Twice, It's Alright'. Perhaps—as this track reveals—if Elvis had relied upon his instincts, rather than allowing himself to be railroaded into recording yet another Christmas album (and another devoted to religious incantations), he might have averted disaster. As it subsequently transpired, only 'Merry Christmas Baby' escaped the inbuilt redundancy of this project. But it would appear that, from the outset, Elvis wasn't remotely interested in the chore. Within hours of the commencement of the sessions, he was attempting to alleviate the acute 'tween-takes boredom by persuading his musicians to jam like fury on whatever old rock song immediately sprang to mind. It was during one such refuelling break that 'Don't Think Twice, It's Alright' resulted. This extract illustrates that the voice and the great sense of humour was still there and that when the spirit moved him, Elvis still possessed the ability to reach out and touch the listener. So why, one asks, if he was so disenchanted with the original task at hand, didn't Elvis scrap his nauseous and bogus repertoire and return to the rough-hewn and totally original style of yesteryear?

And why did none of the musicians have the guts to speak up and question why they were

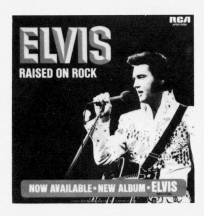

'Raised On Rock' (James) CPA5 4767
'For Old Times Sake' (White) CPA5 4768
(US) RCA APBO-0088
Released: September 1973

Elvis Presley (vcl), James Burton, Reggie Young,
Charlie Hodge, (gtr), Bobby Wood (pno),
Bobby Emmons (o), Tommy Cogbill (bs),
Jerry Carrigan, Ronnie Tutt (dms),
Joe Esposito (perc), J.D. Sumner & The Stamps,
Kathy Westmoreland, Jeannie Green,
Mary & Ginger Holladay (bv)
Recorded: Stax Studios, Memphis, July 23, 1973

Being forced to contrive what was once second nature underlines the state of Elvis' artistic impotence at this all-time nadir in his career.

October 11th, 1973:
Elvis and Priscilla legally divorced.

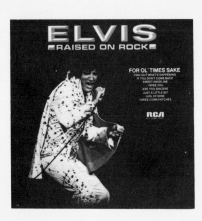

'RAISED ON ROCK' (LP)
(US) RCA APL-1-0388
Released: October 1973

Side 1
*** 'Raised On Rock' (James) CPA5 4767
****** 'Are You Sincere' (Walker) CPA5 4775
** 'Find Out What's Happening' (Crutchfield)
CPA5 4764
****** 'I Miss You' (Sumner) CPA5 4774
**** 'Girl Of Mine' (Reed, Mason) CPA5 4769
Side 2
*** 'For Ol' Times Sake' (White) CPA5 4768
* 'If You Don't Come Back' (Leiber, Stoller)
CPA5 4761
** 'Just A Little Bit'
(Thornton, Brown, Bass, Worthington)
CPA5 4766
***** 'Sweet Angeline' (Arnold, Martin, Morrow)
CPA5 4772
* 'Three Corn Patches' (Leiber, Stoller)
CPA5 4762

Elvis Presley (vcl, gtr), James Burton,
Reggie Young, Charlie Hodge (gtr),
Bobby Wood (pno), Bobby Emmons (o),
Tommy Cogbill (bs), Ronnie Tutt,
Jerry Carrigan (dms), Joe Esposito (perc),
J. D. Sumner & The Stamps,
Kathy Westmoreland, Jeannie Green,
Mary Holladay, Ginger Holladay (bv)
*Recorded: Stax Studio, Memphis, Tennessee,
July 21, 1973. **July 22, 1973. ***July 23, 1973
Elvis Presley (vcl, gtr), Bobby Manuel,
Johnny Christoper, Charlie Hodge (gtr),
Bobby Wood (pno), Bobby Emmons (o),
Donald "Duck" Dunn (bs), Al Jackson Jr,
Jerry Carrigan (dms), Joe Esposito (perc),
J. D. Sumner & The Stamps,
Kathy Westmoreland, Jeannie Green,
Mary & Ginger Holladay (bv)
****Recorded: Stax Studio, Memphis,
Tennessee, July 24, 1973. *****July 25, 1973
Elvis Presley (vcl, gtr), The Voice (bv),
remaining musicians unidentified
******Recorded: Elvis Presley's Palm Springs
home, California, September 24, 1973

Risking an album's chances by depending upon such a disastrous title track shows about as much foresight as renaming an ocean liner *Titanic*. It was doomed to instant failure. Moreover, a bunch of tawdrily performed R&B standards (that took up most of the second side) didn't improve matters. The album sold poorly, was quickly deleted from the catalogue and conveniently forgotten.

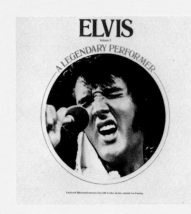

**'ELVIS – A LEGENDARY PERFORMER.
VOLUME I'** (LP)
(US) RCA CPL-1-0341
Released: January 1974

Side 1
'That's All Right (Mama)' (Crudup)
* 'I Love You Because' (Payne) G2WB 1080
'Heartbreak Hotel' (Axton, Durdon, Presley)
'Excerpt From "Elvis Sails"'
'Don't Be Cruel' (Blackwell)
*** 'Love Me' (Leiber, Stoller) WPA1 8119
*** 'Trying To Get To You' (Singleton, McCoy)
WPA1 8119
Side 2
'Love Me Tender' (Presley, Matson)
'(There'll Be) Peace In The Valley (For Me)'
(Dorsey)
'Excerpt From "Elvis Sails"'
'(Now And Then There's) A Fool Such As I'
(Trader)
** 'Tonight's All Right For Love'
(Wayne, Silver, Lilley) WPA1 8124
*** 'Are You Lonesome Tonight?' (Turk, Handman)
WPA1 8116
'Can't Help Falling In Love'
(Peretti, Creatore, Weiss)

Elvis Presley (vcl, gtr), Scotty Moore (gtr),
Bill Black (bs)
*Recorded: Memphis Recording Service,
Memphis,
July 5, 1954
Elvis Presley (vcl, gtr), Scotty Moore,
Tiny Timbrell, Neil Mathews (gtr),
Dudley Brooks (pno), Ray Siegel (bs),
D.J. Fontana, Bernie Mattinson (dms),
Jimmie Haskell (acc), Hoyt Hawkins (tam),
The Jordanaires (bv)
**Recorded: Radio Recorders, Hollywood,
May 6, 1960
Elvis Presley (vcl, gtr), Scotty Moore,
Charlie Hodge (gtr), D.J. Fontana (dms),
Alan Fortas (tam)
***Recorded: NBC Sound Studios, Burbank,
June 27, 1968

Even for the most discerning of fans, at whom this splendidly packaged collection was obviously aimed, the *Legendary Performer* series promised much more than was actually delivered.

The inclusion of the original unedited Sun recording of 'I Love You Because', plus three informal acoustic NBC-TV Special leftovers ('Love Me', 'Trying To Get To You' and 'Are You Lonesome Tonight?') couldn't camouflage the truth—that this was just another early Greatest Hits variant, complete with album-sized illustrated scrapbook. It was at moments like this that one genuinely regretted the phasing-out of the all-purpose EP. These four essential tracks would have been infinitely more appreciated in splendid isolation. Honestly, is there anyone whose life would be incomplete without the *sixth* re-issue of 'Heartbreak Hotel'?

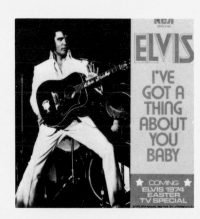

* **'I've Got A Thing About You Baby'** (White)
CPA5 4765
** **'Take Good Care Of Her'** (Warren, Kent)
CPA5 4763
(US) RCA APB0-0916
Released: January 1974
(for personnel see 'Raised On Rock' LP)
*Recorded: Stax Studios, Memphis,
July 22, 1973
**July 21, 1973

Considering that Tony Joe White's material was ideally suited to the distinctive Presley style, it's extraordinary that Elvis didn't delve further into the excellent whomper-stomper albums of Southern roots music White recorded for both Monument and Warner Brothers. Or, better still, commission this highly-imaginative artist to custom-write songs specifically for him. Indeed, White once declared openly that he would be willing to consider such a proposition.

By comparison, the depressive flip sounds strained and shoddy.

'GOOD TIMES' (LP)
(US) RCA CLP-0475
Released: March 1974
Side 1
* 'Take Good Care Of Her' (Warren, Kent)
CPA5 4763
**** 'Loving Arms' (Jans) CPA 1626
*** 'I Got A Feelin' In My Body' (Linde) CPA5 1618
****** 'If That Isn't Love' (Rambo) CPA5 1632
****** 'She Wears My Ring' (Boudleaux, Bryant)
CPA5 1634
Side 2
** 'I've Got A Thing About You Baby'
(White, Putnam, Malone, Young, Briggs)
CPA5 4765
**** 'My Boy' (Martin, Coulter) CPA5 1625
****** 'Spanish Eyes' (Kaempfert, Singleton, Snyder)
CPA5 1633
***** 'Talk About The Good Times' (Reed)
CPA5 1628
**** 'Good Time Charlie's Got The Blues' (O'Keefe)
CPA5 1627

Elvis Presley (vcl, gtr), James Burton,
Reggie Young, Charlie Hodge (gtr),
Bobby Wood (pno), Bobby Emmons (o),
Tommy Cogbill (bs), Jerry Carrigan,
Ronnie Tutt (dms), Joe Esposito (perc),
J.D. Sumner & The Stamps, Kathy Westmoreland,
Jeannie Green, Mary & Ginger Holladay (bv)
*Recorded: Stax Studio, Memphis, July 21, 1973
**July 22, 1973
Elvis Presley (vcl, gtr), James Burton,
Johnny Christoper (gtr), David Briggs,
Per Erik Hallin (pno, o), Norbert Putnam (bs),
Ronnie Tutt (dms), J.D. Sumner & The Stamps,
The Voice, Kathy Westmoreland, Jeannie Green,
Mary Holladay, Susan Pilkington (bv)
***Recorded: Stax Studios, Memphis,
December 10, 1973.
****December 13, 1973.
*****December 14, 1973.
******December 16, 1973.

A most inappropriate album title if ever there was one. To paraphrase The Kinks' Ray Davies, more like 'Where Have All The Good Times Gone?' Like so many artists before and since, Elvis Presley had fallen victim to a genuinely pathetic fallacy, that of his own artistic invincibility. The American Studio and RCA marathons (1969 and 1970 respectively) may have produced a preponderance of excellent finished masters, but Elvis was now under the grand delusion that quantity and quality were the same.

Whatever usable material had emanated from the July and December '73 Stax sessions had already been spread far too thinly over both *Raised On Rock* and *The Promised Land* and an exhumation order on the remains failed to produce anything of genuine merit.

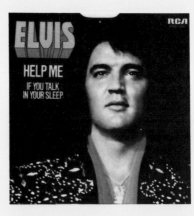

* **'If You Talk In Your Sleep'**
(West, Christopher) CPA5 1620
** **'Help Me'** (Gatlin) CPA5 1624
(US) RCA APBO-0208
Released: May 1974

Elvis Presley (vcl), James Burton,
Johnny Christopher (gtr), David Briggs,
Per Erik Hallin (pno, o), Norbert Putnam (bs),
Ronnie Tutt (dms), J.D. Sumner & The Stamps,
The Voice, Kathy Westmoreland, Jeannie Green,
Mary Holladay, Susan Pilkington (bv)
*Recorded: Stax Studios, Memphis,
December 11, 1973
**December 12, 1973

An irrelevant, clichéd account of the self-inflicted hazards of extra-marital shenanigans. The frailty of the song is further exposed by the over-arranged garishness of the instrumental accompaniment. The B-side is the studio version of the song premiered on *Recorded Live On Stage In Memphis*.

'RECORDED LIVE ON STAGE IN MEMPHIS' (LP)
(US) RCA CLP-1-0606
Released: June 1974

Side 1
'See See Rider' (Rainey) DPA5 0903
'I Got A Woman' (Charles) DPA5 0904
'Love Me' (Leiber, Stoller) DPA5 0905
'Trying To Get To You' (McCoy, Singleton)
DPA5 0906
Medley
'Long Tall Sally' (Johnson, Penniman, Blackwell)
'Whole Lotta Shakin' Goin' On' (Williams, David)
'Your Mama Don't Dance' (Loggins, Messina)
'Flip, Flop And Fly' (Turner)
'Jailhouse Rock' (Leiber, Stoller)
'Hound Dog' (Leiber, Stoller) DPA5 0911
'Why Me, Lord?' (Kristofferson) DPA5 0914
'How Great Thou Art' (Hine) DPA5 0915
Side 2
Medley
'Blueberry Hill' (Lewis, Stock, Rose)
'I Can't Stop Loving You' (Gibson) DPA5 0918
'Help Me' (Gatlin) DPA5 0919
'An American Trilogy' (Newbury) DPA5 0920
'Let Me Be There' (Rostill) DPA5 0921
'My Baby Left Me' (Crudup) DPA5 0926
'Lawdy, Miss Clawdy' (Price) DPA5 0927
'Can't Help Falling In Love'
(Peretti, Creatore, Weiss) DPA5 0929
'Closing Vamp' DPA5 0930

Elvis Presley (vcl,gtr), James Burton,
John Wilkinson (gtr), Charlie Hodge (gtr, vcl),
Glen D. Hardin (pno), Duke Bardwell (bs),
Ronnie Tutt (dms), J.D. Sumner & The Stamps,
The Voice, The Sweet Inspirations,
Kathy Westmoreland (bv),
Joe Guercio & His Orchestra
Recorded: Mid-South Coliseum, Memphis
March 20, 1974

It was now becoming evident that Elvis was troubled by the allegations and speculations of gossip columnists about his private life. This induced recurring bouts of paranoid rage, which, on occasions, erupted on stage. During a 1974 Las Vegas season, Elvis went so far as to stop the show to deliver a tirade against press stories which dealt with a paternity suit against him and alleged that he was using heroin.

First, Elvis introduced John O'Grady, the head of the Los Angeles Narcotics Division, to the audience, and then, holding aloft a pre-publication copy of O'Grady's memoirs, he claimed, "There's three chapters in here about the recent paternity suit filed against me. *He*," Elvis continued, pointing at O'Grady, "handled it, and it turned out to be a complete

1974

conspiracy and hoax. I had my picture taken with this chick – that's *all*."

If Elvis was succinct about that allegation, he was much more verbally aggressive about those rumours of his dabbling with drugs, and specifically that he cancelled shows not because of 'flu, but because he was smashed.

"From three different sources," ranted Elvis, "I heard that I was strung out on heroin . . . I've never been strung out in my life. They don't give you a Black Belt if you're strung out. These reports", he emphasized, "are damaging to my little daughter [Lisa Marie], to Priscilla, to my father, my doctor, my friends, everyone on stage and", he motioned to the audience, "to YOU." Whipping out a certificate and holding it up for inspection, he boasted, "This is from the International Narcotics Enforcement Association. *This*", he explained, flapping it around, "awards special honours and life membership of the Association . . . to ME!"

Perhaps, in his (often fuzzy) state of mind, Elvis genuinely believed that he didn't have a drug problem – an illusion common to heavy users. Though he never meddled with Heroin, drug abuse was cited by many as being the alleged cause of Elvis' death. During an hour-long investigation screened by NBC-TV in September 1979, claims of a cover-up were made by the channel, and Presley's personal doctor, Dr George Nichopoulos, was accused by NBC reporters of alleged professional neglect in that he regularly and grossly over-prescribed drugs to Presley – charges of which he was later cleared.

This album represents the first occasion in thirteen years that Elvis had chosen to perform on stage in his hometown of Memphis. An event of such importance, decided the Presley organization, should be preserved for posterity. It may well have been Elvis' second live album in 16 months, but it was assumed that his triumphant homecoming point-of-sales pitch would be sufficient in itself to drive the product up the charts. Actually, this album records the second of the three shows that Elvis gave in Memphis during the month of March (20–21). The first of the three shows was given on March 16–17. As both the *Madison Square Garden* and *Aloha From Hawaii* one-offs had emphasized, the problem of recording any Presley concert was that he was obliged to include many of his greatest hits, be it by full-blown treatments or in the form of a medley. They couldn't be axed, and though duplication of songs was kept to a reasonable minimum, this album was still primarily a back-catalogue re-run. The fact that it was presented with more enthusiastic commitment than either of his last two outings wasn't recommendation enough. It actually failed to repeat the success of his last two live albums (it reached No. 33) even though there was the consolation that it greatly outsold *Good Times*. Since sales response indicated that the live album formula lived no more, RCA made it clear that henceforth they'd pass on all in-concert collections until Elvis had worked-up a much stronger contemporary repertoire and a more positive, creative attitude to recording.

N.B. Anticipating that with sufficient radio exposure, Elvis' rendition of Olivia Newton-John's 'Let Me Be There' (one of the few *new* songs on this album), might create a demand for its single release, the publisher – Al Gallico Music Corp – decided to distribute 2,000 RCA promo-only singles of both the mono and stereo mixes of the song (RCA JH-10951).

It proved a wasted effort.

* **'Promised Land'** (Berry) CPA5 1629
** **'It's Midnight'** (Wheeler, Chestnut) CPA5 1618
(US) RCA PB-10074
Released: October 1974

Personnel: See 'Promised land' (LP)
*Recorded: Stax Studios, Memphis, December 15, 1973. **December 10, 1973

'Promised Land', apart from being arguably the best rocker that Elvis Presley released during the seventies, is an illustration of the total unpredictability of Presley when he was in a recording studio. Producer Felton Jarvis describes how one day (during a six-day session at Stax Studios in Memphis, in December 1973) had been arbitrarily set aside by Tom Parker for Elvis to cut a number of religious songs. When Jarvis arrived at the studio, Presley and his rhythm section were amusing themselves playing all the Chuck Berry songs they knew, and weren't about to break it up for any gospel session.

"Elvis didn't like to overdub. He figured it lost a whole lot of the spontaneity of the thing. He liked to sing right along with the band, move around and get those little extra accents and things. He'd move, and the drummer would add something. That was the way that Elvis liked to work on a song."

On 'Promised Land' Elvis seemed to have seized a unique chance to work on a classic rock 'n' roll song without anything to hamper him. One obvious question was – why didn't Presley have the chance more often? Felton Jarvis again:

"I'd have liked to have got him to do more rock stuff, things like 'Burning Love'. For a while it looked as though Elvis wanted to get back into rock 'n' roll. For the last couple of years, all he really wanted to do was ballads. I guess that he was down over his divorce or something, and ballads were closer to what he was feeling."

'HAVING FUN WITH ELVIS ON STAGE'
(LP)
(US) RCA CPM-0818
Released: October 1974

What other artists normally throw away as being worthless, the Presley organization kept and transformed into profit. Bottom-of-the-barrel scrapings of the worst kind. Nothing more illuminating than the in-between-song banter that had been edited out of the live albums, and originally sold exclusively at Elvis gigs on The Colonel's Box Car label. All one can add is that if God had wanted Elvis to be a professional comedian, he would have given him a funny nose, baggy pants, a banana skin, and an exploding guitar.

1975

'THE BRIGHTEST STARS OF CHRISTMAS' (LP)
(US) RCA DPL-1-0086
Released: November 1974

Side 1
'We Wish You A Merry Christmas'
Eugene Ormandy & The Philadelphia Orchestra
'Here Comes Santa Claus' *Elvis Presley*
'Winter Wonderland' *Danny Davis &*
'Winter Wonderland' *Danny Davis &*
The Nashville Brass
'Home For The Holidays' *Perry Como*
'Medley: It Came Upon A Midnight Clear/
Away In A Manger/The First Noel'
Henry Mancini & Chorus
Side 2
'Jingle Bells' *Julie Andrews*
'Joy To The World' *Ed Ames*
'Sleigh Ride' *Arthur Fiedler &*
The Boston Pops Orchestra
'Christmas In My Home Town' *Charlie Pride*
'Christmas Hymn—Hark! The Herald Angels Sing'
Robert Shaw Chorale
'Silent Night' *Sergio Franchi*

A *Various Artists* compilation sold exclusively at all J.C. Penney Stores

'PROMISED LAND' (LP)
(US) RCA APL-1-0873
Released: January 1975

Side 1
**** 'Promised Land' (Berry) CPA5 1629
**** 'There's A Honky Tonk Angel
      (Who'll Take Me Back In)' (Seals, Rice)
      CPA5 1631
*** 'Help Me' (Gatlin) CPA5 1624
*** 'Mr. Songman' (Sumner) CPA5 1621
*** 'Love Song Of The Year' (Christian) CPA5 1623
      Side 2
* 'It's Midnight' (Wheeler, Chesnut) CPA5 1618
*** 'Your Love's Been A Long Time Coming'
      (Bourke) CPA5 1630
** 'If You Talk In Your Sleep' (West, Christopher)
      CPA5 1620
*** 'Thinking About You' (Baty) CPA5 1622
** 'You Ask Me To' (Jennings, Shaver) CPA5 1619

Elvis Presley (vcl, gtr), James Burton,
Johnny Christopher (gtr), David Briggs,
Per Erik Hallin (pno, o), Norbert Putnam (bs),
Ronnie Tutt (dms), J.D. Sumner & The Stamps,
The Voice, Kathy Westmoreland, Jeannie Green,
Mary Holladay, Susan Pilkington (bv)
*Recorded: Stax Studio, Memphis,
December 10, 1973 **December 11, 1973
***December 12, 1973
****December 15, 1973

With the exception of the chart-topping *Aloha From Hawaii* (February 1973), Elvis' albums hadn't laid waste the upper reaches of America's charts for many moons.

Of his last six shots, only *Elvis Recorded Live On Stage In Memphis* had seriously bruised the Top 40, and even this, when compared with the impressive sales returns of his previous recorded concert appearances, had been dismissed by the accountants as a turkey. A new strategy was urgently required, but there really didn't seem to be anyone with the authority to introduce one. There was also the unavoidable dilemma of Presley's physical deterioration. On his last tour the very same press that had proclaimed his artistic resurrection a few years before now reported that Elvis was "paranoid, paunchy, worn out and often barely able to move."

In an effort to start the New Year on the right foot and stimulate more than just loyalist sales in Presley product, his last two Top 20 singles, the indifferent 'If You Talk In Your Sleep' and the truly rip-snorting 'Promised Land' (plus respective flips), were added to six December '73 Stax tracks.

The title was completely misleading: more a barren than a promised land. And yet the deficiency in quality is not wholly attributable to the singer; the fault lies largely in the weak choice of songs. Elvis himself was in pretty fine fettle vocally; but except for the diamond-in-the-rust 'There's A Honky Tonk Angel (Who'll Take Me Back In)', the album is an endless round of vapid late-hour country jukebox fodder suitable only for lovelorn winos and insomniacs. Like the authors.

1975

* **'My Boy'** (Martin, Coulter) CPA5 1625
** **'Thinking About You'** (Baty) CPA5 1622
(US) RCA PB-10191
Released: January 1975

Personnel: See 'Promised Land' (LP)
*Recorded: Stax Studios, Memphis,
December 13, 1973. **December 12, 1973

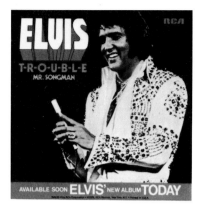

* **'T-R-O-U-B-L-E'** (Chestnut) EPA3 1599
** **'Mr Songman'** (Sumner) CPA5 1621
(US) RCA PB-10278
Released: April 1975

Elvis Presley (vcl), James Burton, John Wilkinson,
Charlie Hodge (gtr), Glen D. Hardin (pno),
David Briggs (clav), Duke Bardwell (bs),
Ronnie Tutt (dms).
Overdubbed at a later session: The Voice,
Millie Markham, Mary & Ginger Holladay,
Lea Jane Berinati (bv)
*Recorded: RCA Studios, Hollywood,
March 10–11, 1975
Personnel: See 'Promised Land' (LP)
**Recorded: Stax Studios, Memphis,
December 12, 1973

A former 1971 chart entry for hell-raising movie actor Richard Harris (the original hit recorder of 'MacArthur Park'). It's to Elvis' credit that he avoids over-dramatizing the obvious sentimentality of the song to concentrate on a controlled interpretation which was good enough to reinstate him quickly in the US Top 20. It was the very last time a single was to do so during his life.

First heard on *Good Times*, the track's selection as a US single (it had already been issued in the UK the previous October) was probably determined by the fact that months prior to its commercial release, Special Products' pressing (RCA 2458-EX) of 'My Boy' backed by another *Good Times* track, 'Loving Arms', was circulated around radio stations. However, a *Promised Land* track, 'Thinking About You', was chosen for US copies, spotlighting a superb (albeit extremely low-profile) performance by Elvis of what, in the hands of a much lesser talent, would have proved just an imponderable country song.

Not the malevolent *King Creole* classic of the same title, but a mercurial three-minute-flat spring-heeled barroom bopper, identical in style to the kind of salvo upon which Jerry Lee Lewis built his Wild Man Of Rock reputation. A blockbusting performance from everyone involved. 'T-R-O-U-B-L-E' evoked the same combustible intensity Elvis had rarely triggered since his NBC-TV Special. Spurred on by Ronnie Tutt's demented drumming. Elvis fired straight from the hip with covering fire from the duelling pianistics of David Briggs and Glen D. Hardin. This was rock 'n' roll as it was originally conceived and, coupled with his recent hit, 'Promised Land', this track dispelled persistent rumours that Elvis was too sick to cut the mustard. 'T-R-O-U-B-L-E' offered sufficient evidence that Elvis had caught a second breath, picked up the thread and was still capable of mixing it in the roughest of company. So why this remarkable single didn't top the charts, instead of crawling no higher than No. 35, remains to this day a perplexing unsolved mystery. At the time of its release Elvis was out on the road, packing in the SRO crowds nightly on a Southern trek, generating scenes of mass hysteria and grossing more greenbacks than most other rock groups of the time. It's inexplicable that not only the American public but the world at large didn't recognize a stone solid Elvis Presley classic when it bulldozed right over them. If that was the case, they didn't deserve better.

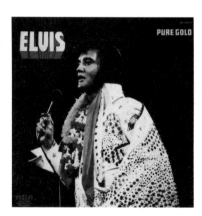

'PURE GOLD' (LP)
(US) RCA ANL-1-0971
Released: March 1975

Side 1
'Kentucky Rain' (Rabbit, Heard)
'Fever' (Davenport, Cooley)
'It's Impossible' (Wayne, Manzanera)
'Jailhouse Rock' (Leiber, Stoller)
'Don't Be Cruel' (Blackwell, Presley)
Side 2
'I Got A Woman' (Charles)
'All Shook Up' (Blackwell, Presley)
'Loving You' (Leiber, Stoller)
'In The Ghetto' (Davis)
'Love Me Tender' (Presley, Matson)

Instead of handing these titles over to Camden, attempting to collate a *Gold Records Volume 5*, or, better still, forgetting the whole idea, RCA carelessly put together ten unrelated tracks—many of which self-respecting Presleyophiles already owned in triplicate—and sold them at budget price.

'ELVIS TODAY' (LP)
(US) RCA APL-1-1039
Released: May 1975
Side 1
*** 'T-R-O-U-B-L-E' (Chestnut) EPA3 1599
*** 'And I Love You So' (McLean) EPA3 1597
*** 'Susan When She Tried' (Reid) EPA3 1598
** 'Woman Without Love' (Chestnut) EPA3 1600
** 'Shake A Hand' (Morris) EPA3 1601
Side 2
**** 'Pieces Of My Life' (Seals) EPA3 1603
* 'Fairytale' (Pointer, Pointer) EPA3 1594
* 'I Can Help' EPA3 1596
** 'Bring It Back' (Gordon) EPA3 1602
* 'Green Green Grass Of Home' (Putnam Jr) EPA3 1595

Elvis Presley (vcl, gtr), James Burton,
John Wilkinson, Charlie Hodge (gtr),
Glen D. Hardin (pno), David Briggs (el.pno),
Duke Bardwell (bs), Ronnie Tutt (dms),
The Voice, Mary & Ginger Holladay,
Millie Kirkham, Lea Jane Berinati (bv),
remaining musicians unidentified
*Recorded: RCA Studios, Nashville,
March 10, 1975. **March 11, 1975.
***March 10–11, 1975. ****March 12, 1975.

Elvis' last-ever official studio date (henceforth he'd only agree to record within the sanctuary of Graceland), and an album made under sufferance in Hollywood in four days flat.

The Man and his musicians were due in Las Vegas on March 18 for a season, after which they'd hit the road for 51 cross-country concerts before again returning to Sin City USA on

1975

August 18. During this gruelling itinerary the media unmercifully bad-mouthed Elvis for being pathetically out-of-shape. They implied that his stage show had become a sad parody of his many *Tribute To Elvis* imitators. By the time he reached Vegas in August, he was demoralized, ill and exhausted from the heavy work schedule and his frantic attempts at dieting. After three days, Elvis collapsed. The season was cancelled, and he checked into The Baptist Hospital in Memphis to recuperate.

Though his album sales had slipped drastically, three out of Presley's last four 45s ('If You Talk In Your Sleep', 'Promised Land' and 'My Boy') had still managed to scrape into the Top 20, and RCA desperately required a new consignment of Presley product if they were to try to sustain this modicum of success.

Given such short notice, this was one of the rare occasions when Elvis would employ the services of his entire regular road crew for a studio date. Perhaps it was the empathy that obviously existed between them that enabled Elvis to turn out a slightly more varied album than one would normally have predicted. Nevertheless, it still gave the distinct impression that he had become just as apathetic towards making records as he previously became to churning out conveyor belt movies.

Today was the second Elvis album in under six months that kicked off with a true-grit rocker ('T-R-O-U-B-L-E'). Whereas its predecessor (*Promised Land*) had careered downhill straight after the last strains of the Chuck Berry title-track had faded, *Today* took slightly longer to descend the slippery slope. This was simply because Elvis' balladeering on both Don McLean's 'And I Love Her So' and Porter Wagoner's 'Green Green Grass Of Home' was marginally more competent than one had now come to expect, while, for a change, his choice of The Statler Brothers' 'Susan When She Cried' and Billy Swan's 'I Can Help' affirmed that, contrary to belief, he was only besotted with *country* mawkishness. As recently as 1972 Elvis had publicly admitted the difficulty of securing good new material. "The people that are writing the songs", Elvis claimed, "are recording them."

Not so. On several occasions the likes of John Lennon, Paul McCartney, Bruce Springsteen, Roy Wood, Dave Edmunds and Nick Lowe had declared that they would be only too willing to write songs exclusively for Elvis. Led Zeppelin went even further. After meeting The Man, they went on record as saying that, if invited, they'd also be quite prepared to act as a house band on a record date.

Maybe he was never aware of such gestures. Certainly he never took up any of these offers. Meanwhile, it had become apparent that though the name Elvis Presley might still pull the concert crowds, the record buyers had deserted him.

* **'Pieces Of My Life'** (Seals) EPA3 1603
** **'Bring It Back'** (Gordon) EPA3 1062
(US) RCA PB-1-0401
Released: October 1975

Elvis Presley (vcl), James Burton, John Wilkinson, Charlie Hodge (gtr), Glen D. Hardin (pno), David Briggs (clav), Duke Bardwell (bs), Ronnie Tutt (dms).
Overdubbed at a later session: The Voice, Millie Kirkham, Mary & Ginger Holladay, Lea Jane Berinati (bv)
*Recorded: RCA Studios, Hollywood, March 12, 1975. **March 11, 1975

Seems that, with few respites, Elvis was either indulging himself in performing songs concerned with the tragedy of lost love or, as 'Pieces Of My Life' firmly illustrates, market-testing autobiographical man-of-the-world numbers in the hope that one of them would become as synonomous with his career as 'My Way' had become with Frank Sinatra's.

'ELVIS SINGS FLAMING STAR' (LP)
(US) Pickwick CAS-2304
'LET'S BE FRIENDS' (LP)
(US) Pickwick CAS-2408
'ALMOST IN LOVE' (LP)
(US) Pickwick CAS-2440
'ELVIS' CHRISTMAS ALBUM' (LP)
(US) Pickwick CAS-2428
'YOU'LL NEVER WALK ALONE' (LP)
(US) Pickwick CAS-2472
'C'MON EVERYBODY' (LP)
(US) Pickwick CAS-2518
'I GOT LUCKY' (LP)
(US) Pickwick CAS-2533
'ELVIS SINGS HITS FROM HIS MOVIES. VOLUME I' (LP)
(US) Pickwick CAS-2567
'BURNING LOVE AND HITS FROM HIS MOVIES. VOLUME 2' (LP)
(US) Pickwick CAS-2595
'SEPARATE WAYS' (LP)
(US) Pickwick CAS-2611
All released: December 1975

In August 1975 the Pickwick organization acquired the entire Camden budget line catalogue, and four months later re-issued all the Elvis albums under their own logo.

'DOUBLE DYNAMITE (LP)
(US) Pickwick DL2-5001
Released: December 1975

Side 1
'Burning Love' (Linde)
'I'll Be There (If Ever You Want Me)'
(Gabbard, Price)
'Fools Fall In Love' (Leiber, Stoller)
'Follow That Dream' (Wise, Weisman)
'You'll Never Walk Alone'
(Rodgers, Hammerstein)
Side 2
'Flaming Star' (Wayne, Edwards)
'Yellow Rose Of Texas/The Eyes Of Texas'
(Wise, Starr)
'Old Shep' (Foley)
'Mama' (O'Curren, Brooks)
Side 3
'Rubberneckin'' (Jones, Warren)
'US Male' (Hubbard)
'Frankie And Johnny'
(Gottlieb, Karger, Weisman)
'If You Think I Don't Need You' (West, Cooper)
'Easy Come, Easy Go' (Weisman, Wise)
Side 4
'Separate Ways' (West, Mainegra)
'(There'll Be) Peace In The Valley (For Me)'
(Dorsey)
'Big Boss Man' (Smith, Dixon)
'It's A Matter Of Time' (Westlake)

Multiplication is the name of the game!

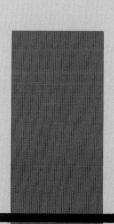

1976

**'ELVIS—A LEGENDARY PERFORMER.
VOLUME 2'** (LP)
(US) RCA CPL-1-1349
Released: January 1976

Side 1
* 'Harbour Lights' (Kennedy, Williams) EPA3 2742
'Interview With Elvis—Jay Thompson,
Wichita Falls, Texas. April 10, 1956.' EPA3 2744
** 'I Want You, I Need You, I Love You' (Alt. take)
(Mysels, Kosloff) G2WB 0270
'Blue Christmas' (Hayes, Johnson)
'Jailhouse Rock' (Leiber, Stoller)
'It's Now Or Never' (Schroeder, Gold, Di Capua)
Side 2
*** 'A Cane And A High Starched Collar'
(Tepper, Bennett) SPA3 6743
'Presentation Of Awards To Elvis—Pearl
Harbour, Hawaii. March 25, 1961.' EPA3 2743
***** 'Blue Hawaii' (Robin, Rainger) CPA5 4756
'Such A Night' (Chase)
**** 'Baby, What You Want Me To Do' (Reed)
WPA1 8120
'How Great Thou Art' (Hine)
'If I Can Dream' (Brown)

Elvis Presley (vcl, gtr), Scotty Moore (gtr),
Bill Black (bs)
*Recorded: Memphis Recording Service,
Memphis, (possibly) July 1954
Elvis Presley (vcl, gtr), Scotty Moore,
Chet Atkins (gtr), Marvin Hughes (pno),
Bill Black (bs), DJ Fontana (dms), Gordon Stoker,
Ben & Brock Speer (bv)
**Recorded: RCA Studios, Nashville,
April 11, 1956
Elvis Presley (vcl, gtr), Scotty Moore,
Tiny Timbrell, Neal Mathews (gtr),
Dudley Brooks (pno), Ray Siegel (bs),
DJ Fontana (dms), Jimmie Haskell (acc),
The Jordanaires (bv),
remaining musicians unidentified
***Recorded: 20th Century Fox Studios,
Hollywood, August 12, 1960
Elvis Presley (vcl, gtr), Scotty Moore,
Charlie Hodge (gtr), DJ Fontana (dms),
Alan Fortas (tam)
****Recorded: NBC Studios, Burbank,
June 27, 1968
Elvis Presley (vcl, gtr), James Burton,
John Wilkinson, Charlie Hodge (gtr),
Glen D. Hardin (pno), Jerry Scheff (bs),
Ronnie Tutt (dms), J. D. Sumner & The Stamps,
The Sweet Inspirations,
Kathy Westmoreland (bv)
*****Recorded: Honolulu International Centre,
Honolulu, January 14, 1973

'THE SUN SESSIONS' (LP)
(US) RCA APM-1-1675
Released: March 1976

Side 1
'That's All Right' (Crudup)
'Blue Moon Of Kentucky' (Monroe)
'I Don't Care If The Sun Don't Shine' (David)
'Good Rockin' Tonight' (Brown)
'Milkcow Blues Boogie' (Arnold)
'You're A Heartbreaker' (Sallee)
'I'm Left, You're Right, She's Gone'
(Kesler, Taylor)
'Baby, Let's Play House' (Gunter)
Side 2
'Mystery Train' (Parker, Phillips)
'I Forget To Remember To Forget'
(Kesler, Feathers)
'I'll Never Let You Go (Little Darlin')' (Wakely)
'I Love You Because' (1st version) (Payne)
'Trying To Get To You' (Singleton-McCoy)
'Blue Moon' (Rodgers, Hart)
'Just Because' (Shelton, Shelton, Robin)
'I Love You Because' (2nd version) (Payne)

Compiled and annotated by Roy Carr, the original intention of this project was to obtain official access to RCA's vaults and, if sufficient unreleased Sun material was to be found, use it to transform this package into a double album.

If, upon investigation, a companion-album's-worth of tracks wasn't forthcoming, other ideas were mooted: to include a "bonus" EP comprising various studio out-takes and false starts, similar to those that had previously appeared on the Dutch *Good Rockin' Tonight* bootleg or, if this were not acceptable, to settle for a single that coupled the hitherto twice-withdrawn 'Tennessee Saturday Night' with the original slow version of 'Blue Moon Of Kentucky'.

All these ideas were rejected. Moreover, despite the fact that RCA's British division were pushing for a Sun Sessions album, even the concept of gathering together all the previously released Sun sides was vetoed. As a result, it took almost two years before the initial idea became vinyl reality.

The reason why 'Tomorrow Night' was dropped from the final selection was purely a question of aesthetics. As the original Sam Phillips-produced backing track had been rearranged and refurbished by Chet Atkins in 1965, it no longer qualified for the album's state-of-the-art concept.

This album was originally released in Britain in August 1975 to launch RCA's Starcall budget series. Entitled *The Elvis Presley Sun Collection* (RCA HY-1001), the initial copies had an advertisement for other albums in the Starcall series printed on the rear sleeve as opposed to the familiar discography and sleeve notes. This album, complete with a different cover design, didn't appear in RCA's US catalogue until March of the following year, entering the charts the same month and peaking at No. 48.

In Britain, 'Blue Moon', 'You're A Heartbreaker' and 'I'm Left, You're Right, She's Gone' were released as a maxi-single.

Once again, just an EP's-worth of Presleyrama is fleshed out to make an album.

As with Volume 1, a solitary Sun track, in this case the hitherto unknown recording of the plaintive ballad 'Harbour Lights' (later a hit for The Platters), is dangled as the price of admission. (This track came to light when, following the death of Steve Sholes, the tape was discovered amongst his personal effects. In 1981, it was issued in Britain as a single.) The essential extras come in the guise of the familiar version of 'Such A Night' (but this time including the revealing false-starts to takes three and four) and, to complete the foursome, two more surplus acoustic NBC-TV out-takes: 'Blue Suede Shoes' and 'Baby, What You Want Me To Do'.

Considering that there were quite a number of takes from the Elvis TV Special still in the can, surely it would have been better to release them all at once, rather than filtering them out in twos and threes.

It needs to be said that only the bootleggers have an acceptable attitude to packaging such material.

N.B. On the inner-sleeve 'A Cane And A High Starched Collar' is given a recording date of February 9, 1961. It is commonly believed that this song was recorded on August 12, 1960, and that the February date refers to the time when 20th Century Fox handed over the tape to RCA-Victor.

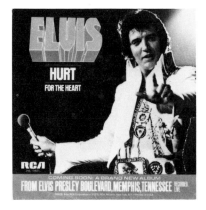

'Hurt' (Craine, Jacobs) FWA5 0672
'For The Heart' (Linde) FWA5 0671
(US) RCA PB-1-0601
Released: March 1976

Elvis Presley (vcl, gtr), James Burton,
John Wilkinson, Charlie Hodge (gtr),
Glen D. Hardin (pno), David Briggs (clav),
Jerry Scheff (bs), Ronnie Tutt (dms),
J. D. Sumner & The Stamps,
Kathy Westmoreland, Myrna Smith (bv).
Overdubbed at a later session: Chip Young (gtr),
Dennis Linde (bs), Shane Keister (synth),
Farrell Morris (cong, tymp), Wendellyn Suits,
Dolores Edgin, Hurschel Wiginton (bv)
Recorded: Graceland, Memphis,
February 5–6, 1976

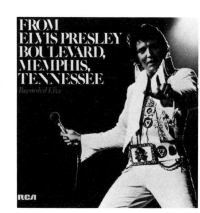

'FROM ELVIS PRESLEY BOULEVARD, MEMPHIS, TENNESSEE' (LP)
(US) RCA APL-1-1506
Released: May 1976
Side 1
**** 'Hurt' (Crane, Jacobs) FWA5 0672
***** 'Never Again' (Wheeler, Chesnut) FWA5 0674
****** 'Blue Eyes' (Rose) FWA5 0676
**** 'Danny Boy' (Weatherley) FWA5 0673
* 'The Last Farewell' (Whittaker, Webster) FWA5 0667
Side 2
**** 'For The Heart' (Linde) FWA5 0671
* 'Bitter They Are' (Gatlin) FWA5 0665
** 'Solitaire' (Sedaka, Cody) FWA5 0668
***** 'Love Coming Down' (Chestnut) FWA5 0675
*** 'I'll Never Fall In Love Again' (Donegan, Currie) FWA5 0670

Elvis Presley (vcl, gtr), James Burton,
John Wilkinson, Charlie Hodge (gtr),
Glen D. Hardin (pno), David Briggs (el pno),
Jerry Scheff (bs), Ronnie Tutt (dms),
J.D. Sumner & The Stamps, Kathy Westmoreland,
Myrna Smith (bv), Overdubbed at a later session:
Chip Young (gtr), Dennis Linde (bs),
Shane Keister (synth),
Farrell Morris (cong, tymp), Wendellyn Suits,
Dolores Edgin, Hurschel Wiginton (bv)
Recorded: Graceland, Memphis,
*February 2 & 3, 1976. **February 3 & 4, 1976.
***February 4 & 5, 1976. ****February 5 & 6,
1976. *****February 6 & 7, 1976
Elvis Presley (vcl, gtr), Bill Sanford,
John Wilkinson, Charlie Hodge (gtrs),
David Briggs (pno), Bobby Emmons (el pno),
Norbert Putnam (bs), Ronnie Tutt (dms),
J.D. Sumner & The Stamps, Kathy Westmoreland,
Myrna Smith (bv). Overdubbed at a later session:
Chip Young (gtr), Wendellyn Suits,
Dolores Edgin, Hurschel Wiginton (bv)
Recorded: Graceland, Memphis,
******February 8, 1976

For his first single of the year, Elvis feverishly raked the classic 1961 Timi Yuro heartbreaker over the emotional coals. Despite a psychotic, lip-quivering, over-the-top performance which all but resembles a P.J. Proby parody, it was again viewed by many as being autobiographical. Maybe it was a thinly-veiled plea for a reconciliation with Priscilla. Who knows! The fact was that Presley would now only agree to record within the guarded walls of his Graceland home, and thus such maudlin melodrama may have been a reflection of his depressive and often drugged state. The album which it previewed would reveal infinitely more. By comparison, 'For The Heart' was a much lighter shade of blue.

'HIS HAND IN MINE' (LP)
(US) RCA ANL-1-1319
Released: March 1976

This 'Pure Gold' budget release contains the same track listing to be found on RCA LSP/LPM 2328.

Taken purely at face value, just another in the line of predictable Presley packages, with the artist (attired in his familiar rhinestone combat catsuit) gracing the cover in characteristic carefree manner. Well, so it seemed. But the few who paid the price of admission discovered Elvis suffering from a most disturbing bout of melancholia.

For the first of his two at-home Graceland sessions (February 1976), Elvis planned to record a collection of predominantly forlorn slowies. "One of the problems", confided one of the musicians imported from New York for this date, "is he [Elvis] doesn't like fast songs anymore. He's just doing love ballads." What in fact emerged was an album of tortured, emotive blues wailing.

Plagued from the outset by persistent technical problems, Presley suddenly decided that he no longer liked his newly-constructed $200,000 home studio, or his musicians, or most of all, the way his records weren't selling. Particularly since the Graceland backing tracks had to be re-recorded, either in part or entirely, elsewhere. It seemed that Elvis was pining for the Nashville sound, Nashville musicians and the old RCA Studio where he had recorded so many of his earliest (and biggest) hits. Frustration, his explosive temper and erratic behaviour quickly got the better of him. One day Elvis bounded into the hated studio brandishing a loaded shotgun and threatening to blast the playback speakers and demolish all the rest of the costly recording hardware. He had gone beyond reason, and eventually had to be physically restrained.

Coupled with Elvis' losing battle with his weight problem, recurring bouts of ill-health and manic drug intake, this incident prompted musicians to claim that he was becoming extremely "difficult" to work with in the studio. And, they added, the range of his once magnificent voice had decreased. Perhaps slow songs were the only things Elvis could tackle comfortably!

Nevertheless, Elvis tries harder than he'd done in years on this album. The result is that the songs are laced with anxiety and tension. Finding himself against the ropes, Elvis totters precariously over the narrow ground that separates self-parody and prime-cut Presley.

Sometimes he can't cut it the way he used to, but when he catches a second breath he delivers with a positive vengeance.

Gone were the days when Elvis Presley could cruise through a record date on overdrive. He was now faced with the dilemma of fighting for artistic self-respect.

For all its misgivings, its lack of charm and humour, this is an album that reveals great courage. A blues collection which painfully exposes the soul of the man and, despite the depressing overtones, is required un-easy listening.

But this wasn't the side of their hero that most Elvis fans wanted to hear. The album only sold 400,000 copies, which, by Presley's standards, was close to a total disaster.

Soon after the album was released, to critical moans and groans, one of Presley's associates revealed: "Elvis really needs a hit record. His last album was cut at his place and it didn't sell well. And for him, that's not good enough.

"Oh sure, there were some songs on it that hit the charts – but not anything like he wanted. Elvis", he concluded, "is still thinking about those days back in '71, when each new record still sold a million."

Sadly, it was too late in the day for anyone to do anything about it.

'FRANKIE AND JOHNNY' (LP)
(US) Pickwick ACL-7007
Released: November 1976

Side I
'Frankie And Johnny'
(Gottlieb, Karger, Weisman)
'Come Along' (Hess)
'What Every Woman Lives For' (Pomus, Shuman)
'Hard Luck' (Weisman, Wayne)
'Please Don't Stop Loving Me' (Byers)
Side 2
'Down By The Riverside'/'When The Saints Go Marching In' (Trad: arr Giant, Baum, Kaye)
'Petunia, The Gardeners Daughter'
(Tepper, Bennett)
'Beginner's Luck' (Tepper, Bennett)
'Shout It Out' (Giant, Baum, Kaye)

Considering its superficiality, it's difficult to appreciate the commercial longevity of this particular Presley vehicle. Quite frankly, it doesn't even possess the perverse fascination to qualify for a so-bad-it's-good citation. In this mid-price manifestation, three tracks – 'Chesay', 'Look Out Broadway' and 'Everybody Come Abroad' – have been chopped. They're not missed.

* **'Moody Blue'** (James) FWA5 0669
** **'She Thinks I Still Care'** (Duffy, Lipscombe)
FWA5 0666
(US) RCA PB-10857
Released: December 1976

Personnel: See 'From Elvis Presley Boulevard' (LP)

*Recorded: Graceland, Memphis,
February 4 & 5, 1976
**February 2 & 3, 1976

This was the period when innumerable new releases (preferably in brightly coloured limited editions) were reduced to mere inanimate objects, suitable only for investment purposes, and not for actual spinning. The industry was quick to capitalize on this short-lived fad, which sometimes proved to be an artificial aid to an initial chart entry.

The first pressing of the *Moody Blue LP* was scheduled to be on royal blue vinyl, but for some reason the 'Moody Blue' single was used to experiment with various vinyl dyes. In all, 60 singles were manufactured – a dozen each in white, red, green, yellow and, naturally, blue. During the process, 25 percent of these samples were discovered to be defective and were promptly destroyed. The remaining 45 copies were then distributed amongst RCA company executives as keepsakes!

Closer to home, there were more immediate problems than the proposed gimmicky release of this boisterous singalong which, for all its Christmas cake frippery, relied far too heavily upon a painting-by-numbers formula favoured by chest-wigged Elvis supper-club clones, rather than an inspired performance from the man himself. Sadly, a gung-ho work-out wasn't forthcoming. Rumours had spread fast around Memphis that both Elvis Presley's mental and physical condition had now degenerated from bad to worse to terminal. When such news reached Elvis' long-time friend and professional adversary Jerry Lee Lewis, the self-proclaimed, "Killer", (who for years had indulged exessively in booze 'n' barbs but – due to a cast-iron metabolism – hadn't quite been reduced to a wreck), he took it upon himself to "save" Elvis.

Jerry Lee phoned Elvis and got himself invited over to Graceland before Elvis was due to leave the next day for an engagement in Reno. Hours later (at 3.07 am on November 23 to be exact), Jerry Lee was to be heard raising an unholy ruckus at Graceland's locked gates. He was as drunk as a skunk, and brandishing a loaded .32 Derringer pistol. The purpose of his appearance, the "Killer" duly informed security guard Robert Lloyd, was to speak and sing with his ol' buddy Elvis. The very next minute he was claiming, somewhat loudly, that his true intention was to either liberate or assassinate The King. It seems he couldn't quite make up his mind! When Lloyd informed Elvis of Mr Lewis' "condition", he was instructed to ignore Lewis who, no doubt, would soon drift back to wherever he'd emerged from. Jerry Lee refused to be either budged or humoured. Sometime later, Memphis patrolman B. J. Kirkpatrick arrived on the scene, and Lewis was promptly arrested (for the second time in 24 hours) for all manner of disorderly conduct. When bail was granted, Jerry Lee again turned up at Graceland, by which time Elvis had split. They never met up again.

Had they parlayed, perhaps they may have seen in one another the inevitability of their ways, promptly cleaned up both their acts and, as is often the case, been *born again*. On the other hand, with their shared fondness for pharmaceuticals and fire-arms, they might have embarked upon a crash-course of total self-destruction!

Jerry Lee Lewis – despite recent hospitalization – is still alive and still rockin'.

1977

'WELCOME TO MY WORLD' (LP)
(US) RCA APL-1-2274
Released: March 1977

Side 1
'Welcome To My World' (Winkler, Hathcock)
'Help Me Make It Through The Night'
(Kristofferson)
'Release Me (And Let Me Love Again)'
(Miller, Stevenson)
'I Really Don't Want To Know'
(Barnes, Robertson)
'For The Good Times' (Kristofferson)
Side 2
'Make The World Go Away' (Cochran)
'Gentle On My Mind' (Hartford)
'I'm So Lonesome I Could Cry' (Williams)
'Your Cheatin' Heart' (Williams)
'I Can't Stop Loving You' (Gibson)

Elvis Presley (vcl, gtr), James Burton,
John Wilkinson, Charlie Hodge (gtr),
Glen D. Hardin (pno), Jerry Scheff (bs),
Ronnie Tutt (dms), J.D. Sumner & The Stamps,
The Sweet Inspirations,
Kathy Westmoreland (bv),
Joe Guercio & His Orchestra
Recorded: Madison Square Garden, New York
City, June 10, 1972

Since RCA had received only a solitary album of brand new material from Elvis since June 1975, they desperately needed something (anything!) to try to prop up Presley's popularity as a recording artist.

Nothing was delivered.

Having been given the word that Elvis would henceforth record only in his home at Graceland, RCA had absolutely no alternative but to knock together a quick compilation of previously available material to cover everyone's embarrassment.

Half studio, the other half live, and a cover that didn't suggest this was a recycle job, its only real value to the Elvis fan who just had to have *everything* is the inclusion of 'I Can't Stop Loving You', which was extracted from the unreleased afternoon concert of the two shows recorded for the *Elvis As Recorded At Madison Square Garden* album.

While rummaging through those tapes, they should also have extracted the unreleased recording of 'Reconsider Baby'.

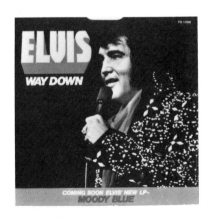

'Way Down' (Martine, Jr) FWA5 1049
'Pledging My Love' (Washington, Robey)
FWA5 1050
(US) RCA PB-10998
Released: June 1977

Elvis Presley (vcl), James Burton (ld gtr),
John Wilkinson, Chip Young, Charlie Hodge (gtr),
Tony Brown (pno), David Briggs (clav),
Jerry Scheff (bs), Ronnie Tutt (dms), J.D. Sumner
& The Stamps, Kathy Westmoreland,
Myrna Smith, Sherrill Nielsen (bv). Overdubbed
at a later session: the entire instrumental and
vocal backtrack with the exception of Charlie
Hodge, J.D. Sumner and Kathy Westmoreland.
Also, the following musicians were added:
Weldon Myrick (stl gtr), Shane Keister (synth),
Randy Cullers (perc)
Recorded: Graceland, Memphis,
October 29 & 30, 1976

From the tawdry evidence that has over-saturated the world's scandal sheets, by this late stage in the game, Elvis may well have been whacked out of his gourd on various lethal pharmaceutical cocktails, but his instinct for artistic survival hadn't altogether been rendered impotent. He could, as 'Way Down' indicated, still momentarily rise to the occasion. At a time when he was drowning in a sea of schmaltz, 'Way Down' depicts Elvis in the now uncharacteristic role of a rock 'n' roller – a bull-lung bellow slung over a crisp rock shuffle, with J.D. Sumner's sublime rich bass voice supplying the appropriate punctuation.

If, as subsequent events proved, it was checking-out time, then at least Elvis did it in style.

In Britain, 'Way Down' proved to be one of the biggest Elvis singles in living memory. It went to the very top of the charts on September 3 for one week, but on October 1, recaptured the top slot for a further fortnight. Meanwhile, the flip, Johnny Ace's 'Pledging My Love' suffers from some heavy-handed piano and a strained vocal. Overall, it's devoid of the lustre that Elvis was able to give such material at the time of the *From Elvis In Memphis* sessions.

'MOODY BLUE' (LP)
(US) RCA AFL-1-2428
Released: July 1977

Side 1
**** 'Unchained Melody' (North, Zaret) GWA5 2576
**** 'If You Love Me' (Rostill) GWA5 2574
**** 'Little Darlin'' (Williams) GWA5 2575
*** 'He'll Have To Go' (Allison, Allison) FWA5 1051
* 'Let Me Be There' (Rostill) DPA5 0921
Side 2
*** 'Way Down' (Martine Jr) FWA5 1049
*** 'Pledging My Love' (Robey, Washington)
FWA5 1050
** 'Moody Blue' (James) FWA5 0669
** 'She Thinks I Still Care' (Duffy, Lipscomb)
FWA5 0666
*** 'It's Easy For You' (Webber, Rice) FWA5 1048

Elvis Presley (vl, gtr), John Wilkinson,
Charlie Hodge (gtr), Glen D. Hardin (pno),
Duke Bardwell (bs), Ronnie Tutt (dms),
J.D. Sumner & The Stamps, The Voice,
The Sweet Inspirations,
Kathy Westmoreland (bv),
Joe Guercio & His Orchestra.
*Recorded: Midsouth Coliseum, Memphis,
Tennessee, March 20, 1974.
Elvis Presley (vcl, gtr), James Burton,
John Wilkinson, Charlie Hodge (gtr),
Glen D. Hardin (pno), David Briggs (el pno),
Jerry Scheff (bs), Ronnie Tutt (dms),
J.D. Sumner & The Stamps, Kathy Westmoreland,
Myrna Smith (bv). Overdubbed at a later session:
Chip Young (gtr), Dennis Linde (bs),
Shane Keister (Synth),
Farrell Morris (cong, tymp), Wendellyn Suits,
Dolores Edgin, Hurschel Wiginton (bv).
**Recorded: Graceland, Memphis, Tennessee.
'She Thinks I Still Care' – February 2 & 3, 1976
'Moody Blue' – February 3 & 4, 1976
'Moody Blue' February 3 & 4, 1976
Elvis Presley (vcl, gtr), James Burton,
John Wilkinson, Charlie Hodge, Chip Young (gtr),
Tony Brown (pno), David Briggs (el pno),
Jerry Scheff (bs), Ronnie Tutt (dms),
J.D. Sumner & The Stamps, Kathy Westmoreland,
Myrna Smith, Sherrill Nielson (bv).
The entire backing tracks, with the exception of
Charlie Hodge, J.D Sumner and Kathy
Westmoreland were completely overdubbed at
a later session, with the addition of:
Weldon Myrick (stl gtr), Shane Keister (synth),
Randy Cullers (perc).
***Recorded: Graceland, Memphis, Tennessee.
'Way Down', 'Pledging My Love' & 'It's Easy For
You' – October 29 & 30, 1976.
'He'll Have To Go' – October 30 & 31, 1976.
Elvis Presley (vcl, gtr), James Burton,
John Wilkinson (gtr), Tony Brown (pno),
Bobby Ogdin (el pno), Jerry Scheff (bs),
Ronnie Tutt (dms), J.D. Sumner & The Stamps,
The Sweet Inspirations, Kathy Westmoreland,
Sherill Nielsen (bv), Joe Guercio & his Orchestra.
Overdubbed at a later session: Alan Rush (gtr),
Bobby Ogdin (pno), Tony Brown (o),
Dennis Linde, Norbert Putnam (bs),
Randy Cullers (dms), Farrell Morris (perc & bells).
****Recorded: Civic Centre, Saginaw, April 25,
1977.

If, towards the end of his increasingly troubled life, Elvis Presley developed an abhorrence towards recording within the confines of a studio, he made no secret of his objections to having his concerts *officially* taped as an emergency product safeguard.

Whilst out on the road, Elvis would sometimes go as far as to harangue producer Felton Jarvis and his technicians over the microphone, truculently cut short many songs, intentionally mess up others, passing off his *playfulness* as self-mocking humour, and refuse to include more than a few token new songs (usually other artists' oldies) in his repertoire. Such perverse methods of complete artistic control were not only self-defeating, but meant that there was insufficient unheard *new* material readily available for commercial means.

Maybe it had slipped Elvis' opiated mind, but RCA had made it quite clear, some time back, that they didn't want another in the series of decreasingly-popular, repetitive live albums.

However, the theory that his reluctance to record was because the incontinence of his bizarre lifestyle had ravaged both his voice and once-handsome appearance is put in dispute by the fact that he not only continued to tour extensively, but had also agreed to allow CBS to film an *Elvis In Concert* TV Special to be transmitted in October.

Perhaps, illogically, Elvis Presley assumed that he now transcended both recording and movies as a satisfactory means of communication. It seems that his only gratification came from personal contact and the resulting hysterical scenes of fan worship that still accompanied the Messianic pomp of his in-person appearances before his followers. Around this time, Elvis said of his subjects, "I appreciate their wanting to see me and their loyalty. I intend to continue to perform as long as I'm able and for as long as they want me. I really love singing for my fans. It's my life. I want them to be excited and to go away saying 'Man! Wow!' I like to think that they remember us with pleasure, and look forward to us coming again. It's ironic, but it appears that history is repeating itself. My career is again as hectic as it was in the '50s. The people mob every arena. It's frightening. Somehow it doesn't seem normal. I'm grateful for their loyalty, but it's scary. I wonder what's next!"

This is the last Elvis Presley album released during his lifetime.

However, with only two unreleased Graceland titles at their disposal (a perfunctory 'It's Easy For You' and Jim Reeves' persuasive 'He'll Have To Go'), RCA had no option but to round up Elvis' last two Graceland session singles: 'Moody Blue'/'She Thinks I Still Care' (PB-10857), 'Way Down'/'Pledging My Love' (PB-10998), pilfer 'Let Me Be There' from the 1974 album *Elvis As Recorded Live On Stage In Memphis*, and pad it out with three hitherto unreleased songs they'd taped on April 25, 1977 at the Saginaw Civic Centre: Olivia Newton John's 'If You Love Me', 'Little Darlin' (a song first recorded in 1957 by The Gladiolas, and transformed into a world-wide chart-topper by The Diamonds) and finally, the much-covered Al Hibbler standard, 'Unchained Melody'.

It wasn't quite as simple as that.

On stage, Elvis had chosen to perform 'Unchained Melody' with only his own piano accompaniment. However, when it came to readying both this and the other two Saginaw songs for release, a rhythm section was over-dubbed, and extra instrumental tracks were re-cut to beef up the backings of both the chirpy country singalong 'If You Love Me' and the tongue-in-cheek 'Little Darlin'. Incidentally, when, after Elvis' death, RCA's Canadian cousins released a special limited edition white vinyl single of 'Unchained Melody' (11212), not only did they prefer to use the full 3.26 minute version (the album cut is noticeably truncated), but back it up with an *unobtainable-elsewhere* Elvis concert recording of Matt Monro's 15-year old British hit, 'Softly As I Leave You'. This is arguably one of the most eccentric of all Elvis' recordings. A me-and-my-shadow arrangement featuring Sherrill Nielsen's eerie wailing vocal, and Elvis intimately reciting the lyric. A tinkling piano plays, in what sounds like the next apartment!

Even though he was but a few months away from death, all three Saginaw songs, which open this album, corroborate eye-witness reports, that despite the slothfulness of his movements, there were still evenings when Elvis could summon together his artistic senses into some acceptable semblance of co-ordination, and redeem himself. But despite his aforementioned eagerness to appear in public, precisely why Elvis was allowed to tax his alarming physical condition nightly on stage remains unanswered. One can only assume that he was beyond reasoning with, and that nobody possessed either the authority or courage to ground him. However, despite his wish to continue until his fans no longer wanted him, in May of the previous year Elvis had confided to friends that the (100 concerts in 85 days) 1976 tour would most definitely be his last!

"This is the Bicentennial Year," said Elvis, "so if I hit 'em all, I can retire and not feel like I short-changed anybody. Physically," he admitted, "I'm not well enough to continue to keep doin' this." The poor state of his health wasn't the sole reason for Elvis to formulate retirement plans. Whenever Elvis toured, his daughter Lisa went to stay with her mother. "I think," said a tired but optimistic Elvis, "when we quit doing the road shows and everything, Priscilla and Lisa will move back home. It's always been the major problem. I wasn't home enough."

The Bicentennial Tour finished in Pittsburg on New Year's Eve. On February 12, 1977, Elvis was back out on the road, working an average of ten cities each month, and looking even worse than before. He gave his last concert in Indianapolis on June 26, 1977. Elvis Presley collapsed and died in his Graceland mansion on August 16, 1977.

The Graceland Sessions

FWA5 0665 'Bigger They Are, Harder They Fall'	February 2 & 3	APL-1-1506
FWA5 0666 'She Thinks I Still Care'	February 2 & 3	APL-1-2428
FWA5 0667 'The Last Farewell'	February 2 & 3	APL-1-1506
FWA5 0668 'Solitaire'	February 3 & 4	APL-1-1506
FWA5 0669 'Moody Blue'	February 4 & 5	AFL-1-2428
FWA5 0670 'I'll Never Fall In Love Again'	February 4 & 5	APL-1-1506
FWA5 0671 'For The Heart'	February 5 & 6	APL-1-1506
FWA5 0672 'Hurt'	February 5 & 6	APL-1-1506
FWA5 0673 'Danny Boy'	February 5 & 6	APL-1-1506
FWA5 0674 'Never Again'	February 6 & 7	APL-1-1506
FWA5 0675 'Love Comin' Down'	February 6 & 7	APL-1-1506
FWA5 0676 'Blue Eyes Crying In The Rain'	February 8	APL-1-1506
FWA5 1048 'It's Easy For You'	October 29 & 30	AFL-1-2428
FWA5 1049 'Way Down'	October 29 & 30	AFL-1-2428
FWA5 1050 'Pledging My Love'	October 29 & 30	AFL-1-2428
FWA5 1051 'There's A Fire Down Below'	October 30 & 31	unreleased
FWA5 1052 'He'll Have To Go'	October 30 & 31	AFL-1-2428

1977

'ELVIS IN CONCERT' (LP)
(US) RCA APL2-2587
Released: October 1977

Side 1
Elvis' Fans Comments/Opening Riff
'Also Sprach Zarathustra' (Strauss) GPA5 0435
'See See Rider' (Rainey) GPA5 0423
'That's All Right (Mama)' (Crudup) GPA5 0425
'Are You Lonesome Tonight' (Turk, Handman)
GPA5 0426
Medley
'(Let Me Be Your) Teddy Bear' (Mann, Lowe)/
'Don't Be Cruel' (Blackwell, Presley) GPA5 0434
Elvis' Fans Comments
'You Gave Me A Mountain' (Robbins)
GPA5 0429
'Jailhouse Rock' (Leiber, Stoller) GPA5 0430
Side 2
Elvis' Fans Comments
'How Great Thou Art' (Hine) GPA5 0448
Elvis' Fans Comments
'I Really Don't Want To Know'
(Barnes, Robertson) GPA5 0440
Elvis Introduces His Father
'Hurt' (Crane, Jacobs) GPA5 0441
'Hound Dog' (Leiber, Stoller) GPA5 0442
'My Way' (Anka, Revaux, Francois) GPA5 0436
'Can't Help Falling In Love'
(Peretti, Creatore, Weiss) GPA5 0444
Closing Riff
Special Message From Elvis' Father
Side 3
Medley
'I Got A Woman' (Charles)/'Amen' (Trad)
GPA5 0424
Elvis Talks
'Love Me' (Leiber, Stoller) GPA5 0427
'If You Love Me (Let Me Know)' (Rostill)
GPA5 0428
Medley:
'O Sole Mio'/'It's Now Or Never' (Di
Capua, Capurro, Schroeder, Gold) GPA5 0431
'Trying To Get To You' (McCoy, Singleton)
GPA5 0432
Side 4
'Hawaiian Wedding Song'
(King, Hoffman, Manning) GPA5 0433
'Fairytale' (Pointer, Pointer) GPA5 0445
'Little Sister' (Pomus, Shuman) GPA5 0446
'Early Mornin' Rain' (Lightfoot) GPA5 0437
'What'd I Say' (Charles) GPA5 0438
'Johnny B. Goode' (Berry) GPA5 0439
'And I Love You So' (McLean) GPA5 0447

Elvis Presley (vcl, gtr), James Burton,
John Wilkinson, Charlie Hodge (gtr),
Tony Brown (pno), Jerry Scheff (bs),
Larry Londin (dms), J.D. Sumner & The Stamps,
The Sweet Inspirations, Kathy Westmoreland,
Sherrill Nielsen (bv), Joe Guercio & His
Orchestra
Recorded: Omaha, June 19, 1977; Rapid City,
June 21, 1977

The four majestic full-colour portraits of Elvis Presley that adorn this sleeve offer absolutely no indication of the tragedy hidden within.

This album was recorded in June 1977. Two months later, The King Of Rock 'N' Roll was dead.

This is the sound of his death-rattle, although prior to his demise it was not scheduled for commercial release.

In the mid-'50s, television had been instrumental in propagating the Presley phenomenon on an unprecedented national scale. Furthermore, in both 1960 and 1968 the medium was effectively employed to instigate crucial public comebacks. Once again, in 1973, television gave Elvis a new, if short-term, career lease, when the money-spinning *Aloha From Hawaii* project catapulted the accompanying soundtrack souvenir to the very summit of the international charts. It was assumed, erroneously, that if supported by sufficient promotional drum-beating, a similar TV Special could reinstate Elvis' reputation while successfully appropriating the domestic dollar. The trouble was, that Elvis was no

longer the performer he was in 1973. Bloated to the point of grotesquerie, his once leonine physical charisma and dazzling voice had all but deserted him.

Instead he was jaded, breathless, exhausted and so old beyond his years that he was hardly able to move. He also encountered great difficulty in remembering his lyrics, hitherto one of his more dependable virtues. Sensing, no doubt, that they were accompanying a dying man, Elvis' band and singers formed a united-front, making every conceivable attempt to tighten his laborious task. If ever a band earned their wages, they did so on this album.

Obviously, Elvis shouldn't have been performing in such a terrible condition. Out of respect to his memory, both the CBS-TV Special and this, the soundtrack, should have been scrapped.

It has been alleged that having seen some of the rushes, horrified CBS executives held top-level discussions about postponing the project and reshooting it later, should Elvis get himself back into shape.

But Elvis was dead and buried when this travesty was screened, allegedly because of its "historic significance"! Had it been shown during his lifetime, it would have caused more irrevocable damage to what was left of his career than almost a decade of starring in third-rate movies.

At the conclusion of this TV Special, Elvis Presley's distraught father, Vernon, went before the cameras and, fighting back the tears, explained that the viewers had just witnessed his son's last public performance. He concluded by thanking everyone for their condolences in his time of grief.

On June 26, 1979 Vernon Presley died, aged 63, of a broken heart.

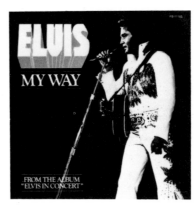

* **'My Way'** (Anka, Revaux, Francois) GPA5 0436
* **'America'** (Trad: arranged Presley)
CPKM 3809
(US) RCA PB-11165
Released: October 1977

Elvis Presley (vcl), James Burton (ld gtr),
John Wilkinson, Charlie Hodge (gtr),
Tony Brown (pno), Jerry Scheff (bs),
Larry Londin (dms), Joe Guercio & His
Orchestra, The Sweet Inspirations, J.D. Sumner
& The Stamps, Kathy Westmoreland,
Sherrill Nielsen (bv)
*Recorded: Either Omaha, June 19, 1977 or
Rapid City, June 21, 1977
Elvis Presley (vcl), James Burton (ld gtr),
John Wilkinson, Charlie Hodge (gtr),
Glen D. Hardin (pno), Jerry Scheff (bs),
Ronnie Tutt (dms), Joe Guercio & His Orchestra,
The Sweet Inspirations, J.D. Sumner &
The Stamps, Kathy Westmoreland,
Sherrill Nielsen (bv)
**Recorded: No details are known, but believed
to have been recorded in Las Vegas with
(possibly) the line-up above in either December
1975 or 1976

So that it wouldn't seem too blue a Christmas without him, Elvis' first posthumous single was now released.

It didn't much matter that this dour paean to self-glorification had, over the years, been mauled beyond all semblance of recognition by every two-bit bar-fly. Under the circumstances, it seemed reasonably appropriate that Elvis' interpretation should be employed as a vinyl epitaph.

The anthemic 'America' further emphasized the muffled-drum solemnity of the occasion. Here Presley's red-blooded patriotism was run up the flagpole in a veritable blaze of wide-screen pomp, that eclipsed even 'An American Trilogy' for stoically formularized stars 'n' stripes ostentation.

1978

'HE WALKS BESIDE ME—FAVOURITE SONGS OF FAITH AND INSPIRATION'
(LP)
(US) RCA AFL-1-2772
Released: February 1978

Side I
'He Is My Everything' (Frazier)
'Miracle Of The Rosary' (Denson)
'Where Did They Go, Lord?' (Frazier, Owens)
'Somebody Bigger Than You And I'
(Heath, Burke, Lange)
'An Evening Prayer' (Battersby, Gabriel)
** 'The Impossible Dream (The Quest)'
(Leight, Darion) BPA5 1146
Side 2
* 'If I Can Dream' (Brown)
'Padre' (Romans, LaRue, Webster)
'Known Only To Him' (Hamblen)
'Who Am I?' (Goodman)
'How Great Thou Art' (Hine)

Elvis Presley (vcl, gtr), Tommy Tedesco,
Mike Deasy (gtr), Don Randi (pno),
Larry Knechtal (bs), Hal Blaine (dms),
The Blossoms (bv), The NBC Orchestra
conducted by W. Earl Brown, Musical Direction:
William Goldenberg
*Recorded: NBC Studios, Burbank,
June 29, 1968
Elvis Presley (vcl, gtr), James Burton,
John Wilkinson (gtr), Charlie Hodge (gtr, vcl),
Glen D. Hardin (pno), Jerry Scheff (bs),
Ronnie Tutt (dms), Joe Esposito (perc),
J.D. Sumner & The Stamps,
The Sweet Inspirations,
Kathy Westmoreland (bv),
Joe Guercio & His Orchestra.
**Recorded: Hilton Hotel, Las Vegas,
February 16, 1972

If you believed that Elvis had only shuffled off this mortal coil so that he could front The Big G's rapidly-expanding celestial house band, this posthumous release offered some small comfort.

But when you found that apart from alternate in-concert takes of two hitherto available songs ('The Impossible Dream' and 'If I Can Dream') all the remaining tracks had been borrowed from six in-catalogue albums, consolation gave way to resentment.

'ELVIS SINGS FOR CHILDREN AND GROWNUPS TOO!' (LP)
(US) RCA CPL-1-2901
Released: July 1978

Side I
'(Let Me Be Your) Teddy Bear' (Mann, Lowe)
'Wooden Heart'
(Wise, Weisman, Twomey, Kaempfert)
'Five Sleepyheads' (Tepper, Bennett)
'Puppet On A String' (Tepper, Bennett)
'Angel' (Tepper, Bennett)
'Old McDonald' (Starr)
Side 2
'How Would You Like To Be' (Raleigh, Barkan)
'Cotton Candy Land' (Batchelor, Roberts)
'Old Shep' (Foley)
'Big Boots' (Wayne, Edwards)
'Have A Happy' (Weisman, Kaye, Fuller)

Elvis Presley was now worth more dead than when he was alive. This wasn't hearsay, but a proven financial statistic. During the twelve month period immediately following his death, Elvis sold more records than in any of the previous ten years. And there was no reason to believe that he wouldn't continue to do so. Therefore, to commemorate the first anniversary of his death (August 16, 1978), RCA launched its extensive *Always Elvis* sales campaign. To quote: "A theme that reflects the strong and enduring quality of Elvis' music through his catalogue". Included among the *celebrations* was a three hour ABC Radio

Network Special (August 13) which featured Priscilla Presley among others, while from September 1–10, the Las Vegas Hilton played host to the multi-dimensional First Annual Elvis Fan Summer Festival. During this 10-day convocation, a lifesize bronze statue of Elvis was unveiled, and the room in the luxury hotel where he often performed in public was re-named in his honour.

RCA's contribution was an album, *Elvis Sings For Children And Grownups Too!*, and the inauguration of the limited edition Collectors' Series—the re-issue of fifteen of Elvis' most popular singles in their original sleeves. Available either separately, or as a $15.98 deluxe Pre-Pak, they were the very same records still to be found in the Gold Standard series catalogue.

As it happens, RCA's British affiliate had put out a similar sixteen singles set fourteen months earlier, and managed to get at least half-a-dozen of them on the charts.

'Hound Dog' (Leiber, Stoller)
'Don't Be Cruel' (Blackwell, Presley)
(US) RCA PB-1-1099
Released: July 1978

'In The Ghetto' (Davis)
'Any Day Now' (Hilliard, Bacharach)
(US) RCA PB-1-1100
Released: July 1978

'Jailhouse Rock' (Leiber, Stoller)
'Treat Me Nice' (Leiber, Stoler)
(US) RCA PB-1-1101
Released: July 1978

'Can't Help Falling In Love'
(Perretti, Creatore, Weiss)
'Rock-A-Hula Baby' (Wise, Weisman, Fuller)
(US) RCA PB-1-1102
Released: July 1978

'Suspicious Minds' (James)
'You'll Think Of Me' (Shuman)
(US) RCA PB-1-1103
Released: July 1978

'Are You Lonesome Tonight'
(Turk, Handman)
'I Gotta Know' (Evans, Williams)
(US) RCA PB-1-1104
Released: July 1978

'Heartbreak Hotel' (Axton, Presley, Durden)
'I Was The One'
(Schroeder, DeMetrius, Blair, Peppers)
(US) RCA PB-1-1105
Released: July 1978

'All Shook Up' (Blackwell, Presley)
'That's When Your Heartaches Begin'
(Fisher, Hill, Raskin)
(US) RCA PB-1-1106
Released: July 1978

'Blue Suede Shoes' (Perkins)
'Tutti Frutti' (LaBostrie, Penniman, Lubin)
(US) RCA PB-1-1107
Released: July 1978

'Love Me Tender' (Presley, Matson)
'Any Way You Want Me (That's How I Will Be)' (Schroeder, Owens)
(US) RCA PB-1-1108
Released: July 1978

'(Let Me Be Your) Teddy Bear'
(Mann, Lowe)
'Loving You' (Leiber, Stoller)
(US) RCA PB-1-1109
Released: July 1978

'It's Now Or Never' (Schroeder, Gold)
'A Mess Of Blues' (Pomus, Shuman)
(US) RCA PB-1-1110
Released: July 1978

'Return To Sender' (Blackwell, Scott)
'Where Do You Come From'
(Batchelor, Roberts)
(US) RCA PB-1-1111
Released: July 1978

'I Got Stung' (Schroeder, Hill)
'One Night' (Bartholomew, King)
(US) RCA PB-1-1112
Released: July 1978

'Crying In The Chapel' (Glenn)
'I Believe In The Man In The Sky' (Howard)
(US) RCA PB-1-1113
Released: July 1978

1979

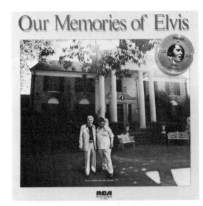

'OUR MEMORIES OF ELVIS. VOLUME I'
(LP)
(US) RCA AQL-1-3279
Released: February 1979

Side I
'Are You Sincere' (Walker) HPKS 6376
'It's Midnight' (Wheeler, Chesnut) HPKS 6377
'My Boy' (Francois, Bourtayre, Martin, Coulter) HPKS 6378
'Girl Of Mine' (Reed, Mason) HPKS 6379
'Take Good Care Of Her' (Warren, Kent) HPKS 6380
'I'll Never Fall In Love Again' (Donegan, Currie) HPKS 6381
Side 2:
'Your Love's Been A Long Time Coming' (Bourke) HPKS 6382
'Spanish Eyes' (Kaempfert, Singleton, Snyder) HPKS 6383
'Never Again' (Wheeler, Chesnut) HPKS 6384
'She Thinks I Still Care' (Duffy, Lipscomb) HPKS 6385
'Solitaire' (Sedaka, Cody) HPKS 6386

For reasons never satisfactorily explained, quite a number of Elvis' latter studio sessions suffered noticeably from inferior technical quality. Quite often, the basic backing tracks had to be severely overdubbed (and in some instances, re-recorded) to render them remotely acceptable.

The *Our Memories Of Elvis* series is supposed to rectify this sad state of affairs. The reverse-sleeve carries a personal message from Elvis' dad and The Colonel.

"Many fans have asked over the years why we didn't release an album of just Elvis singing as he did in the recording studio. To them we dedicate this album – *the pure Elvis* without additional accompaniment." Cursory investigation of these pre-surgery tapes reveal this to be an utterly pointless exercise in keeping the legend simmering. The inherent problem is, that as these weren't premium Presley performances, stripping the multi-tracks down still doesn't improve the quality, or offer the same fly-on-the-wall perspective as one has come to expect from some of the more recent bootlegs.

'Are You Sincere' (Walker) HPKS 6376
'Solitaire' (Sedaka, Cody) HPKS 6386
(US) RCA PB-11533
Released: March 1979

During the July 21–25, 1973, Stax sessions, Elvis only completed nine of the 13 songs tackled. When, for the last two days of recording, guitarists Bobby Manuel and Johnny Christopher were drafted in to replace James Burton and Reggie Young, and the usually dependable Booker T & The MGs' rhythm section of bassist Duck Dunn and drummer Al Jackson Jr were added, things just fell to pieces. This was the notorious date when the musicians became so totally over-awed by Elvis' actual physical presence in the studio that they completely blew it. In the end, the only means of saving the session from being a total write-off was for Elvis to split, as opposed to following his usual practice of cutting each vocal track live with the band. Even so, only one track was salvaged from the July 24 debacle, whilst by the end of the following day, four songs were left in various stages or disarray: 'Good, Bad, But Beautiful' (CPA5 4770), 'Colour My Rainbow' (CPA5 4771),

'Sweet Angeline' (CPA5 4772) and 'The Wonders You Perform' (CPA5 4773).

On September 24, 1973, Elvis and friends set about re-recording a new vocal track for 'Sweet Angeline' in the privacy of his Palm Springs retreat. Once that chore was completed, as far as we know, Elvis dashed off two more titles, 'I Miss You' and 'Are You Sincere'. Two months later, all three tracks had been over-dubbed and included on the unremarkable *Raised On Rock* LP. In retrospect, the pleading 'Are You Sincere', was one of the album's few redeeming moments. This version is the undubbed track used to open side one of the first "au naturel" *Our Memories Of Elvis* (Vol.1) compilations. Now it's probably just coincidental (but then one never knows!), but both 'Are You Sincere' and 'Solitaire' had previously been huge international hits for crooner Andy Williams in 1958 and 1973 respectively.

'I Got A Feelin' In My Body' (Linde)
JPA5 6060
'There's A Honky Tonk Angel (Who Will Take Me Back In)' (Seals, Rice)
JPA5 6066
(US) RCA PB-1-1679
Released: July 1979

Two tracks from the second volume of the posthumous *Our Memories Of Elvis* series, that were pitched at country music fans. That being the case, it's surprising that 'I Got A Feelin' In My Body' (not one of Dennis Linde's better songs) took promotional preference over the vastly superior and neglected 'There's A Honky Tonk Angel'.

'OUR MEMORIES OF ELVIS. VOLUME 2'
(LP)
(US) RCA CPL-1-3448
Released: September 1979

Side I
'Got A Feelin' In My Body' (Linde) JPA5 6060
'Green Green Grass Of Home' (Putnam) JPA5 6061
'For The Heart' (Linde) JPA5 6062
'She Wears My Ring' (Bryant, Bryant) JPA5 6063
'I Can Help' (Swain) JPA5 6064
Side 2
'Way Down' (Martine) JPA5 6065
'There's A Honky Tonk Angel (Who'll Take Me Back In)' (Seals, Rice) JPA5 6066
'Find Out What's Happening' (Crutchfield) JPA5 6067
'Thinking About You' (Baty) JPA5 6068
* 'Don't Think Twice, It's Alright' (Dylan) JPA5 6069
Elvis Presley (vcl, gtr), James Burton, Chip Young, Charlie Hodge, Joe Esposito (gtrs), David Briggs (pno), Norbert Putnam (bs), Jerry Carrigan or Kenneth Buttrey (dms).
*Recorded: RCA Studios, Nashville, May 16, 1971

RCA take a leaf out of the bootleggers' ever-expanding catalogue and belatedly release the complete, unedited May 16, 1971 impromptu studio jam of Bob Dylan's 'Don't Think Twice, It's Alright', which first appeared (in truncated form) on *Elvis* (APL-1-0283).

Apart from this titbit, there's still nothing new to report from the company vaults. Is RCA's tape cupboard really as bare as both the unsatisfactory *Legendary Performer* and *Our Memories Of Elvis* series would have one believe?

1979

There is apparently much concern amongst the RCA hierarchy regarding the vast quantity of unreleased Elvis master tapes that have gone AWOL through the back door of the studios in which they were originally recorded (only to promptly reappear in the shape of exquisitely packaged bootlegs). Can the loyal Elvis fan, who doesn't acquire bootlegs from record collector fairs, now only look forward to alternate studio takes and "live" Vegas re-runs of previously available material? Or are the rumours true – that RCA reissue producer Joan Deary has been given a huge unspecified budget to purchase *privately recorded tapes*(!) from fans, for possible legitimate release?

At the time of this release, there could be a logical explanation for the famine. When, in 1973, Colonel Parker sold Elvis' entire back-catalogue to RCA for five million dollars, the transaction didn't cover any hitherto *unreleased* material.

As the Colonel's agreements with RCA allegedly came up for renewal sometime in 1980, it was rumoured that he could well be in possession of a cache of unknown studio masters, impromptu jams (like that which had produced 'Don't Think Twice, It's Alright'), and home-made tracks.

It's no secret that a number of both pre and post Army Elvis concerts were filmed and recorded. There are also the dozen CBS and NBC epochal television appearances from the mid-'50s, plus hours of dynamic jams from the June 1968 NBC-TV *Elvis* comeback Special.

If this is the case, it would place the Colonel in a position to negotiate possibly the most lucrative deal ever made on behalf of a deceased client!

'ELVIS – A LEGENDARY PERFORMER. VOLUME 3' (LP)
(US) RCA CPL-1-3082
Released: November 1979

Side 1
'Hound Dog' (Leiber, Stoller)
Excerpts From An Interview With Elvis And The Colonel – TV Guide interview by Paul Wilder, Lakeland, Florida. August 1956 HPA5 6337
* 'Danny' (Wise, Weisman) WPKM 8123
'Fame And Fortune' (Alt. take) (Wise, Weisman) HPA5 6335
'Frankfort Special' (Alt. take) (Wayne, Edwards) HPA5 6334
** 'Britches' (Wayne, Edwards) SPA3 6744
'Crying In The Chapel' (Glenn)
Side 2
'Surrender'
(DeCurtis, Pomus, Shuman, DeCurtis)
'Guadalajara' (Alt. take) (Guizar) PPA3 4433
** 'It Hurts Me' (Byers, Daniels) WPKM 8113
*** 'Let Yourself Go' (Byers) WPKM 8112
'In The Ghetto' (Davis)
**** 'Let It Be Me' (Becaud, Delanoe, Curtis) HPA5 6336

Elvis Presley (vcl, gtr), Scotty Moore (gtr),
Bill Black (bs), D.J. Fontana (dms),
The Jordanaires (bv),
remaining musicians unidentified
*Recorded: Radio Recorders, Hollywood, January 1958
Elvis Presley (vcl, gtr), Scotty Moore,
Tiny Timbrell, Neal Mathews (gtr),
Dudley Brooks (pno), Ray Siegel (bs),
D.J. Fontana (dms), Jimmie Haskell (acc),
The Jordanaires (bv),
remaining musicians unidentified
**Recorded: 20th Century Fox Studios, Hollywood, August 8, 1960
Elvis Presley (vcl, gtr), Tom Tedesco,
Mike Deasy (gtr), Don Randi (pno, o),
Larry Knechtal (bs), Hal Blaine (dms),
The Blossoms (bv),
The NBC Orchestra conducted by W. Earl Brown,
Musical Director: William Goldenberg
***Recorded: NBC Studios, Burbank, June 27, 1968
Elvis Presley (vcl, gtr), James Burton,
John Wilkinson (gtr), Charlie Hodge (gtr, vcl),
Glen D. Hardin (pno), Jerry Scheff (bs),
Bob Lanning (dms), The Imperials,
The Sweet Inspirations, Millie Kirkham (bv)
****Recorded: International Hotel, Las Vegas, February 1970

This differs from the first two volumes in this rather patchy series, in that no unreleased Sun sides – though some do exist – were dusted off as bait. It was just an innocuous bunch of alternate takes salvaged from various soundtracks, the NBC-TV Special, the farcical 'Britches' (a song rightly junked from *Flaming Star*), plus extracts from the exceptionally rare August 1956 *TV Guide* interview with Elvis and the Colonel.

In every instance, the stealthy bootleggers had beaten RCA to the vaults. Fortunately, in their haste, these larcenous brigands had overlooked this album's one true major work, 'Danny'. Initially, 'Danny' was custom-written by Fred Wise and Ben Weisman as the possible title song for the Paramount movie *A Stone For Danny Fisher*. It was subsequently dropped and the duty re-assigned to Leiber & Stoller, when this screen adaptation of Harold Robbins' novel was first altered to *Sing You Sinners*, before the title of *King Creole* was permanently attached to it.

A typical self-pitying Presley-style woeful big beat ballad, it received preferential treatment from both Elvis and The Jordanaires, which only adds to the mystery as to why it was not only scratched from the *King Creole* soundtrack, but shelved for all of 22 years! Few people are aware that the song actually appeared in January 1960 under the title of 'Lonely Blue Boy' (MGM 12857) giving Conway Twitty an unexpected Top 10 hit.

This album is also available as a limited edition picture disc (RCA CLP-1-3078).

SIDE A

© 1978 RCA RECORDS TMK(S) ® RCA CORP • Made in Canada

'ELVIS, SCOTTY & BILL – THE FIRST YEAR' (LP)
(US) Very Wonderful Golden Editions. King.1
Released: November 1979

Side 1
Biff Collie Interview
* 'Good Rockin' Tonight' (Brown)
* 'Baby, Let's Play House' (Gunter)
* 'Blue Moon of Kentucky' (Monroe)
* 'I Got A Woman' (Charles)
* 'That's All Right (Mama)' (Crudup)
Elvis Presley Interview
Side 2
Scotty Moore Tells The Story Of The First Year

Elvis Presley (vcl, gtr), Scotty Moore (gtr),
Bill Black (bs).
*Recorded: Eagle's Hall, Houston, Texas, March 1955.

The various interviews and personal reminiscences that account for three-quarters of this album tend to overshadow the historic significance of what remains.

Assuming that most people don't have access to *unauthorized* bootlegs, this album (itself, initially a bootleg!) offers the general record buyer the earliest commercially available document of Elvis Presley in a concert situation – to be precise, a Thursday night dance held in March 1955 at The Eagle's Hall, Houston, Texas.

For all its patchy short-wave fidelity (could it have been a broadcast?), the five live tracks faithfully capture Elvis, Scotty and Bill at a pivotal point in their first 12-months together.

Just one month after recording the epochal 'Baby, Let's Play House' and 'Mystery Train', this is a typical out-of-town Elvis one-nighter of the period. Outside of the South, Elvis may still have been comparatively unknown, but nonetheless the hyped-up "Bopping Hillbilly" (as he is introduced to the demonstrative crowd), immediately takes command and slays the enthusiastic beer drinkers with the same degree of unabashed self-assertiveness with which he'd conquer the rest of the country within a year.

Despite the aural background smog, one can clearly detect, that even this early in his career, the screamers were an integral part of any Presley performance, as he boldly bops where no one had bopped before through 'Good Rockin' Tonight', 'Baby, Let's Play House' (still a month away from being released), 'Blue Moon Of Kentucky', 'I Got A Woman' (which he wouldn't record until he'd signed with RCA) and 'That's All Right (Mama)'.

Though none of the five songs on this album deviate from the familiar studio versions, the added dimension of a live performance, plus the realisation that Elvis is completely aware of his potency – note the ecstatic female response to his 'That's All Right (Mama)' call – substantiates that nothing short of a holocaust was about to prevent this 20-year old ex-trucker from fulfilling his destiny.

File under: indispensable.

'ELVIS ARON PRESLEY' (8-LPs)
(US) RCA CPL8-3699
Released: August 1980.

Album 1
Side 1
'AN EARLY LIVE PERFORMANCE'
* 'Heartbreak Hotel' (Axton, Durden, Presley) KPA5-9538
* 'Long Tall Sally' (Johnson, Penniman, Blackwell) (KPA5-9539)
* 'Blue Suede Shoes' (Perkins) KPA5-9540
* 'Money Honey' (Stone) KPA5-9541
Side 2
'MONOLOG'
** An Elvis Monolog KPA5-9542

Elvis Presley (vcl, gtr), Scotty Moore (gtr),
Bill Black (bs), D.J. Fontana (dms) plus
Freddy Martin's Orchestra.
*Recorded: The Venus Room, The New Frontier Hotel, Las Vegas, Nevada, April 24–30, 1956.
Elvis Presley (narrative)
**Recorded: On a United Artists' movie set, 1962.

Album 2
Side 1
'AN EARLY BENEFIT PERFORMANCE – PART ONE'
'Heartbreak Hotel' (Axton, Durden, Presley) KPA5-9543
'All Shook Up' (Blackwell, Presley) KPA5-9544
'A Fool Such As I' (Trader) KPA5-9545
'I Got A Woman' (Charles) KPA5-9546
'Love Me' (Leiber, Stoller) KPA5-9547
Introductions KPA5-9548
'Such A Night' (Chase) KPA5-9549
'Reconsider Baby' (Fulson) KPA5-9550
Side 2
'AN EARLY BENEFIT PERFORMANCE – CONCLUSION'
'I Need Your Love Tonight' (Wayne, Reichner) KPA5-9551
'That's All Right (Mama)' (Crudup) KPA5-9552
'Don't Be Cruel' (Blackwell) KPA5-9553
'One Night' (Bartholomew, King) KPA5-9554
'Are You Lonesome Tonight?' (Turk, Handman) KPA5-9555
'It's Now Or Never' (Schroeder, Gold) KPA5-9556

'Swing Down Sweet Chariot' (Trad: arranged/adapted Presley) KPA5-9557
'Hound Dog' (Leiber, Stoller) KPA5-9558

Elvis Presley (vcl, gtr), Scotty Moore,
Hank Garland (gtr), Floyd Cramer (pno),
Bob Moore (bs), D.J. Fontana (dms),
Homer "Boots" Randolph (ts),
The Jordanaires (bv).
Recorded: USS Arizona Memorial Benefit Concert, The Bloch Arena, Pearl Harbour, Honolulu, Hawaii, March 25, 1961.

Album 3
Side 1
'COLLECTORS' GOLD FROM THE MOVIE YEARS'
* 'They Remind Me Too Much Of You' (Robertson) PPA3-2725
** 'Tonight Is So Right For Love' (Wayne, Silver) KPA5-9559
*** 'Follow That Dream' (Wise, Weisman) M2WW-0874

**** 'Wild In The Country' (Peretti, Creatore, Weiss) L2PB-5383
***** 'Datin' (Wise, Starr) KPA5-9560
Side 2
'COLLECTORS' GOLD FROM THE MOVIE YEARS'
** 'Shoppin' Around' (Tepper, Bennett, Schroeder) KPA5-9561
****** 'Can't Help Falling In Love' (Peretti, Creatore, Weiss) M2PB-2988
***** 'A Dog's Life' (Wayne, Weisman) KPA5-9562
* 'I'm Falling In Love Tonight' (Robertson) PPA3-2719
******* 'Thanks To The Rolling Sea' (Batchelor, Roberts) KPA5-9563

Elvis Presley (vcl, gtr), Scotty Moore,
Barney Kessel, Tiny Timbrell (gtr),
Dudley Brooks (pno), Bob Moore,
Ray Siegel (bs), D.J. Fontana, Hal Blaine (dms),
The Mello Men (bv), remaining musicians unidentified.
*Recorded: MGM Sound Studios, Hollywood, California, September 22, 1962.
Elvis Presley (vcl, gtr), Scotty Moore,
Tiny Timbrell, Neil Mathews (gtr),
Dudley Brooks (pno), Ray Siegel (bs),
D.J. Fontana, Bernie Mattinson (dms),
Jimmie Haskell (acc), Hoyt Hawkins (tam),
The Jordanaires (bv).
**Recorded: Radio Recorders, Hollywood, California. May 6, 1960.
Elvis Presley (vcl, gtr), Scotty Moore,
Hank Garland, Neil Mathews (gtr),
Floyd Cramer (pno), Bob Moore (bs),
D.J. Fontana, Murrey "Buddy" Harman (dms).
***Recorded: United Artists Studios, Hollywood, California, July 2, 1961.
Elvis Presley (vcl,gtr), Scotty Moore (gtr),
Floyd Cramer, Dudley Brooks (pno),
Bob Moore (bs), D.J. Fontana,
Murrey "Buddy" Harman (dms),
The Jordanaires (bv), remaining musicians unidentified.
****Recorded: 20th Century Fox Studios, Hollywood, California, November 7, 1960.
Elvis Presley (vcl,gtr), Scotty Moore,
Barney Kessel, Charlie McCoy (gtr),
Barnie Lewis (st gtr), Larry Muhoberac (pno),
Ray Siegel, Keith Mitchell (bs), D.J. Fontana,
Hal Blaine, Victor Feldman (dms).
*****Recorded: Radio Recorders, Hollywood, California, August 4, 1965.
Elvis Presley (vcl, gtr), Scotty Moore,
Hank Garland, Tiny Timbrell (gtr),
Floyd Cramer (pno), Dudley brooks (pno, cel),
Bob Moore (bs), D.J. Fontana, Hal Blaine,
Bernie Mattinson (dms), Bernie Lewis (st gtr),
Homer "Boots" Randolph (ts),
George Fields (har), The Jordanaires,
The Surfers (bv).
******Recorded: Radio Recorders, Hollywood, California, March 23, 1961.
Elvis Presley (vcl,gtr), Scotty Moore,
Barney Kessel, Tiny Timbrell (gtr),
Dudley Brooks (pno), Ray Siegel (bs),
D.J. Fontana, Hal Blaine, Bernie Mattinson (dms),
Homer "Boots" Randolph (ts),
The Jordanaires (bv).
*******Recorded: Radio Recorders, Hollywood, California. March 27, 1962.

Album 4
Side 1
'THE TV SPECIALS'
** 'Jailhouse Rock' (Leiber, Stoller) WPA1 8037
*** 'Suspicious Minds' (James) (CPA5 4740)
* Medley
'Lawdy Miss Clawdy' (Price)
'Baby What You Want Me To Do' (Reed) KPA5 9564
* 'Blue Christmas' (Hayes, Johnson) WPA1 8062
Side 2
'THE TV SPECIALS'
*** 'You Gave Me A Mountain' (Robbins) CPA5 4727

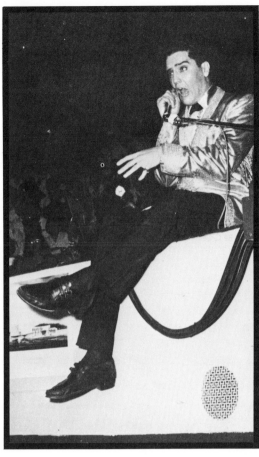

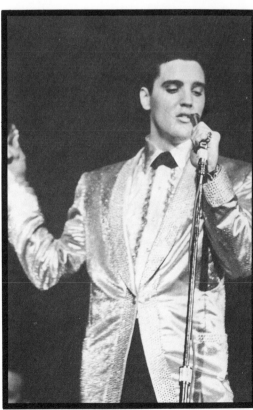

*** 'Welcome To My World' (Winkler, Hathcock) CPA5 4739
**** 'Trying To Get To You' (McCoy, Singleton) GPA5 0432
*** 'I'll Remember You' (Lee) CPA5 4742
**** 'My Way' (Anka, Revaux, Francois) GPA5 0436

Elvis Presley (vcl,gtr), Scotty Moore,
Charlie Hodge (gtr), D.J. Fontana (dms),
Alan Fortas (tam).
*Recorded: NBC Studios, Burbank, California,
June 27, 1968.
Elvis Presley (vcl,gtr), Tom Tedesco,
Mike Deasy (gtr), Don Randi (pno, o),
Larry Knechtal (bs), Hal Blaine (dms),
The Blossoms (bv),
The NBC Orchestra conducted by W. Earl Brown,
Musical Direction: William Goldenberg.
**Recorded: NBC Studios, Burbank, California,
June 28, 1968.
Elvis Presley (vcl, gtr), James Burton,
John Wilkinson (gtr), Charlie Hodge (gtr, vcl),
Glen D. Hardin (pno), Jerry Scheff (bs),
Ronnie Tutt (dms), J.D. Sumner & The Stamps,
The Sweet Inspiration,
Kathy Westmoreland (bv),
Joe Guerico & his Orchestra.
***Recorded: Honolulu International Centre,
Honolulu, January 14, 1973.
Elvis Presley (vcl,gtr), James Burton,
John Wilkinson, Charlie Hodge (gtr),
Tony Brown (pno), Jerry Scheff (bs),
Larry Londin (dms), J.D. Sumner & The Stamps,
The Sweet Inspiration, Kathy Westmoreland,
Sherrill Nielsen (bv),
Joe Guerico & his Orchestra.
****Recorded: Omaha, Nebraska, June 19,
1977. Rapid City, South Dakota, June 21, 1977.

Album 5
Side 1
'THE LAS VEGAS YEARS'
** 'Polk Salad Annie' (White) KPA5-9565
** 'You've Lost That Lovin' Feelin''
(Mann, Weil, Spector) KPA5-9566
** 'Sweet Caroline' (Diamond) KPA5-9567
*** 'Kentucky Rain' (Rabbitt, Heard) KPA5-9568
* 'Are You Lonesome Tonight?' (Turk, Handman)
KPA5-9569
Side 2
'THE LAS VEGAS YEARS'
* 'My Babe' (Dixon) KPA5-9570
* 'In The Ghetto' (Davis) KPA5-9571
** 'An American Trilogy' (Newbury) KPA5-9572
Medley
**** 'Little Sister' (Pomus, Shuman)
'Get Back' (Lennon, McCartney) KPA5-9573
* 'Yesterday' (Lennon, McCartney) KPA5-9574

Elvis Presley (vcl, gtr), James Burton,
John Wilkinson (gtr), Charlie Hodge (gtr, vcl),
Larry Muhoberac (pno ,o – August 1969
recordings only), Glen D. Hardin (pno – February
1970 & August 1970 recordings only),
Jerry Scheff (bs), Ronnie Tutt (dms – August 1969
& August 1970 recordings only),
Bob Lanning (dms – February 1970 recordings
only), The Imperials, The Sweet Inspirations,
Millie Kirkham (bv),
Bobby Morris & His Orchestra (August 1969 &
February 1970 recordings only),
Joe Guerico & His Orchestra (August 1970
recordings only).
*Recorded: International Hotel, Las Vegas,
Nevada.
August 22–26, 1969, **February 16–19, 1970,
***February 18, 1970, ****August 13, 1970.

Album 6
Side 1
'THE LOST SINGLES'
(a) 'I'm Leavin'' (Jarrett, Charles)
(b) 'The First Time Ever I Saw Your Face'
(MacColl)
(c) 'Hi-Heel Sneakers' (Higginbotham)
(d) 'Softly As I Leave You' (DeVite, Shaper)

Side 2
'THE LOST SINGLES'
(e) 'Unchained Melody' (North, Zaret)
(f) 'Fool' (Sigman, Last)
(g) 'Rags To Riches' (Adler, Ross)
(h) 'It's Only Love' (James, Tyrell)
(i) 'America The Beautiful' (Trad: arr Presley)
Original source
(a) 47-9998
(b) 74-0672
(c) 47-9425
(d) PB-11212
(e) PB-11212
(f) 74-0910
(g) 47-9980
(h) 48-1017
(i) PB-11165

Album 7
Side 1
'ELVIS AT THE PIANO'
** 'It's Still There' (Hunter) KPA5-9575
** 'I'll Take You Home Again Kathleen'
(Trad: arr Presley) APA4-1283
* 'Beyond The Reef' (Pitman) TPA4-0919
** 'I Will Be True' (Hunter) APA4-1284

Elvis Presley (vcl, pno), Scotty Moore,
Chip Young (gtr), Pete Drake (stl gtr),
Bob Moore (bs), D.J. Fontana (dms),
The Jordanaires (bv).
*Recorded: RCA Studios, Nashville, Tennessee,
May 27, 1966.
Elvis Presley (vcl, pno).
**Recorded: RCA Studios, Nashville, Tennessee,
May 19, 1971.

Side 2
'THE CONCERT YEARS – PART 1'
'Also Sprach Zarathustra' (Strauss) KPA5-9576
'See See Rider' (Trad: arr Presley) KPA5-9577
Medley
'I Got A Woman' (Charles)
'Amen' (Hairston)
'I Got A Woman' (Charles) KPA5-9578
'Love Me' (Leiber, Stoller) KPA5-9579
'If You Love Me' (Rostill) KPA5-9580
'Love Me Tender' (Presley, Matson) KPA5-9581
'All Shook Up' (Blackwell, Presley) KPA5-9582
Medley
'(Let Me Be Your) Teddy Bear' (Mann, Lowe)
'Don't Be Cruel' (Blackwell) KPA5-9583

Album 8
Side 1
'THE CONCERT YEARS – PART 2'
'Hound Dog' (Leiber, Stoller) KPA5-9584
'The Wonder Of You' (Knight) KPA5-9585
'Burning Love' (Linde) KPA5-9586
'Dialogue – introductions – Johnny B. Goode'
(Berry) KPA5-9587
'Introductions – Long Live Rock And Roll'
(Colyer) KPA5-9588
'T-R-O-U-B-L-E' (Chesnut) KPA5-9589
'Why Me Lord' (Kristofferson) KPA5-9590
Side 2
'THE CONCERT YEARS – PART 3'
'How Great Thou Art' (Hine) KPA5-9591
'Let Me Be There' (Rostill) KPA5-9592
'An American Trilogy' (Newbury) KPA5-9593
'Funny How Time Slips Away' (Nelson) KPA5-9594
'Little Darlin'' (Williams) KPA5-9595
Medley
'Mystery Train' (Phillips, Parker)
'Tiger Man' (Lewis, Burns, Phillips) KPA5-9596
'Can't Help Falling In Love'
(Peretti, Creatore, Weiss)

Elvis Presley (vcl, gtr), James Burton,
John Wilkinson (gtr), Charlie Hodge (gtr, vcl),
Glen D. Hardin (pno), Jerry Scheff (bs),
Ronnie Tutt (dms), J.D. Sumner & The Stamps,
The Sweet Inspirations, Voice, Kathy Westmoreland (bv),
Joe Guerico & His Orchestra.
Recorded: 1975 – date and locations unknown.

Dateline: August 16, 1980.

To commemorate the third anniversary of Elvis Presley's death, whilst simultaneously popping a cork to celebrate 25-years of (still) having him under exclusive contract, RCA produced *Elvis Aron Presley*—a 250,000 limited edition, eight-album deluxe package, containing 87 different performances of 78 different songs, plus interviews and monologues adding up to a (not over-generous) playing time of four hours and twenty-six minutes.

Scratch the embossed imitation silver gun-metal surface, and it becomes very apparent that, despite the advance ballyhoo, this was not the long-awaited treasure trove product-hungry fans were subtly railroaded into believing.

With top-heavy duplication of previously issued material, TV and movie out-takes, it also includes *five* entire sides of '70s concert appearances which, by 1974, had been offered up once too often to attract anyone other than the completist.

The genuinely collectable material contained herein could have quite easily been accommodated on a double album.

One must appreciate that, from the outset, *Elvis Aron Presley* was conceived as a sophisticated monument to high-powered marketing strategy, as much as an over-stuffed tribute to The Man's accomplishments. Maximum media impact appears to be the only desired objective.

The real bait—and the only material present never to have been bootlegged—is the illuminating 13½ minutes of Elvis in the spotlight during his less-than-successful April 1956 stint at The New Frontier Hotel, Las Vegas. This being the occasion when Elvis was cruelly referred to as "a jug of corn liquor at a champagne party."

The last show of the final night of his truncated season, it's painfully apparent that Elvis is uncomfortable in his surroundings. As any stray screamers had long since been packed off to their rooms, for the first time since hitting the big-time, Elvis wasn't playing to *his* audience, but mere curiosity seekers having a late drink before once more trying to take on the house at the gaming tables.

When Elvis sings, it's without the gale-force accompaniment of hysterical young girls. When he finishes, it's to nothing more than a ripple of polite applause.

If 'Heartbreak Hotel' and 'Long Tall Sally' sound cautious, there's every indication that when Elvis bops into 'Blue Suede Shoes' and finally, 'Money Honey', the more easy-to-please onlookers have begun to warm to his in between-song crackerbarrel attempts to break the ice.

For his efforts, one reviewer claimed, "His [Elvis'] musical sound with the combo of three is uncouth, matching to a great extent the lyric content of 'Long Tall Sally', 'I Got A Woman', 'Money Honey' and other such ditties."

In tandem with Elvis' March 25, 1961, USS *Arizona* Memorial Benefit Concert in Honolulu—by the sound of it dubbed directly from the same flawed source as the familiar lavishly-packaged bootleg—these are (to date) the earliest *official* evidence of full-blown Presleymania.

Whereas the 1956 tape depicts the novice working under extreme stress, five years later in Honolulu, the warrior just home from the (cold) wars once again erupts like one of the island's dormant volcanoes. His pacing is beyond reproach, selecting an excellent 45-minute cross-section from his extensive back-catalogue. For the last time, until his return to the stage eight years later, here is Elvis still consciously proving his supremacy to perfection. Amidst scenes of mass-meyhem, Elvis follows a provocative 'Such A Night' with a steamy 'Reconsider Baby', replete with "Boots" Randolph's hackle-raisin' tenor sax solo. Later on, Elvis drives the audience even further to distraction with a version of 'One Night' which leaves very little to the imagination.

Of the remaining material scattered around this eight-pack, even the hitherto solitary unreleased tune, 'Beyond The Reef'—as with the two sides of a waggish Elvis screwin' up soundtrack fillers like 'Datin''—was a readily available under-the-counter purchase.

The reflective 'Beyond The Reef' is the stand out track on the otherwise unremarkable short 12-minute side, *Elvis At The Piano*. The remaining three tracks have been lifted from off the deleted *Fool* LP—the only difference being that 'I'll Take You Home Again, Kathleen' is minus the overdubbed strings.

The appearance of *Elvis Aron Presley* achieved its desired (commercial) objective. Over-subscribed before actual release (equivalent to 2-million LPs sold), it also redirected a considerable amount of revenue out of the hands of the bootleggers, and (with the spate of scurrilous exposés starting to distract public attention from the merits Elvis possessed as a performer) garnered much needed "positive" press coverage and airplay.

RCA demonstrated to the world that, three years after his death, Elvis could be even more spectacular than when he was alive. Furthermore, as the individual eight sleeves confirm, they could freeze-frame his image at its best.

When evaluating precisely what's on offer, there's no reason to suppose that such an exercise can't be repeated indefinitely (whenever a suitable anniversary presents itself!)

To begin with, there's those elusive Sun sides, the *Louisiana Hayride* airshots, the remainder of the 1956 TV shows, the Timex-sponsored/Frank Sinatra-hosted Army homecoming, innumerable alternate takes from Hollywood (in particular the 'Loving You' sessions), seven years worth of Elvis in Vegas and on tour . . . oh yes, and the 31 takes of 'Hound Dog'.

Place your order now!

N.B. Although Elvis always spelled his middle name "Aron", it appears on his birth certificate as "Aaron".

1981

* **'Guitar Man'** (Hubbard) KWA5-8566-1
** **'Faded Love'** (Wills, Wills) KWA5-8562
RCA PB-12158
Released: January 1981

Re-recorded:
*October 16, 1980. **October 15, 1980
Young 'un Sound Studio, Nashville, Tennessee.

Taking into account the bizarre circumstances surrounding the appearance of this track, it's best discussed within the framework of the album of the same title with which it was simultaneously released.

'GUITAR MAN' (LP)
RCA AHL1-3917
Released: January 1981

Side I
*** (a) 'Guitar Man' (Hubbard) KWA5-8566
**** (b) 'After Loving You' (Miller, Lantz)
        KWA5-8571
* (c) 'Too Much Monkey Business' (Berry)
        KWA5-8556
* (d) 'Just Call Me Lonesome' (Griffin)
        KWA5-8553
***** (e) 'Lovin' Arms' (Jans) KWA5-8591
Side 2
* (f) 'You Asked Me To' (Jennings, Shaver)
        KWA5-8558
**** (g) 'Clean Up Your Own Backyard' (Strange,
        Davis) KWA5-8572
** (h) 'She Still Thinks I Care' (Lee) KWA5-8564
** (i) 'Faded Love' (Wills, Wills) KWA5-8562
* (j) 'Help Me' (Gatlin) KWA5-8555

Re-recorded
*October 14, 1980. **October 15, 1980.
***October 16, 1980. ****October 17, 1980.
*****November 11, 1980
Young 'un Sound Studio, Nashville, Tennessee

Original source
(a) CLAMBAKE (LPM/LSP.3892) & single
    (47-9425)
(b) FROM ELVIS IN MEMPHIS (LSP.4155)
(c) SINGER PRESENTS ELVIS SINGING
    FLAMING STAR AND OTHERS (PRS.279)
(d) CLAMBAKE (LPM/LSP.3892)
(e) GOOD TIMES (CPL1-0475)
(f) PROMISED LAND (APL1-0873)
(g) single (47-9747)
(h) MOODY BLUE (AFL1-2428) &
    single (PB-10857)
(i) ELVIS COUNTRY (LSP-4460)
(j) FROM ELVIS IN MEMPHIS (LSP-4155)

Right up until his death at the age of 46, on January 3, 1981 from a stroke, record producer Felton Jarvis had been engaged on two new Presley projects of questionable validity.

The first one, begun around February 1980, reportedly had Felton coaxing Neil Diamond, Tony Joe White, Dolly Parton and a number of country stars into a Nashville studio for the unique "privilege" of taking turns to *duet* with Elvis on some of the late King's former glories!

It could well be that such a preposterous idea – which years earlier had *re-united* Hank Williams Jr in the studio with his late father – stemmed from Ray Quinn, D-J on station WCBM in Baltimore. Noting the similarity in key, tempo and phrasing of Linda Ronstadt's

wistful rendition of 'Love Me Tender' to Elvis' original, Quinn took both records and electronically transformed them into an intriguing romantic duet.

Despite instant public demand for this cute novelty, the Elvis and Linda duet was never officially forthcoming from either RCA or Asylum, thus giving *carte blanche* to enterprising bootleggers to circulate quantities of this unsanctioned single. They didn't stop there, producing far less satisfactory Elvis duets with the likes of Buddy Holly, Bill Haley and Shirley Bassey!

As for Felton's second project – the only one to so far surface – it wasn't Elvis' voice that was being tampered with.

Not content with stripping the backing tracks of familiar country-flavoured Elvis recordings right down to the bone, as he'd done for two *Our Memories Of Elvis* collections, Felton retained *only* Elvis' original vocal track, carefully resetting it over newly-recorded "contemporized" instrumental backings.

In itself, by no means an innovation in tape surgery. During the early '60s, such techno-trickery enabled Buddy Holly to achieve numerous posthumous hits in Europe, though in the late '70s such procedure proved most disadvantageous when applied to unreleased Jimi Hendrix tapes.

Here, it amounts to somewhat of a non-event.

The title track, 'Guitar Man', encapsulates the most obvious errors of artistic judgement, in that Jerry Reed's humorously nimble acoustic guitar pickin' is dumped in favour of an up-front "treated" electric model with a guts 'n' glory rhythm section in support. As if to further prove an unsubtle point, everything within earshot is pushed way up in the final "bright-sounding" mix.

Neither have the ten tracks been selected haphazardly. It's all part of a premeditated master-plan to make the renovated Thoroughly Modern Elvis competitive when programmed for radio alongside such amped-up country-rockers as Waylon Jennings, Willie Nelson, Merle Haggard and whoever else automatically makes the play-lists.

Outside of North America, Elvis Presley may still be honoured primarily as a rocker – indeed, at the time of writing, his pre-Army image is much favoured amongst Britain's new wave quiffabilly bands – but in the States, that particular form of surreal nostalgia is regarded as faddish, and of little appeal to a well-heeled mass market.

Corporate strategy decrees that if the Presley legend is to flourish (and remain lucrative), then it must be channeled through the more traditionally conservative folk-hero realms that only Country Music can offer.

John Wayne and Elvis Presley are arguably the closest thing to natural-born Royalty that America has produced this century, and as such are to be remembered as patriarchs and Southern Gentlemen. (Elvis will *not* be remembered as a greasy punk, anymore than John Wayne will be remembered as Genghis Khan.)

Theoretically, Felton Jarvis completed his given task on 'Guitar Man'. However, by the very nature of the exercise, the overall feeling is one of professional conveyor-belt expertise bereft of any true individuality.

* 'Loving' Arms' (Jans) KWA5-8591
** 'You Asked Me To' (Jennings, Shaver)
KWA5-8558
RCA PB-12205
Released: March 1981

Re-recorded
*November 11, 1980, **October 14, 1980
Young 'un Sound Studios, Nashville, Tennessee

The Oct '74 British B-side of 'My Boy'. Almost a decade on, there's nothing in this refurbished second-coming to suggest that it has gained genuine A-side aspirations.

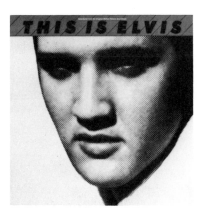

THIS IS ELVIS (LP)
RCA CPL2-4031
Released: March 1981

Side 1
'(Marie's The Name) His Latest Flame'
(Pomus, Shuman)
'Moody Blue' (James)
'That's All Right (Mama)' (Crudup)
Medley
  * 'Shake, Rattle And Roll' (Calhoun)
  * 'Flip, Flop And Fly' (Calhoun, Turner)
LPA5-5807
 ** 'Heartbreak Hotel' (Axton, Durden, Presley)
LPA5-5808
*** 'Hound Dog' (Leiber, Stoller) LPA5-5809
**** Excerpt from the Hy Gardner Interview
LPA5-5810

Elvis Presley (vcl, gtr), Scotty Moore (gtr),
Bill Black (bs), D.J. Fontana (dms),
*Recorded: Tommy & Jimmy Dorsey TV Show,
CBS Studios, New York City, February 11, 1956
Elvis Presley (vcl, gtr), Scotty Moore (gtr),
Bill Black (bs), D.J. Fontana (dms) plus
The Dorsey Brothers Orchestra
**Recorded: Tommy & Jimmy Dorsey TV Show,
CBS Studios, New York City, March 17 1956
Elvis Presley (vcl, gtr), Scotty Moore (gtr),
Bill Black (bs), D.J. Fontana (dms) plus
NBC Studio Orchestra
***Recorded: Milton Berle TV Show, NBC
Studios, Hollywood, California, June 5, 1956
****Television Interview, July 1, 1956

Side 2
***** 'Merry Christmas Baby' (Baxter, Moore)
LPA5-5811
 ** 'Mean Woman Blues' (De Metrius) LPA5-5812
  * 'Don't Be Cruel' (Blackwell, Presley)
LPA5-5813
'(Let Me Be Your) Teddy Bear' (Mann, Lowe)
'Jailhouse Rock' (Leiber, Stoller)
*** Army Swearing In LPA5-5814
'GI Blues' (Tepper, Bennett)
Excerpt from 'Departure For Germany Press
Conference' ("Elvis Sails")
**** Excerpts from 'Home From Germany Press
Conference' LPA5-5815

Elvis Presley (vcl, gtr), Scotty Moore (gtr),
Bill Black (bs), D.J. Fontana (dms),
The Jordanaires (bv)
*Recorded: Ed Sullivan's *Toast Of The Town* TV
Show, CBS Studios, New York City,
January 6, 1957
Elvis Presley (vcl, gtr), Scotty Moore (gtr),
Bill Black (bs), D.J. Fontana (dms),

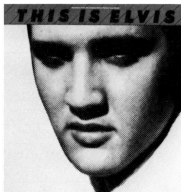

The Jordanaires plus unidentified Paramount
Pictures studio chorus (bv)
**Recorded: Radio Recorders, Hollywood,
California, February 1957
***Memphis, Tennessee, March 24, 1958
****Gracelands, Memphis, Tennessee,
March 8, 1960
Elvis Presley (vcl, gtr), James Burton, Chip Young,
Charlie Hodge, Joe Esposito (gtr),
David Briggs (pno, o), Joe Moscheo (p),
Charlie McCoy (o), Norbert Putnam (bs),
Jerry Carrigan, Kenneth Buttrey (dms)
*****Recorded: RCA Studios, Nashville,
Tennessee, May 15, 1971

Side 3
  * 'Too Much Monkey Business' (Berry)
LPA5-5816
'Love Me Tender' (Presley, Matson)
'I've Got A Thing About You Baby' (White)
'I Need Your Love Tonight' (Wayne, Reichner)
 ** 'Blue Suede Shoes' (Perkins) LPA5-5817
'Viva Las Vegas' (Pomus, Shuman)
*** 'Suspicious Minds' (James) LPA5-5818
**** JC's Award To Elvis As One Of The Outstanding
Men Of The Year LPA5-5819
'Promised Land' (Berry)

Elvis Presley (vcl, gtr), Scotty Moore,
Chip Young, Jerry Reed (gtr), Pete Drake (stl gtr),
Floyd Cramer (pno), Charlie McCoy (har),
Bob Moore (bs), D.J. Fontana,
Murrey "Buddy" Harman (dms)
*Recorded: RCA Studios, Nashville, Tennessee,
January 13, 1968
Elvis Presley (vcl, gtr). This is a sliced version
featuring two entirely different combos:
(a) Scotty Moore, Charlie Hodge (gtr),
D.J. Fontana (dms), Alan Fortas (tam),
(b) Tom Tedesco, Mike Deasy (gtr),
Don Randi (pno, o), Larry Knechtal (bs),
Hal Blaine (dms) plus The NBC Orchestra:
conductor, W. Earl Brown.
Mucial Director: William Goldenberg
**Recorded: NBC Studios, Burbank, California,
June 27, 1968
Elvis Presley (vcl, gtr), James Burton,
James Wilkinson (gtr), Charlie Hodge (gtr, vcl),
Glen D. Hardin (pno), Jerry Scheff (bs),
Ronnie Tutt (dms), J.D. Sumner & The Stamps,
The Sweet Inspirations,
Kathy Westmoreland (bv),
Joe Guercio & His Orchestra
***Recorded: possibly Virginia-Texas section of
April 1972 tour
****Memphis, Tennessee, January 9, 1971

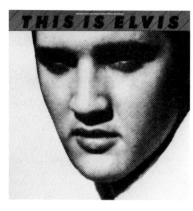

Side 4
*** Excerpt from the Madison Square Garden Press
Conference LPA5-5820
  * 'Always On My Mind' (Thompson, James,
Christopher) LPA5-5821
'Are You Lonesome Tonight?' (Turk, Hardman)
'My Way' (Francois, Revaux, Thibaut, Anka)
 ** 'An American Trilogy' (Newbury)
'Memories' (Strange, Davis)

Elvis Presley (vcl, gtr), James Burton,
John Wilkinson (gtr), Glen D. Hardin (pno),
Emory Gordy (bs), Ronnie Tutt (dms),
J.D. Sumner & The Stamps (bv)
*Recorded: RCA Studios, Hollywood, California,
March 30, 1972
Elvis Presley (vcl, gtr), James Burton,
John Wilkinson (gtr), Charlie Hodge (gtr, vcl),
Glen D. Hardin (pno), Jerry Scheff (bs),
Ronnie Tutt (dms),
J.D. Sumner & The Stamps,
The Sweet Inspirations,
Kathy Westmoreland (bv),
Joe Guercio & His Orchestra
**Recorded: possibly Virginia-Texas section of
April 1972 tour
***New York City, June 8, 1972

This Is Elvii would have been a far more apt title for this, Presley's 34th motion picture.

No less than *five* persons – including the genuine article – are required to portray the lead in this *officially* blessed one-dimensional "docudrama". The Colonel gets his usual technical adviser credit.

When there isn't sufficient available footage for this predictable re-telling of the legend (which is often the case), enter the appropriate stand-in, switch to a gauze-covered soft-focus lens, and cue the disembodied voiceover of "Elvis" (Ral Donner) to confidentially utter edited extracts from old interviews and liner notes, or read some of the most asinine dialogue since Louise Fazenda cussed, "Well, suck my corn!" in *Swing Your Lady*. At least Shelley Winters wasn't called upon to take her hands out of the pickle barrel to repeat her (classically miscast) role as Gladys.

Save for snippets of wobbly home-movies, there's nothing on offer here that hasn't been re-cycled previously, either in Elvis movie documentaries or TV tributes. Nevertheless, the clips from his chaotic 1956 appearances on The Dorsey Brothers, Milton Berle, Steve Allen and Ed Sullivan shows forever excite and enthral – in particular his memorable June 5 guest shot with Milton Berle when, in a jacket so big it could have doubled as a day-bed, a self-mocking Elvis blatantly bumps, grinds and grins his way through 'Hound Dog', cutting the studio audience up by deliberately stretching it out into a burlesque half-tempo ending.

At the other extreme, 21-years to the month later, there is the saddening spectre of a sweat-soaked, obese, and prematurely aged Elvis floundering like a beached whale through 'Are You Lonesome Tonight?' One still cannot entirely accept the pathetic excuses frequently given as to precisely why a person in such alarming physical and mental condition was ever allowed to exhibit himself in public.

Naturally, every Elvis movie has to have a soundtrack album – in this instance, a double.

Perhaps it has something to do with equalizing the soundtrack for movie theatres, but on occasion, the mastering appears to leave something to be desired. Surprisingly, it's the 1956 TV transcriptions that come off best, which is just as well, because this, together with Elvis' rousing movie version of 'Mean Woman Blues' (*Loving You*), is the only way one can *legally* acquire such extensively bootlegged gems.

As there still remain 30 performances of 16 different songs from the 1956 TV shows, hopefully when RCA release them it will be as one self-contained package and not, as has become the case with the 1968 NBC-TV alternate takes, served up piecemeal.

N.B. As only a fraction of known Elvis film footage was incorporated into this movie, can we soon expect to have it resold to the public along similar lines to *Close Encounters Of The Third Kind* – a spot of slick re-editing, the addition of whole new sequences and a *This Is Elvis – The Special Edition* tag!

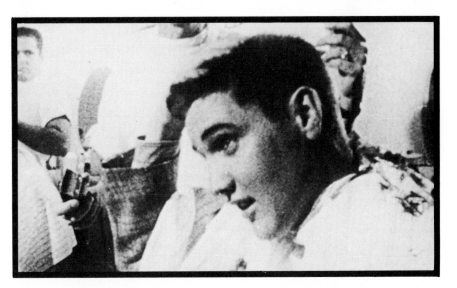

THIS IS ELVIS/
Warner Brothers

Cast
Elvis Presley.............................Himself
Elvis Presley (aged 10).......................
.... Paul Boensch III
Elvis Presley (aged 18). David Scott
Elvis Presley (aged 35)........................
.... Dana MacKay
Elvis Presley (aged 42).......................
.... Johnny Harra
Elvis Presley (narration)....................
.... Ral Donner

Written, Produced, Directed...........
.... Malcolm Leo, Andrew Solt
Running Time: 88 minutes
Released: April 3, 1981

'MILLION DOLLAR QUARTET' (LP)
(UK) SUN 1006.
Released: 1 April, 1981

Side 1
'Just A Little Talk With Jesus' (Trad: arr, Young)
'Walk That Lonesome Valley' (Trad: arr, Young)
'I Shall Not Be Moved' (Trad: arr, Young)
'(There'll Be) Peace In The Valley (For Me)'
(Dorsey)
Side 2
'Down By The Riverside' (Trad: arr, Young)
'I'm With The Crowd But Oh So Alone'
(Tubb, Story)
'Father Along' (Trad: arr, Young)
'Blessed Jesus Hold My Hand' (Trad: arr, Young)
'As We Travel Along On The Jericho Road'
(Trad: arr, Young)
'I Just Can't Make It By Myself' (Unknown)
'Little Cabin On The Hill' (Unknown)
'Summertime Has Passed And Gone' (Unknown)
'I Hear A Sweet Voice Calling' (Unknown)
'And Now Sweetheart You've Done Me Wrong'
(Unknown)
'Keeper Of The Keys' (Brewer, Shipley)
'Crazy Arms' (Mooney, Seals)
'Don't Forbid Me' (Singleton)

Elvis Presley (vcl, gtr, pno),
Jerry Lee Lewis (vcl, pno), Carl Perkins (vcl, gtr),
Johnny Cash (though present, there's some
debate as to whether he actually participated),
Jay Perkins (gtr), Clayton Perkins (bs),
W.S. Holland (dms)
Recorded: Memphis Recording Service,
Memphis, Tennessee, December 4, 1956

In search of rock 'n' roll's Holy Grail . . .

For a quarter-of-a-century, The Million Dollar Quartet was the group that every card-carrying Elvis fan had heard about but, right up until the spring of 1981, never *actually* heard!

On Tuesday, December 4, 1956, while Carl Perkins and his band were recording in Sun Records' hole-in-the-wall studio, a somewhat *euphoric* Elvis Presley cruised through the door with 19-year-old Las Vegas showgirl Marilyn Evans on his arm and sidekick Cliff Gleaves in tow. Seems Elvis had already commenced celebrating his Christmas vacation. After horsing around, Elvis eased the then still relatively little known Jerry Lee Lewis off the piano stool and, with spectator Johnny Cash later making up a foursome, spent the entire afternoon *speeding* through traditional gospel songs and current juke box hits. Pictures were snapped and columnist Robert Johnson filed a brief report for the local Memphis *Press-Scimitar*, which concluded: "If Sam Phillips had been on his toes, he'd have turned the recorder on when that very unrehearsed but talented bunch got to cutting up on 'Blueberry Hill' and a lot of other songs. That quartet could sell a million." Johnson greatly underestimated Phillips' sense of occasion, because for the duration, Sam The Man kept the tapes rolling. "Who knows", he told engineer Jack Clement, "we may never have these people together again!" But Elvis had transferred from Sun to RCA a year earlier, and with the off-the-cuff nature of the session, the tapes were felt to have no real commercial viability and were promptly shelved and forgotten. Forgotten, that is, by everyone except the fans of all four participants. Over the next 25 years the legend of The Million Dollar Quartet perpetuated, with much speculation as to precisely what songs were performed (either in full or in part) and whether it truly was, as Sam Phillips always insisted, a spiritual awakening, or just a bunch of cat-clothed pill-poppers rockin' and holy rollin'!

"That was probably the highlight of my life," Phillips recalled 25 years later, "having all of them in the same studio singing and playing together. The atmosphere that afternoon was of an old time revival meeting—just the four boys fooling around and having fun together. Even though by this time Elvis was the biggest star of the four . . . already making movies, he just loved to bounce things off Carl, Jerry Lee and Johnny and, in turn, they did the same to him, especially Jerry Lee . . . their voices sounded so good together. It wasn't just because they were all successful that made what happened that day such a unique event," insists Phillips, "each in his own way was a highly distinctive artist, and there was this feeling of artistic freedom in the studio that afternoon, purely as a result of their mutual respect for one another's talent. They may have only been making some impromptu music together, but the only way I can best describe what was happening is to liken it to a spiritual awakening. Had this been a properly arranged session, with all the material selected beforehand and rehearsed, then there's no doubt that it would have produced something so remarkable as to never be equalled."

A couple of years before Elvis died, there had been rumours that these tapes (which Shelby Singleton Jr had acquired when he purchased Sun in July 1969) were to be released. However, there was a series of legal shuffles concerning precisely who had the legal authority to press and sell such an album. Carl Perkins seemed to be the obvious claimant, by virtue of the fact that he was said to have paid for the studio costs on the day in question; Johnny Cash and Jerry Lee Lewis may have been contracted Sun recording artists at the time. The main obstacle appeared to be Elvis' exclusive contract with RCA. Allegedly, before the tapes could be released, written permission had to be given by all four. Seemingly, it was being whispered, there were those who wanted it on sale and those (unless the price was right) who didn't. But before anything was close to being finalised, Elvis made his Grand Exit. A few months later, it was announced that highlights from this legendary session would be released on December 15, 1977. First RCA Records and then Johnny Cash prevented that happening. Nothing else was heard until the summer of 1981, when a bootleg album began circulating, quickly followed by a commercial release on the Sun Label (through the UK-based Charly Record Company). At the time of writing, this album *hasn't* been withdrawn from sale.

Prior to ever being heard, The Million Dollar Quartet—like a proposed Beatles Reunion—had taken on almost mystical significance. Was it worth holding one's breath for so many years? Was all revealed? Of course not. It's obvious, that by the very nature of the circumstances under which it was recorded, this low-fidelity 30-minute extract couldn't possibly hope to live up to the expectations. Predominantly gospel, Elvis leads most of the time, whilst Carl and Jerry Lee harmonize on such inspirational cuts as 'Just A Little Walk With Jesus', '(There'll Be) Peace In The Valley (For Me)' (which Elvis performed on the *Ed Sullivan Show* four weeks later) and 'Farther Along'. Much of the remaining material is only performed in part: Elvis gets around to mimicking Hank Snow on 'I'm With The Crowd But So Alone', and Bill Monroe on 'Little Cabin On The Hill'. Prior to crooning 'Don't Forbid Me', he claims that it was originally written for him, not Pat Boone—"it laid over my house for ages man, I never did see it . . . so much junk . . ." Elsewhere, Jerry Lee takes over to passionately warble 'I Walk That Lonesome Valley' and Carl delivers a spirited 'I Shall Not Be Moved'. The fourth "Millionaire", Johnny Cash, is nowhere to be heard at all! In the final analysis, it's true historical value is as a revealing fly-on-the-wall curio. Most definitely worth acquiring, but doubtful if it'll realise its expected Million Dollars. On the other hand, there's still sufficient material in the can for at least another four albums. Or is that just another myth?

For those requiring such details, here is a break-down of who does what:

'Just A Little Talk With Jesus'
 Elvis and Jerry Lee (split lead vocal), Carl (guitar).
'Walk That Lonesome Valley'
 Jerry Lee and Elvis (split lead vocal), Carl (guitar).
'I Shall Not Be Moved'
 Carl, Elvis and Jerry Lee (split lead vocal), Carl (guitar).
'(There'll Be) Peace In The Valley (For Me)'
 Elvis (lead vocal), Jerry Lee and Carl (back-up vocal), Carl (guitar).
'Down By The Riverside'
 Elvis (lead vocal), Jerry Lee (back-up vocal), Carl (guitar).
'I'm With The Crowd But Oh So Alone'
 Elvis (lead vocal).
'Farther Along'
 Elvis, Carl and Jerry Lee (split lead vocal).

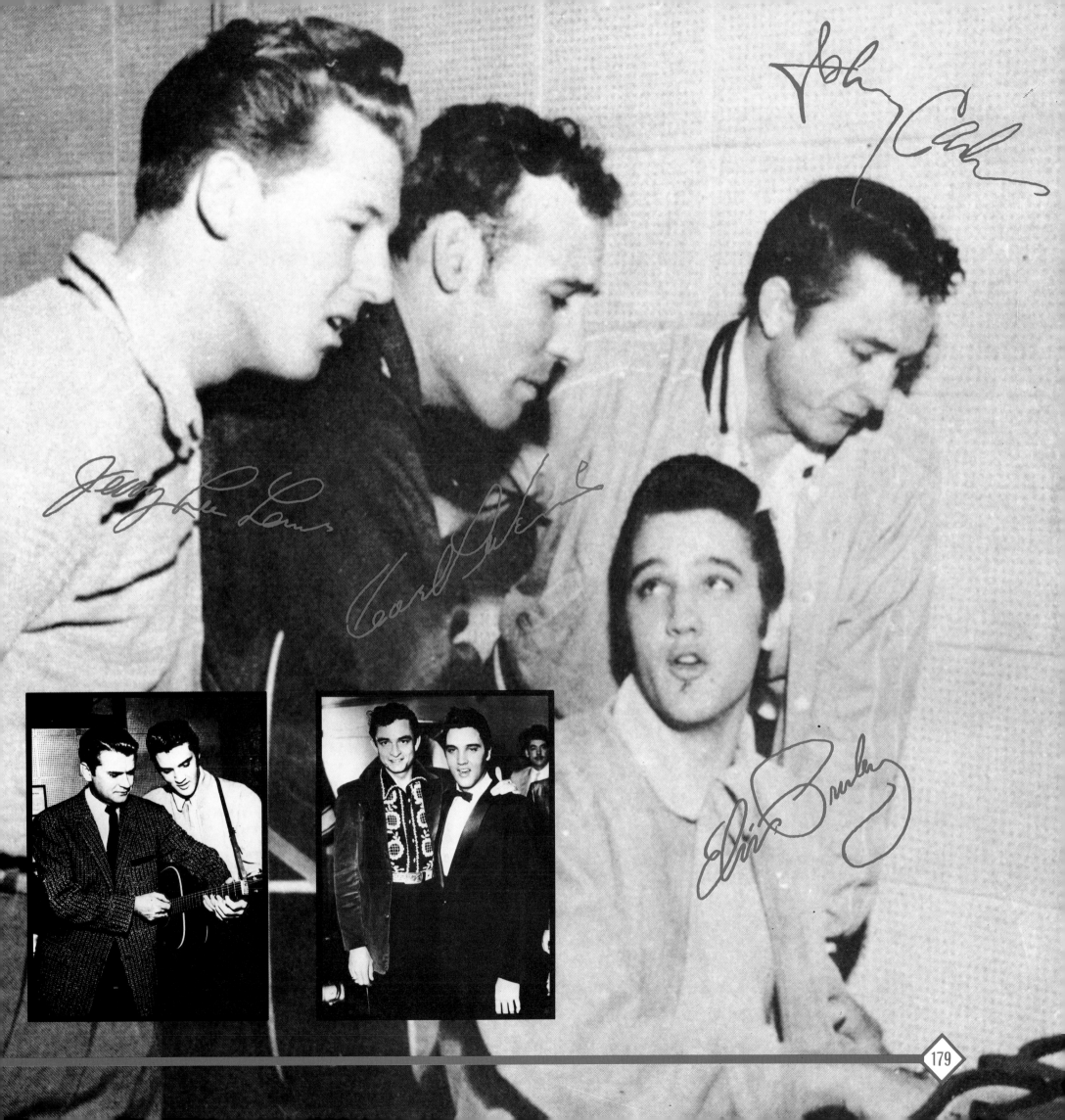

'Blessed Jesus Hold My Hand'
  Elvis, Jerry Lee and Carl (split lead vocal).
'As We Travel Along On The Jericho Road'
  Elvis and Jerry Lee (split lead vocal), Elvis (guitar).
'I Just Can't Make It By Myself'
  Elvis and Jerry Lee (split lead vocal), Elvis (guitar).
'Little Cabin On The Hill'
  Elvis (lead vocal and guitar).
'Summertime Has Passed And Gone'
  Elvis, Jerry Lee and Carl (split lead vocal).
'I Hear A Sweet Voice Calling'
  Elvis, Jerry Lee and Carl (split lead vocal), Elvis (guitar).
'And Now Sweetheart You've Done Me Wrong'
  Elvis (lead vocal and guitar).
'Keeper Of The Keys'
  Carl (lead vocal), Elvis and Jerry Lee (back-up vocal), Elvis (guitar), Jerry Lee (piano).
'Crazy Arms'
  Elvis and Jerry Lee (split lead vocal), Elvis (guitar).
'Don't Forbid Me'
  Elvis (lead vocal and guitar).
  Other titles believed to have been recorded at this session, either in part or in total: 'Isle Of Golden Dreams', 'I Won't Have To Cross Jordan Alone', 'Vacation In Heaven', 'That Old Rugged Cross', 'Blueberry Hill', 'Cry, Cry, Cry', 'Down The Line', 'Strange Things Happening'.

N.B. The only other known recordings on which Presley guests are:-

Ray Harris
* **'Greenback Dollar, Watch And Chain'**
(Harris)
'Foolish Heart'
(US) Sun 272
Released: 1957

Ray Harris (vcl, gtr), Wayne Cogswell (gtr), Elvis Presley (pno), Bill Lee Riley (bs), James Van Eaton (dms)
*Recorded: Memphis Recording Service, Memphis, Possibly June 1957

Jerry Lee Lewis
'A TASTE OF COUNTRY' (LP)
(US) Sun LP-114
Released: 1971
'Am I To Be The One' (Blackwell)

Jerry Lee Lewis (vcl, pno),
Elvis Presley (vcl harmony), Roland Janes (gtr), Dudley Brooks (pno), James Van Eaton (dms)
Recorded: Memphis Recording Service, Memphis, Date unknown. Though Elvis Presley is listed in the Sun files as having been present on this track, Jerry Lee Lewis has claimed that the vocal harmony was in fact sung by Charlie Rich. Charlie!

ELVIS–GREATEST HITS. VOLUME I (LP)
RCA AHLI/2347
Released: October 1981

Side I
'The Wonder Of You' (Baker, Knights)
** 'A Big Hunk O' Love' (Schroeder, Wyche)
BPA5 1144
'There Goes My Everything' (Frazier)
'Suspicious Minds' (James)
**** 'What'd I Say' (Charles) LPA5 907

Side 2
* 'Don't Cry Daddy' (Scott, Davis) LPA5 5902
*** 'Steamroller Blues' (Taylor) CPA5 4706
'The Sound Of Your Cry' (Giant, Baum, Kaye)
'Burning Love' (Linde)
'You'll Never Walk Alone' (Rodgers, Hammerstein)

Elvis Presley (vcl,gtr), James Burton, John Wilkinson, Charlie Hodge (gtr), Glen D. Hardin (pno), Jerry Scheff (bs), Bob Lanning (dms), Bob Harris & His Orchestra, The Imperials, Sweet Inspirations, Millie Kirkham (bv).
*Recorded: The International Hotel, Las Vegas, Nevada. February 16–19, 1970.

Elvis Presley (vcl, gtr), James Burton, John Wilkinson, Charlie Hodge (gtr), Glen D. Hardin (pno), Jerry Scheff (bs), Ronnie Tutt (dms), Joe Esposito (per- Feb 15, 1972 only). Joe Guercio & His Orchestra, J.D. Sumner & The Stamps, Sweet Inspirations, Kathy Westmoreland (bv).
**Recorded: The Hilton Hotel, Las Vegas, Nevada. February 15, 1972. ***The H.I.C. Arena, Honolulu, Hawaii. January 13, 1973. ****Nashville, Tennessee. July 2, 1973.

Following a flood of squalid revelations, Elvis Presley's virtues as a performer have become somewhat neglected–to the extent of their being of secondary importance. His posthumous role is currently that of grand prize, in what is squaring up to be arguably both the most murky and complex of all showbiz litigations. As we write, various parties lay claim to all or part of the Presley finances.

Lawyers acting in the interests of Lisa Marie Presley–Elvis' 14-year-old daughter and sole beneficiary–have filed suit against Colonel Tom Parker, charging that he acted as the singer's manager in the State of California without being duly licensed.

The suit against the Colonel seeks to have all agreements declared void, and asks for the recovery of all sums of money Parker received from 1972 onwards. The claim is that these contracts–of which the Colonel received a 50 percent managerial cut–were signed in California, where he was not legally licensed to represent his client.

In a counter suit filed March 12, 1982 in the District Court of Las Vegas, (a town which the Colonel insists was designated as the principal place of business for their joint venture– of which he is the sole surviving partner), the Colonel asks the court to confirm his right, power and authority to possess and control the assets of the joint venture's enterprises, in order to wind up its affairs.

The Colonel is further asking the court to order interfering parties and entities to cease their activities immediately, and allow him to liquidate and sell all remaining assets of the joint venture and to desist further activities.

The Colonel's lawsuit claims that, "such interference had had an adverse effect upon the values of the assets owned by the Estate and the Colonel", causing the amount of income received by both the Estate and the Colonel to have been "substantially reduced".

At the present time, the Presley Estate is valued at $31 million, for which the IRS have sent in their bill for a cool $17 million as settlement.

As to the record itself, don't be misled by the title. Predictable Las Vegas standards hardly fall under the category of "Greatest Hits". However, facts must be faced. Short of endless re-packaging (which, as RCA UK have demonstrated, could be handled with infinitely more flair–and understanding–than is evident here), the output of Elvis Presley records will cease forever. Unless, that is, RCA or the Colonel are in possession of some hitherto unknown material. Meanwhile, one seriously wonders exactly who records like this are aimed at.

N.B.: The UK equivalent, *The Sound Of Your Cry* (RCA 3060), comprises one dozen tracks, and definitely has the edge. Both 'There Goes My Everything' and 'The Wonder Of You' are dropped and replaced by 'It's Only Love' (extended Version) and 'Angel' (US stereo version), whilst two cuts from the 8-LP set, *Elvis Aron Presley*, 'Are You Lonesome Tonight?' (the laughing version) and 'Kentucky Rain' round off the collection.

'There Goes My Everything' (Frazier)
'You'll Never Walk Alone' (Rodgers, Hammerstein)
(US) RCA PB-13058
Released: February 1982

Familiar as the 1970 flip of, 'I Really Don't Want To Know' and a countryfied standard, instantly indentified with Engelbert more than with Elvis.

I'm Left, You're Right, He's Gone.

Despite the many mistakes, mishandlings and miscalculations that dogged his career, in the final analysis no one individual can be blamed for the disasters that hallmark the last years of Elvis Presley. Elvis was one of those paradoxical combinations – he had talent, charisma and magnetism, but at the same time he was cripplingly shy and insecure. Had he been more confident in his own abilities, there wouldn't have been the need for the drugs, the constant promiscuity and the continual companionship of hired flunkies and yes-men.

The personality split between talent and insecurity is not that unique – it killed Judy Garland, pushed Bob Dylan from drugs to religion, and has dogged the lives of many lesser artists. Nobody, however, had to carry quite the same load that was placed on Elvis Presley's shoulders. He may not have been the inventor of rock 'n' roll, but he was its very first superstar – no individual has equalled his stature as an entertainer. The Beatles and the Rolling Stones may have come close, but with the Beatles and the Rolling Stones there was always more than one person to carry the weight. The Beatles were a team, but Elvis Presley was on his own.

In Presley's early days he was vilified and called a corrupter of youth and an agent of the Devil. He was the first symbol, the first rallying point in what would later be called youth revolt, the generation gap. He was an object of desire for countless thousands of women. Equally, countless thousands of young men wanted nothing more than to be Elvis Presley. The legend became so big, so quickly, that it was impossible to control. In fact, nobody really tried to control it. For most of his life, he was surrounded by small minded men with small dreams and small horizons. The majority of the time they were busy protecting their own petty interests and investments. None seem to have been really capable of managing the Presley legend, let alone helping Elvis Presley the individual come to terms with that legend.

In the whole story of Elvis Presley there are just too many "what if's?" What if he had had more sensitive creative management? What if he had been presented with better material? What if he had not squandered his talent on all those awful movies? What if friends, or professional help could have done something to mitigate his horrendous drug habit and almost pathological self destruction?

Speculation however, has little point. The Elvis Presley story is over. It could be that the Presley legend was so great that it would never have been possible for the man and the myth to be reconciled; that walking around with the full burden of being Elvis Presley would have broken any human being.

All we can concentrate on now is the legacy of music that is left behind. Although flawed, it is without parallel in the history of popular music. Sinatra may have survived, the Beatles and Bob Dylan may have been more creative, but *nobody* had the power to affect an audience like Elvis Presley. It is no exaggeration to say that he changed lives, and actually affected the course of human affairs. Now he has gone, he has left a space in the popular culture of our planet that can in no way be filled by a substitute. In the end, this has to be the true measure of the man.

RCA

GOLD STANDARD SERIES

‖‖‖‖‖‖‖‖‖‖‖‖‖‖‖‖‖‖‖‖‖‖‖‖

'Mystery Train'/
'I Forgot To Remember To Forget'
RCA 447-0600
'That's All Right (Mama)'/
'Blue Moon Of Kentucky'
RCA 447-0601
'I Don't Care If The Sun Don't Shine'/
'Good Rockin' Tonight'
RCA 447-0602
'Milkcow Blues Boogie'/
'You're Heartbreaker'
RCA 447-0603
'Baby Let's Play House'/
'I'm Left, You're Right, She's Gone'
RCA 447-0604
'Heartbreak Hotel'/'I Was The One'
RCA 447-0605
'I Want You, I Need You, I Love You'/
'My Baby Left Me'
RCA 447-0607
'Hound Dog'/'Don't Be Cruel'
RCA 447-0608
'Blue Suede Shoes'/'Tutti Frutti'
RCA 447-0609
'I Got A Woman'/'I'm Counting On You'
RCA 447-0610
'I'll Never Let You Go (Little Darlin')'/
'I'm Gonna Sit Right Down and Cry (Over
You)'
RCA 447-0611
'I Love You Because'/
'Trying To Get To You'
RCA 447-0612
'Blue Moon'/'Just Because'
RCA 447-0613
'One Sided Love Affair'/'Money Honey'
RCA 447-0614
'Shake, Rattle And Roll'/
'Lawdy, Miss Clawdy'
RCA 447-0615
'Love Me Tender'/'Anyway You Want Me
(That's How I Will Be)'
RCA 447-0616
'Too Much'/'Playing For Keeps'
RCA 447-0617
'All Shook Up'/
'That's When Your Heartaches Begin'
RCA 447-0618
'Jailhouse Rock'/'Treat Me Nice'
RCA 447-0619

'(Let Me Be Your) Teddy Bear'/'Loving You'
RCA 447-0602
'Don't'/'I Beg Of You'
RCA 447-0621
'Wear My Ring Around Your Kneck'/
'Doncha' Think It's Time'
RCA 447-0622
'Hard Headed Woman'/'Don't Ask Me Why'
RCA 447-023
'One Night'/'I Got Stung'
RCA 447-0624
'(Now And Then There's) A Fool Such As I'/
'I Need Your Love Tonight'
RCA 447-0625
'A Big Hunk O' Love'/'My Wish Came True'
RCA 447-0626
'Stuck On You'/'Fame And Fortune'
RCA 447-0627
'It's Now Or Never'/'A Mess Of Blues'
RCA 447-0628
'Are You Lonesome Tonight'/'I Gotta Know'
RCA 447-0629
'Surrender'/'Lonely Man'
RCA 447-0630
'I Feel So Bad'/'Wild In The Country'
RCA 447-0631
'(Marie's The Name) His Latest Flame'/
'Little Sister'
RCA 447-0634
'Can't Help Falling In Love'/
'Rock-A-Hula Baby'
RCA 447-0635
'Good Luck Charm'/
'Anything That's Part Of You'
RCA 447-0636
'She's Not You'/
'Just Tell Her Jim Said Hello'
RCA 447-0637
'Return To Sender'/
'Where Do You Come From'
RCA 447-0638
'Kiss Me Quick'/'Suspicion'
RCA 447-0639
(RCA-Victor Gold Standard Original)
'One Broken Heart For Sale'/
'They Remind Me Too Much Of You'
RCA 447-0640
'(You're the) Devil In Disguise'/
'Please Don't Drag That String Around'
RCA 447-0641
'Bossa Nova Baby'/'Witchcraft'
RCA 447-0642
'Blue Christmas'/'Wooden Heart'
RCA 447-0702
(RCA-Victor Gold Standard Original with special
catalogue number)
'Crying In The Chapel'/
'I Believe In The Man In The Sky'
RCA 447-0643
(RCA-Victor Gold Standard Original)
'Kissin' Cousins'/'It Hurts Me'
RCA 447-0644
'Such A Night'/'Never Ending'
RCA 447-0645
'Viva Las Vegas'/'What'd I Say'
RCA 447-0646
'Blue Christmas'/
'Santa Claus Is Back In Town'
RCA 447-0647
(RCA-Victor Gold Standard Original)
'Do The Clam'/'You'll Be Gone'
RCA 447-0648
'Ain't That Loving You Baby'/'Ask Me'
RCA 447-0649
'Wooden Heart'/'Puppet On A String'
RCA 447-0650
(RCA-Victor Gold Standard Original)
'Joshua Fit The Battle'/'Known Only To Him'
RCA 447-0651
(RCA-Victor Gold Standard Original)
'Milky White Way'/
'Swing Down Sweet Chariot'
RCA 447-0652
(RCA-Victor Gold Standard Original)
'(Such An) Easy Question'/'It Feels So Right'
RCA 447-0653
'(It's A) Long Lonely Highway'/'I'm Yours'
RCA 447-0654
'Tell Me Why'/'Blue River'
RCA 447-0655
'Frankie And Johnny'/
'Please Don't Stop Loving Me'.
RCA 447-0656
'Love Letters'/'Come What May'
RCA 447-0657
'Spinout'/'All That I Am'
RCA 447-0658
'Fools Fall In Love'/'Indescribably Blue'

RCA 447-0659
'Long Legged Girl (With The Short Dress
on)'/'That's Someone You Never Forget'
RCA 447-0660
'There's Always Me'/'Judy'
RCA 447-0661
'Big Boss Man'/'You Don't Know Me'
RCA 447-0662
'Guitar Man'/'High Heel Sneakers'
RCA 447-063
'US Male'/'Stay Away'
RCA 447-0664
'You'll Never Walk Alone'/'We Call On Him'
RCA 447-0665
'You're Time Hasn't Come Yet, Baby'/
'Let Yourself Go'
RCA 447-0666
'Almost In Love'/
'A Little Less Conversation'
RCA 447-0667
'If I Can Dream'/'Edge Of Reality'
RCA 447-0668
'Memories'/'Charro'
RCA 447-0669
'His Hand In Mine'/'How Great Thous Art'
RCA 447-0670
'In The Ghetto'/'Any Day Now'
RCA 447-0671
'Clean Up Your Own Backyard'/
'The Fair Is Moving On'
RCA 447-0672
'Suspicious Minds'/'You'll Think Of Me'
RCA 447-0673
'Don't Cry Daddy'/'Rubberneckin''
RCA 447-0674
'Kentucky Rain'/'My Little Friend'
RCA 447-0675
'The Wonder Of You'/
'Mama Liked The Roses'
RCA 447-0676
'I've Lost You'/'The Next Step Is Love'
RCA 447-0677
'You Don't Have To Say You Love Me'/
'Patch It Up'
RCA 447-0678
'There Goes My Everything'/
'I Really Don't Want To Know'
RCA 447-0679
'Rags To Riches'/'Where Did They Go, Lord'
RCA 447-0680
'If Everyday Was Like Christmas'/
'How Would You Like To Be'
RCA 447-0681
'Life'/'Only Believe'
RCA 447-0682
'I'm Leavin'/'Heart Of Rome'
RCA 447-0683
'It's Only Love'/'The Sound Of Your Cry'
RCA 447-0684
'An American Trilogy'/
'Until It's Time For You To Go'
RCA 447-0685
(RCA-Victor Gold Standard Original)
'Steamroller Blues'/'Burning Love'
RCA 447-10156
(RCA-Victor Gold Standard Original)
'Raised On Rock'/'If You Talk In Your Sleep'
RCA GB-10157
(RCA-Victor Gold Standard Original)
'Take Good Care Of Her'/
'I've Got A Thing About You Baby'
RCA GB-10485
'Seperate Ways'/'Always On My Mind'
RCA GB-10486
'T-R-O-U-B-L-E'/'Mr. Songman'
RCA GB-10487
'Promised Land'/'It's Midnight'
RCA GB-10488
'My Boy'/'Thinking About You'
RCA GB-10489
'The Real Elvis'
(US)RCA EPA-5120
(same as EPA-940)
'Peace In The Valley'
(US)RCA EPA-5121
(same as EPA-4054)
'King Creole Volume I'
(US)RCA EPA-5122
(same as EPA-4319)
'Elvis Sails'
(US)RCA EPA-5157
(same as EPA-4325)
'A Touch Of Gold Volume I'
(US)RCA EPA-5088
'A Touch Of Gold Volume 2'
(US)RCA EPA-5101
'A Touch Of Elvis Volume 3'
(US)RCA EPA-5141

SPOKEN WORD RECORDS

'Elvis Presley: The Truth About Me'
Rainbo Records 78 rpm
Pressed on gold cardboard, this record came
with the 1956 fan publication, *Elvis Presley
Speaks*. It reappeared again as a gold cardboard
Rainbo Records release, under the title, 'Elvis
Speaks—In Person!!'
Teen Parade was the next magazine to offer
this record to its readers. This time it was
produced as a 45 rpm plastic flexidisc entitled
'Elvis Speaks!! The Truth About Me'. The initial
pressings had a blue label and were
manufactured by Lynchburg Audio of
Lynchburg, Virginia, while subsequent copies
had a black label. In Britain it was offered to
readers of *Weekend Mail* as a 6-inch vinyl
pressing
'TV Guide Presents Elvis Presley'
RCA G8MW 8705. 45 rpm
Pelvis Nickname/Adults' Reaction/First Public
Appearance/How 'Rockin' Motion' Started
'THE ELVIS TAPES' (LP)
Official Press Conference. Vancouver, Canada.
August 22, 1957
Redwood 1
**'ELVIS EXCLUSIVE LIVE PRESS
CONFERENCE'** (LP)
Memphis, February 1961
Greenvalley GV-2001
A flexidisc featuring extracts appeared in *Elvis
Collectors' Issue* magazine in 1978
**'ELVIS PRESLEY—INTERVIEWS AND
MEMORIES OF THE SUN YEARS'** (LP)
Sun 1001
The Sun Years: Contains parts of recording
sessions with the voices of Sam Phillips and Elvis
Presley, plus excerpts of Elvis Presley's Sun
Recordings, issued and unissued
Interviews and Music: Contains interviews by
Jay Thompson at Wichita Falls, Charlie Walker
at San Antonio Texas, plus various other rare
Elvis Presley talking intros on stage and
television.
This album was withdrawn from circulation
due to litigation with RCA Records
'ELVIS: IN DAYS GONE BY' (Double EP)
Elvis Always Record Club
Press Conference: Portland, Oregon/Press
Conference: San Antonio/Elvis In The Army/
Elvis Talks About His Career/Aloha From
Hawaii Press Conference. January 1973

BOOT-LEGS

The practice of bootlegging is immoral, illegal and – despite increased pressures brought to bear by the recording industry – still very much a flourishing business. For instance, in 1979 well in excess of $50 million worth of illegal counterfeiting and tape duplicating equipment, bootleg/counterfeit records, tapes and cassettes, and related materials were confiscated in America alone by the FBI and local law enforcement agencies working with the Recording Industry Association of America (RIAA).

Bootlegs enable the insatiable Elvis fan to purchase – usually at extortionate prices – rare moments in live performances (the 1961 Hawaii Benefit Concert), television appearances (the Dorsey Brothers Show, etc.), radio broadcasts (the Louisiana Hayride) plus hitherto unreleased studio material, soundtracks, demos, out-takes, jam sessions and sweepings from the studio floor, which, for one reason or a dozen, have been rejected for commercial consideration.

In every instance these recordings were illegally procured. Indeed, the professional quality of both pressing and packaging of recent releases leads one to believe that the rumours of tape thefts and an organized crime connection can't altogether be ruled out. Furthermore, the fact that throughout his career Elvis never released a *live* album that captured the mayhem of his electrifying pre-Army concert performances has, since his death, created an even greater world-wide demand for such recordings.

Since them, the number of Elvis bootlegs has proliferated at such an alarming rate that it has been estimated that there are well over 200 different albums in circulation. However, many of these are duplications of existing bootlegs with a new sleeve or just a different permutation of familiar material. With the exception of the electronically-produced Elvis Presley-Linda Ronstadt 'Love Me Tender' duet (Duet 101), all bootleg singles have been culled from bootleg albums.

Whilst choosing to offer an editorial selection of some of the most comprehensive Elvis Presley bootlegs, the authors wish to state that they are not prepared to enter into any correspondence concerning bootlegs – their quality or availability.

SECOND PRESSINGS

Second Pressing doesn't mean a legitimate re-issue. It's a thoroughly misleading term for a counterfeit. In other words, collectors jargon for identifying near-perfect facsimiles of rare and costly originals (i.e. the five Sun singles or British and French 10″ LPs).

However, though the majority of under-the-counter retailers make it quite clear to would be customers that they're being sold a forgery, there are instances where guileless collectors have been duped into believing that they are being offered a mint original and have paid hundreds of dollars for records that cost only a few cents to counterfeit. Watch out!

'GOOD ROCKING TONIGHT' (LP)
Bopcat LP-100
Side 1: 'Good Rockin' Tonight'/'My Baby's Gone'/'I Don't Care If The Sun Don't Shine' (two false starts and complete take)/'Blue Moon Of Kentucky' (slow version)/'I'll Never Let You Go Little Darlin''/'Mystery Train'/'I Forgot To Remember To Forget'
Side 2: Jerry Lee Lewis, Warren Smith, Billy Lee Riley

'ELVIS PRESLEY DORSEY SHOWS' (LP)
Golden Archives GA-100
The Dorsey Brothers Shows: 'Blue Suede Shoes''Heartbreak Hotel' (January 28, 1956); 'Tutti Frutti'/'I Was The One' (February 4, 1956); 'Shake, Rattle And Roll'/'Flip, Flop And Fly'/'I Got A Woman' (February 11, 1956); 'Baby, Let's Play House'/'Tutti Frutti' (February 18, 1956); 'Blue Suede Shoes'/'Heartbreak Hotel' (March 17, 1956); 'Money Honey'/ 'Heartbreak Hotel' (March 24, 1956)

'TV GUIDE PRESENTS ELVIS' (LP)
'Hound Dog' HD-1000
Steve Allen TV Show, July 1, 1956: 'I Want You, I Need You, I Love You'/'Hound Dog'/'Comedy sketch with Elvis Presley, Steve Allen, Imogene Coca and Andy Griffith
TV Guide Presents Elvis (interview): "Pelvis" Nickname/Adults Reaction/First Public Appearance/How "Rockin' Motion" Started Hy Gardner Calling – 1958 Interview on WABD-TV, New York City
Frank Sinatra Timex TV Special, May 12, 1960: 'Fame And Fortune'/'Stuck On You'/ 'Witchcraft-Love Me Tender' (Presley-Sinatra duet)

'FROM THE WAIST UP' (LP)
Golden Archives GA-150
The Ed Sullivan Shows: 'Don't Be Cruel'/'Love Me Tender'/'Ready Teddy'/'Hound Dog' (Sept 9, 1956); 'Don't Be Cruel'/'Love Me Tender'/ 'Love Me'/'Hound Dog' (Oct 28, 1956); 'Hound Dog'/'Love Me Tender'/'Heartbreak Hotel'/ 'Don't Be Cruel'/'(There'll Be) Peace In The Valley (For Me)'/'Too Much'/'When My Blue Moon Turns To Gold Again' (Jan 6, 1957)

'GOT A LOT O' LIVIN' TO DO!' (LP)
Pirate PR-101
Jailhouse Rock Soundtrack: 'Young And Beautiful'/'I Wanna Be Free'/'Young And Beautiful'/'Don't Leave Me Now'/'Treat Me Nice'/'Jailhouse Rock'/'Baby I Don't Care'/ 'Young And Beautiful'
The Dick Clark Interview
Loving You Soundtrack: 'Loving You' (fast version)/'Got A Lot O' Livin' To Do'/'Party'/ Medley: 'Party – (Let Me Be Your) Teddy Bear' – 'Got A Lot O' Livin' To Do-Hot Dog' – 'Lonesome Cowboy'/'Hot Dog'/'Mean Woman Blues'/'(Let Me Be Your) Teddy Bear'/'Loving You' (slow version)/'Got A Lot O' Livin' To Do'
Brief excerpts of Elvis Presley Live In Vancouver, Canada, September 1, 1957: 'Heartbreak Hotel'/'I Was The One'/'I Got A Woman'/'That's When Your Heartaches Begin'

'I WANNA BE A ROCK 'N' ROLL STAR' (LP)
Viktorie NS-13026.
The Truth About Me (Elvis Speaks)/'My Baby's Gone' (unissued Sun track)/Press Interview (Brooklyn Army Terminal, September 22, 1958)/'(Let Me Be Your) Teddy Bear' (soundtrack)/'Got A Lot O' Livin' To Do' (soundtrack)/'Treat Me Nice' (soundtrack)/ 'Jailhouse Rock' (soundtrack)/Pat Hernon Interviews Elvis/'Fame and Fortune' (Frank Sinatra Special)/'Stuck On You' (Frank Sinatra

Special)/'A Cane And Highstarched Collar' (soundtrack)/'The Lady Loves Me' (soundtrack)/ 'C'Mon Everybody' (soundtrack)/'Dominique' (soundtrack)/'Baby What You Want Me To Do' (NBC-TV Special)/1967-68 Elvis Tribute programme Interviews/'Wild In The Country' (1961 single version)

'VIVA LAS VEGAS' (LP)
Lucky LR-711
Radio spot No. 1/'Viva Las Vegas'/'Yellow Rose Of Texas' – 'The Eyes Of Texas'/'The Lady Loves Me'/'C'Mon Everybody'/'Today, Tomorrow And Forever'/'Cheek To Cheek'/ 'What'd I Say'/'Santa Lucia'/'If You Think I Don't Need You'/Radio Spot No. 2/'Appreciation'/ 'Viva Las Vegas'/'I Need Somebody To Lean On'/'My Rival'/'Viva Las Vegas'/'If You Think I Don't Need You' (three takes)

'THE BURBANK SESSIONS VOLUME 1 JUNE 27, 1968' (2-LPs)
Audifon AFNS-62768
The 6-00 p.m. Show: Dialogue/'That's All Right (Mama)'/'Heartbreak Hotel'/'Love Me'/'Baby What You Want Me To Do'/Dialogue/'Blue Suede Shoes'/'Baby What You Want Me To Do'/Dialogue/'Lawdy, Miss Clawdy'/'Are You Lonesome Tonight?'/'When My Blue Moon Turns To Gold Again'/'Blue Christmas'/'Tryin' To Get To You'/'One Night'/'Baby What You Want Me To Do'/Dialogue/'One Night'/ 'Memories'
The 8-00 p.m. Show: Dialogue/'Heartbreak Hotel'/'Baby What You Want Me To Do'/ Dialogue/'That's All Right (Mama)'/'Are You Lonesome Tonight?'/'Baby What You Want Me To Do'/'Blue Suede Shoes'/'One Night'/'Love Me'/Dialogue/'Tryin' To Get To You'/'Lawdy, Miss Clawdy'/'Santa Claus Is Back In Town'/'Blue Christmas'/'Tiger Man'/'When My Blue Moon Turns To Gold Again'/'Memories'

'THE BURBANK SESSIONS VOLUME 2 JUNE 29, 1968' (2-LPs)
Audifon AFNS-62968
The 6-00 p.m. Show: Intro & Dialogue/ 'Heartbreak Hotel'/'One Night'/Medley: 'Heartbreak Hotel' – 'Hound Dog' – 'All Shook Up'/'Can't Help Falling In Love'/'Jailhouse Rock'/ 'Don't Be Cruel'/'Blue Suede Shoes'/'Love Me Tender'/Dialogue/'Trouble'/Dialogue/'Baby What You Want Me To Do'/'If I Can Dream'.
The 8-00 p.m. Show: Intro & Dialogue/Medley: 'Heartbreak Hotel' – 'Hound Dog' – 'All Shook Up'/'Can't Help Falling In Love'/'Jailhouse Rock'/ 'Don't Be Cruel'/'Blue Suede Shoes'/'Love Me Tender'/Dialogue/'Trouble No. 1'/Dialogue/ 'Trouble – Guitar Man'/Dialogue/'Trouble – Guitar Man'/Dialogue/'If I Can Dream'

'THE '68 COMEBACK' (LP)
Memphis MKS 101
Medley: 'Nothingsville' – 'Guitar Man' – 'Yourself Go' – 'Guitar Man' – 'Big Boss Man'/'If I Can Dream' (instrumental)/'Memories'/'Let Yourself Go' (instrumental)/'It Hurts Me'/'Trouble' – 'Guitar Man'/Medley: 'Sometimes I Feel Like A Motherless Child' – 'Where Could I Go But To The Lord' – 'Up Above My Head' – 'Saved'/'A Little Less Conversation' (instrumental)
NBC-TV Special June 27 & 29, 1968

'THE LEGEND LIVES ON' (LP)
Golden Archives PCS-1001
Las Vegas 1969: Elvis Talks About His Career/ 'Yesterday'/'Hey Jude'/Introductions/'Happy Birthday' (James Burton)/'In The Ghetto'/ 'Suspicious Minds'.
Las Vegas 1972: 'What'd I Say'/'Can't Help Falling In Love'/'It's Over'/'A Big Hunk O' Love'/ 'It's Impossible'/'The Impossible Dream'/'Bridge Over Troubled Water' (studio take, June 5, 1970)

'FROM THE DARK TO THE LIGHT!' (LP)
Tiger TR-101
Soundtracks of both 'That's The Way It Is' and 'Elvis On Tour.'

'BEHIND CLOSED DOORS – UNRELEASED STUDIO/LIVE CONCERT MASTERS 1960–1972' (4-LP Boxed Set)
Audifon AFNS-66072-4
'Lonely Man'/'I Slipped, I Stumbled, I Fell' (three takes)/'Wild In The Country' (two takes)/'In My Way'/'Forget Me Never' (two takes)/'Hawaiian Wedding Song'/'Island Of Love' (two takes)/ 'Steppin' Out Of Line' (two takes)/'Almost Always True' (two takes)/'Moonlight Swim' (two takes)/'Can't Help Falling In Love' (four takes)/'Beach Boy Blues' (two takes)/'King Of The Whole Wide World'/'This Is Livin''/'Home Is Where The Heart Is'/'I Got Lucky'/'A Whistling

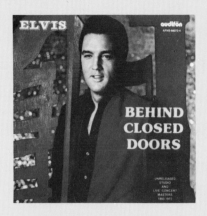

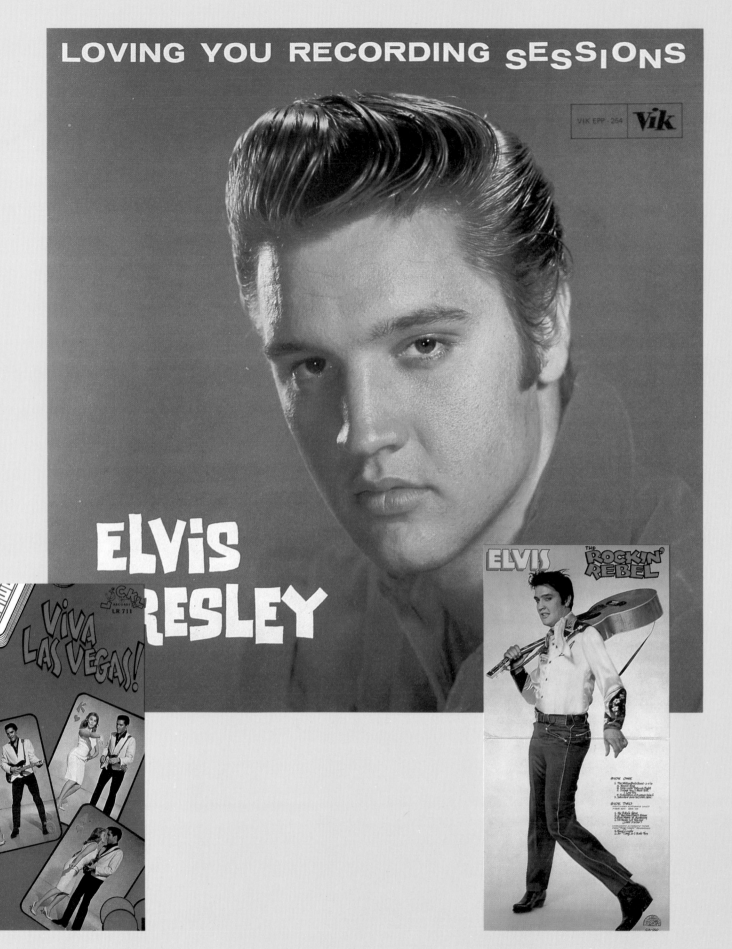

Tune' (three takes)/'Drums Of The Islands'
(three takes)/'This Is My Heaven'/'Swing Down
Sweet Chariot'/'Almost'/'Sign Of The Zodiac'/
'Wiffenpoof Song'/'Violet'/'Gentle On My Mind'/
'Faded Love'/'*I Got A Woman' (Aug 22, '69)/
'Suspicious Minds' (Feb 16, '70)/'Don't Cry
Daddy' (Feb 17, '70)/*'Kentucky Rain' (Feb 18,
'70)/*'Polk Salad Annie' (Feb 18, '70)/'It's Your
Baby, You Rock It'/'Tomorrow Never Comes'/
'Funny How Time Slips Away'/'I Washed My
Hands In Muddy Water'/'The First Time Ever I
Saw Your Face'/'Don't Think Twice, It's Alright'
*Recorded in concert
**'ROCKIN' WITH ELVIS NEW YEAR'S
EVE'** (2-12" LPs)
Spirit Of America HNY-7677
'Also Sprach Zarathustra'/'See See Rider'/'I Got
A Woman'/'Amen'/'Big Boss Man'/'Love Me'/
'Fairytale'/'Lord, You Gave Me A Mountain'/
'Jailhouse Rock'/'Presentation Of Liberty Bell by
Jim Curtin'/'It's Now Or Never' (featuring
Sherril Nielson)/'My Way'/'Funny How Time
Slips Away'/'Auld Lang Syne'/'Introduction of
Vernon and Lisa Marie Presley'/'Blue Suede
Shoes'/'Trying To Get To You'/'Polk Salad
Annie'/'Introductions to the band'/'Early Morning
Rain'/'What'd I Say'/'Johnny B. Goode'/'Ronnie
Tutt drum solo'/'Jerry Scheff bass solo'/'Sonny
Brown piano solo'/'Love Letters'/'Hail, Hail,
Rock 'N' Roll'/'Fever'/'Hurt'/'Hound Dog'/'Are
You Lonesome Tonight?'/'Reconsider Baby'/
'Little Sister'/'Unchained Melody'/'Rags To
Riches'/'Can't Help Falling In Love'/'Closing
Vamp'
Pittsburg, December 31, 1976

MAIL ORDER RECORDS

||||||||||

||||||||||

'WORLDWIDE GOLD AWARD HITS PARTS 1 & 2'
RCA Record Club R.213690
This double album comprises the first four sides from the boxed set *Worldwide 50 Gold Award Hits Vol. 1* (RCA LPM-6401), released 1970

'WORLDWIDE GOLD AWARD HITS PARTS 3 & 4'
RCA Record Club R.214657
This double album comprises the four remaining sides from the boxed set *Worldwide 50 Gold Award Hits Vol. 1* (RCA LPM-6401), released 1970

'FROM ELVIS WITH LOVE' (1978)
RCA Record Club R.234340
Side 1
'Love Me Tender'/'Can't Help Falling In Love'/'The Next Step Is Love'/'I Need Your Love Tonight'/'I Can't Stop Loving You'
Side 2
'I Want You, I Need You, I Love You'/'I Love You Because'/'Love Letters'/'A Thing Called Love'/'A Big Hunk O'Love'
Side 3
'Love Me'/'Without Love'/'Faded Love'/'Loving You'/'You've Lost That Lovin' Feeling'
Side 4
'Have I Told You Lately That I Love You'/'You Don't Have To Say You Love Me'/'True Love'/'Ain't That Loving You Baby'/'Please Don't Stop Loving Me'

'ELVIS' (LP)
(US) RCA DPL 2-0056
Released: August 1973

Side 1
'Hound Dog' (Leiber, Stoller)
'I Want You, I Need You, I Love You' (Mysels, Kosloff)
'All Shook Up' (Blackwell, Presley)
'Don't' (Leiber, Stoller)
'I Beg Of You' (McCoy, Owens)

Side 2
'A Big Hunk O'Love' (Schroeder, Wyche)
'Love Me' (Leiber, Stoller)
'Stuck On You' (Schroeder, Leslie, McFarland)
'Good Luck Charm' (Schroeder, Gold)
'Return To Sender' (Blackwell, Scott)
Side 3
'Don't Be Cruel' (Blackwell, Presley)
'Loving You' (Leiber, Stoller)
'Jailhouse Rock' (Leiber, Stoller)
'Can't Help Falling In Love' (Peretti, Creatore, Weiss)
'I Got Stung' (Schroeder, Hill)
Side 4
'(Let Me Be Your) Teddy Bear' (Mann, Lowe)
'Love Me Tender' (Presley, Matson)
'Hard Headed Woman' (DeMetrius)
'It's Now Or Never' (Schroeder, Gold, Di Capua)
'Surrender' (Pomus, Shuman, De Curtis)

It's generally reckoned that TV-advertised album collections are aimed at that section of the public who normally don't buy records. This heavily-promoted mail-order 20 Greatest Hits double album, licensed by RCA to the Brookville Marketing Corporation, quickly added a further two million album units to Elvis' impressive grand total.

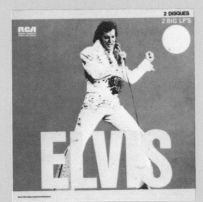

'ELVIS IN HOLLYWOOD' (LP)
(US) RCA DPL.2-0168
Released: January 1976

Side 1
'Jailhouse Rock' (Leiber, Stoller)
'Rock-A-Hula Baby' (Wise, Weisman, Fuller)
'GI Blues' (Tepper, Bennett)
'Kissin' Cousins' (Wise, Starr)
'Wild In The Country' (Peretti, Creatore, Weiss)
Side 2
'King Creole' (Leiber, Stoller)
'Blue Hawaii' (Robin, Rainger)
'Fun In Acapulco' (Weisman, Wayne)
'Follow That Dream' (Wise, Weisman)
'Girl! Girls! Girls!' (Leiber, Stoller)
Side 3
'Viva Las Vegas' (Pomus, Shuman)
'Bossa Nova Baby' (Leiber, Stoller)
'Flaming Star' (Wayne, Edwards)
'Girl Happy' (Pomus, Meade)
'Frankie And Johnny' (Gottlieb, Karger, Weisman)
Side 4
'Roustabout' (Giant, Baum, Kaye)
'Spinout' (Wayne, Weisman, Fuller)
'Double Trouble' (Pomus, Shuman)
'Charro' (Strange, Davis)
'They Remind Me Too Much Of You' (Robertson)
The specially-priced companion set to Elvis's, first, and highly lucrative, RCA-Brookville TV-promoted mail-order double album. ('Elvis', RCA DPL 2-0056; August 1973.)

'THE ELVIS PRESLEY STORY' (1977)
Candlelite Music RCA DML5-0263
Side 1
'It's Now Or Never'/'Treat Me Nice'/'For The Good Times'/'I Got Stung'/'Ask Me'/'Return To Sender'
Side 2
'The Wonder Of You'/'Hound Dog'/'Make The World Go Away'/'(Marie's The Name) His Latest Flame'/'Loving You'
Side 3
'One Night'/'You Don't Know Me'/'Blue

Christmas'/'Good Luck Charm'/'Blue Suede Shoes'/'Surrender'
Side 4
'In The Ghetto'/'Too Much'/'Help Me Make It Through The Night'/'I Was The One'/'Love Me'/'Little Sister'
Side 5
'Can't Help Falling In Love'/'Trouble'/'Memories'/'Wear My Ring Around Your Neck'/'Blue Hawaii'/'Burning Love'
Side 6
'Love Me Tender'/'Stuck On You'/'Funny How Time Slips Away'/'All Shook Up'/'Puppet On A String'/'Jailhouse Rock'
Side 7
'Heartbreak Hotel'/'I Just Can't Help Believin''/'I Beg Of You'/'Don't Cry Daddy'/'Hard Headed Woman'/'Are You Lonesome Tonight?'
Side 8
'(Let Me Be Your) Teddy Bear'/'Hawaiian Wedding Song'/'A Big Hung O'Love'/'I'm Yours'/'A Fool Such As I'/'Don't'
Side 9
'I Want You, I Need You, I Love You'/'Kissin' Cousins'/'I Can't Stop Lovin' You'/'(You're The) Devil In Disguise'/'Suspicious'/'Don't Be Cruel'
Side 10
'She's Not You'/'From A Jack To A King'/'I Need Your Love Tonight'/'Wooden Heart'/'Have I Told You Lately That I Love You'/'You Don't Have To Say You Love Me'
Special Bonus Album:
'ELVIS–HIS SONGS OF INSPIRATION'
Candlelite Music RCA DML-1-0264
Side 1
'Crying In The Chapel'/'Put Your Hand In The Hand'/'I Believe'/'How Great Thou Art'/'If I Can Dream'
Side 2
'(There'll Be) Peace In The Valley (For Me)'/'Amazing Grace'/'An American Trilogy'/'Follow That Dream'/'You'll Never Walk Alone'

The Elvis Presley Story/Candlelite Music-Mail Order (Aug 77)
There can't be too many American families who aren't conversant with Candlelite Music–the TV mail order company who specialise in selling millions of budget price "Showcase Presentation Edition" album sets to people who normally wouldn't budge out of their easy-chair to buy records. Which ever way you look at it, $26.64 for a boxed set of five Greatest Hits LPs, plus the bonus of a specially compiled album, *Elvis–His Songs Of Inspiration*, is just too good an offer to pass up.

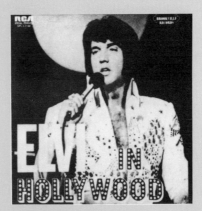

'MEMORIES OF ELVIS' (1978)
Candlelite Music RCA DML 5-0347
Side 1
'One Broken Heart For Sale'/'Young And Beautiful'/'A Mess Of Blues'/'The Next Step Is Love'/'I Gotta Know'/'Love Letters'
Side 2
'When My Blue Moon Turns To Gold Again'/'If Everyday Was Like Christmas'/'Steamroller Blues'/'Anyway You Want Me'/'(Such An) Easy Question'/'That's When Your Heartaches Begin'
Side 3
'Kentucky Rain'/'Money Honey'/'My Way'/'Girls! Girls! Girls!'/'Lonely Man'/'US Male'
Side 4
'My Wish Came True'/'Kiss Me Quick'/'As Long As I Have You'/'Bossa Nova Baby'/'I Forgot To Remember To Forget'/'Such A Night'

Side 5
'I Really Don't Want To Know'/'Doncha' Think It's Time'/'His Hand In Mine'/'That's All Right (Mama)'/'Nothingsville Medley'/'Baby, I Don't Care'
Side 6
'Playing For Keeps'/'King Of The Whole Wide World'/'Don't Ask Me Why'/'Flaming Star'/'I'm Left, You're Right, She's Gone'/'What'd I Say'
Side 7
'There Goes My Everything'/'Patch It Up'/'Reconsider Baby'/'Good Rockin' Tonight'/'You Gave Me A Mountain'/'Rock-A-Hula Baby'
Side 8
'Mean Woman Blues'/'It Hurts Me'/'Fever'/'I Want To Be Free'/'Viva Las Vegas'/'Old Shep'
Side 9
'Anything That's Part Of You'/'My Baby Left Me'/'Wild In The Country'/'Memphis, Tennessee'/'Don't Leave Me Now'/'I Feel So Bad'
Side 10
'Separate Ways'/'Polk Salad Annie'/'Fame And Fortune'/'Trying To Get To You'/'I've Lost You'/'King Creole'

Special Bonus Album:
'THE GREATEST SHOW ON EARTH'
Candlelite Music RCA DML1-0348
Side 1
'I'll Remember You'/'Without Love'/'Gentle On My Mind'/'It's Impossible'/'What Now My Love'
Side 2
'Until It's Time For You To Go'/'Early Morning Rain'/'Something'/'The First Time Ever I Saw Your Face'/'The Impossible Dream'

'LEGENDARY CONCERT PERFORMANCES' (1978)
RCA Record Club RCA R-244047
Side 1
'Blue Suede Shoes'/'Sweet Caroline'/'Burning Love'/'My Babe'
Side 2
'Johnny B. Goode'/'Yesterday'/'Medley: Mystery Train-Tiger Man'/'You Gave Me A Mountain'/'Never Been To Spain'
Side 3
'See See Rider'/'Words'/'Proud Mary'/'Walk A Mile In My Shoes'/'Steamroller Blues'
Side 4
'Polk Salad Annie'/'Something'/'Let It Be Me'/'The Impossible Dream'/'My Way'

'ELVIS' COUNTRY MEMORIES' (1978)
RCA Record Club RCA R-244069
Side 1
'I'll Hold You In My Arms'/'Welcome To My World'/'It Keeps Right On A-Hurtin''/'Release Me'/'Make The World Go Away'
Side 2
'Snowbird'/'Early Morning Rain'/'I'm So Lonesome I Could Cry'/'Funny How Time Slips Away'/'I'm Movin' On'
Side 3
'Help Me Make It Through The Night'/'You Don't Know Me'/'How Great Thou Art'/'I Washed My Hands In Muddy Water'/'I Forgot To Remember To Forget'
Side 4
'Your Cheatin' Heart'/'Baby, Let's Play House'/'Whole Lotta Shakin' Goin' On'/'Gentle My Mind'/'For The Good Times'

UK DISCOGRAPHY

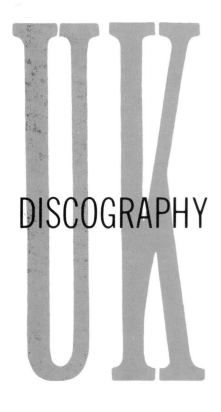

'Heartbreak Hotel'/'I Was The One'
HMV POP-182 (78); 7M-385 (45)
Released: March 1956
'Blue Suede Shoes'/'Tutti Frutti'
HMV POP-213 (78); 7M-405 (45)
Released: June 1956
'I Want You, I Need You, I Love You'/
'My Baby Left Me'
HMV POP-235 (78); 7M-424 (45)
Released: July 1956
'Hound Dog'/'Don't Be Cruel'
HMV POP-249
Released: September 1956

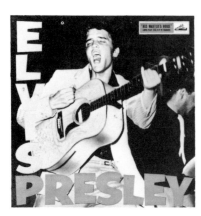

'ROCK 'N' ROLL. No.I' (LP)
HMV CLP-1093
Released: October 1956
'Blue Suede Shoes'/
'I Got A Sweetie (I Got A Woman)'/
'I'm Counting On You'/
'I'm Left, You're Right, She's Gone'/
'That's All Right (Mama)'/'Money Honey'/
'Mystery Train'/
'I'm Gonna Sit Right Down And Cry Over You'/
'One-Sided Love Affair'/
'Lawdy, Miss Clawdy'/'Shake, Rattle And Roll'
'Blue Moon'/
'I Don't Care If The Sun Don't Shine'
HMV POP-272
Released: November 1956
'Love Me Tender'/'Anyway You Want Me'
HMV POP-253
Released: December 1956

'LOVE ME TENDER' (EP)
HMV 7EG-8199
Released: December 1956
'Love Me'/'Mystery Train'
HMV POP-295
Released: February 1957
'ROCK 'N' ROLL. No. 2' (LP)
HMV CLP-1105
Released: April 1957
Rip It Up/Love Me/When My Blue Moon Turns
To Gold Again/Long Tall Sally/First In Line/
Paralysed/So Glad You're Mine/Old Shep/Ready
Teddy/Anyplace Is Paradise/How's The World
Treating You/How Do You Think I Feel.
'Playin' For Keeps'/'Too Much'
HMV POP-330
Released: May 1957
'All Shook Up'/
'That's When Your Heartaches Begin'
HMV POP-359
Released: June 1957
'PEACE IN THE VALLEY' (EP)
RCA RCX-101
Released: June 1957
'Loving You'/'Teddy Bear'
RCA 1013
Released: July 1957
'Paralysed'/
'When My Blue Moon Turns To Gold Again'
HMV POP-378
Released: August 1957
'GOOD ROCKING TONIGHT' (EP)
HMV 7EG-8256
Released: September 1957
'Good Rocking Tonight'/'Blue Moon Of
Kentucky'/'Milkcow Blue Boogie'/
'Just Because'.
'THE BEST OF ELVIS' (10-inch LP)
HMV DLP-1159
Released: October 1957
'Heartbreak Hotel'/'I Don't Care If The Sun
Dont' Shine'/'Blue Moon'/'Tutti Frutti'/'All
Shook Up'/'Hound Dog'/'Too Much'/'Anyway
You Want Me'/'Dont Be Cruel'/'Playin' For
Keeps'.
'Lawdy, Miss Clawdy'/'Tryin' To Get To You'
HMV POP-408
Released: October 1957
'Got A Lot O' Livin' To Do'/'Party'
RCA 1020
Released: October 1957
'LOVING YOU' (10-inch LP)
RCA RC-24001
Released: October 1957
'Mean Woman Blues'/'Teddy Bear'/
'Loving You'/'Got A Lot O'Livin' To Do'/
'Lonesome Cowboy'/'Hot Dog'/'Party'/'True Love'.

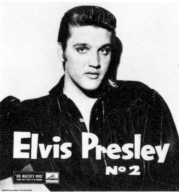

'ELVIS PRESLEY' (LP)
RCA RCX-104
Released: October 1957
'I Need You So'/
'Have I Told You Lately That I Love You'/
'Blueberry Hill'/'Don't Leave Me Now'
'Santa Bring My Baby Back'/
'Santa Claus Is Back In Town'
RCA 1025
Released: November 1957
'ELVIS' CHRISTMAS ALBUM' (LP)
RCA RD-27052
Released: November 1957
'Jailhouse Rock'/'Treat Me Nice'
RCA 1028
Released: January 1958
'JAILHOUSE ROCK' (EP)
RCA RCX-106

Released: January 1958
'Wear My Ring Around Your Neck'/
'Doncha' Think It's Time'
RCA 1058
Released: April 1958
'Hard Headed Woman'/'Don't Ask Me Why'
RCA 1070
Released: July 1958
'KING CREOLE VOLUME I' (EP)
RCA RCX-117
Released: September 1958
'KING CREOLE VOLUME 2' (EP)
RCA RCX-118
Released: September 1958
King Creole/Dixieland Rock
RCA 1081
Released: October 1958
'ELVIS' GOLDEN RECORDS. VOL.I' (LP)
RCA RB-16069
Released: October 1958
'Hound Dog'/'I Love You Because'/
'All Shook Up'/'Heartbreak Hotel'/
'You're A Heartbreaker'/'Love Me'/
'Too Much'/'Don't Be Cruel'/
'That's When You're Heartaches Begin'/
'I'll Never Let You Go'/'Love Me Tender'/
'I Forgot To Remember To Forget'/
'Anyway You Want Me (That's How I Will Be)'/
'I Want You, I Need You, I Love You'
'ELVIS SINGS CHRISTMAS SONGS' (EP)
RCA RCX-121
Released: November 1958
'ELVIS SAILS' (EP)
RCA RCX-13
Released: November 1958
'Hound Dog'/'Blue Suede Shoes'
RCA 1095
Released: December 1958
'One Night'/'I Got Stung'
RCA 1100
Released: January 1959
'ELVIS IN TENDER MOOD' (EP)
RCA RCX-135
Released: February 1959
'Young And Beautiful'/'True Love'/'Lover Doll'/
'Love Me Tender'
'A Fool Such As I'/
'I Need Your Love Tonight'
RCA 1113
Released: April 1959
'ELVIS' (LP)
RCA RD-27120
Released: May 1959
'That's All Right (Mama)'/'Lawdy, Miss Clawdy'/
'Mystery Train'/'Playing for Keeps'/'Poor Boy'/
'Money Honey'/'I'm Counting On You'/
'My Baby Left Me'/'I Was The One'/
'Shake, Rattle and Roll'/
'I'm Left, You're Right, She's Gone'/
'You're A Heartbreaker'/'Trying To Get To You'/
'Blue Suede Shoes'
'A Big Hunk O'Love'/'My Wish Came True'
RCA 1136
Released: July 1959
'A DATE WITH ELVIS' (LP)
RCA RD-27128
Released: September 1959
'Blue Moon Of Kentucky'/'Milkcow Blues Boogie'/
'Baby, Let's Play House'/
'I Don't Care If The Sun Don't Shine'/
'Tutti Frutti'/
'I'm Gonna Sit Right Down And Cry Over You'/
'I Got A Woman'/'Good Rockin' Tonight'/
'Is It So Strange'/'We're Gonna Move'/'Blue Moon'/
'Just Because'/'One-Sided Love Affair'/'Let Me'
'A TOUCH OF GOLD. VOL.I' (EP)
RCA RCX-1045
Released: November 1959
'Hard Headed Woman'/'Good Rockin' Tonight'/
'Don't'/'Teddy Bear'
'STRICTLY ELVIS' (EP)
RCA RCX-175
Released: December 1959
'A TOUCH OF GOLD VOL.2' (EP)
RCA RCX-1048
Released: February 1960
Stuck On You/Fame And Fortune
RCA 1187
Released: April 1960
'ELVIS' GOLDEN RECORDS. VOL.2' (LP)
RCA RD-27159
Released: June 1960
'I Need Your Love Tonight'/'Don't'/
'Wear My Ring Around Your Neck'/
'My Wish Came True'/'I Got Stung'/'Loving You'/
'(Let Me Be Your) Teddy Bear'/'One Night'/
'A Big Hunk O'Love'/'I Beg Of You'/
'A Fool Such As I'/'Doncha' Think It's Time'/

'Jailhouse Rock'/'Treat Me Nice'
'A Mess Of Blues'/
'The Girl Of My Best Friend'
RCA 1194
Released: July 1960
'It's Now Or Never'/'Make Me Know It'
RCA 1207
Released: October 1960
'SUCH A NIGHT' (EP)
RCA RCX-190
Released: November 1960
'Such A Night'/'It Feels So Right'/
'Like A Baby'/'Make Me Know It'
'Are You Lonesome Tonight'/'I Gotta Know'
RCA 1216
Released: January 1961
'Wooden Heart'/
'Tonight Is So Right For Love'
RCA 1226
Released: March 1961
'HIS HAND IN MINE' (LP)
RCA RD-27211/SF-5094
Released: May 1961
'Surrender'/'Lonely Man'
RCA 1227
Released: May 1961
'Wild In The Country'/'I Feel So Bad'
RCA 1244
Released: September 1961
'(Marie's The Name) His Latest Flame'/
'Little Sister'
RCA 1258
Released: October 1961
'SOMETHING FOR EVERYBODY' (LP)
RCA RD-27244/SF-5106
Released: October 1961
'Rock-A-Hula Baby'/
'Can't Help Falling In Love'
RCA 1270
Released: January 1962
'Good Luck Charm'/
'Anything That's Part Of You'
RCA 1280
Released: May 1962
'FOLLOW THAT DREAM' (EP)
RCA RCX-211
Released: May 1962
'POT LUCK' (LP)
RCA RD-27265/SF-5135
Released: July 1962
'She's Not You'/
'Just Tell Her Jim Said Hello'
RCA 1303
Released: August 1962
'KID GALAHAD' (EP)
RCA RCX-7106
Released: October 1962
'Return To Sender'/
'Where Do You Come From'
RCA 1320
Released: November 1962
'GIRLS! GIRLS! GIRLS!' (LP)
RCA RD-7534/SF-7534
Released: January 1963
'One Broken Heart For Sale'/
'They Remind Me Too Much Of You'
RCA 1337
Released: February 1963
'IT HAPPENED AT THE WORLD'S FAIR'
(LP)
RCA RD-7565/SF-7565
Released: May 1963
'(You're The) Devil In Disguise'/
'Please Don't Drag That String Around'
RCA 1355
Released: June 1963
'Bossa Nova Baby'/'Witchcraft'
RCA 1374
Released: October 1963
'ELVIS' GOLDEN RECORDS. VOLUME 3'
(LP)
RCA RD-7630/SF-7030
Released: November 1963
'Kiss Me Quick'/'Something Blue'
RCA 1375
Released December 1963
'FUN IN ACAPULCO' (LP)
RCA RD-7609/SF-7609
Released: December 1963
'Viva Las Vegas'/'What'd I Say'
RCA 1390
Released: February 1964
'LOVE IN LAS VEGAS' (EP)
RCA RCX-7141
Released: February 1964
'ELVIS FOR YOU. VOLUME I' (EP)
RCA RCX-7142
Released: May 1964

'PROMISED LAND' (LP)
RCA-APL-1-0873
Released: January 1975
'EASY COME, EASY GO' (LP)
RCA Camden CDS-1146
Released: February 1975
'C'Mon Everybody'/'A Whistling Tune'/'I'll Be There'/'I Love Only One Girl'/'Easy Come, Easy Go'/'Santa Lucia'/'Tonight Is So Right For Love'/'Guadalajara'/'Angel'/'A Little Less Conversation'/'Follow That Dream'/'Long Legged Girl'
'HAVING FUN WITH ELVIS ON STAGE' (LP)
RCA APM-1-0818
Released: March 1975
'ELVIS PRESLEY'S GREATEST HITS' (LP)
RCA-Reader's Digest RDS-9001/7
Released: May 1975
Volume 1
'Heartbreak Hotel'/'I Was The One'/'I'm Left, You're Right, She's Gone'/'Tutti Frutti'/'Blue Suede Shoes'/'Don't Be Cruel'/'I Want You, I Need You, I Love You'/'My Baby Left Me'/'Hound Dog'/'Ready Teddy'/'I Love You Because'/'Anyway You Want Me (That's How I Will Be)'/'Money Honey'/'I'm Gonna Sit Right Down And Cry Over You'/'Blue Moon/Rip It Up'
Volume 2
'Long Tall Sally'/'Shake, Rattle And Roll'/'Old Shep'/'Lawdy, Miss Clawdy'/'Playing For Keeps'/'All Shook Up'/'That's When Your Heartaches Begin'/'Too Much'/
'Mean Woman Blues'/'Blueberry Hill'/'Lonesome Cowboy'/'(Let Me Be Your) Teddy Bear'/'Paralysed'/'Let's Have A Party'/'Got A Lot O' Livin' To Do'/'Trying To Get To You'
Volume 3
'Baby I Don't Care'/'(There'll Be) Peace In The Valley (For Me)'/'Don't Wear My Ring Around Your Neck'/'Hard Headed Woman'/'I Got Stung'/'One Night'/'A Fool Such As I'/'I Need Your Love Tonight'/'A Big Hunk O' Love'/'Milkcow Blues Boogie'/'Good Rockin' Tonight'/'Stuck On You'/'Fever'/'Soldier Boy'/'It Feels So Right'
Volume 4
'The Girl Of My Best Friend'/'A Mess Of Blues'/'It's Now Or Never'/'I Gotta Know'/'Are You Lonesome Tonight?'/'Surrender'/'I Feel So Bad'/'His Latest Flame'/
'Can't Help Falling In Love'/'Good Luck Charm'/'Anything That's Part Of You'/'She's Not You'/'One Broken Heart For Sale'/'(You're The) Devil In Disguise'/'Kiss Me Quick'/'Such A Night'
Volume 5
'Ain't That Loving You Baby'/'Crying In The Chapel'/'Your Cheating Heart'/'Tell Me Why'/'Love Letters'/'All That I Am'/'Frankie And Johnny'/'Long-Legged Girl (With The Short Dress On)'/
'U.S. Male'/'Just Tell Her Jim Said Hello'/'If I Can Dream'/'In The Ghetto'/'Suspicious Minds'/'Don't Cry Daddy'/'The Wonder Of You'/'I've Lost You'
Volume 6
'Proud Mary'/'Kentucky Rain'/'You Don't Have To Say You Love Me'/'Patch It Up'/'There Goes My Everything'/'Rags To Riches'/'You've Lost That Lovin' Feelin''/'I'm Leavin''/
'I Just Can't Help Believing'/'Until It's Time For You To Go'/'Bridge Over Troubled Water'/'American Trilogy'/'The Next Step Is Love'/'Burning Love'/'Always On My Mind'
Volume 7: Bonus LP
'ELVIS IN THE MOVIES'
'Love Me Tender'/'Loving You'/'Jailhouse Rock'/'King Creole'/'Wooden Heart'/'Flaming Star'/'Wild In The Country'/'Rock-A-Hula Baby'/'Return To Sender'/'Bossa Nova, Baby'/'Viva Las Vegas'/'Kissing' Cousins'/'Do The Clam'/'Double Trouble'/'Guitar Man'/'It's A Wonderful World'
'T-R-O-U-B-L-E'/'Mr Songman'
RCA 2562
Released: May 1975
'TODAY' (LP)
RCA RS-1011
Released: June 1975
'THE US MALE' (LP)
RCA Camden CDS-1150
Released: June 1975
'US Male'/'We'll Be Together'/'It's A Matter Of Time'/'Almost In Love'/'Let's Forget About The Stars'/'My Little Friend'/'If I'm A Fool'/'I'll Take Love'/'Today, Tomorrow And Forever'/'Let's Be Friends'/'No More'/'Burning Love'

'THE ELVIS PRESLEY SUN COLLECTION' (LP)
RCA-Starcall HY-1001
Released: August 1975
'Blue Moon'/'You're A Heartbreaker'/
'I'm Left, You're Right, She's Gone'
RCA 2601
Released: September 1975
'Green, Green Grass Of Home'/
'Thinking About You'
RCA 2635
Released: November 1975
'PICTURES OF ELVIS' (LP)
RCA HY.1023
Released: November 1975
'Return To Sender'/'Roustabout'/'Little Egypt'/'Paradise Hawaiian Style'/'Girls! Girls! Girls!'/'Double Trouble'/
'Do The Clam'/'Fun In Acapulco'/'Bossa Nova, Baby'/'Clambake'/'Girl Happy'/'Rock-A-Hula Baby'
'I GOT LUCKY' (LP)
RCA Camden CDS-1154
Released: November 1975
'I Got Lucky'/'What A Wonderful Life'/'I Need Somebody To Lean On'/'Yoga Is As Yoga Does'/'Riding The Rainbow'/'Fools Fall In Love'/'The Love Machine'/'Home Is Where The Heart Is'/'You Gotta Stop'/'If You Think I Don't Need You'
'ELVIS—A LEGENDARY PERFORMER. VOLUME 2' (LP)
RCA CPL-1-1-1349
Released: January 1976
'THE ELVIS PRESLEY COLLECTION. VOLUME I' (LP)
RCA Camden PDA-009
Released: February 1976
A double album that combines, 'You'll Never Walk Alone' (CDM-1088) and 'Elvis Sings Hits From His Movies' (CDS-1110).
'Hurt'/'For The Heart'
RCA 2674
Released: April 1976
'FROM ELVIS PRESLEY BOULEVARD, MEMPHIS, TENNESSEE' (LP)
RCA RS-1060
Released: May 1976
'The Girl Of My Best Friend'/
'Mess Of Blues'
RCA 2729
Released: August 1976
'Suspicion'/'It's A Long Lonely Highway'
RCA 2768
Released: November 1976
'ELVIS IN DEMAND' (LP)
RCA PL-42003
Released: January 1977
'Suspicion'/'Hi-Heel Sneakers'/'Got A Lot O' Livin' To Do'/'Have I Told You Lately That I Love You'/'Please Don't Drag That String Around'/'It's Only Love'/'The Sound Of Your Cry'/'Viva Las Vegas'/'Do Not Disturb'/'Tomorrow Is A Long Time'/'(A) Long Lonely Highway'/'Puppet On A String'/'The First Time Ever I Saw Your Face'/'Summer Kisses, Winter Tears'/'It Hurts Me'/'Let It Be Me'
'Moody Blue'/'She Still Thinks I Care'
RCA 0857
Released: February 1977
'All Shook Up'/'Heartbreak Hotel'
RCA 1694
Released: May 1977
'Jailhouse Rock'/'Treat Me Nice'
RCA 2695

Released: May 1977
'I Got Stung'/'One Night'
RCA 2696
Released: May 1977
'A Fool Such As I'/
'I Need Your Love Tonight'
RCA 2697
Released: May 1977
'It's Now Or Never'/'Make Me Know It'
RCA 2698
Released: May 1977
'Are You Lonesome Tonight'/
'I Gotta Know'
RCA 2699
Released: May 1977
'Wooden Heart'/
'Tonight Is So Right For Love'
RCA 2700
Released: May 1977
'Surrender'/'Lonely Man'
RCA 2701
Released: May 1977
'(Marie's The Name) His Latest Flame'/
'Little Sister'
RCA 2702
Released: May 1977
'Rock-A-Hula Baby'/
'Can't Help Falling In Love'
RCA 2703
Released: May 1977
'Good Luck Charm'/
'Anything That's Part Of You'
RCA 2704
Released: May 1977
'She's Not You'/
'Just Tell Her Jim Said Hello'
RCA 2705
Released: May 1977
'Return To Sender'/
'Where Do You Come From'
RCA 2706
Released: May 1977
'(You're The) Devil In Disguise'/
'Please Don't Drag That String Around'
RCA 2707
Released: May 1977
'Crying In The Chapel'/
'I Believe In The Man In The Sky'
RCA 2708
Released: May 1977
'The Wonder Of You'/
'Mama Liked The Roses'
RCA 2709
Released: May 1977
'Way Down'/'Pledging My Love'
RCA PB-0998
Released: July 1977
'WELCOME TO MY WORLD' (LP)
RCA PL-12274
Released: July 1977
'MOODY BLUE' (LP)
RCA PL-12428
Released: August 1977
'GIRLS! GIRLS! GIRLS!' (LP)
RCA PL-42354
Released: October 1977
'KISSIN' COUSINS' (LP)
RCA PL-42355
Released: October 1977
'ROUSTABOUT' (LP)
RCA PL-42356
Released: October 1977
'FUN IN ACAPULCO' (LP)
RCA PL-42357
Released: October 1977
'LOVING YOU' (LP)
RCA PL-42358
Released: October 1977
'Mean Woman Blues'/'Teddy Bear'/'Loving You'/'Got A Lot O' Livin' To Do'/'Lonesome Cowboy'/'Hot Dog'/'Party'/'Blueberry Hill'/'True Love'/'Don't Leave Me Now'/'Have I Told You Lately That I Love You?'/'I Need You So'
'ELVIS IN CONCERT' (LP)
RCA PL-02587
Released: October 1977
'My Way'/'America'
RCA PB-1165
Released: November 1977
'ELVIS—THE '56 SESSIONS VOLUME I' (LP)
RCA PL-42101
Released: February 1978
'I Got A Sweetie (I Got A Woman)'/'Heartbreak Hotel'/'Honey Honey'/'I'm Counting On You'/'I Was The One'/'Blue Suede Shoes'/'My Baby Left Me'/'One-Sided Love Affair'/
'So Glad You're Mine'/'I'm Gonna Sit Right

Down And Cry Over You'/'Tutti Frutti'/'Lawdy, Miss Clawdy'/'Shake, Rattle And Roll'/'I Want You, I Need You'/'Hound Dog'/'Don't Be Cruel'
'HE WALKS BESIDE ME' (LP)
RCA PL-12772
Released: March 1978
'Don't Be Cruel'/'Hound Dog'
RCA 9265
Released: June 1978
'THE ELVIS PRESLEY COLLECTION. VOLUME 2' (LP)
RCA Camden PDA-042
Released: June 1978
A double album that combines, 'Separate Ways' (CDS-1118) and 'Easy Come, Easy Go' (CDS-1146)
'ELVIS NBC-TV SPECIAL' (LP)
RCA PL-42370
Released: August 1978
'ELVIS' 40 GREATEST' (LP)
RCA PL-42691
Released: October 1978
Same track listing as RCA-Arcade ADE.P-12 (released October '74), but this time around, not only was an entirely new sleeve design produced, but the albums were pressed in pink vinyl
'Old Shep'/'Paralysed'
RCA 9334
Released: November 1978
'ELVIS—A LEGENDARY PERFORMER. VOLUME 3' (LP)
RCA PL-13082
Released: January 1979
'THE ELVIS COLLECTION VOLUME 3' (LP)
RCA Camden PDA-054
Released: April 1979
A double album that combines Please Don't Stop Loving Me (CDS-1175) and Flaming Star (CDS-1185)
'ELVIS—THE '56 SESSIONS VOLUME 2' (LP)
RCA 42102
Released: May 1979
'Anyway You Want Me (That's How I Will Be)'/'Love Me Tender'/'We're Gonna Move'/'Poor Boy'/'Let Me'/'Playing For Keeps'/'Love Me'/'Paralysed'/'How Do You Think I Feel?'/
'How's The World Treating You?'/'When My Blue Moon Turns To Gold Again'/'Long Tall Sally'/'Old Shep'/'Too Much'/'Any Place Is Paradise'/'Ready Teddy'/'First In Line'/'Rip It Up'
'OUR MEMORIES OF ELVIS. VOLUME 2' (LP)
RCA PL-13448
Released: September 1979
'ELVIS LOVE SONGS' (LP)
K-Tel NE-1062
Released: November 1979
'It's Now Or Never'/'She's Not You'/'Love Letters'/'Anything That's Part Of You'/'Surrender'/'Kentucky Rain'/'Suspicious Minds'/'You Don't Have To Say You Love Me'/'I Just Can't Help Believing'/'The Wonder Of You'/'Can't Help Falling In Love'/'Always On My Mind'/'Love Me Tender'/'Loving You'/'I Want You, I Need You, I Love You'/'Wooden Heart'/'Are You Lonesome Tonight?'/'Just Pretend'/'Until It's Time For You To Go'/'Memories'
'ELVIS, SCOTTY & BILL—THE FIRST YEAR' (LP)
Very Wonderful Golden Editions. King 1
Released: November 1979
'Biff Collie Interview'/'Good Rockin' Tonight'/'Baby, Let's Play House'/'Blue Moon Of Kentucky'/'I Got A Woman'/'That's All Right (Mama)'/'Elvis Presley Interview'/'Scotty Moore Tells The Story Of The First Year'
'It Won't Seem Like Christmas (Without You)'/'Merry Christmas Baby'
RCA PC-9464 (12")
Released: December 1979
'ELVIS SINGS THE WONDERFUL WORLD OF CHRISTMAS' (LP)
RCA PL-42371
Released: December 1979
'ELVIS PRESLEY—TWIN PACK (LP)
RCA NL-43054
Released: December 1979
'Blue Suede Shoes'/'That's All Right (Mama)'/'Blue Moon Of Kentucky'/'Any Way You Want Me'/'Mystery Train'/'Long Tall Sally'/'Shake, Rattle And Roll'/'Lawdy, Miss Clawdy'/'I Don't Care If The Sun Don't Shine'/'Old Shep'/'Good Rockin' Tonight'/'Heartbreak Hotel'/'Separate Ways'/'Are You Lonesome Tonight?'/'A Fool Such As I'/'Crying In The Chapel'/'How Great Thou Art'/'Rip It Up'/'The Wonder Of You'/'Sweet Caroline'/'American Trilogy'